Chapter-wise Physics MCQs

Volume – 1

Highly Useful for Class XI Students

and NEET Aspirants

Amit Gorain

First Edition : 2022

Second Edition : 2025

Contents

Preparatory Unit

Sub-unit - 1 : Physical World & Measurement

(1) Physical World	(2) Unit System
(3) Dimensional Analysis	(4) Error in Measurement

Physical World

Origin of the word "Science", is from Latin Word, "Scientia" which means "to Know".

In the nineteenth century, physical sciences were divided into five distinct disciplines : Physics, Chemistry, Astronomy, Geology and Meteorology. The most fundamental of these is the Physics.

(1) Physics :

Physics is the branch of science that deals with the study of basic laws of nature and their manifestation in various natural phenomena.

In physics, we study matter, energy and their interaction. The laws and principles of physics help us to understand nature.

Two principal thrusts in physics are unification and reductionism .

(a) Unification : In physics, attempt is made to explain various physical phenomena in terms of just few concepts and laws. We try to see the physical world as manifestation of some universal laws.

(b) Reductionism : In physics, attempt is made to explain a macroscopic system in terms of its microscopic constituents.

(2) Different Branches of Physics :

Mechanics : It is the stud of motion of objects, its cause and effects.

Heat : It deals with nature of heat, modes of transfer and effect of heat.

Sound : It deals with the physical aspects of sound waves, their production, properties and applications.

Light (Optics) : It deals with the physical aspects of light, its properties, working and use of optical instruments.

Electricity & magnetism : It is the study of the charges at rest and in motion, their affects and their relationship with magnetism.

Atomic Physics : It is the study of the structure and properties of atoms.

Nuclear Physics : It deals with the properties and behavior of nuclei and the particles within the nuclei.

Plasma Physics : It is the study of production, properties of the ionic state of matter-the fourth state of matter.

Geophysics : It is the study of the internal structure of the earth.

Unit System

(3) Physical Quantity

A quantity which can be measured and by which various physical happenings can be explained and expressed in form of laws is called a physical quantity.

For example length, mass, time, force *etc*.

(4) Types of Physical Quantities

[a] Fundamental quantities :

The physical quantities which can be treated independently as basic quantities and not usually defined in terms of other physical quantities are called fundamental quantities

e.g. length, mass, time etc. Only four additional quantities temperature, current, luminous intensity and amount of substance are needed to deal with all other branches of physics.

[b] Derived quantities :

The physical quantities which can be defined using fundamental quantities are called derived quantities.

e.g. speed, volume, force etc

(5) Unit

- Unit is defined as the standard of measurement of quantity.
- To determine the magnitude of a physical quantity we need (1) the unit in which it is measured, (2) the number of times that unit is contained in the quantity.

Measurement of Physical Quantity = Numerical Value (n) × Unit (u)

e.g., measurement of a physical quantity = 1 m

Here, n = 1 and u = m.

The units selected for the measurement of the base quantities are known as the base units or absolute units or **fundamental units**.

The units of all those quantities which can be obtained from the fundamental units are called **derived units**.

It follows that if the size of the chosen unit is small, then the numerical value of the quantity will be larger and vice-versa. But the measurement of the physical quantity is always same i.e. n u = constant

- **Characteristics of a Standard Unit :**

It should be - (i) well defined
(ii) of suitable size
(iii) easily accessible and reproducible at all places.

It should not -(iv) change with time and from place to place.
(v) not change with change in its physical conditions, like temperature, pressure etc.

(6) System of Units

- A complete set of base and derived units called as system of units.
- A few common systems of units are given below : [a] CGS system
[b] FPS system
[c] MKS system
[d] International system of units (SI).

(7) Symbol of Units

Wrong Approaches	Correct Approaches	
c.m or c.m.	cm	There is no dot(.) within the symbol or at the end. However, if a sentence ends with a symbol then a full stop should be used to indicate end of the sentence.
10 gs 10 meter	10 g 10 meters	"s" and "es" is not used in a symbol to represent plural. But if the symbol is written in words and magnitude is more than 1(one), plural from can be used.
n	N	Symbol of units named after scientists should have only the first letter capital.

Newton	**newton**	But if the name is written instead of the symbol, it should start with small letter.
m	m	The symbol of unit should be represented in regular font, not in italics. Even when the whole sentence is written in italics, symbols must be in roman. In general, physical quantities are represented in italics, but this is not mandatory. Example : Representation of mass : *m* (italic), but metre : m (roman)
300°K	**300 K**	In thermometry, kelvin cannot be used with a degree (°) sign.
3 Mkm	**3 × 10⁶ km**	The use of double prefixes is conventionally prohibited.
mN (for newton meter)	**N m**	Since "m" is symbol for both meter and milli, the symbol for meter i.e. m should never be written before the symbol of another unit.
gm amp sec sq. mm mps cc	g A s mm^2 or square millimetre m s^{-1} cm^3	

(8) Operation of units :

[a] Multiplication and division of units follow general algebraic rules.
Example : 10 ms^{-1} × 2 s = 20 m.

[b] A space should be inserted between two adjacent symbols to indicate multiplication. However, the use of "." Or dot is more prevalent. Again, to indicate division we can use the per or "/" sign or the dot inverse sign.
Example : J / (m^2 . s) or J . m^{-2} . s^{-1}

[c] It is improper to use a hyphen in between the number and the unit when the number is used as an adjective. There is a space between the numerical value and unit symbol except in the case superscript units for plane angle.
Example : 14-mm film is improper, but 14 mm film is proper.

Dimensional Analysis

(9) Dimensions :

Dimensions of a physical quantity are expressed as the powers to which the fundamental units of mass, length, time etc. must be raised to obtain the derived unit of the quantity.

Example : speed = $\frac{distance}{time}$
So, speed is said to possess zero dimension in mass, one dimension in length and -1 dimension in time.

(10) Dimensional Formula :

Dimensional formula is an expression which shows how and which of the fundamental units are required to represent the unit of a physical quantity.

Example : Dimensional formula of speed = $\frac{[L]}{[T]} = [LT^{-1}]$

(11) Dimensional Equation :

Dimensional equation is the equation obtained by equating the physical quantity with its dimensional formula.
Example : The dimensional equation of speed is given as under : $[V] = [LT^{-1}]$

(12) Dimensional Formula for Different Physical Quantities

Physical Quantity	Relation	Dimensional Formula	SI Unit
Area	A = Length (a) × breath(b)	$[L^2]$	m^2
Volume	V = Length (a) × breath (b) × height (c)	$[L^3]$	m^3
Density	$D = \frac{\text{Mass } (m)}{\text{Volume } (V)}$	$\frac{[M]}{[L^3]} = [ML^{-3}]$	$kg\ m^{-3}$
Velocity	$v = \frac{\text{Displacement } (\Delta S)}{\text{time } (\Delta t)}$	$\frac{[L]}{[T]} = [LT^{-1}]$	$m\ s^{-1}$
Acceleration	$a = \frac{\text{Change in velocity } (\Delta v)}{\text{time } (\Delta t)}$	$\frac{[LT^{-1}]}{[T]} = [LT^{-2}]$	$m\ s^{-2}$
Force	F = Mass (m) × Acceleration (a)	$[M][LT^{-2}] = [MLT^{-2}]$	$kg\ m\ s^{-2}$ or N
Pressure	$P = \frac{\text{Force } (F)}{\text{Area } (A)}$	$\frac{[MLT^{-2}]}{[L^2]} = [ML^{-1}T^{-2}]$	$kg\ m^{-1}\ s^{-2}$ or Nm^{-2}

Momentum	p = Mass (m) × Velocity (v)	$[M][LT^{-1}] = [M LT^{-1}]$	$kg\ m\ s^{-1}$
Work done	W = Force (F) × Displacement (s)	$[M LT^{-2}][L] = [M L^2T^{-2}]$	$kg\ m^2\ s^{-2}$ or J
Energy	E = Force (F) × Displacement (s)	$[M LT^{-2}][L] = [M L^2T^{-2}]$	$kg\ m^2\ s^{-2}$ or J
Power	$P = \frac{\text{Work}(\Delta W)}{\text{Time}(\Delta t)}$	$\frac{[M L^2 T^{-2}]}{[T]} = [M L^2T^{-3}]$	$kg\ m^2\ s^{-3}$ or $J\ s^{-1}$
Surface Tension	$S = \frac{\text{Force}(F)}{\text{Length}(l)}$	$\frac{[M L T^{-2}]}{[L]} = [M T^{-2}]$	$g\ s^{-2}$ or $N\ m^{-1}$
Moment of Inertia	I = Mass (m) × [distance $(r)]^2$	$[M][L^2] = [M L^2]$	$kg\ m^2$
Stress	$S = \frac{\text{Force}(F)}{\text{Area}(A)}$	$\frac{[M L T^{-2}]}{[L^2]} = [M L^{-1} T^{-2}]$	$kg\ m^{-1}\ s^{-2}$ or Nm^{-2}
Longitudinal Strain	$e = \frac{\text{Change in length}(\Delta l)}{\text{Initial length}(l)}$	$\frac{[L]}{[L]} = 1$	1
Young's Modulus	$Y = \frac{\text{Longutudinal stress}(s)}{\text{Longitudinal strain}(e)}$	$\frac{[M L^{-1} T^{-2}]}{1} = [M L^{-1} T^{-2}]$	$kg\ m^{-1}\ s^{-2}$ or Nm^{-2}

1	**Gravitational Constant (G) :**
Gravitational Force : $F = \frac{Gm_1m_2}{r^2}$ $\therefore G = \frac{F r^2}{m_1 m_2}$	$[G] = \frac{[M L T^{-2}][L^2]}{[M][M]} = [M^{-1} L^3 T^{-2}]$
2	**Co-efficient of viscosity (η)**
Stokes' Law : Viscous force $F = 6\pi \eta r v$ $\therefore \eta = \frac{F}{6\pi r v}$	$[\eta] = \frac{[M L T^{-2}]}{[L][L T^{-1}]} = [M L^{-1} T^{-1}]$
3	**Specific Heat (C)**

Q = m c ΔT [Where, c = specific heat] $\therefore c = \frac{\Delta Q}{m\, \Delta T}$	$[\,c\,] = \frac{[Q]}{[m]\,[\Delta T]}$ $= \frac{[M L^2 T^{-2}]}{[M][\theta]} = [L^2 T^{-2} \theta^{-1}]$
4 Latent Heat (L)	
Latent heat (L) = $\frac{Q}{m}$	$[\,latent\ heat\,] = \frac{[Q]}{[m]} = \frac{[M L^2 T^{-2}]}{[M]}$ $= [L^2 T^{-2}]$
5 Universal Gas Constant (R)	
Ideal gas equation : p V = μ R T $\therefore R = \frac{p V}{\mu T}$	$[R] = \frac{[M L^{-1} T^{-2}][L^3]}{[N][\theta]}$ $= [M L^2 T^{-2} N^{-1} \theta^{-1}]$
6 Boltzmann Constant (K_B)	
k (or K_B) = $\frac{R}{N_A}$ [$K_B = 1.38 \times 10^{-16}$ erg $K^{-1} = 1.38 \times 10^{-23}$ J K^{-1}]	$[K_B] = \frac{[M L^2 T^{-2} N^{-1} \theta^{-1}]}{[N^{-1}]}$ $= [M L^2 T^{-2} \theta^{-1}]$
7 Thermal Conductivity (K)	
Q = $\frac{K A \Delta T\, t}{d}$ [Where, K = coefficient of thermal conductivity] $\therefore K = \frac{Q L}{A \Delta T\, t}$	$[K] = \frac{[Q]\,[d]}{[A]\,[\Delta T]\,[t]}$ $= \frac{[M L^2 T^{-2}]\,[L]}{[L^2]\,[\theta]\,[T]} = [M L T^{-3} \theta^{-1}]$
8 Stefan's Constant (σ)	
Stefan's Law : E = σT^4 $\therefore \sigma = \frac{E}{T^4}$ Where, E = energy radiated per unit area per unit time	$[\sigma] = \frac{[M L^2 T^{-2} L^{-2} T^{-1}]}{[\theta^{-4}]} = [M T^{-3} \theta^{-4}]$

(13) Quantities having Same Dimensional Formula

Quantities	Dimensional Formula
Distance, Displacement, Length, Wave length	[L]

Mass, Inertial Mass, Gravitational Mass	$[M]$
Speed, Velocity	$[LT^{-1}]$
Force, Weight, Tension	$[MLT^{-2}]$
Linear momentum, Impulse	$[MLT^{-1}]$
Work, Energy, Torque, Heat, Moment of Couple	$[ML^2T^{-2}]$
Pressure, Stress, Young Modulus, Bulk Modulus	$[ML^{-1}T^{-2}]$
Plank's Constant, Angular momentum	$[ML^2T^{-1}]$

(14) Principle of Homogeneity of Dimension

A given physical relation is dimensionally correct if the dimensions of the various terms on either side of the relation are the same.

This principle is based on the fact that two quantities of the same nature only can be added up. The resulting quantity is also of the same nature.

(15) Use of Dimensional Equations

(a) To mention the unit of a physical quantity.
(b) To check the dimensional correctness of a given physical relation ;
(c) To find the dimensions of constants or variables in an equation ;
(d) To convert a physical quantity from one system of units to another ;
(e) To establish relation between different physical quantities.

[a] To mention the unit of a physical quantity:

Physical Quantity	Dimensional Symbol	SI Unit
Gravitational Constant	$[M^{-1} L^3 T^{-2}]$	$m^3\, kg^{-1}\, s^{-2}$
Co-efficient of Viscosity	$[M L^{-1} T^{-1}]$	$kg\, m^{-1}\, s^{-1}$
Linear momentum	$[M L T^{-1}]$	$kg\, m\, s^{-1}$

[b] To check the dimensional correctness of a given physical relation:

Illustration : $s = u\,t + \frac{1}{2} a\, t^2$

$[s] : [L]$

$[ut] = [LT^{-1}][T] = [L]$
$[\frac{1}{2} at^2] = [LT^{-2}][T^2] = [L]$

The dimensional formulae of every term in the given physical relation are the same.
So, according to the principle of homogeneity of dimensions, the given physical relation $s = ut + \frac{1}{2} at^2$ is **dimensionally** correct.

Limitation: It can only check whether a physical relation is dimensionally correct or not. It cannot tell whether the relation is absolutely correct or not.

Example : The equation : $s = ut + \frac{1}{4}at^2$ is dimensionally correct but it is actually wrong equation because the correct equation is $s = ut + \frac{1}{2}at^2$.

[c] To find the dimensions of constants of variables in an equation :

Q : The equation of state of some gases can be expressed as $(P + \frac{a}{V^2})(V - b) = RT$. Here P is the pressure, V the volume, T the absolute temperature and a, b are constants. What are the dimensional formula of 'a' and 'b' ?

Solution : Given, $(P + \frac{a}{V^2})(V - b) = RT$

Since quantities of only the like nature can be added therefore the dimensional formula of $\frac{a}{V^2}$ is the same as that of pressure.

$\therefore \frac{[a]}{[V^2]} = [M L^{-1} T^{-2}]$

$[a] = [M L^{-1} T^{-2}][L^3]^2 = [M L^5 T^{-2}]$

Also the dimensional formula of b is the same as that of volume.

$[b] = [L^3]$

Unit of a is kg $m^5 s^{-2}$ and unit of b is m^3.

[d] To convert a physical quantity from one system of units to another

The method of dimensional analysis may be used to convert the value of a physical quantity in one system of units to another.

Let us consider, a physical quantity P whose dimensional formula is : $[M^x L^y T^z]$

Let us assume N_1 be its numerical value in a system of fundamental units m_1, l_1 and t_1 then

$$P = N_1 (m_1^x l_1^y t_1^z) \text{ ....(1)}$$

N_2 be its numerical value in another system of fundamental units m_2, l_2 and t_2 then

$$P = N_2 (m_2^x l_2^y t_2^z) \text{ .... (2)}$$

Since the value of the physical quantity is the same in all systems,

$\therefore N_1(m_1^x l_1^y t_1^z) = N_2(m_2^x l_2^y t_2^z)$

$\therefore N_2 = N_1 \left(\frac{m_1}{m_2}\right)^x \left(\frac{l_1}{l_2}\right)^y \left(\frac{t_1}{t_2}\right)^z$

[e] To establish relation between different physical quantities

Q : For a small sphere falling through a viscous medium, the opposing force (F) is directly proportional to the terminal velocity (v), the coefficient of viscosity (η)of the medium and radius (r) of the sphere. From dimensional analysis establish Stokes' formula.

Let us assume, $F \propto \eta^a r^b v^c$ (a, b and c are unknowns power to be determined)

or, $F = k \eta^a r^b v^c$ [k is a dimensionless constant]

Writing down the dimensional formulae of all quantities of both sides of the equation

$$[MLT^{-2}] = [ML^{-1}T^{-1}]^a [L]^b [LT^{-1}]^c$$
$$= [M^a L^{-a+b+c} T^{-a-c}]$$

Comparing dimensions,

[M] : $a = 1$ ....(1)
[L] : $-a + b + c = 1$ ....(2)
[T] : $-a - c = -2$ ....(3)

Putting $a = 1$ in equation (3), we get c = 1
Again putting **a** = 1 and b = 1 in equation (2) we get, $-1 + b + 1 = 1$
or, $b = 1$

$\therefore a = 1, b = 1, c = 1$
Hence, $F = k\eta r v$
The value of k as found experimentally comes out to be $k = 6\pi$
$\therefore F = 6\pi\eta r v$

(16) Limitations of Use of Dimensional Equations :

(a) It supplies no information about dimensionless constants. They have to be determined either by experiments or by mathematical investigation.
(b) This method cannot be used to derive the composite relations. Such as $s = ut + \frac{1}{2}at^2$ which contain more than one term on one side by the usual method.
(c) This method cannot be used to derive a relation in the cases where trigonometric or exponential functions are involved.

(d) If a physical quantity depends on three physical quantities out of which two have same dimensions, the formula cannot be derived by dimensional analysis.

Error in Measurement

(17) Error, Accuracy and Precision

The exact measurement of a physical quantity is not possible. This uncertainty in the measurement is called the error.

The **accuracy** of a measurement is a measure of how closed the measured value is to the true value of the quantity.

Precision tells us to what resolution or limit the quantity is measured.

Explanation : If the true value of a certain length is 5.374 m and two instruments with different resolutions, up to one and two decimal places respectively, are used. If first measures the length as 5.2 and the second as 5.15 then the first has more accuracy but less precision while the second has less accuracy but more precision.

(18) Significant Number

Significant figure in a measured value of any physical quantity is the number of digits in which we have a confidence of their accurate value.
More the number of significant figure, more is the accuracy of the measured value. Conversely, a measurement made only to a few significant figures is not a very accurate one even if all care is taken to make the measurement.

Rules for counting significant figures :

[1] All non-zero digits are significant. e.g.,

Number	Significant figures
12.43	4

[2] Zeros ?

Trapped Zero (All zeros appearing between two non-zero digits)	Significant	Number: 500.09 — Significant figures: 5
Leading Zero	Not Significant	Number: 0.003 — Significant figures: 1
Trailing Zeros (a) With decimal Point (b) Without decimal Point	 Significant NOT Significant	Number: 750 — Significant figures: 2 Number: 50.400 — Significant figures: 5

[3] The power of 10 is not counted as significant figure. e.g.,

Number	Significant figures
500.09×10^5	5

[4] A change of unit of a physical quantity does not change the number of significant digits or figures in a measurement. e.g. 431 cm has 3 significant digits. The same measurement expressed as either 4.31 m or 43100 mm or 0.00431 km also has 3 significant figures.
[Use scientific notation to report measurement, Like $x \times 10^y$, to avoid the confusion arising due to change in the units of the measured quantity.]

[5] The pure or exact numbers appearing in the mathematical formulae of various physical quantities have infinite number of significant figures.

(19) Rounding Off the Digit

(a) If the digit to be dropped is smaller than 5, then the preceding digit should be left unchanged.

(b) If the digit to be dropped is greater than 5, then the preceding digit should be raised by 1.

(c) If the digit to be dropped is 5 followed by digits other than zero then the preceding digit should be raised by 1 .

(d) If the digit to be dropped is 5 or 5 followed by zeros then the preceding digit is not changed if it is even.

(e) If the digit to be dropped is 5 or 5 followed by zeros then the preceding digit is raised by 1 if it is odd.

[Rules (4) and (5) are based on the convention that the number is to be rounded off to the nearest even number.]

Example :

Number	After rounding off
15.654 to 4 digits	15.65
15.656 to 4 digits	15.66
15.656 to 3 digits	15.7
15.65 to 3 digits	15.6
15.75 to 3 digits	15.8

(20) Scientific Notation

Scientific notation or **standard form** is a way of expressing numbers that are too big or too small to be conveniently written in decimal form.

In scientific notation, all numbers are written in the form : $\boldsymbol{x \times 10^y}$

Where, $1 \leq x \leq 10$ and y is a positive or negative integer.

If x is less than or equal to 5, then order of number is y and if x is greater than 5 then order of the number is $(y + 1)$. [because in order to get an approximate idea of the number we may round off the number x to 1 (for $x \leq 5$) and to 10 (for $5 < x \leq 10$)]

Example : we can write 12345 as 1.2×10^4 in scientific notation.

(21) Rules For Arithmetic Operations (With Significant Figures)

(a) In **addition or subtraction**, the final result should retain as many decimal places as are there in the number with the **least decimal places**.

(b) In **multiplication or division**, the final result should retain as many significant figures as are there in the original number with the **least significant figures**.

Example : The length and width of a rectangular sheet are measured as 25.326 cm and 10.6 cm. Taking care of significant figures, calculate its (a) perimeter and (b) area.

Length : x = 25.326 cm and width y = 10.6 cm

[a] Perimeter = 25.326 + 25.326 + 10.6 + 10.6 = 71.852
On rounding off one decimal place, we get the answer as 71.9 cm

[b] Area = (25.325 × 10.6) cm^2
= 268.4562 cm^2
On rounding off to three significant figure, we get the answer 268 cm^2

Note : we always try to measure directly the difference between two nearly equal quantities instead of measuring the quantities and the calculating their differences because subtraction of two nearly equal quantities destroys accuracy.

(22) Error in Measurement

It is the difference between the measured value and the true value of a physical quantity. It gives an indication of the limits within which the true value may lie.
There are **three types** of error : **[a]** Systematic error **[b]** Random error **[c]** Gross error

[a] Systematic errors : Errors whose causes are known are called systematic errors. These errors can be minimized by improving experimental techniques, selecting better instruments and removing personal bias as far as possible.
Systematic errors are various types :
[i] Errors due to external factors,
[ii] Errors due to imperfection,
[iii] Instrumental errors,
[iv] Personal errors.

[b] Random errors : Errors occur randomly. The causes of such type of errors are not known precisely. Hence, it is not possible to eliminate the random errors. For example, same person repeating the same experiment may get different readings each time.
These errors can be minimized by repeating the experiment and taking the arithmetic mean of all the observations. The mean value should be close to the accurate value.

Mathematically, $\bar{a} = \frac{a_1 + a_2 + a_3 + \ldots\ldots + a_n}{N} = \frac{1}{N}\sum_{i=1}^{N} a_i$

[C] Gross errors : These errors arise on the account of shear carelessness of the observer.
For example: (i) Reading an instrument without setting it properly.
(ii) Recording the observations wrongly without caring for the sources of errors.
(iii) Using wrong values of the observations in calculations.
These errors can be minimized only if observer is sincere and mentally alert.

(23) Some Important Terms Related to Random Errors

[a] Measurement Value :	It is value obtained in a measurement and is denoted by a_i.

[b] Arithmetic Mean :

Let us consider, the values obtained in several measurements be $a_1, a_2, a_3 \ldots\ldots\ldots a_n$. Then the arithmetic mean of these values is given by :

$$\bar{a} \text{ or } a_m \text{ or, } a_{av} = \frac{a_1 + a_2 + a_3 + \ldots\ldots + a_n}{n}$$

$$= \frac{1}{n} \sum_{i=1}^{n} a_i$$

[c] True Value

Actual value is something which nobody knows because no instrument is dead accurate. Every instrument has least count which gives the degree of its accuracy. So arithmetic mean of all measured values is taken as the true value (a_m).

True Value = $\bar{a}$ or a_m

$$= \frac{a_1 + a_2 + a_3 + \ldots\ldots + a_n}{n}$$

$$= \frac{1}{n} \sum_{i=1}^{n} a_i$$

[d] Absolute Error :

It is magnitude of the difference between true and the measured value of a physical quantity.

The error in the individual measured value is denoted by $\Delta a_i = |a_m - a_i|$

i.e. **absolute error = true value or arithmetic mean – measured value**

[e] Mean Absolute Error :

It is the arithmetic mean of absolute errors.

$$\Delta a_m \text{ or } \overline{\Delta a} = \frac{\sum_{i=1}^{n} |\Delta a_i|}{n}$$

[f] Relative Error Or Fractional Error :

It is the ratio of the (mean) absolute error (Δa_m) to the mean value or true value (a_m) of the quantity measured.

Relative error or fractional error

$$= \frac{(\text{mean})\text{ absolute error } (\Delta a_m)}{(\text{mean})\text{ value or true value } (a_m)}$$

Percentage error = $\frac{\Delta a_m}{a_m} \times 100$

i.e. P.E. = $\frac{(\text{mean})\text{ absolute error}}{(\text{mean})\text{ value or true value } (a_m)} \times 100$

The final result of measurement can be written as : $\boldsymbol{a = a_m \pm \Delta a_m}$

or, $\boldsymbol{a = a_m}$ ± (Percentage Error)

This means that the value of a is likely to lie between $a_m - \Delta a_m$ and $a_m + \Delta a_m$.

(24) Propagation and Combination of Error

[a] Error of a Sum or a Difference :

When two quantities are added or subtracted, the absolute error in the final result is the sum of the absolute errors in the individual quantities.

When a quantity is expressed as A = x + y

then, $\Delta A_m = \Delta x_m + \Delta y_m$

When a quantity is expressed as A = x − y

then, $\Delta A_m = \Delta x_m + \Delta y_m$

[b] Error of a Product or a Quotient :

When two quantities are multiplied or divided, the (relative or) percentage error in the final result is the sum of the (relative or) percentage errors in the individual quantities.

[c] Error in Quantity Raised to Some Power :

When a quantity is expressed as :

$$Z = A^a B^b C^c$$

Then to find the maximum error in Z, we write a relation as,

$$\frac{\Delta Z_m}{Z_m} = a\,\frac{\Delta A_m}{A_m} + b\,\frac{\Delta B_m}{B_m} + c\,\frac{\Delta C_m}{C_m}$$

[Where, a, b and c are numbers which could be positive or negative.]

Here, the maximum percentage error in Z is equal to the sum of modulus of power times maximum percentage error in quantities A, B and C.

[Thus in an experiments the quantity, which occurs with higher power in the formula for the result, should be measured with the maximum accuracy]

(25) Propagation and combination can be summarised in the table given below:

Operation	**Formula**	**Absolute error** [ΔA_m]	**Relative error** $[\frac{\Delta A_m}{A_m}]$	**Percentage error** $[\frac{\Delta A_m}{A_m}] \times 100$
Sum	$x + y$	$\Delta x_m + \Delta y_m$	$\frac{\Delta x_m + \Delta y_m}{x_m + y_m}$	$\frac{\Delta x_m + \Delta y_m}{x_m + y_m} \times 100$
Difference	$x - y$	$\Delta x_m + \Delta y_m$	$\frac{\Delta x_m + \Delta y_m}{x_m - y_m}$	$\frac{\Delta x_m + \Delta y_m}{x_m - y_m} \times 100$
Multiplication	$x \times y$	$x\,\Delta y + y\,\Delta x$	$\frac{\Delta y_m}{y_m} + \frac{\Delta x_m}{x_m}$	$(\frac{\Delta y_m}{y_m} + \frac{\Delta x_m}{x_m}) \times 100$
Division	$\frac{x}{y}$	$\frac{x\,\Delta y + y\,\Delta x}{x^2}$	$\frac{\Delta y_m}{y_m} + \frac{\Delta x_m}{x_m}$	$(\frac{\Delta y_m}{y_m} + \frac{\Delta x_m}{x_m}) \times 100$
Power	x^n	$n\,x^{n-1}\,\Delta x$	$n\,\frac{\Delta x_m}{x_m}$	$n\,\frac{\Delta x_m}{x_m} \times 100$
Root	$x^{\frac{1}{n}}$	$\frac{1}{n}\,x^{\frac{1}{n-1}}\Delta x$	$\frac{1}{n}\,\frac{\Delta x_m}{x_m}$	$\frac{1}{n}\,\frac{\Delta x_m}{x_m} \times 100$

Solved Examples & Exercise

On finding the dimensional formula and units of constants or variables in an equation

Q : What is the dimensional formula of co-efficient of viscosity.

Ans : Viscous force $F = 6\,\pi\,\eta\,r\,v$

$$\therefore \eta = \frac{F}{6\,\pi\,r\,v}$$

$$[\eta] = \frac{[M\,L\,T^{-2}]}{[L]\,[L\,T^{-1}]} = [M\,L^{-1}\,T^{-1}]$$

Try Yourself

---

(1) Find the dimensional formula of the following constants :

(a) Gravitational constant

(b) Planck's constant

(c) Universal gas constant

Q : If x = a + bt + ct^2, where x is in metres and t in seconds, find the units of b.

Ans : Given, $x = a + bt + ct^2$

From principle of dimensional homogeneity, $[bt] = [x]$

$$\text{or, } [b] = \frac{[x]}{[t]}$$

$$\text{or, } [b] = \frac{[L]}{[T]}$$

$$\therefore [b] = [L\,T^{-1}]$$

∴ The unit of b is $m\,s^{-1}$

Try Yourself

---

(2) If $t = a + bx + cx^2$, where x is in metres and t in seconds, find the units of b.

Q : Relation between force and time is given by the relation : $F = Pt^{-1} + Qt$. Which quantity has the same unit that of the P?

Ans : Given, $F = Pt^{-1} + Qt$

From Principle of dimensional homogeneity, $[Pt^{-1}] = [F]$

$$\text{or, } [P] = \frac{[F]}{[t^{-1}]}$$

$$\text{or, } [P] = \frac{[M L\,T^{-2}]}{[T^{-1}]}$$

$$\therefore [P] = [M\,L\,T^{-1}]$$

∴ P has the dimensional formula same that of linear momentum. So, P has the same unit that of linear momentum and the SI unit is $kg\,m\,s^{-1}$.

Try Yourself

---

(3) Write the dimensions of $\frac{a}{b}$ in the relation: $F = a\sqrt{x} + bt^2$, where F is force, x is distance and t is time.

(4) In the equation y = a sin (ωt – kx), t and x stand for time and distance respectively. Obtain the dimensional formula of ω and k.
(5) In the equation r = m^2 sin pt, t is time, if N be the unit of m, then what will be the unit of r?

Q : What is the dimensional formula of $\frac{1}{\mu_0 \varepsilon_0}$? where symbols have their usual meanings.

Ans : Velocity of electromagnetic wave in vacuum, $c = \frac{1}{\sqrt{\mu_0 \varepsilon_0}}$

or, $\frac{1}{\mu_0 \varepsilon_0} = c^2$

$\therefore [\frac{1}{\mu_0 \varepsilon_0}] = [\mathrm{L\,T^{-1}}]^2 = [\mathrm{L^2\,T^{-2}}]$

Q : What is the dimensional formula of proportionality constant if force is proportional to square of velocity?

Ans : According to the problem, $F \propto v^2$

or, $F = kv^2$

or, $k = \frac{F}{v^2}$

$\therefore [k] = \frac{[\mathrm{M\,L\,T^{-2}}]}{[\mathrm{L^2\,T^{-2}}]} = [\mathrm{M\,L^{-1}}]$

Try Yourself

---

(6) The energy of a system E = $av^2 + kx^2$, where v is velocity and x is distance. Determine the units of a and k.
(7) An unknown quantity x multiplied by velocity equal to power. Identify x, using method of dimensions.
(8) The equation of state of some gases can be expressed as $(P + \frac{a}{V^2})(V - b) = RT$. Here P is the pressure, V the volume, T the absolute temperature and a, b are constants. What are the dimensional formula of 'a' and 'b' ?

On Checking the Correctness of a Relation

Q : Check the dimensional consistency in the case of the following equations: $v^2 = u^2 + 2as$ (where, the symbols have their usual meanings)

Ans : Given, $v^2 = u^2 + 2as$
Now, $[v^2] = [\mathrm{L\,T^{-1}}]^2 = [\mathrm{L^2\,T^{-2}}]$
$[u^2] = [\mathrm{L\,T^{-1}}]^2 = [\mathrm{L^2\,T^{-2}}]$
and $[2as] = [\mathrm{L\,T^{-2}}][\mathrm{L}] = [\mathrm{L^2\,T^{-2}}]$

$\therefore$ The given equation is dimensionally correct.

Try Yourself

---

(9) Test by using dimensional analysis, the accuracy of the relation :
[a] $\lambda = \frac{h}{mv}$
[b] $s = ut + \frac{1}{2}at^2$
[c] $\rho = \frac{3g}{4\pi R G}$
[d] $v^2 = u^2 + 2as$

[e] $v_c = \frac{k\eta}{\rho r}$

[where the letters have their usual meanings]

(10) Verify dimensionally the relation: $t = 2\pi\sqrt{\frac{l}{g}}$ for the time period of a simple pendulum. Where, l is the length of the pendulum and g is the acceleration due to gravity.

(11) Time period of an oscillating drop of radius r, density ρ and surface tension s is $t = k\sqrt{\frac{\rho r^3}{s}}$ Check the correctness of the relation.

(12) Check the dimensional consistency in the case of the following equations:

[i] $\tau = I\alpha$

[where, τ is the torque acting on a body, I is the moment of inertia and α is the angular acceleration]

[ii] $h = \frac{r\rho g}{2S\cos\theta}$

[where, h is height, r is radius, ρ is density, s is surface tension and g is the acceleration due to gravity]

On Conversion From One Unit System To Another

Q : Convert 2 N into dyne with the help of dimensional analysis.

Ans : Dimensional formula of force is : $[MLT^{-2}]$

If the fundamental units in SI are m_1, l_1 and t_1 then F = $2\,(m_1 l_1 t_1^{-2})$ ....(1)

Let us consider, x be its numerical value in CGS and the fundamental units are m_2, l_2 and t_2 then

F = $x\,(m_2 l_2 t_2^{-2})$ .... (2)

Since the value of the physical quantity is the same in all systems,

$\therefore x\,(m_2 l_2 t_2^{-2}) = 2\,(m_1 l_1 t_1^{-2})$

or, $x = 2\left(\frac{m_1}{m_2}\right)^1\left(\frac{l_1}{l_2}\right)^1\left(\frac{t_1}{t_2}\right)^{-2}$

or, $x = 2\left(\frac{1\text{ kg}}{1\text{ g}}\right)^1\left(\frac{1\text{ m}}{1\text{ cm}}\right)^1\left(\frac{1\text{ s}}{1\text{ s}}\right)^{-2}$

or, $x = 2\left(\frac{1000\text{ g}}{1\text{ g}}\right)^1\left(\frac{100\text{ cm}}{1\text{ cm}}\right)^1\left(\frac{1\text{ s}}{1\text{ s}}\right)^{-2}$

$\therefore x = 2\times 10^3 \times 10^2 = 2\times 10^5$

Hence, 2 N = 2×10^5 dyn

Try Yourself

(13) In CGS system value of the gravitational constant G is 6.67×10^{-8}. Convert this value in SI.

[Ans : 6.67×10^{-11} N m^{-2} kg^{-2}]

(14) In CGS the density of mercury is 13.6 g cm^{-3}, what is the value of the density in SI ?

[Ans : 13.6×10^3 kg m^{-3}]

On Deriving Physical Relation

Q : Using the method of dimensions, derive an expression for the centripetal force F acting on a particle of mass m moving with velocity v in a circle of radius r.

Ans : Let us assume, $F \propto m^a v^b r^c$ (a, b and c are unknown powers to be determined) or, $F = k\, m^a\, v^b\, r^c$ ....(1) (k is a non-zero dimensionless constant)

Writing down the dimensional formulae of all quantities of both sides of the equation

$[\mathrm{M\,L\,T^{-2}}] = [\mathrm{M}]^a\,[\mathrm{L\,T^{-1}}]^b\,[\mathrm{L}]^c$

$= [\mathrm{M}^a\,\mathrm{L}^{b+c}\,\mathrm{T}^{-b}]$

Comparing dimensions,

[M] : $a = 1$ ....(2)

[L] : b + c = 1 ....(3)

[T] : − b = −2 ....(4)

From (2), we get, $a = 1$

From (4), we get, b = 2

Putting b = 2 in equation (3) we get,

c = − 1

∴ $a = 1$, b = 2, c = −1

Hence, $F = \mathrm{k}\,\mathrm{m}^1\,v^2\,r^{-1} = \frac{k\,m\,v^2}{r}$

Try Yourself

---

(15) Position of a body with acceleration a is given by $x = K\,a^m\,t^n$. Here t is time. Find the values of m and n.
[Ans : m = 1 and n = 2]

(16) The velocity of a body which has fallen freely under gravity varies as $g^p h^q$, where g is acceleration due to gravity at a place and h is the height which the body has fallen from. Determine the values of p and q.
[Ans : $p = \frac{1}{2}$ and $q = \frac{1}{2}$]

(17) Units of X, Y and Z are g $cm^2\,s^{-5}$, g s^{-1} and cm s^{-2} respectively. Find out the mathematical relation between them.
[Ans : $X = k\,Y\,Z^2$]

(18) The velocity (v) of sound through a medium may be assumed to depend on (1) the density (e) of the medium and (2) modulus of elasticity (E). If the dimensions for elasticity are $[ML^{-1}T^{-2}]$, deduce the formula for the velocity of sound by the method of dimensions.

[Ans : $v = k\sqrt{\frac{E}{e}}$]

(19) Deduce the expression of critical velocity by the method of dimensions.
[Ans : $v_c = \frac{k\,\eta}{\rho\,r}$]

(20) The escape velocity (v) of a body depends upon : (i) the acceleration due to gravity (g) of the planet, (ii) the radius (r) of the planet. Establish dimensionally the relationship between them.
[Ans : $v = k\sqrt{g\,r}$]

(21) Velocity (v) of water waves may depend upon their wavelength (λ), the density of water (ρ) and the acceleration due to gravity (g). Find the relation between these quantities by the method of dimension.
[Ans : $v = k\sqrt{g\,\lambda}$]

(22) Assuming that the frequency (n) of a vibrating string depends upon the load (F) applied, length of the string (l) and mass per unit length (m), prove that n = $\frac{k}{l}\sqrt{\frac{F}{m}}$. where k is a dimensionless constant.

Q : If energy (E), velocity (V) and the force (F) be the fundamental quantities, then what will be the dimensional formula of mass?

Let us assume, $m = k\, E^a\, V^b\, F^c$

(where, a, b and c are unknowns power to be determined and k is a non-zero dimensionless constant)

Writing down the dimensional formulae of all quantities of both sides of the equation

$[\,M\,] = [M\,L^2\,T^{-2}\,]^a\,[\,L\,T^{-1}\,]^b\,[\,M\,L\,T^{-2}\,]^c$

$= [\,M^{a+c}\,L^{2a+b+c}\,T^{-2a-b-2c}\,]$

Comparing dimensions,

[M] : a + c = 1 ....(1)

[L] : 2 a + b + c = 0 ....(2)

[T] : – 2a – b – 2 c = 0 ....(3)

From (1), we get, $a = 1 - c$

Putting the value of a in (3) we get, – 2 (1 – c) – b – 2 c = 0

or, – 2 – b = 0

or, b = – 2

Now putting the value of a and b in (3) we get, 2 (1 – c) + (– 2) + c = 0

or, – c = 0

∴ c = 0

Putting c = 2 in equation (1) we get, a = 1

∴ a = 1, b = – 2, c = 0

Hence, [m] = $[\,E^1\,V^{-2}\,F^0\,]$

Try Yourself

---

(23) If the velocity of light c, gravitational constant G and Planck's constant h are chosen as fundamental units, find the dimensions of length in the new system.
[Ans : [L] = $[\,c^{-\frac{3}{2}}\,G^{\frac{1}{2}}\,h^{\frac{1}{2}}\,]$]

(24) The energy (E), angular momentum (L) and universal gravitational constant (G) are chosen as fundamental quantities. Find the dimensions of universal gravitational constant in the dimensional formula of Planck's constant (h).
[Ans : [h] = $[\,E^0 L^1\,G^0]$]

(25) If velocity (v), acceleration (A) and force (F) be the fundamental quantities, then determine the dimensional formula for Young's modulus.
[Ans : [Y] = $[\,v^{-4}\,A^2\,F^1]$]

(26) If force (F), length (L) and time (T) be the fundamental quantities, then what will be the dimensional formula for mass?
[Ans : [m] = [$F L^{-1} T^2$]]

(27) If energy (E), velocity (v) and the force (F) be the fundamental quantities, then what will be the dimensional formula of mass?
[Ans : [m] = [$E v^{-2} F^0$]]

On Number of Significant figures

Q : State the number of significant figures in the following:
(a) 33.7
(b) 6700 kg
(c) 76.0
(d) 0.0046

Ans :

(a) 33.7 has three significant figures. (RULE : All non-zero digits are significant.)

(b) 6700 kg has two significant figures. (RULE : In a number without decimal point, trailing zero is not significant)

(c) 76.0 has three significant figures. (RULE : In a number with decimal point, trailing zero is significant)

(d) 0.0046 has two significant figures. (RULE : Leading zeros are not significant)

Q : How many significant figures are there in the value 3.50 × 10^{10} m ?

Ans : 3.50 × 10^{10} m has three significant figures.

(RULES : All non-zero digits are significant.)

(RULE : In a number with decimal point, trailing zero is significant)

(RULE : The power of 10 is not counted as significant figure.)

Q : How many zeros are significant in the following measured values ?
(a) 760050
(b) 0.009700

Ans : (a) 760050 has two significant zeros. (76**00**50)

(b) 0.009700 has two significant zeros. (0.0097**00**)

Try Yourself

---

(28) State the number of significant figures in the following:
[a] 12.34
[b] 2.26 × 10^{24} kg,
[c] 4200
[d] 0.34
[e] 0.007 m^2
[f] 4.2370 g cm^{-3}
[g] 6.032 N m^{-2}

[h] 0.0006032

(29) What is the uncertain digit in the measurement of length reported as 41.68 cm ?

(30) What is the number of significant zeros present in the measured value of 0.020040 ?

(31) What is the number of significant figures in a pure number 410 ?

Q : Round off the following numbers as indicated :
[a] 7.37 to 2 digits
[b] 6.32 to 2 digits
[c] 15.654 to 3 digit
[d] 15.75 to 3 digits
[e] 15.85 to 3 digits

Ans : [a] 7.3
[b] 6.3
[c] 15.7
[d] 15.8
[e] 15.8

Q : Round 451.45 to four, three, and two significant digits.

Ans : (a) 451.4
(b) 451
(c) 450

Q : Express the following in the scientific notation with 2 significant figures-
(a) 0.0032
(b) 58600
(c) 100.0

Ans : (a) 3.2×10^{-3}
(b) 5.9×10^{4}
(c) 1.0×10^{2}

Try Yourself

---

(32) Round off the following numbers as indicated :
[a] 6.36 to 2 digits
[b] 6.32 to 2 digits
[c] 15.654 to 3 digit
[d] 15.75 to 3 digits
[e] 15.85 to 3 digits
[f] 5.996×10^{4} to 3 digits
[g] 0.779 to 1 digit
[h] 132667 to 5 digits

(33) Round off to three significant digits :
[a] 0.03927 kg
[b] 4.085×10^{8} s
[c] 20.96 meter

[d] 4996 × 10^4
[e] 6.032 N m^{-2}

On Rules for Arithmetic Operation with Significant Figures

Q : If A = 4.213 kg and B = 3.21 kg, then find A + B.

Ans : Given, A = 4.213 kg → three decimal places
and B = 3.21 kg → two decimal place

Now, A + B = (4.213 + 3.21) kg

= 7.423 kg

But the answer should be expressed as 7.42 kg.

Q : A particle of mass 3.513 kg is moving along x axis with velocity 5.00 m s^{-1}. Calculate its linear momentum.

Ans : Given, mass (m) = 3.513 kg → four significant figure
and velocity (v) = 5.00 m s^{-1} → three significant figure

Now, Linear momentum : p = mv = 3.513 × 5.00 kg m s^{-1}

= 17.565 kg m s^{-1}

= 17.6 kg m s^{-1} (rounding off to three significant figure)

Try Yourself

---

(34) If A = 4.213 kg and B = 3.21 kg, then find A + B.
[Ans : 7.42 kg]

(35) Subtract 0.2 J from 7.26 J and express the result with correct number of significant figure.
[Ans : 7.1 J]

(36) A particle of mass 3.513 kg is moving along x axis with velocity 5.00 m s^{-1}. Calculate its linear momentum.
[Ans : 17.6 kg m s^{-1}]

(37) Each side of a cube is measured to be 7.20 m. What are the total surface area and the volume of the cube to appropriate significant figure?
[Ans : 311 m^2, 373 m^3]

(38) 5.74 g of a substance occupied a volume of 1.2 cm^3. Calculate its density with due to regard for significant figures.
[Ans : 4.8 g cm^{-3}]

(39) The time taken by a pendulum to complete 25 vibrations is 88.0 seconds. Calculate the time period of the pendulum in second.
[Ans : 3.52 s]

(40) The radius of a circle is 0.51 cm. calculate its area with due regard to significant figures. Given π = 3.14.
[Ans : 0.82 cm^2]

(41) Given : π = 3.14. Determine π^2 with due regards for significant figure.
[Ans : 9.86]

(42) Solve the following with due regard to significant figures: $\frac{0.9996 \times 3.52}{1.758}$
[Ans : 2.00]

On Rules for Arithmetic Operation with Scientific Notation

Q : Add 1.1 × 10^4 with 1.23 × 10^3

Ans : $1.1 \times 10^4 + 1.23 \times 10^3$
$= 1.1 \times 10^4 + 0.123 \times 10^4$
$= 1.223 \times 10^4$
$= 1.2 \times 10^4$ (after rounding off to one decimal place)

Try Yourself

---

(43) Add 6.75×10^3 cm to 4.52×10^2 cm.
(44) Subtract 3.2×10^{-6} from 4.7×10^{-4} with due to regard to significant figures.

On Error in Measurement

Q : **In an experiment, the value of refractive index of glass was found to be 1.54, 1.53, 1.54 and 1.56 in successive measurement.**

Calculate (1) the mean value of refractive index of glass, (2) absolute error in each measurement (3) mean absolute error, (4) relative error, (5) percentage error.

Ans : Measurement Value : $\mu_1 = 1.54$,

$\mu_2 = 1.53$,

$\mu_3 = 1.54$ and

$\mu_4 = 1.56$

[1] Mean value of refractive index of glass : $\mu_m = \frac{1.54 + 1.53 + 1.54 + 1.56}{4} = 1.5425$

[2] Absolute Error :

$\Delta \mu_1 = |1.5425 - 1.54| = 0.0025$

$\Delta \mu_2 = |1.5425 - 1.53| = 0.0125$

$\Delta \mu_3 = |1.5425 - 1.54| = 0.0025$

$\Delta \mu_4 = |1.5425 - 1.56| = 0.0175$

[3] Mean Absolute Error : $\Delta \mu_m = \frac{\sum_{i=1}^{n} |\Delta \mu_i|}{n}$

$= \frac{0.0025 + 0.0125 + 0.0025 + 0.0175}{4} = 0.0088$

[4] Relative Error : Relative error $= \frac{0.0088}{1.5425} = 0.0057$

[5] Percentage error = $0.0057 \times 100 = 0.57$

Try Yourself

(45) In an experiment, the value of refractive index of glass was found to be 1.54, 1.53, 1.44, 1.54, 1.56 and 1.45 in successive measurement. Calculate (1) the mean value of refractive index of glass, (2) absolute error in each measurement (3) mean absolute error, (4) relative error, (5) percentage error.

(46) The successive measurement of time period of simple pendulum in a simple pendulum experiment come out to be 2.63 s, 2.56 s, 2.42 s, 2.71s and 2.80 s.
(1) What is the mean period of oscillation of pendulum?
(2) What is the arithmetic mean of all absolute errors ?
(3) Calculate the percentage error?

On Error propagation in addition and subtraction Formula

Q : The volumes of two bodies are measured to be V_1 = (10.2 $\pm$ 0.02) $\mathrm{cm^3}$ and V_2 = (6.4 $\pm$ 0.01) $\mathrm{cm^3}$. Calculate sum and difference in volume with error limits.

Ans : Given, V_1 = (10.2 $\pm$ 0.02) $\mathrm{cm^3}$

and V_2 = (6.4 $\pm$ 0.01) $\mathrm{cm^3}$

$\therefore V' = V_1 + V_2$
= { (10.2 $\pm$ 0.02) + (6.4 $\pm$ 0.01)} $\mathrm{cm^3}$
= 16.6 $\pm$ 0.03 $\mathrm{cm^3}$

Again, $V'' = V_1 - V_2$
= {(10.2 $\pm$ 0.02) − (6.4 $\pm$ 0.01)} $\mathrm{cm^3}$ = 3.8 $\pm$ 0.03 $\mathrm{cm^3}$

Try Yourself

(47) The lengths of two rods are recorded as 25.2 $\pm$ 0.1 cm and 16.8 $\pm$ 0.1 cm. Find the sum of the lengths of two rods with the limits of error.
[Ans : 42.0 $\pm$ 0.2 cm]

(48) The initial and final temperature of a liquid in a container are observed to be 76.3 $\pm$ 0.4 °C and 67.7 $\pm$ 0.3 °C. Determine the fall in temperature of the liquid.
[Ans : 8.6 $\pm$ 0.7 °C]

(49) The volumes of two bodies are measured to be V_1 = (10.4 $\pm$ 0.01) $\mathrm{cm^3}$ and V_2 = (6.4 $\pm$ 0.01) $\mathrm{cm^3}$. Calculate sum and difference in volume with error limits.
[Ans : 16.8 $\pm$ 0.02 $\mathrm{cm^3}$ and 4.0 $\pm$ 0.02 $\mathrm{cm^3}$]

On Error propagation in product of quantities

Q : A capacitor of capacitance C = (2.0 $\pm$ 0.1) µF is charged to a voltage V = (20 $\pm$ 0.2) volt. What will be the charge Q on the capacitor ? Use Q = CV

Ans : Given, C = (2.0 $\pm$ 0.1) µF and V = (20 $\pm$ 0.2) volt

We know that Q = CV

$\therefore Q_m = C_m V_m$ = 2.0 × 20 = 40

Again, $\frac{\Delta Qm}{Qm} = \frac{\Delta Cm}{Cm} + \frac{\Delta Vm}{Vm}$

$= \frac{0.1}{2} + \frac{0.2}{20}$

$= 0.05 + 0.01 = 0.06 = 6\%$

∴ Charge Q on the capacitor is given by : Q = $Q_m \pm$ (Percentage Error) = 40 $\pm$ 6%

Try Yourself

---

(50) A capacitor of capacitance C = (2.0 $\pm$ 0.1) μF is charged to a voltage V = (20 $\pm$ 0.2) volt. What will be the charge Q on the capacitor ? Use Q = CV

(51) The resistance R = $\frac{V}{I}$, where V = (100 $\pm$ 5) volt and I = (10 $\pm$ 0.2) A. Find the percentage error in V, I and R.

(52) A rectangular plate has a length of (21.3 $\pm$ 0.2) cm and a width of (9.80 $\pm$ 0.10) cm. Calculate the area of the plate and also percentage error.

Q: **An experiment measures quantities a, b, c and X is calculated from the formula X = $\frac{a\,b^2}{c^3}$. The percentage errors in a, b and c are $\pm$ 1 %, $\pm$ 3% and $\pm$ 2% respectively. What is the percentage error of X?**

Ans : Given, x = $\frac{a\,b^2}{c^3}$

∴ $\frac{\Delta Xm}{Xm} = \frac{\Delta am}{am} + 2\frac{\Delta bm}{bm} + 3\frac{\Delta cm}{cm}$

= 1% + 2× 3% + 3×2%

= 13%

Try Yourself

---

(53) Find the relative error in Z if Z = $A^4\,B^{1/3}\,C\,D^{3/2}$

(54) A physical quantity is represented by : x = $M^a L^b T^c$. If the percentage error in measurement of M, L and T are α, β and γ respectively, then what is the total percentage error in the measurement of the physical quantity?

(55) An experiment measures quantities a, b, c and X is calculated from the formula X = $\frac{a^{\frac{1}{2}}\,b^2}{c^4}$.The percentage errors in a, b and c are $\pm$ 1 %, $\pm$ 2% and $\pm$ 2% respectively. What is the percentage error of X?

(56) The centripetal force is given by F = $\frac{mv^2}{r}$. The mass, velocity and radius of the circular path of an object are 0.5 kg, 10 ms^{-1} and 0.4 m respectively. Find the percentage error in force. Given: m, v and r are measured to accuracies of 0.005 kg, 0.01 ms^{-1} and 0.01 m respectively.

(57) The radius of a sphere is measured to be 5.3 $\pm$ 0.1 cm. Calculate the percentage error in volume.

(58) The period of oscillation of a simple pendulum is T = $2\pi\sqrt{\frac{L}{g}}$. Measured value of L is 20.0 cm known to 1 mm accuracy and time for 100 oscillations of the pendulum is found to be 90 s using a wrist watch of 1 s resolution. What is the accuracy in the determination of g .

Q : **Two resistors of resistances R_1 = (100 $\pm$ 3) ohm and R_2 = (200 $\pm$ 4) ohm are connected (a) in series, (b) in parallel. Find the equivalent resistance of the series combination and parallel combination.**

Ans : Given, R_1 = (100 $\pm$ 3) ohm and R_2 = (200 $\pm$ 4) ohm

(a) Equivalent resistant in series : $R_{series} = R_1 + R_2$

= (100 + 200) $\pm$ (3 + 4) ohm

= 300 $\pm$ 7 ohm

(b) Let us, equivalent resistant in parallel combination is R_p

Now, $(R_p)_m = \frac{(R_1)\,m\,(R_2)m}{(R_1)\,m + (R_1)\,m}$

$= \frac{100 \times 200}{100 + 200} = \frac{20000}{300}$ = 67.7 ohm

Again from, $\frac{1}{R_p} = \frac{1}{R_1} + \frac{1}{R_2}$

or, $\frac{(\Delta R_p)_m}{(R_p)_m^{\;2}} = \frac{(\Delta R_1)m}{(R_1)m^2} + \frac{(\Delta R_2)m}{(R_2)m^2}$

or, $\frac{(\Delta R_p)_m}{(R_p)_m^{\;2}} = \frac{3}{100^2} + \frac{4}{200^2}$

or, $\frac{(\Delta R_p)_m}{(R_p)_m^{\;2}} = \frac{3}{100^2} + \frac{4}{200^2}$

or, $(\Delta R_p)_m = (\frac{3}{10000} + \frac{4}{40000})\ (67.7)^2$

$= \frac{16}{40000}\ (67.7)^2 = 1.83$

$\therefore R_p = (R_p)_m \pm (\Delta R_p)_m$

= (67.7 $\pm$ 1.83) ohm

Try Yourself

(59) Two resistors of resistances R_1 = (100 $\pm$ 3) ohm and R_2 = (200 $\pm$ 4) ohm are connected (a) in series, (b) in parallel. Find the equivalent resistance of the series combination and parallel combination.

(60) Calculate focal length of a spherical mirror from the following observations. Object distance u = (50.1 $\pm$ 0.5) cm and image distance v = (20.1 $\pm$ 0.2) cm

MCQ – 1 : Physical World & Measurement

Physics MCQ || Class – XI	Physical World & Measurement
	Topic : Unit & Unit System

Important Points

Important Units :

Gravitational Constant (G) : N m^2 kg^{-2}
Universal Gas Constant (*R*) : J K^{-1} mol^{-1}
Stefan's Constant : J m^{-2} s^{-1} K^{-4}
Thermal Conductivity (K) : W $m^{-1}K^{-1}$
Planck's constant (h) : J s

Important Facts :

- Measurement of Physical Quantity = Numerical Value (n) × Unit (u)

(1) The base quantity among the following is
(a) Speed
(b) Weight
(c) Length
(d) Area

(2) Number of fundamental units in SI is
(a) 3
(b) 4
(c) 7
(d) 5

(3) Which of the following sets cannot enter into the list of fundamental quantities in any system of units ?
(a) Length, time and velocity
(b) Length, mass and velocity
(c) Mass, time and velocity
(d) Length, time and mass

(4) A physical quantity is measured and its value is found to be nu. Where, n = numerical value and u = unit. Then which of the following relation is true ?
(a) n ∝ u^2
(b) n ∝ u
(c) n ∝ $\sqrt{u}$
(d) n ∝ $\frac{1}{u}$

(5) If u_1 and u_2 are the units selected in two systems of measurement and n_1 and n_2 their numerical values, then
(a) $n_1u_1 = n_2u_2$
(b) $n_1u_1 + n_2u_2 = 0$
(c) $n_1n_2 = u_1u_2$
(d) $n_1 + u_1 = n_2 + u_2$

(6) Which of the following is not a unit of time?
(a) Second
(b) Minute
(c) Hour
(d) Light year

(7) Which of the following is a unit of force?
(a) N m
(b) mN
(c) nm
(d) Ns

(8) 'Torr" is the unit of which of the following?
(a) Pressure
(b) volume
(c) density
(d) flux

(9) Unit of surface tension is
(a) N m^{-1}
(b) N m^{-2}
(c) N^2 m^{-1}
(d) N m^{-3}

(10) A suitable unit for gravitational constant is
(a) kg m s^{-1}
(b) N m^1 s
(c) N m^2 kg^{-2}
(d) J s

(11) The SI unit of universal gas constant (*R*) is
(a) W K^{-1} mol^{-1}
(b) N K^{-1} mol^{-1}
(c) J K^{-1} mol^{-1}
(d) erg K^{-1} mol^{-1}

(12) The unit of impulse per unit area is as same that of
(a) Viscosity
(b) Surface tension
(c) Bulk modulus
(d) Force

(13) Unit of Stefan's constant is
(a) J s^{-1}
(b) J m^{-2} s^{-1} K^{-4}
(c) J m^{-2}
(d) J s

(14) The unit of thermal conductivity is
(a) W $m^{-1}K^{-1}$
(b) J m K^{-1}
(c) J m^{-1} K^{-1}
(d) W m K^{-1}

(15) The unit of the Stefan-Boltzmann's constant is
(a) W $m^{-2}K^{-4}$
(b) W m^{-2}
(c) W m^{-2} K^{-1}
(d) W $m^{-2}K^{-2}$

(16) The unit of permittivity of free space ε_0, is
(a) coulomb / newton-meter
(b) newton-metre^2/ coulomb^2
(c) coulomb^2/newton – meter^2
(d) coulomb^2/ (newton – meter)^2

(17) The unit of Planck's constant is
(a) Joule
(b) J s^{-1}
(c) J m^{-1}
(d) J s

(18) Ampere-hour is the unit of
(a) quantity of charge
(b) potential
(c) energy
(d) current

(19) Hertz is the unit of
(a) frequency
(b) force
(c) electric charge
(d) magnetic flux

(20) Unit of magnetic moment is
(a) A m^2
(b) A m
(c) Wb m^2
(d) Wb m^{-1}

(21) The unit of resistance is
(a) ohm
(b) volt
(c) mho
(d) N

(22) The unit of absolute permittivity is
(a) farad meter
(b) farad m^{-1}
(c) farad m^{-2}
(d) farad

(23) Faraday is the unit of
(a) Charge
(b) Mass
(c) emf
(d) Energy

 # Important Points

$\frac{L}{R}$ / RC / $\sqrt{LC}$ = Time Constant
Unit : second
Where, R = resistance
L = Inductance
C = Capacitance

(24) The unit of $\frac{L}{R}$ is (where L = inductance and R = resistance)
(a) second
(b) second^{-1}
(c) volt
(d) ampere

(25) One astronomical unit is a distance equal to
(a) 9.46×10^{15} m
(b) 1.496×10^{11} m
(c) 3×10^{8} m
(d) 3.08×10^{16} m

(26) Which of the following practical units of length is not correct?
(a) 1 fm = 10^{-15} m
(b) 1 astronomical unit = 1.496×10^{11} m
(c) 1 parsec = 3.26 light year
(d) 1 light year = 9.46×10^{12} m

(27) One unified atomic mass unit representation a mass of magnitude
(a) 10^{-30} kg
(b) 1.66×10^{-27} kg

(c) 1.66×10^{-27} m
(d) 10^{30} kg

(28) Curie is a unit of
(a) Frequency
(b) Half life
(c) Radioactivity
(d) Intensity of γ rays

(29) If the average life of a person is taken as 100 s, the age of the universe on this scale is of the order
(a) 10^{10} s
(b) 10^{8} s
(c) 10^{7} s
(d) 10^{9} s

(30) The value of 60° in radian is
(a) $\frac{\pi}{2}$
(b) $\frac{\pi}{3}$
(c) $\frac{\pi}{4}$
(d) $\frac{\pi}{5}$

(31) Total plane angle subtended by a circle at its centre is
(a) π rad
(b) 2π rad
(c) $\frac{2\pi}{3}$ rad
(d) $\frac{\pi}{2}$ rad

(32) Which of the following pairs is wrong
(a) Pressure – Barometer
(b) Relative density – Pyrometer
(c) Temperature – Thermometer
(d) Earthquake – Seismograph

(33) The exchange of particles responsible for weak interactions are
(a) Gluons
(b) π meson
(c) photon
(d) W and Z bosons

(34) Which of the following does not experience strong nuclear force?
(a) Leptons
(b) Baryons
(c) Hadrons
(d) Proton

(35) Maxwell unified
(a) Electricity and gravitation
(b) Electricity and magnetism
(c) Electromagnetism with optics
(d) Electromagnetism with weak force

(36) Which of the following is not a derived force?
(a) Tension in a string
(b) Electrostatics force between proton and proton
(c) Vander waal force
(d) Nuclear force between proton-proton

(37) Which of the following is not true about electric charge?
(a) Charge on a body is always integral multiple of certain charge known as charge of electron
(b) Charge is a scalar quantity.
(c) Net charge on an isolated system is always conserved.
(d) Charge can be converted into energy and energy can be converted into charge.

Answer

Physical World & Measurement

Topic : Unit & Unit System

Q	Ans	Q	Ans	Q	Ans	Q	Ans	Q	Ans
(1)	(c)	(9)	(a)	(17)	(d)	(25)	(b)	(33)	(d)
(2)	(c)	(10)	(c)	(18)	(a)	(26)	(d)	(34)	(a)
(3)	(a)	(11)	(c)	(19)	(a)	(27)	(b)	(35)	(c)
(4)	(d)	(12)	(a)	(20)	(a)	(28)	(c)	(36)	(b)
(5)	(a)	(13)	(b)	(21)	(a)	(29)	(a)	(37)	(d)
(6)	(d)	(14)	(a)	(22)	(b)	(30)	(b)		
(7)	(c)	(15)	(a)	(23)	(a)	(31)	(b)		
(8)	(a)	(16)	(c)	(24)	(a)	(32)	(b)		

Physics MCQ | | Class – XI

Physical World & Measurement

Topic : Dimension Finding of a Physical Quantity

 # Important Points

Important Dimensional Formulae :

- [Gravitational Constant] = [$M^{-1} L^3 T^{-2}$]
- [Universal Gas Constant] = [$M L^2 T^{-2} N^{-1} \theta^{-1}$]
- [Thermal Conductivity] = [$M L T^{-3} \theta^{-1}$]
- [Impulse] = [$ML T^{-1}$]
- [Planck's constant] = [$M L^2 T^{-1}$]
- [Solar Constant] = [$M^1 T^{-3}$]
- [Co-efficient of Viscosity] = [$M L^{-1} T^{-1}$]
- [Specific Heat] = [$L^2 T^{-2} \theta^{-1}$]
- [Latent Heat] = [$L^2 T^{-2}$]
- [Boltzmann Constant] = [$M L^2 T^{-2} \theta^{-1}$]
- [Stefan's Constant] = [$M T^{-3} \theta^{-4}$]

(1) Two physical quantities A and B have different dimensions. Which mathematical operation given below is physically possible?
(a) $\sqrt{AB}$
(b) A (1 + B)
(c) A – B
(d) A + B

(2) Two physical quantities A and B have different dimensions. Which mathematical operation given below is physically meaningful?
(a) $\frac{A}{B}$
(b) A + B
(c) A – B
(d) None

(3) If A, B and C are physical quantities, having different dimensions, which of the following combinations can never be a meaningful quantity ?
(a) $\frac{A-B}{C}$
(b) $\frac{AB}{C}$
(c) AB – R
(d) $\frac{AC-B^2}{C}$

(4) What are the dimensions of the change in velocity?
(a) [$M^0 L^0 T^0$]
(b) [$M^1 L^2 T^{-2}$]
(c) [$L^1 T^{-1}$]
(d) [$L T^{-2}$]

(5) Which of the following has the dimension of pressure
(a) [$M L T^{-2}$]
(b) [$M L^{-1} T^{-2}$]
(c) [$M L^{-2} T^{-2}$]
(d) [$M^{-1} L^{-1}$]

(6) The dimensional formula for energy is
(a) [$M L T^{-2}$]
(b) [$M L^2 T^{-2}$]
(c) [$M^{-1} L^2 T$]
(d) [$M L^2 T$]

(7) The dimensions of potential energy of an object in mass, length and time are respectively
(a) 2, 2, 1
(b) 1, 2, - 2
(c) – 2, 1, 2
(d) 1, - 1, 2

(8) The dimensions of time in energy are
(a) 0
(b) – 2
(c) 2
(d) 1

(9) The dimensional formula for impulse is
(a) [$M L T^{-2}$]
(b) [$ML T^{-1}$]
(c) [$M L^2 T^{-1}$]
(d) [$M^2 L T^{-1}$]

(10) The unit of angular frequency is rad s^{-1}. Its dimension is
(a) [L]
(b) [$L T^{-2}$]
(c) [T]
(d) [T^{-1}]

(11) The dimensional formula for angular momentum is
(a) [$M^{-1} L^3 T^{-2}$]
(b) [$M L^2 T^{-1}$]

(c) [$M^{-2} L^3 T^{-2}$]
(d) [$M^1 L^2 T^{-2}$]

(12) What is the dimensions of surface tension?
(a) [$M L^1 T^0$]
(b) [$M^1 L^1 T^{-1}$]
(c) [$M L^0 T^{-2}$]
(d) [$M L T^{-2}$]

(13) The dimensional formula of solar constant (energy falling on earth per second per unit area) are
(a) [$M^0 L^0 T^0$]
(b) [$M L T^{-2}$]
(c) [$M^1 L^2 T^{-2}$]
(d) [$M^1 T^{-3}$]

(14) Dimensional formula for r.m.s. (root mean square) velocity is
(a) [$M^0 L T^{-1}$]
(b) [$M^0 L^0 T^{-2}$]
(c) [$M^0 L^0 T^{-1}$]
(d) [$M^1 L^1 T^{-3}$]

(15) The dimensional formula of universal gravitational constant is
(a) [$M^0 L^2 T^{-2}$]
(b) [$M^0 L^2 T^{-1}$]
(c) [$M^1 L^1 T^{-1}$]
(d) [$M^{-1} L^3 T^{-2}$]

(16) Dimensional formula of K in the equation $W = \frac{1}{2} K x^2$ is
(a) [$M^1 L^0 T^{-2}$]
(b) [$M^0 L^1 T^{-2}$]
(c) [$M^1 L^1 T^{-1}$]
(d) [$M^1 L^0 T^{-1}$]

(17) The dimensional formula for coefficient of viscosity is
(a) [$M^{-1} L^3 T^{-2}$]
(b) [$M^1 L^{-1} T^{-1}$]
(c) [$M^1 L^0 T^0$]
(d) [$M^1 L^1 T^{-1}$]

(18) The dimensional formula of coefficient of thermal conductivity is
(a) [$M L^2 T^{-2} K^{-1}$]
(b) [$M L T^{-3} K^{-1}$]
(c) [$M L T^{-2} K^{-1}$]
(d) [$M^1 L^1 T^{-3} K$]

(19) The dimensional symbol of the ratio of angular to linear momentum is
(a) [$M^0 L^1 T^0$]
(b) [$M^1 L^1 T^1$]
(c) [$M^1 L^2 T^{-1}$]
(d) [$M^{-1} L^{-1} T^{-1}$]

(20) If η denotes coefficient of viscosity and G denotes gravitational constant then $G \times \eta$ yields the dimension
(a) [$M^2 L^0 T^{-3}$]
(b) [$M^1 L^1 T^{-3}$]
(c) [$M^1 L^2 T^{-2}$]
(d) [$M^0 L^2 T^{-3}$]

(21) The dimension of stress and coefficient of viscosity are given by [S] and [η] respectively, then
(a) $\frac{[S]}{[\eta]} = \frac{1}{T}$
(b) $\frac{[S]}{[\eta]} = T$
(c) $[S] = \frac{1}{[\eta]}$
(d) $[S][\eta] = T$

(22) E, m, J and G denote energy, mass, angular momentum and gravitational constant respectively. The dimension of $\frac{E J^2}{m^5 G^2}$ are same as of
(a) Angle
(b) Length
(c) Mass
(d) Time

(23) The ratio of the dimensions of Planck's constant and that of the moment of inertia is the dimension of
(a) Frequency
(b) Velocity
(c) Angular momentum
(d) Time

(24) If the dimensions of a physical quantity are given by [$M^a L^b T^c$], then the physical quantity will be
(a) velocity if a = 1, b = 0 and c = - 1
(b) acceleration if a = 1, b = 1 and c = - 2
(c) force if a = 0, b = - 1 and c = - 2
(d) pressure a = 1, b = - 1 and c = - 2

(25) The dimensional formula [$M L^{-1} T^{-2}$] is for the quantity
(a) Force
(b) Acceleration
(c) Pressure
(d) Work

(26) The dimensional formula for relative refractive index is
(a) [$M^1 L^1 T^1$]
(b) [$M^0 L^0 T^0$]

(c) $[M^1 L^0 T^0]$
(d) $[M^1 L^1 T^{-1}]$

(27) The dimensional formula of electric potential is
(a) $[M^1 L^2 T^{-3} I^{-1}]$
(b) $[M^1 L^1 T^{-2} I^{-1}]$
(c) $[M^1 L^2 T^{-1} I]$
(d) $[M^1 L^2 T^{-2} I]$

(28) The dimensional formula of magnetic flux is
(a) $[M^0 L^{-2} T^2 I^{-2}]$
(b) $[M^1 L^0 T^{-2} I^{-2}]$
(c) $[M^1 L^2 T^{-2} I^{-1}]$
(d) $[M^1 L^2 T^{-1} I^3]$

(29) The dimensional formula of μ_0 is
(a) $\left[M^1 L^{-\frac{1}{2}} T^{\frac{1}{2}}\right]$
(b) $\left[M^1 L^{\frac{1}{2}} T^{-\frac{1}{2}}\right]$
(c) $[L^{-1} T]$
(d) $[M^1 L^1 T^{-2} I^{-2}]$

(30) The dimensional formula of $(\mu_0 \varepsilon_0)^{-\frac{1}{2}}$ is
(a) $\left[L^{-\frac{1}{2}} T^{\frac{1}{2}}\right]$
(b) $\left[L^{\frac{1}{2}} T^{-\frac{1}{2}}\right]$
(c) $[L^{-1} T]$
(d) $[L T^{-1}]$

(31) The dimension of $\frac{1}{2} \varepsilon_0 E^2$, where ε_0 is permittivity of free space and E is electric field, is
(a) $[M L^2 T^{-2}]$
(b) $[M L^{-1} T^{-2}]$
(c) $[M L^2 T^{-3}]$
(d) $[M L T^{-1}]$

(32) The focal power of a lens has the dimensions
(a) $[L]$
(b) $[L^{-1}]$
(c) $[M^1 L^2 T^{-3}]$
(d) $[M^1 L^1 T^{-3}]$

(33) Dimensions of resistance in an electric circuit, in terms of dimension of mass M, of length L, of time T and of current I, would be
(a) $[M L^2 T^{-3} I^{-2}]$
(b) $[M L^2 T^{-3} I^{-1}]$
(c) $[M L^2 T^{-2}]$
(d) $[M L^2 T^{-1} I^{-1}]$

(34) The dimensions of RC is
(a) Square of time
(b) Square of inverse time
(c) Time
(d) Inverse time

(35) Which of the following dimensions will be the same as that of time ?
(a) LC
(b) $\frac{C}{L}$
(c) $\frac{L}{R}$
(d) $\frac{R}{L}$

(36) If L, R and C stand for inductance, resistance and capacitance respectively, which of the following have the dimension of time ?
(a) LR
(b) $\frac{L}{R}$
(c) CR
(d) LCR

(37) In the formula, $X = 3YZ^2$; X has dimensions of capacitance and Z has dimensions of magnetic induction. The dimension of Y are
(a) $[M^{-3} L^{-2} T^{-2} A^4]$
(b) $[M^1 L^{-2} T^2 A^2]$
(c) $[M^{-3} L^{-2} A^4 T^4]$
(d) $[M^{-3} L^{-2} T^8 A^4]$

Important Points

Dimensionless Physical Quantity :

- Relative density or Specific gravity
- Refractive index
- Relative permittivity or Dielectric constant
- Relative permeability
- Plane angle and solid angle
- Strain (Longitudinal strain, Volume strain, Shearing strain)
- Poisson's ratio

(38) A dimensionless quantity
(a) may have a unit
(b) never has a unit
(c) always has a unit
(d) does not exist

(39) A unitless quantity
(a) may have a non-zero dimension
(b) always has a non-zero dimension
(c) never has a non-zero dimension
(d) does not exist

(40) Which one of the following is NOT dimensionless
(a) Relative density
(b) Relative velocity
(c) Refractive index
(d) Relative permittivity

(41) Which of the following is a dimensional constant?
(a) refractive index
(b) poission's ratio
(c) relative density
(d) gravitational constant

(42) Which of the following is a dimensional constant?
(a) Magnification
(b) Relative error
(c) Relative density
(d) Gravitational constant

(43) Which one of the following is dimensionless physical quantity?
(a) Velocity gradient
(b) Stress
(c) Force gradient
(d) Angle

(44) Which of the following does not have the dimensions of force?
(a) weight
(b) rate of change of momentum
(c) work per unit length
(d) work done per unit charge

(45) The dimensional formula for impulse is the same as the dimensional formula for
(a) Linear momentum
(b) Force
(c) Rate of change of momentum
(d) Torque

(46) The dimensions of impulse are equal to that of
(a) Pressure
(b) Force
(c) Linear momentum
(d) Angular momentum

(47) The dimensions of Planck's constant are same as
(a) Energy
(b) Power
(c) Linear momentum
(d) Angular momentum

(48) Dimensional formula for electromotive force is same as that of
(a) Potential
(b) Current
(c) Force
(d) Energy

(49) The dimensions of potential are the same as that of
(a) work
(b) electric field per unit charge
(c) work per unit charge
(d) force per unit charge

(50) Surface tension has the same dimensions as that of
(a) Co-efficient of viscosity
(b) Impulse
(c) Momentum
(d) Spring constant

(51) The modulus of elasticity is dimensionally equivalent to
(a) Force
(b) Stress
(c) Strain
(d) co-efficient of viscosity

(52) The pairs of quantities having same dimensions is
(a) displacement, velocity
(b) time and frequency
(c) wavelength, focal length
(d) force, acceleration

(53) The pair of quantities having same dimensions is
(a) Young's modulus and energy
(b) Impulse and Surface tension
(c) Angular momentum and work
(d) Work and torque

(54) Which two of the following five physical quantities have the same dimensions? (1) Energy density, (2) Refractive index, (3) Dielectric constant, (4) Young's modulus, (5) Magnetic field
(a) (1) and (5)
(b) (2) and (4)
(c) (3) and (5)
(d) (1) and (4)

(55) Which pair does not have equal dimensions?
(a) Energy and Torque
(b) Force and Impulse
(c) Angular momentum and Planck's constant

(d) Elastic modulus and Pressure

(56) Select the pair whose dimensions are same

(a) Pressure and stress
(b) Momentum and impulse
(c) Torque and energy
(d) All of these

Answer

Physical World & Measurement

Topic : Dimension Finding of a Physical Quantity

(1) (a)	(13) (d)	(25) (c)	(37) (d)	(49) (c)
(2) (a)	(14) (a)	(26) (b)	(38) (a)	(50) (d)
(3) (a)	(15) (d)	(27) (a)	(39) (c)	(51) (b)
(4) (c)	(16) (a)	(28) (c)	(40) (b)	(52) (c)
(5) (b)	(17) (b)	(29) (d)	(41) (d)	(53) (d)
(6) (b)	(18) (b)	(30) (d)	(42) (d)	(54) (d)
(7) (b)	(19) (a)	(31) (b)	(43) (d)	(55) (b)
(8) (b)	(20) (d)	(32) (a)	(44) (d)	(56) (d)
(9) (b)	(21) (a)	(33) (a)	(45) (c)	
(10) (d)	(22) (a)	(34) (c)	(46) (c)	
(11) (b)	(23) (a)	(35) (c)	(47) (d)	
(12) (c)	(24) (d)	(36) (b)(c)	(48) (a)	

Physics MCQ || Class – XI	Physical World & Measurement
	Topic : Unit Finding & Unit Conversion

 # Important Point

Principle of Dimensional Homogeneity :

A given physical relation is dimensionally correct if the dimensions of the various terms on either side of the relation are the same. This principle is based on the fact that two quantities of the same nature only can be added up. The resulting quantity is also of the same nature.

(1) The equation $(P + \frac{a}{V^2})(V - b)$ = constant. The units of a is
(a) dyn cm^2
(b) dyn cm^4
(c) dyn m^{-3}
(d) dyn cm^{-2}

(2) If $x = at + bt^2$, where x is the distance travelled by the body in kilometre while t be the time in seconds, then the unit of b are
(a) km s^{-1}
(b) km s
(c) km s^{-2}
(d) km s^2

(3) The damping force on an oscillator is directly proportional to the velocity. The units of the constant of proportionality
(a) kg s^{-1}
(b) kg s
(c) kg m s^{-1}
(d) kg m s^2

(4) The equation of the stationary wave is $y = 2A \sin\left(\frac{2\pi ct}{\lambda}\right)\cos\left(\frac{2\pi x}{\lambda}\right)$, which of the following statements is wrong
(a) The unit of ct is same as that of λ
(b) The unit of x is same as that of λ
(c) The unit of $\frac{2\pi c}{\lambda}$ is same as that of $\frac{2\pi x}{\lambda t}$
(d) The unit of $\frac{c}{\lambda}$ is same as that of $\frac{x}{\lambda}$

(5) The equation $y = x^2 cos^2\left(\frac{2\pi\beta\gamma}{\alpha}\right)$, the units of x, α, β are m, s^{-1} and $(m\,s^{-1})^{-1}$ respectively. The units of y and γ are
(a) m^2, m s^{-1}
(b) m, m s^{-1}
(c) m^2, m
(d) m^2, m s^{-2}

(6) The force F is represented by equation $F = P L^{-1} + Q L$, where L is the length. The unit of P is same as that of
(a) Surface tension
(b) Velocity
(c) Work
(d) Momentum

(7) For a system with variable mass, Newton's second law is given by $F = m\frac{dv}{dt} + v\frac{dm}{dt}$. If for a system $\frac{dm}{dt} = k\,mv$, the SI unit of k is
(a) m^{-1}
(b) m
(c) kg
(d) kg^{-1}

Unit Conversion

(8) When one metre, one kg and one minute are taken as fundamental units, the magnitude of a force is 36 units. What is the value of this force in CGS system?
(a) 10^3 dyne
(b) 10^5 dyne
(c) 10^6 dyne
(d) 10^7 dyne

(9) The density of a material in CGS system of units is 4 g cm^{-3}. In a system of units in which unit of length is 10 cm and unit of mass is 100 g, the value of density of material will be
(a) 400
(b) 0.04
(c) 0.4
(d) 40

(10) The unit of length, velocity and force are doubled. Which of the following is the correct change in the other unit?
(a) unit of time is doubled
(b) unit of mass is doubled
(c) unit of momentum is doubled
(d) unit of energy is doubled

(11) In a practical unit if the unit of mass becomes double and that of time becomes half, then 8 joule will be equal to .... unit of work.
(a) 6
(b) 4
(c) 1
(d) 10

Answer

Physical World & Measurement

Topic : Unit Finding & Unit Conversion

(1)	(b)	(4)	(d)	(7)	(a)	(10)	(c)
(2)	(c)	(5)	(d)	(8)	(a)	(11)	(c)
(3)	(a)	(6)	(c)	(9)	(d)		

Physics MCQ | | Class – XI

Physical World & Measurement

Topic : Finding the Dimensions of Constants or Variables in an Equation

(1) The velocity of a particle (v) at an instant is given by v = $at + bt^2$, the dimension of b is
(a) [L]
(b) [$L T^{-1}$]
(c) [$L T^{-3}$]
(d) [$L T^{-2}$]

(2) The position of the particle moving along Y axis is given by y = $At^2 - B t^3$, where y is measured in meter and t in second. Then, the dimensions of B are
(a) [$L T^{-2}$]
(b) [$L T^{-1}$]
(c) [$L T^{-3}$]
(d) [$ML T^2$]

(3) The dimensions of physical quantity A in the equation force = $\frac{A}{\sqrt{Density}}$ is given by
(a) [$M L^4 T^{-2}$]
(b) [$M^2 L^{-2} T^{-1}$]
(c) $\left[M^{\frac{3}{2}} L^{-\frac{1}{2}} T^{-2}\right]$
(d) [$M L^{-2} T^{-1}$]

(4) The dimensions of $\frac{a}{b}$ in the equation p = $\frac{a - t^2}{bx}$ where, P is pressure, x is distance and t is time, are
(a) [$M^2 L T^{-3}$]
(b) [$M^1 T^{-2}$]
(c) [$L T^{-3}$]
(d) [$M L^3 T^{-1}$]

(5) The dimensions of $\frac{\alpha}{\beta}$ in the equation F = $\frac{\alpha - t^2}{\beta v^2}$, where F is the force, v is velocity and t is time, is
(a) [$ML T^{-1}$]
(b) [$M^1 L^{-1} T^{-2}$]
(c) [$M^1 L^3 T^{-4}$]
(d) [$M L^2 T^{-4}$]

(6) Given that the displacement of an oscillating particle is given by y = A sin (Bx + Ct + D). The dimensional formula for ABCD is
(a) [L^{-1}]
(b) [T^{-1}]
(c) [$L^{-1} T^{-1}$]
(d) [$M^0 L^0 T^0$]

(7) The equation of a wave is given by y = a sin ω ($\frac{x}{V} - k$), where, ω is the angular velocity and v is the linear velocity. The dimension of k will be
(a) [T^{-2}]
(b) [T^{-1}]
(c) [T]
(d) [LT]

(8) The velocity v of a particle at time t is given by v = at + $\frac{b}{t+c}$; where, a, b and c are constants. The dimensions of a, b and c are respectively,
(a) [$L T^{-2}$], [L] and [T]
(b) [L^2], [T] and [$L T^2$]
(c) [$L T^2$], [LT] and [L]
(d) [L], [LT] and [T^2]

(9) The equation of state of a gas is given by (P + $\frac{a}{V^3}$) (V – b^2) = cT where, P, V, T are pressure, volume and temperature respectively and a, b and c are constants. The dimension of a and b are respectively
(a) [$M^1 L^8 T^{-2}$] and $\left[L^{\frac{3}{2}}\right]$
(b) [$M^1 L^5 T^{-2}$] and [L^3]
(c) [$M^1 L^5 T^{-2}$] and [L^6]
(d) [$M^1 L^6 T^{-2}$] and $\left[L^{\frac{3}{2}}\right]$

(10) An equation is given here (P + $\frac{a}{V^2}$) = b $\frac{\theta}{V}$ where, P, V and θ are pressure, volume and absolute temperature respectively. If a and b are constants, the dimension of a will be
(a) [$M^1 L^{-5} T^{-1}$]
(b) [$M^1 L^5 T^{-1}$]
(c) [$M^1 L^5 T^{-2}$]
(d) [$M^{-1} L^5 T^2$]

(11) In the following equation, x, t and F represent respectively displacement, time and force: F = a + bt + $\frac{1}{c + dx}$ + A sin (ωt + Φ). The dimensional formula of A.d is
(a) [T^{-1}]

(b) [L^{-1}]
(c) [M^{-1}]
(d) [$L^{-1}T$]

(12) The potential energy u of a particle varies with distance x from a fixed origin as u = $\frac{A\sqrt{x}}{x+B}$, where A and B are constants. The dimensional formula of A and B are respectively
(a) $\left[ML^{\frac{5}{2}}T^{-2}\right]$, [L]
(b) [ML T^{-2}], [L^2]
(c) [L], $\left[M^1 L^{\frac{3}{2}} T^{-2}\right]$
(d)[L^2], [ML T^{-2}]

(13) The potential energy u of a particle varies with distance x from a fixed origin as u = $\frac{A\sqrt{x}}{x^2+B}$, where A and B are constants. The dimensional formula for AB is
(a) $\left[M L^{\frac{7}{2}} T^{-2}\right]$
(b) $\left[M^1 L^{\frac{11}{2}} T^{-2}\right]$
(c) $\left[M^2 L^{\frac{9}{2}} T^{-2}\right]$
(d) $\left[M L^{\frac{13}{2}} T^{-3}\right]$

(14) Force F and density d are related as F = $\frac{A}{B+\sqrt{d}}$, Find the dimension of A
(a) $\left[M^{\frac{1}{2}} L^{-\frac{1}{2}} T^{-2}\right]$
(b) $\left[M^{\frac{3}{2}} L^{-\frac{1}{2}} T^{2}\right]$
(c) $\left[M^{\frac{3}{2}} L^{-\frac{1}{2}} T^{-2}\right]$
(d) $\left[M^{2} L^{-\frac{1}{2}} T^{2}\right]$

(15) The time dependence of a physical quantity P is given by P = P_0 $e^{\alpha t^2}$, where α is a constant and t is the time. The constant α
(a) is dimensionless
(b) has dimensional formula [T^{-2}]
(c) has dimensional formula [T^2]
(d) has dimensional formula P

(16) A physical quantity P is given by the relation P = $P_0 e^{-\alpha t^2}$. If t denotes time, the dimensions of constant α are
(a) [T]
(b) [T^2]
(c) [T^{-1}]
(d) [T^{-2}]

(17) In a particular system, force is given by, F = A ln ($\alpha \sin Bx$). Which of the following quantities has the same dimension as force ?
(a) Bα
(b) $\frac{\alpha}{B}$
(c) $\frac{A}{\alpha}$
(d) $\alpha^2 B$

(18) Number of particles is given by N = – D $\frac{(N_2 - N_1)}{(Z_2 - Z_1)}$ crossing a unit area perpendicular to z- axis in unit time, where N_1 and N_2 are number of particles per unit volume for the value of z meant to z_1 and z_2 Find dimensions of D called as diffusion constant
(a) [$M^0 L^{-1} T^2$]
(b) [$M^0 L^{-1} T^{-1}$]
(c) [$M^0 L^2 T^{-1}$]
(d) [$M^0 L^2 T^2$]

Answer

Physical World & Measurement

Topic : Finding the Dimensions of Constants or Variables in an Equation

(1)	(c)	(5)	(c)	(9)	(a)	(13)	(b)	(17)	(c)
(2)	(c)	(6)	(b)	(10)	(c)	(14)	(c)	(18)	(c)
(3)	(c)	(7)	(c)	(11)	(b)	(15)	(b)		
(4)	(b)	(8)	(a)	(12)	(a)	(16)	(d)		

Physics MCQ | | Class – XI	Physical World & Measurement
	Topic : Formulae Derivation

(1) An important milestone in the evolution of the universe just after the Big Bang is the Planck time t_p, the value of which depends on three fundamental constants speed of light in vacuum c, Gravitational constant G and Planck's constant h. Then $t_p \propto$

(a) Ghc^5

(b) $\frac{c^5}{Gh}$

(c) $\frac{Gh}{c^5}$

(d) $\left(\frac{Gh}{c^5}\right)^{\frac{1}{2}}$

(2) Planck's constant (h), speed of light in vacuum (c) and Newton's gravitational constant (G) are three fundamentals constants. Which of the following combinations of these has the dimension of length ?

(a) $\frac{\sqrt{hG}}{c^{\frac{3}{2}}}$

(b) $\frac{\sqrt{hG}}{c^{\frac{5}{2}}}$

(c) $\sqrt{\frac{ch}{G}}$

(d) $\sqrt{\frac{Gc}{h^{\frac{3}{2}}}}$

(3) In dimension of critical velocity v_c of a liquid flowing through a tube are expressed as $[\eta^a \rho^b r^c]$, where η, ρ and r are the coefficient of viscosity of liquid, density of liquid and radius of the tube respectively, then the values of a, b and c are given by

(a) 1, 1, 1

(b) 1, - 1, - 1

(c) – 1, - 1, 1

(d) – 1, - 1, - 1

(4) If the buoyant force F acting on an object depends on its volume V immersed in a liquid, the density ρ of the liquid and the acceleration due to gravity g. The correct expression for F can be

(a) $V\rho g$

(b) $\frac{\rho g}{V}$

(c) $\rho g V^2$

(d) $(\rho g V)^{\frac{1}{2}}$

(5) The frequency of vibrations f of a mass m suspended for a spring of spring constant K is given by a relation of type f = c $m^x K^y$, where c is dimensionless constant. The values of x and y are

(a) $x = \frac{1}{2}, y = \frac{1}{2}$

(b) $x = -\frac{1}{2}, y = -\frac{1}{2}$

(c) $x = \frac{1}{2}, y = -\frac{1}{2}$

(d) $x = -\frac{1}{2}, y = \frac{1}{2}$

(6) Let P represent radiation pressure, c represent speed of light and I represent radiation energy striking a unit area per second, then $P^x I^y c^z$ will be dimensionless of

(a) x = 0 , y = z

(b) x = y = z

(c) $x = z = -y$

(d) $x = y = -z$

(7) Even if a physical quantity depends upon three quantities, out of which two are dimensionally same, then the formula cannot be derived by the method of dimensions. This statement

(a) May be true

(b) May be false

(c) Must be true

(d) Must be false

Answer	Physical World & Measurement
	Topic : Formulae Derivation

1.	(d)	3.	(b)	5.	(d)	7.	(c)
2.	(a)	4.	(a)	6.	(c)		

Physics MCQ || Class – XI

Physical World & Measurement

Topic : Finding the Dimensional Formula Taking Different Base Quantity as Fundamental

(1) If energy (E), velocity (V) and time (T) are chosen as the fundamental quantities, the dimensional formula of surface tension will be
(a) $[E^{-2} V^{-1} T^{-3}]$
(b) $[E^{1} V^{-2} T^{-1}]$
(c) $[E^{1} V^{-1} T^{-2}]$
(d) $[E V^{-2} T^{-2}]$

(2) If force (F), velocity (V) and time (T) are taken as fundamental units, then the dimensions of mass are
(a) $[F V T^{-1}]$
(b) $[F V T^{-2}]$
(c) $[F V^{-1} T^{-1}]$
(d) $[F V^{-1} T]$

(3) If force F, area A density D are taken as the fundamental units, the representation of Young's modulus Y will be
(a) $[F^{-1} A^{-1} D^{-1}]$
(b) $[F A^{-2} D^{2}]$
(c) $[F A^{-1} D^{0}]$
(d) $[F A^{-2} D^{0}]$

(4) In a new system of units energy (E), density (d) and power (P) are taken as fundamental units, then the dimensional formula of universal gravitational constant G will be
(a) $[E^{-1} d^{-2} P^{2}]$
(b) $[E^{-2} d^{-1} P^{2}]$
(c) $[E^{2} d^{-1} P^{-1}]$
(d) $[E d^{-2} P^{-2}]$

(5) If pressure P, velocity V and time T are taken as base units, the dimensional formula for the force is
(a) $P V^2 T^2$
(b) $P V T^2$
(c) $P^{-1} V^2 T^{-2}$
(d) $P^{-1} V T^{-2}$

Answer

Physical World & Measurement

Topic : Finding the dimensional formula taking different base quantity as fundamental

1.	(b)	2.	(d)	3.	(c)	4.	(b)	5.	(a)

Physics
MCQ | | Class – XI

Physical World & Measurement

Topic : Number of Significant Figures and Rounding off

 # Important Points

Rules for counting significant figures :

(1) All non-zero digits are significant.
(2) All zeros in between the non-zero digits are significant.
(3) All zeros to the left of non-zero digit (leading zeros) are not significant.
(4) Trailing zeros: with decimal point : Significant
Without decimal point : NOT significant
(5) The power of 10 is not counted as significant figure.
(6) The pure or exact numbers appearing in the mathematical formulae of various physical quantities have infinite number of significant figures.

Rules for rounding off the digits :

(1) If the digit to be dropped is smaller than 5, then the preceding digit should be left unchanged.

(2) If the digit to be dropped is greater than 5, then the preceding digit should be raised by 1.

(3) If the digit to be dropped is 5 followed by digits other than zero then the preceding digit should be raised by 1 .

(4) If the digit to be dropped is 5 or 5 followed by zeros then the preceding digit is not changed if it is even.

(5) If the digit to be dropped is 5 or 5 followed by zeros then the preceding digit is raised by 1 if it is odd.

---

(1) 3.34 is obtained by rounding off the number
(a) 3.346
(b) 3.355
(c) 3.335
(d) 3.334

(2) What is the number of significant figures in 0.310×10^3
(a) 2
(b) 3
(c) 4
(d) 6

(3) The number of significant figure in the measured value 37000 is
(a) Five
(b) Two
(c) Infinite
(d) Three

(4) The respective number of significant figures for the numbers 23.023, 0.0003 and 2.1×10^{-3} are
(a) 5, 1, 2
(b) 5, 1, 5
(c) 5, 5, 2
(d) 4, 4, 2

(5) The number of significant figure in 0.06900 is
(a) 5
(b) 4
(c) 2
(d) 3

(6) The number of significant figures in a pure number 410 is
(a) Two
(b) Three
(c) One
(d) Infinite

(7) The number of significant zeroes present in the measured value 0.030040 is
(a) Five
(b) Two
(c) One
(d) Three

(8) In which of the following number the zero is not significant figure ?
(a) 0.663
(b) 3114
(c) 3.40
(d) 1005

(9) If the number 3.78721 is rounded off to 3 significant figures, it will be
(a) 3.785
(b) 3.787
(c) 3.79
(d) 3.80

(10) The uncertain digit in the measurement of length reported as 41.68 cm is
(a) 4
(b) 1
(c) 6
(d) 8

(11) The number of significant figures in the measured value 4.700 m is the same as that in the value
(a) 4700 m
(b) 0.047 m
(c) 4070 m
(d) 470.0 m

(12) When energy is expressed in J the number of significant figure is 4. If it is expressed in erg the number of significant figure will become
(a) 4
(b) 9
(c) 1
(d) 5

(13) Round off the value 2.845 to three significant figures
(a) 2.85
(b) 2.84
(c) 2.80
(d) 2.83

(14) The decimal equivalent of $\frac{1}{20}$ upto three significant figures is

(a) 0.0500

(b) 0.05000

(c) 0.0050

(d) 5.0×10^{-2}

(15) The mean length of an object is 5 cm. Which of the following measurement is most accurate ?
(a) 4.9 cm
(b) 4.805 cm
(c) 5.25 cm
(d) 5.4 cm

(16) The most accurate reading of the length of a 6.28 cm long fibre is
(a) 6 cm
(b) 6.5 cm
(c) 5.99 cm
(d) 6.0 cm

(17) Which of the following express the most precise measurement of length of a rod?
(a) 500.0 mm
(b) 500 mm
(c) 50 cm
(d) 0.5 m

(18) The most precise reading of the mass of an object, among the following is
(a) 20 g
(b) 20.0 g
(c) 20.01 g
(d) 20×10^{0} g

(19) Which of the following is the most precise measurement ?
(a) 3×10^{-3} m
(b) 0.0030 m
(c) 30×10^{-4} m
(d) 300×10^{-5} m

(20) Which of the following measurement is most precise ?
(a) 5.00 mm
(b) 5.00 cm
(c) 5.00 m
(d) 5.00 km

(21) The values of a number of quantities are used in a mathematical formula. The quantity that should be most precise and accurate in measurement is one
(a) Having smallest magnitude
(b) Having largest magnitude
(c) Used in the numerator
(d) Used in a denominator

Answer

Physical World & Measurement

Topic : Number of Significant Figures and Rounding off

(1)	(c)	(6)	(d)	(11)	(d)	(16)	(b)	(21)	(a)
(2)	(b)	(7)	(d)	(12)	(a)	(17)	(a)		
(3)	(b)	(8)	(a)	(13)	(b)	(18)	(c)		
(4)	(a)	(9)	(c)	(14)	(a)	(19)	(b)		
(5)	(b)	(10)	(d)	(15)	(a)	(20)	(a)		

Physics MCQ		Class – XI	Physical World & Measurement
	Topic : Scientific Notation & Arithmetic Operation

Important Points

Scientific Notation : In scientific notation, all numbers are written in the form : $x \times 10^y$

Where, $1 \le x \le 10$ and y is a positive or negative integer.

If x is less than or equal to 5, then order of number is y and if x is greater than 5 then order of the number is $(y + 1)$.

(1) The order of the magnitude of speed of light in SI unit is
(a) 16
(b) 8
(c) 4
(d) 7

Important Points

• Rules for **Arithmetic Operation** :

(a) In **addition or subtraction**, the final result should retain as many decimal places as are there in the number with the **least decimal places.**

(b) In **multiplication or division**, the final result should retain as many significant figures as are there in the original number with the **least significant figures.**

(2) The addition of three masses 1.6 g, 7.32 g and 4.238 g, addressed upto proper decimal places is
(a) 13.158 g
(b) 13.2 g
(c) 13.16 g
(d) 13.15 g

(3) Three measurements are made as 18.425 cm, 7.21 cm and 5.0 cm. The sum of measurements upto correct number of significant figures is
(a) 30.635 cm
(b) 30.64 cm
(c) 30.63 cm
(d) 30.6 cm

(4) Taking into account the significant figures, what should be the value of 9.99 + 0.0099 ?
(a) 9.9999
(b) 10.00
(c) 10.0
(d) 10

(5) If the mass of a body is 11.079 g and volume 12.7 mL, the number of significant figures in the expression of its density is
(a) 4
(b) 3
(c) 2
(d) 1

(6) If 3.8×10^{-6} is added to 4.2×10^{-5} giving due regard to significant figures, then the result will be
(a) 4.58×10^{-5}
(b) 4.6×10^{-5}
(c) 4.5×10^{-5}
(d) 4.7×10^{-5}

(7) The area of a sheet of length 10.2 cm and width 6.8 cm addressed upto proper number of significant figures is
(a) 6.69 cm^2
(b) 69.4 cm^2
(c) 69 cm^2
(d) 70 cm^2

(8) The radius of disc is 1.2 cm, its area according to idea of significant figures is
(a) 4.5216 cm^2
(b) 4.521 cm^2
(c) 4.52 cm^2
(d) 4.5 cm^2

(9) If 97.52 is divided by 2.54, the correct result in terms of significant figures is
(a) 38.4
(b) 38.3937
(c) 38.394

(d) 38.39

(10) A body of mass m = 3.513 kg is moving along the x-axis with a speed of 5.00 ms^{-1}. The magnitude of its momentum is recorded as
(a) 17.6 kg ms^{-1}
(b) 17.565 kg ms^{-1}
(c) 17.56 kg ms^{-1}
(d) 17.57 kg ms^{-1}

(11) A cube has a side of length 1.2×10^{-2} m. Calculate its volume.
(a) 1.7×10^{-6} m^3
(b) 1.73×10^{-6} m^3
(c) 1.70×10^{-6} m^3
(d) 1.732×10^{-6} m^3

(12) The volume of a cube having sides 1.2 m is appropriately expressed as
(a) 1.728×10^6 cm^3
(b) 1.7×10^6 cm^3
(c) 1.8×10^6 cm^3
(d) 1.73×10^6 cm^3

(13) The time taken by a pendulum to complete 25 vibrations is 88.0 seconds. The time period of the pendulum in second is
(a) 3.52
(b) 3
(c) 3.5
(d) 3.520

Answer

Physical World & Measurement

Topic : Scientific Notation & Arithmetic Operation

(1)	(b)	(4)	(b)	(7)	(c)	(10)	(a)	(13)	(a)
(2)	(b)	(5)	(b)	(8)	(d)	(11)	(a)		
(3)	(d)	(6)	(b)	(9)	(a)	(12)	(b)		

Physics MCQ | | Class – XI	Physical World & Measurement
	Topic : Error in Measurement

Important Points

Important Facts On Error in Measurement :

- A measurement of a physical quantity is said to be accurate if the systematic error in its measurement is relatively very low.
- A measurement of a physical quantity is said to be precise if the random error is small.
- For greater accuracy, the quantity with higher power should have least error.
- The absolute error in each measurement is equal to the least count of the measuring instrument.
- Absolute error has the unit that of the physical quantity but relative error or percentage error is unitless.

(1) Zero error in an instrument introduces
(a) Systematic error
(b) Random error
(c) Least count error
(d) Personal error

(2) We can reduce random errors by
(a) taking large number of observations
(b) corrected zero error
(c) by following proper technique of experiment
(d) both (a) and (c)

(3) A set of defective observation of weights is used by a student to find the mass of an object using a physical balance. A large number of readings will reduce
(a) Random error
(b) Systematic error
(c) Random as well as systematic error
(d) Neither systematic nor random error

(4) In an experiment, refractive index of glass was observed to be 1.45, 1.56, 1.54, 1.44, 1.54 and 1.53. The mean absolute error in the experiment is
(a) $\pm$ 0.04
(b) 0.02
(c) – 0.03
(d) $\pm$ 0.01

(5) The random error in the arithmetic mean of 100 observations is x; then random error in the arithmetic mean of 400 observations would be
(a) $4x$
(b) $\frac{1}{4}x$
(c) 2 x
(d) $\frac{1}{2}x$

(6) The unit of percentage error is
(a) Same as that of physical quantity
(b) Different from that of physical quantity
(c) Percentage error is unit less
(d) Errors have got their own units which are different from that of physical quantity measured

(7) Accuracy of measurement is determined by
(a) Absolute error
(b) Percentage error
(c) Both
(d) None of these

(8) The mean time period of second's pendulum is 2.00 s and mean absolute error on the time period is 0.05 s. To express maximum estimate of error, the time period should be written as
(a) (2.00 $\pm$ 0.01) s
(b) (2.00 +0.025) s
(c) (2.00 $\pm$ 0.05) s
(d) (2.00 $\pm$ 0.10) s

(9) The least count of a stop watch is $\frac{1}{5}$ second. The time of 20 oscillations of a pendulum is measured to be 25 seconds.

The maximum percentage error in the measurement of time will be
(a) 0.1 %
(b) 0.8 %
(c) 1.8 %
(d) 8 %

(10) In the context of accuracy of measurement and significant figures in expressing results of experiment, which of the following is/are correct

(1) Out of the two measurements 50.14 cm and 0.00025 ampere, the first one has greater accuracy

(2) If one travels 478 km by rail and 397 m. by road, the total distance travelled is 478 km.

(a) Only (1) is correct
(b) Only (2) is correct
(c) Both are correct
(d) None of them is correct.

Answer

Physical World & Measurement

Topic : Error in Measurement

(1)	**(a)**	**(3)**	**(a)**	**(5)**	**(b)**	**(7)**	**(c)**	**(9)**	**(b)**
(2)	**(a)**	**(4)**	**(a)**	**(6)**	**(c)**	**(8)**	**(c)**	**(10)**	**(c)**

Physics MCQ | | Class – XI	Physical World & Measurement
	Topic : Error Propagation

Important Points

Rules for Error Propagation in Addition and Subtraction :

- Given, A = $A_m + \Delta A_m$ and B = $B_m + \Delta B_m$

If X = A + B, then $\Delta X_m = \Delta A_m + \Delta B_m$

If Y = A - B, then $\Delta Y_m = \Delta A_m + \Delta B_m$

- Errors are always additive in nature.

(1) If the length of a rod A is 3.25 ± 0.02 cm and that of rod B is 4.19 ± 0.02 cm , then the rod B is longer than rod A by
(a) 0.94 ± 0.00 cm
(b) 0.94 ± 0.05 cm
(c) 0.94 ± 0.04 cm
(d) 0.94 ± 0.004 cm

(2) A packet contains silver powder of mass (20.23 ± 0.01) g. some of the power of mass (5.75 ± 0.01) g is taken out from it. The mass of the powder left back is
(a) (14.48 ± 0.00) g
(b) (14.48 ± 0.02) g
(c) (14.5 ± 0.1) g
(d) (14.5 ± 0.2) g

(3) If x = 10.0 ± 0.1 and y = 10.0 ± 0.1, then 2x – 2y is equal to
(a) 0.0 ± 0.1
(b) zero
(c) 0.0 ± 0.4
(d) 20.0 ± 0.2

Important Points

Rules for Error Propagation in Multiplication and Division of two Quantities :

- Given, A = $A_m + \Delta A_m$ and B = $B_m + \Delta B_m$

If X = A B, then $\frac{\Delta X_m}{X_m} = \frac{\Delta A_m}{A_m} + \frac{\Delta B_m}{B_m}$

If Y = $\frac{A}{B}$, then $\frac{\Delta X_m}{X_m} = \frac{\Delta A_m}{A_m} + \frac{\Delta B_m}{B_m}$

(4) A public park, in the form of a square, has an area of (100 ± 0.2) m^2. The side of park is
(a) (10 ± 0.01) m
(b) (10 ± 0.1) m
(c) (10 ± 0.02) m
(d) (10 ± 0.2) m

(5) A body travels uniformly a distance of (13.8 ± 0.2) m in a time (4.0 ± 0.3) s. The velocity of the body within error limits is
(a) (3.45 ± 0.2) ms^{-1}
(b) (3.45 ± 0.3) ms^{-1}
(c) (3.45 ± 0.4) ms^{-1}
(d) (3.45 ± 0.5) ms^{-1}

(6) If voltage V = (100 ± 5) V and current I = (10 ± 0.2) A , the percentage error in resistance R is
(a) 5.2 %
(b) 25 %
(c) 7 %
(d) 10 %

(7) The percentage error in the measurement of the voltage V is 3% and in the measurement of the current is 2%. The percentage error in the measurement of the resistance is
(a) 3%
(b) 2%
(c) 1%
(d) 5 %

(8) The mass of a body is 20.0 g and its volume is 10.0 cm^3. If possible maximum errors in the measurement of mass of body and volume of body are 0.001 g and 0.01 cm^3 respectively, then the maximum error in the value of density is
(a) 0.001 g cm^{-3}
(b) 0.010 g cm^{-3}

(c) 0.10 g cm^{-3}
(d) none of these

Important Points

Rules for On Error Propagation in Product of Some Powers of the Measured Quantities :

- Given, A = $A_m + \Delta A_m$ and B = $B_m + \Delta B_m$

If X = $A^a B^b$, then $\frac{\Delta X_m}{X_m} = a\frac{\Delta A_m}{A_m} + b\frac{\Delta B_m}{B_m}$

(9) If $x = a^n$, then fractional error $\frac{\Delta X_m}{X_m}$ is equal to
(a) $\pm\left(\frac{\Delta a}{a}\right)^n$
(b) $\pm n\frac{\Delta a}{a}$
(c) $\pm n \log_{10}\frac{\Delta a}{a}$
(c) $\pm n \log_e\frac{\Delta a}{a}$

(10) A physical quantity is given by
$$X = M^a L^b T^c.$$
The percentage error in measurement of M, L and T are α, β and γ respectively. Then the maximum % error in the quantity X is
(a) $a\alpha + b\beta + c\gamma$
(b) $a\alpha + b\beta - c\gamma$
(c) $\frac{a}{\alpha} + \frac{b}{\beta} + \frac{c}{\gamma}$
(d) none of these

(11) In an experiment four quantities a, b, c and d are measured with percentage error 1%, 2%, 3% and 4% respectively. Quantity P is calculated as follows : P = $\frac{a^3 b^2}{c\,d}$, % error in P is
(a) 10%
(b) 7%
(c) 4%
(d) 14%

(12) In an experiment, the percentage of error occurred in the measurement of physical quantities A, B, C and D are 1%, 2%, 3% and 4% respectively. The maximum percentage error in the measurement X, where, X = $\frac{A^2 B^{\frac{1}{2}}}{C^{\frac{1}{3}} D^3}$, will be
(a) 10%
(b) $\frac{3}{13}$%
(c) 16%
(d) – 10 %

(13) In an experiment of simple pendulum, the errors in the measurement of length of pendulum (L) and time period (T) are 3% and 2% respectively. The maximum percentage error in the value of $\frac{L}{T^2}$ is
(a) 5%
(b) 7%
(c) 8%
(d) 1%

Important Points

Volume of a sphere : V = $\frac{4}{3}\pi R^3$

Where, R = radius of the sphere

(14) The radius of a sphere is (2.6 ± 0.1) cm. The percentage error in its volume is
(a) $\frac{0.1}{2.6} \times 100$ %
(b) $3 \times \frac{0.1}{2.6} \times 100$ %
(c) $\frac{0.1}{3 \times 2.6} \times 100$ %
(d) $\frac{0.1}{2.6}$ %

(15) The radius of a sphere is (5.3 ± 0.1) cm. The percentage error in its volume is
(a) $\frac{0.1}{5.3} \times 100$
(b) $3 \times \frac{0.1}{5.3} \times 100$
(c) $\frac{3}{2}\,\frac{0.1}{5.3} \times 100$
(d) $6 \times \frac{0.1}{0.3} \times 100$

(16) If error in radius is 3 %, what is error in volume of sphere?
(a) 3%
(b) 27 %
(c) 9%
(d) 6%

(17) If the error in the measurement of radius of sphere is 2%, then the error in the determination of volume of sphere will be
(a) 2%
(b) 4 %
(c) 6%
(d) 8%

Important Points

Volume of a Cube : V = L^3

Where, L = side of the cube

(18) The relative error in the measurement of the side of a cube is 0.027. The relative error in the measurement of its volume is

(a) 0.027
(b) 0.054
(c) 0.081
(d) 0.046

Important Points

Kinetic energy : $E_k = \frac{1}{2} m v^2 = \frac{P^2}{2m}$

Where, m = mass of the body

v = velocity of the body

P = linear momentum

(19) Percentage errors in the measurement of mass and speed are 2% and 3% respectively. The error in the estimate of kinetic energy obtained by measuring mass and speed will be

(a) 8%
(b) 2 %
(c) 12 %
(d) 10 %

(20) The percentage errors in the measurement of mass and speed are 3% and 4% respectively. How much will be the maximum error in the estimation of the kinetic energy obtained by measuring mass and speed

(a) 11 %
(b) 8 %
(c) 5 %
(d) 1 %

(21) If the percentage error in the measurement of momentum and mass of an object are 2% and 3% respectively, then maximum percentage error in calculated value of its kinetic energy is

(a) 1 %
(b) 2 %
(c) 5 %
(d) 7 %

Important Points

Density of a cube : $\rho = \frac{m}{v} = \frac{m}{L^3}$

Where, m = mass of the body

L = length of the cube

(22) The density of a cube is measured by measuring its mass and length of its sides. If the maximum error in the measurement of mass and lengths are 3% and 2% respectively, the maximum error in the measurement of density would be

(a) 12 %
(b) 14 %
(c) 7 %
(d) 9 %

Important Points

Pressure : $p = \frac{F}{A}$

Where, F = force

A = area of cross-section

(23) If a force F is applied to a square plate of side L. If the percentage error in the determination of L is 2% and that in F is 4%, the possible error in pressure is

(a) 2%
(b) 4 %
(c) 6 %
(d) 8 %

Important Points

Displacement : $s = ut + \frac{1}{2} a t^2$

Where, u = initial velocity

a = constant acceleration

And t = time

(24) A student measures the distance traversed in free fall of a body, initially at rest in a given time. He uses this data to estimate g, the acceleration due to gravity. If the maximum percentage errors in measurement of the distance and the time are e_1 and e_2 respectively, the maximum percentage error in the estimation of g is

(a) $e_1 - e_2$
(b) $e_1 + e_2$
(c) $e_1 - 2e_2$

(d) $e_1 + 2\,e_2$

Important Points

Time period of oscillation of a simple pendulum :

$$T = 2\pi\sqrt{\frac{l}{g}}$$

Where, g = acceleration due to gravity

l = length of the pendulum

(25) The acceleration due to gravity is measured on the surface of earth by using a simple pendulum. If α and β are relative errors in the measurement of length and time period respectively, then percentage error in the measurement of acceleration due to gravity is

(a) $(\alpha + \frac{1}{2}\beta) \times 100$
(b) $(\alpha - 2\beta)$
(c) $(2\alpha + \beta) \times 100$
(d) $(\alpha + 2\beta) \times 100$

(26) The period of oscillation of a simple pendulum is given by $T = 2\pi\sqrt{\frac{l}{g}}$ where l is about 100 cm and is known to 1mm accuracy. The period is about 2s. The time of 100 oscillations is measured by a stop watch of least count 0.1 s. The percentage error in g is

(a) 0.1 %
(b) 1 %
(c) 0.2 %
(d) 0.8 %

(27) While measuring the acceleration due to gravity by a simple pendulum, a student makes a positive error of 1% in the length of the pendulum and a negative error of 3% in the value of time period. His percentage error in the measurement of g by the relation $g = 4\pi^2\left(\frac{l}{T^2}\right)$ will be

(a) 2 %
(b) 4 %
(c) 7 %
(d) 10 %

(28) The value of two resistors are $R_1 = (6 \pm 0.3)$ kΩ and $R_2 = (10 \pm 0.2)$ kΩ. The percentage error in the equivalent resistance when they are connected in parallel is

(a) 5.125 %
(b) 10.125 %
(c) 3.125 %
(d) 7 %

Answer

Physical World & Measurement

Topic : Error Propagation

(1)	(c)	**(7)**	(d)	**(13)**	(b)	**(19)**	(a)	**(25)**	(d)
(2)	(b)	**(8)**	(a)	**(14)**	(b)	**(20)**	(a)	**(26)**	(c)
(3)	(c)	**(9)**	(b)	**(15)**	(b)	**(21)**	(d)	**(27)**	(c)
(4)	(a)	**(10)**	(a)	**(16)**	(c)	**(22)**	(d)	**(28)**	(b)
(5)	(b)	**(11)**	(d)	**(17)**	(c)	**(23)**	(d)		
(6)	(c)	**(12)**	(c)	**(18)**	(c)	**(24)**	(d)		

Physics
MCQ | | Class – XI

Physical World & Measurement

Topic : Measuring Instruments

(1) In a Vernier callipers, N division of Vernier scale coincide with (N – 1) division of main scale (in which one division represents 1 mm). The Vernier constant is (cm)
(a) N
(b) N -1
(c) $\frac{1}{N-1}$
(d) $\frac{1}{10N}$

(2) In a Vernier callipers, one main scale division is x cm and n divisions of the Vernier scale coincide with (n-1) division of main scale. The least count (in cm) of the callipers is
(a) $\left(\frac{n-1}{n}\right)x$
(b) $\left(\frac{nx}{n-1}\right)$
(c) $\left(\frac{x}{n}\right)$
(d) $\left(\frac{x}{n-1}\right)$

Answer

Physical World & Measurement

Topic : Measuring Instruments

(1) (d)
(2) (c)

Vector

(1) Basic Concepts of Vector	(2) Vector Algebra – I (without co-ordinate representation)
(3) Vector Algebra – II (with co-ordinate representation)	

(1) Basic Concepts of Vector

(1) Classification of Quantities :

• **Scalar quantities :** A scalar physical quantity has magnitude only and no direction.
e.g., mass, length, temperature etc.

• **Vector quantities :** A vector quantity has both a magnitude and a direction and obeys the laws of vector mathematics.
e.g., velocity, displacement etc.

• If a physical quantity has magnitude as well as direction but does not add up according to the laws of vector addition, it will not be called vector quantity. e.g., electric current, time etc.

(2) Representation of a Vector :

A vector is represented by an arrow over a letter. (e.g., $\vec{A}$). The magnitude of a vector often called its absolute value is indicated either by modulus sign or by a letter without an arrow over it. (e.g., $|\vec{A}|$ or A)

Geometrically, a vector is represented with directed line segment. The length of the line is proportional to the magnitude of the vector and the direction is represented by the arrowhead.

(3) If a vector is displaced parallel to itself it does not change.

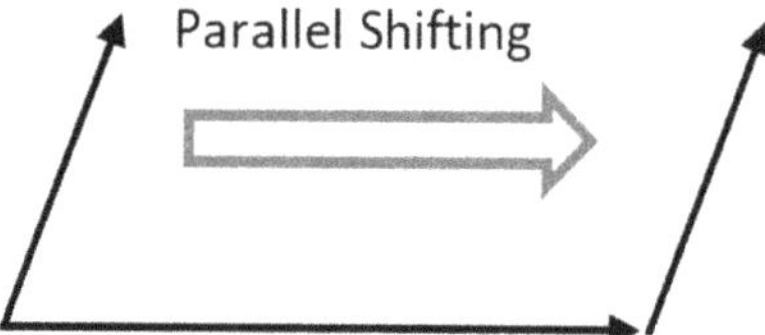

(4) If a vector is rotated through an angle other than multiple of 2π (or, 360º) it changes.

(5) If the frame of reference is translated or rotated the vector does not change (though its component may change).

(6) Angle between two vectors means smaller of the two angles between the vectors when they are placed tail to tail by displacing either of the two vectors parallel to itself. (i.e. $0 \le \theta \le \pi$)

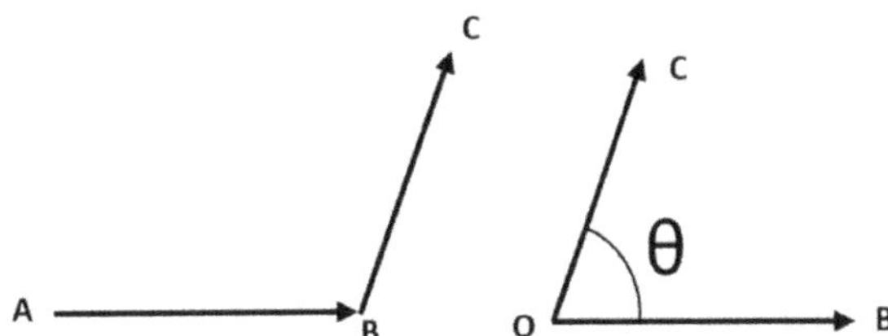

(7) Equal Vectors : Two vectors (representing same physical quantities) are called **equal**, if they have the same magnitude and direction.

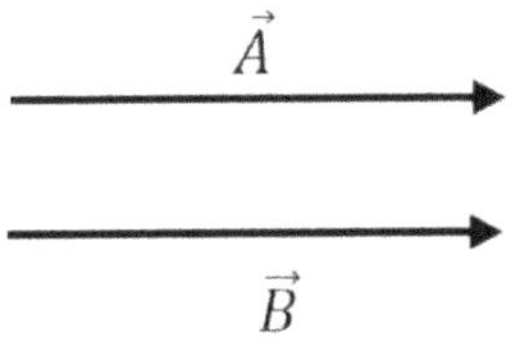

Note : $\vec{A} = \vec{B}$ implies that (a) they have same magnitude
(b) they are in same direction
(c) they are same in nature

(8) Opposite Vectors : Negative (or opposite vector) of a vector is of same magnitude but opposite direction.

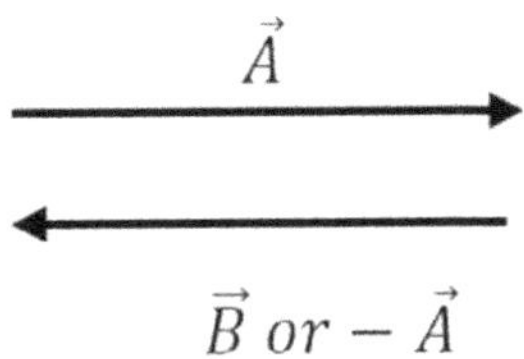

Note : $\vec{A} = -\vec{B}$ implies that (a) they ($\vec{A}$ and $\vec{B}$) have same magnitude
(b) they are in **opposite direction**
(c) they are same in nature

(9) Coplanar vectors : A system of vectors is said to be **coplanar**, if they are parallel to the same plane.

Or, Vectors completely lying on the same plane are called coplanar vectors.

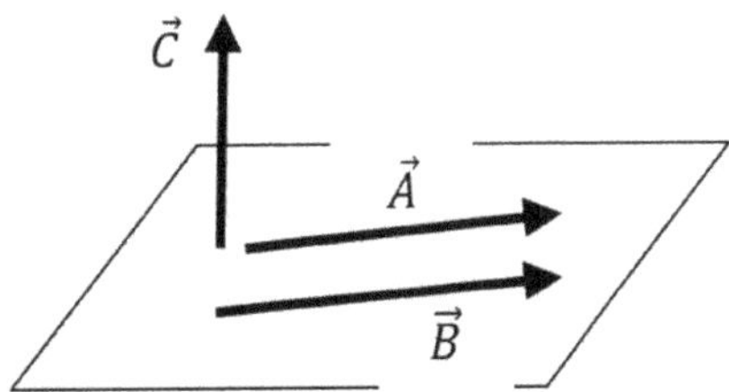

In this figure, vectors $\vec{A}$ and $\vec{B}$ are coplanar but vector $\vec{C}$ is not so.

(10) Collinear vectors : Vectors that are equal or opposite or of different magnitudes, but are parallel to each other are called collinear vectors.

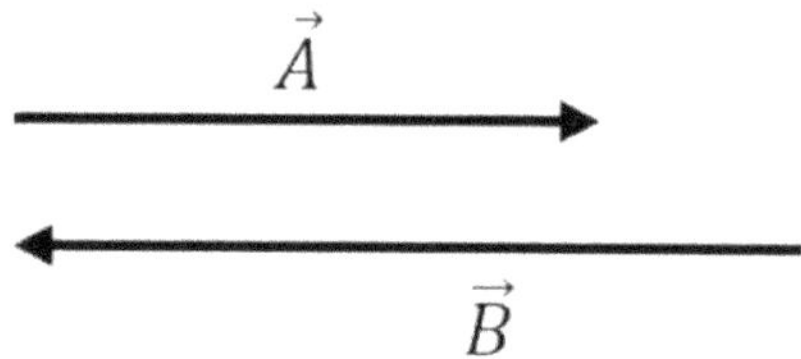

- The angle between collinear vectors is zero or 180º.
- The angle between parallel vectors is zero and the angle between antiparallel vectors is 180º.

(11) Co-initial vectors : Vectors having the same initial point are called **co-initial** vectors.

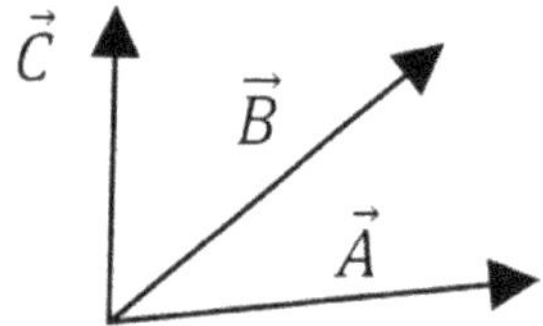

(12) Co-terminus Vectors : Vectors having the same terminal point are called **co-terminus** vectors.

(13) Null vector : Null vector or zero vector is defined as a vector whose magnitude is zero and direction un-determinate.

Note : For any Vector $\vec{A}$,

$\vec{A} + \vec{0} = \vec{A}$

$\vec{A} - \vec{0} = \vec{A}$

$\vec{A} \times \vec{0} = \vec{0}$

Again, for any real number λ, we have $\lambda\,\vec{0} = \vec{0}$

(14) Unit vector : A **unit vector** is a vector of unit magnitude and points in a particular direction.

The unit vector along $\vec{A}$ is given by $\hat{A} = \frac{\vec{A}}{|\vec{A}|}$

Thus, a vector can be represented as $\vec{A} = |\vec{A}|\,\hat{A}$

Unit vectors along the x, y and z axes of a rectangular co-ordinate system are denoted by $\hat{\imath}$, $\hat{\jmath}$ and $\hat{k}$ respectively.

Figure :

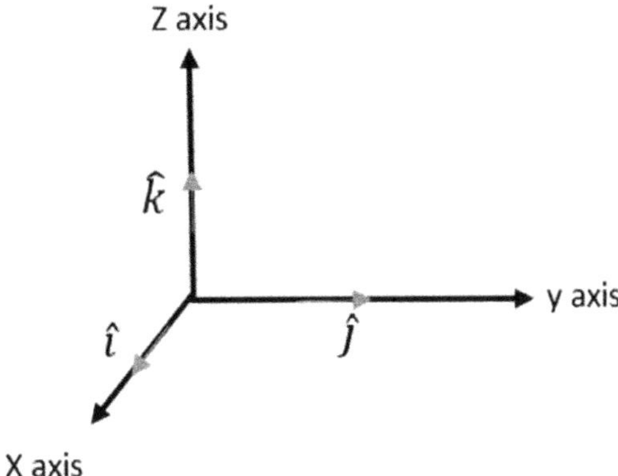

(2) Vector Algebra – I (without co-ordinate representation)

(2.1) Resultant Calculation :

• **Resultant vector :** The resultant of two (or more) vectors is a single vector, which produces the same effect as the individual vector together produce.

• **Geometrical Method for finding resultant of two vectors :** There are two laws which can be used to determine the resultant of two vectors. They are :

(a) Triangle law : *When two vectors in magnitude as well as in direction, are represented by the two adjacent sides of a triangle taken in order, the third side taken in opposite direction, represents the resultant of the two vectors both in direction and in magnitude.*

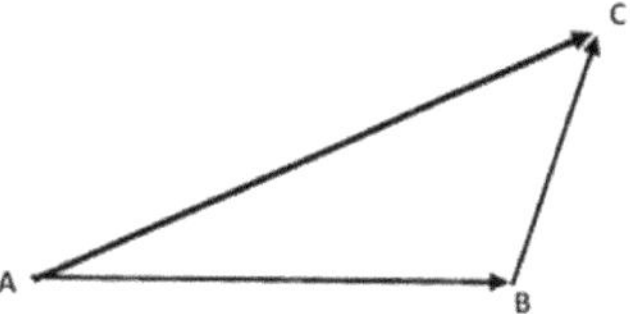

According to triangle law, $\overrightarrow{AB} + \overrightarrow{BC} = \overrightarrow{AC}$

(b) Parallelogram Law : *When two vectors acting simultaneously at a point is represented both in magnitude and direction by the two adjacent sides of a parallelogram, the diagonal of the parallelogram passing through that point represents the resultant of the two vectors both in direction and in magnitude.*

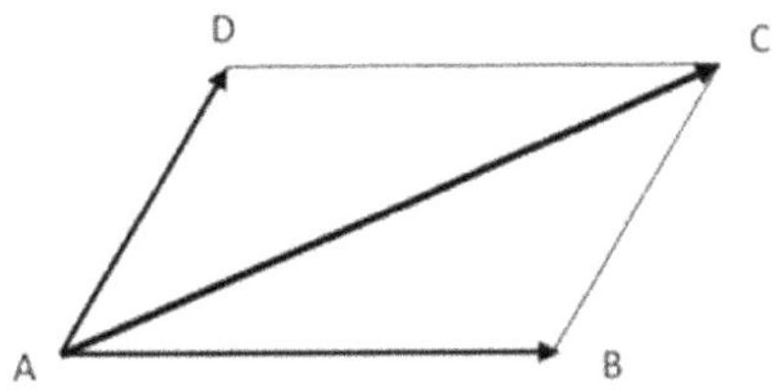

According to parallelogram law of resultant calculation, $\overrightarrow{AB} + \overrightarrow{AD} = \overrightarrow{AC}$

• **Geometrical Method for finding the resultant of more than two vectors : Polygon Law** can be used to determine the resultant of more than two vectors. It states that –

If a number of vectors can be represented in magnitude and direction by the side of a polygon taken in the same order, then their resultant is represented in magnitude and direction by the closing side of the polygon taken in the opposite order.

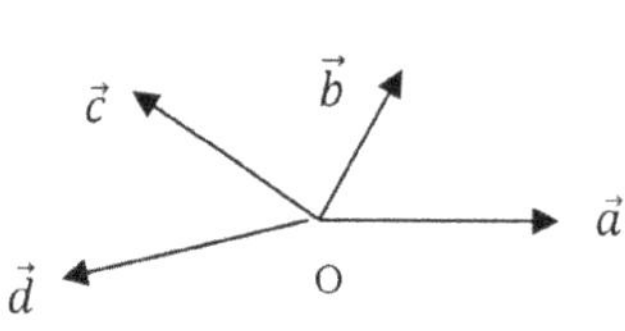

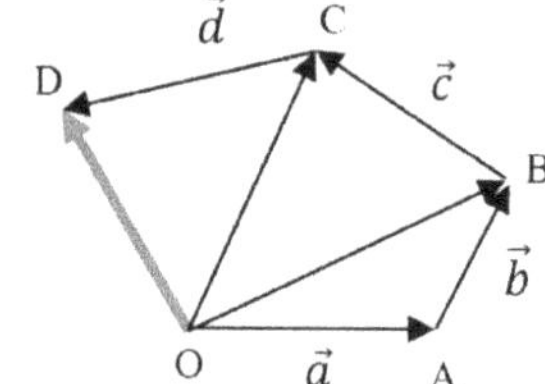

• **Analytical Method for finding resultant of two vectors :**

The magnitude of the resultant of two vectors : $|\vec{R}| = \sqrt{|\vec{A}|^2 + |\vec{B}|^2 + 2|\vec{A}||\vec{B}|\cos\theta}$

The direction of the resultant : If the resultant makes an angle α with vector $\vec{A}$ then

$$\tan\alpha = \frac{|\vec{B}|\sin\theta}{|\vec{A}| + |\vec{B}|\cos\theta}$$

• **Special Cases On Resultant Calculation :**

(a) When two vectors are acting in the same direction:

Magnitude of the resultant : $R = \sqrt{a^2 + b^2 + 2ab\cos 0°}$
$= \sqrt{a^2 + b^2 + 2ab}$
$= \sqrt{(a + b)^2}$
$= a + b$

Direction of the resultant : If the resultant vector $\vec{R}$ makes an angle α with vector $\vec{a}$ then,

$$\tan\alpha = \frac{b\sin 0°}{a + b\cos 0°} = 0$$
$$\therefore \alpha = 0° \text{ or, } 180°$$

Conclusion : When the two vectors are acting in the same direction, the magnitude of the resultant is the sum of magnitudes of the vectors [$R = a + b$] and it is directed along the vectors.

(b) When two vectors are acting in the opposite direction:

Magnitude of the resultant : $R = \sqrt{a^2 + b^2 + 2ab\cos 180°}$
$= \sqrt{a^2 + b^2 - 2ab}$
$= \sqrt{(a - b)^2}$ or, $\sqrt{(b - a)^2}$
$= (a - b)$ or, $(b - a)$

Direction of the resultant : If the resultant vector $\vec{R}$ makes an angle α with vector $\vec{a}$ then

$$\tan\alpha = \frac{b \sin 180°}{a + b \cos 180°} = 0$$
$$\therefore \alpha = 0° \text{ or, } 180°$$

Conclusion : When two vectors are acting in the opposite direction the magnitude of the resultant is the difference in magnitudes of the vectors [R = (a – b) or, (b – a)] and its direction is along the larger vector.

(c) When the two vectors are of equal magnitude and acting in opposite direction :

Magnitude of the resultant : $R = \sqrt{a^2 + a^2 + 2\,a\,a \cos 180°}$
$= \sqrt{2a^2 - 2a^2}$
$= 0$

Conclusion : When the two vectors are of equal magnitude and acting in opposite direction the magnitude of the resultant is zero.

(d) When two vectors are acting at right angles to each other :

Magnitude of the resultant : $R = \sqrt{a^2 + b^2 + 2\,a\,b \cos 90°}$
$= \sqrt{a^2 + b^2}$

Direction of the resultant : If the resultant vector $\vec{R}$ makes an angle α with vector $\vec{a}$ then

$$\tan\alpha = \frac{b \sin 90°}{a + b \cos 90°} = \frac{b}{a}$$

It can, therefore, be concluded that

- ***Maximum possible value of the resultant = sum of the magnitudes of the vectors***
- ***Minimum possible value of the resultant = difference of the magnitudes of the vectors***
- ***If the vectors are equal in magnitude and are oppositely directed, then the resultant is zero.***

- **Properties of Resultant Calculation :**

[a] Commutative rule : $\vec{a} + \vec{b} = \vec{b} + \vec{a}$
[b] Associative rule : $(\vec{a} + \vec{b}) + \vec{c} = \vec{a} + (\vec{b} + \vec{c})$
[c] Distributive law : $n(\vec{a} + \vec{b}) = n\vec{a} + n\vec{b}$

(2.2) Subtraction of Vectors

The subtraction of a vector $\vec{B}$ from vector $\vec{A}$ is defined as the addition of vector $-\vec{B}$ to vector $\vec{A}$.

$$\vec{C} = \vec{A} - \vec{B} = \vec{A} + (-\vec{B})$$

Geometrical Method	Analytical Method

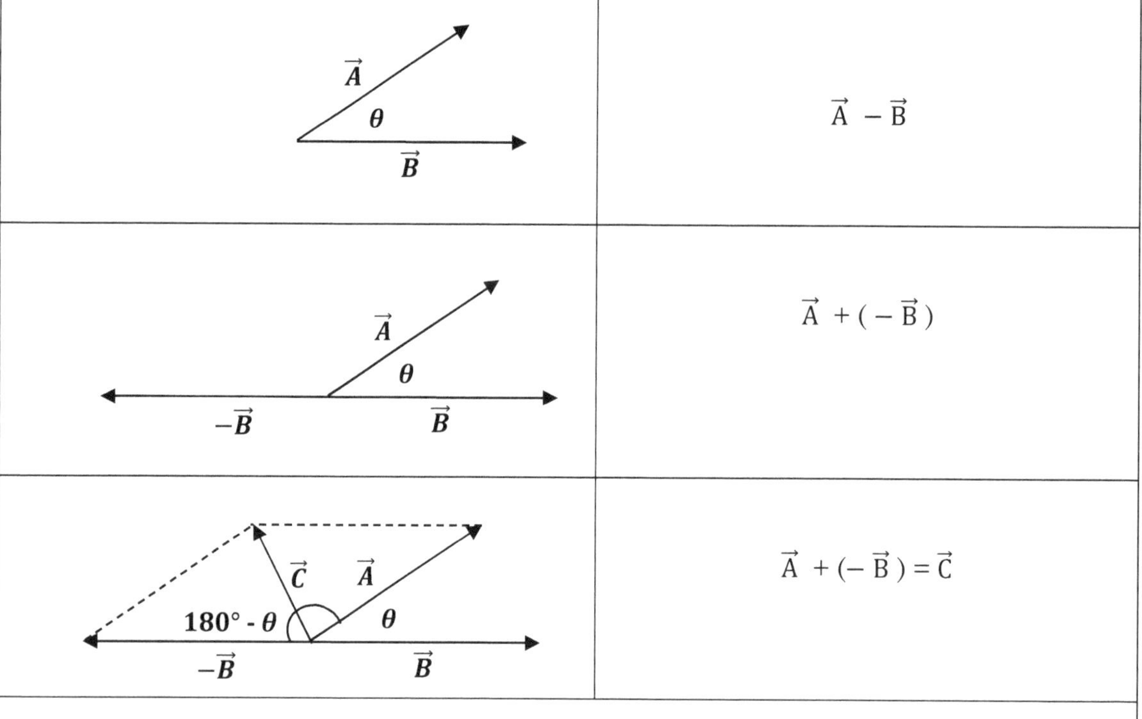

$C^2 = A^2 + B^2 + 2\,A\,B\cos(180° - \theta)$

or, $C^2 = A^2 + B^2 - 2\,A\,B\cos\theta$

$\therefore C = \sqrt{(A^2 - 2\,A\,B\cos\theta + B^2)}$

If $\vec{C}$ vector is inclined at an angle α with $\vec{A}$ then, $\tan\alpha = \frac{B\sin(180° - \theta)}{A + B\cos(180° - \theta)} = \frac{B\sin\theta}{A - B\cos\theta}$

(2.3) Resolution and Components of a Vector

• The resolution of a vector into component vectors is just the converse of the composition of vectors.

• **Resolution of a vector :** The process of splitting up a vector into two or more vectors is known as the resolution of a vector.

The vectors, into which a given vector is split, are called component vectors. **The component of a vector in a given direction gives the measure of the effect of the vector in that direction.**

• **Geometrical Method of Resolution of a vector :**

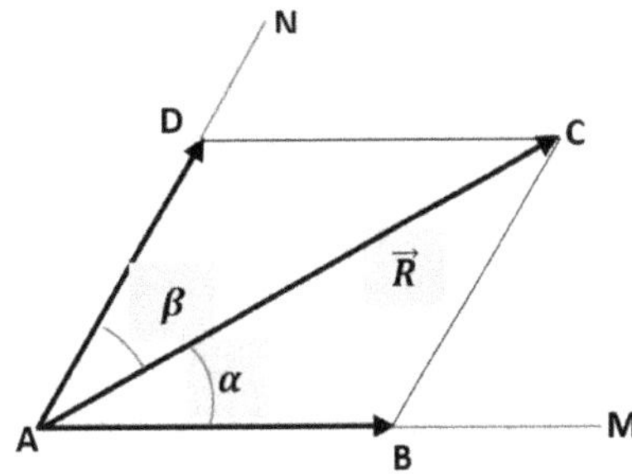

Let us consider, a given vector $\vec{R}$ is represented by $\overrightarrow{AC}$ both in magnitude and direction. AM and AN are inclined to AC by angles α and β respectively. From C, CD parallel to AM and BC parallel to AN are drawn to complete the parallelogram.

Now, from the law of parallelogram of vectors, $\overrightarrow{AB} + \overrightarrow{AD} = \overrightarrow{AC}$

Hence, the two components of $\overrightarrow{AC}$ are $\overrightarrow{AB}$ ($= \vec{a}$) and $\overrightarrow{AD}$ ($= \vec{b}$)

• Analytical Method of Resolution of a vector :

If the components ($\vec{a}$ and $\vec{b}$) of vector $\vec{R}$ makes an angle α and β with with the vector $\vec{R}$, then the magnitude of the components are

$$a = \frac{\sin\beta}{\sin\ (\alpha + \beta)} R \text{ and } b = \frac{\sin\alpha}{\sin\ (\alpha + \beta)} R$$

• Rectangular resolution of a vector :

The resolution of a vector into two mutually perpendicular vectors is called the rectangular resolution of the vector in a plane (two dimension).

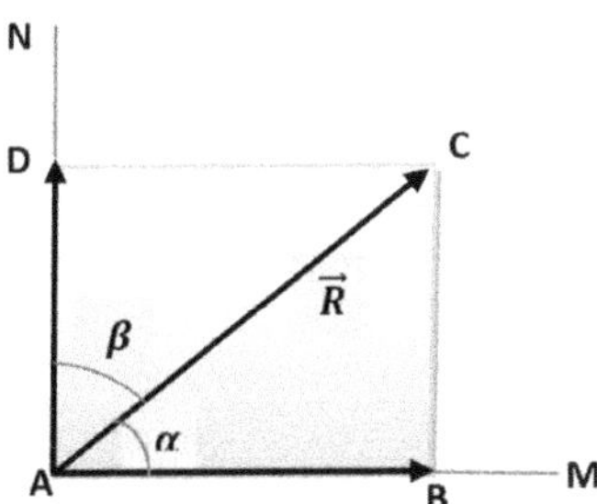

Therefore, in rectangular resolution, $\alpha + \beta = 90°$

Hence, the magnitude of the components are : $a = \frac{R\ \sin\beta}{\sin\ 90°} = R \sin\beta$ and $b = \frac{R\ \sin\alpha}{\sin\ 90°} = R \sin\alpha$

Also, $R = \sqrt{a^2 + b^2}$

• A vector can be resolved into an infinite number of components. However, a vector can have only three rectangular components in space.

Points to Remember :

[1] The component of $\vec{R}$ along a direction which makes an angle θ with $\vec{R}$ is R cos θ and the other component is R sin θ.

Such as, if a vector $\vec{r}$ is inclined at angle θ with x-axis, then magnitude of component of vector $\vec{r}$ along x-axis, $x = r \cos\theta$ and magnitude of component of vector $\vec{r}$ along y-axis, $y = r \sin\theta$

[2] The component (or resolved part) of a vector along its direction is of same magnitude as the vector. [If $\theta = 0°$ then $R_x = R \cos 0° = R$]

[3] There is no component in a direction perpendicular to the vector. [If $\theta = 90°$ then $R_x = R \cos 90° = 0$]

(2.4) Multiplication of a Vector with a Scalar :

When a vector $\vec{A}$ is multiplied with a real number n, it gives a vector $n\vec{A}$ having magnitude n times that of $\vec{A}$ and direction same (if n is positive) or opposite (if n is negative) to that of $\vec{A}$.

(2.5) Multiplication of a Vector with a Vector :

Two vectors, when multiplied may produce either a scalar or a vector. Accordingly they are called scalar or dot product and vector or cross product.

(i) Scalar (or Dot) Product :

■ **Definition :** The scalar product of two vectors $\vec{A}$ and $\vec{B}$ is defined as the product of the magnitudes of the vectors $\vec{A}$ and $\vec{B}$ and the cosine of the angle between them.

If the vectors $\vec{A}$ and $\vec{B}$ are inclined at an angle θ, then $\vec{\mathbf{A}} \cdot \vec{\mathbf{B}} = |\vec{\mathbf{A}}|\,|\vec{\mathbf{B}}| \cos\theta$

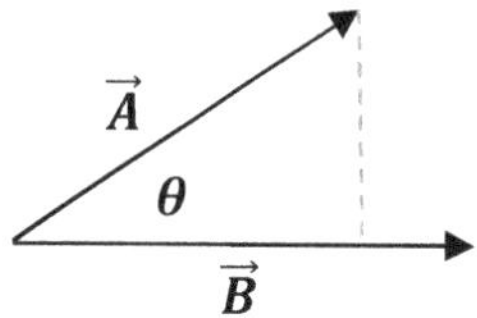

On the other hand, dot product of two vectors is the product of the magnitude of any one of the vectors and the magnitude of component of the other vector in the direction of the first one.

■ **Properties of Dot Product :**

[i] The dot product of two vectors obeys commutative law i.e. $\vec{A} \cdot \vec{B} = \vec{B} \cdot \vec{A}$

[ii] If vectors $\vec{A}$ and $\vec{B}$ are parallel [$\theta = 0°$] then $\vec{A} \cdot \vec{B} = |\vec{A}|\,|\vec{B}| \cos 0° = |\vec{A}|\,|\vec{B}|$

[iii] If vectors $\vec{A}$ and $\vec{B}$ are perpendicular [$\theta = 90°$] then $\vec{A} \cdot \vec{B} = |\vec{A}|\,|\vec{B}| \cos 90° = 0$

[iv] If the vectors $\vec{A}$ and $\vec{B}$ are inclined at an angle θ, then $\vec{A} \cdot \vec{B} = |\vec{A}|\,|\vec{B}| \cos\theta$

$$\text{or, } \cos\theta = \frac{\vec{A} \cdot \vec{B}}{|\vec{A}|\,|\vec{B}|}$$

$$\therefore \theta = \cos^{-1}\left(\frac{\vec{A}.\vec{B}}{|\vec{A}|\,|\vec{B}|}\right)$$

■ **Examples of Dot product :**

(i) Work W = $\vec{F}$. $\vec{s}$ [where, $\vec{F}$ = force and $\vec{s}$ = displacement]
(ii) Power P = $\vec{F}$. $\vec{v}$ [where, $\vec{F}$ = force and $\vec{v}$ = velocity]
(iii) Potential Energy $E_p = -\vec{F}\,.\,\Delta\vec{r}$ [where, $\vec{F}$ = force and $\Delta\vec{r}$ = displacement]

(ii) Vector (or Cross) Product :

■ **Definition :** The vector product of two vectors $\vec{A}$ and $\vec{B}$ is defined as the product of the magnitudes of the vectors $\vec{A}$ and $\vec{B}$ and the sine of the angle between them; and it points in a direction in which a right handed screw will advance, when rotated from the vector $\vec{A}$ to $\vec{B}$ through shortest angel.

■ Mathematically, If the vectors $\vec{A}$ and $\vec{B}$ are inclined at an angle θ, then $\vec{A} \times \vec{B} = |\vec{A}||\vec{B}|\sin\theta\,\hat{n}$

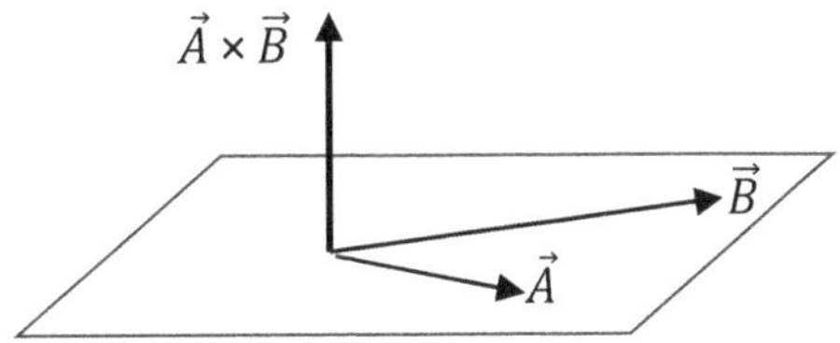

■ **Two rules for determining the direction of the cross product :**

[1] Right Hand Thumb Rule : Curl the fingers of your right hand from $\vec{A}$ to $\vec{B}$ through smallest angel, then the direction of the erect thumb will point in the direction of $\hat{n}$ or $\vec{A} \times \vec{B}$.

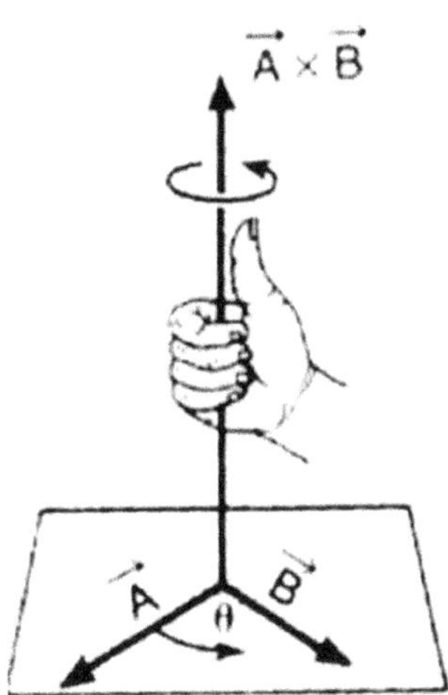

[2] Right Hand Screw Rule : Hold a right hand screw with its axis perpendicular to the plane containing $\vec{A}$ and $\vec{B}$. Now, turn the srew from $\vec{A}$ to $\vec{B}$ through smallest angel. The direction of advance of the screw gives the direction of $\vec{A} \times \vec{B}$.

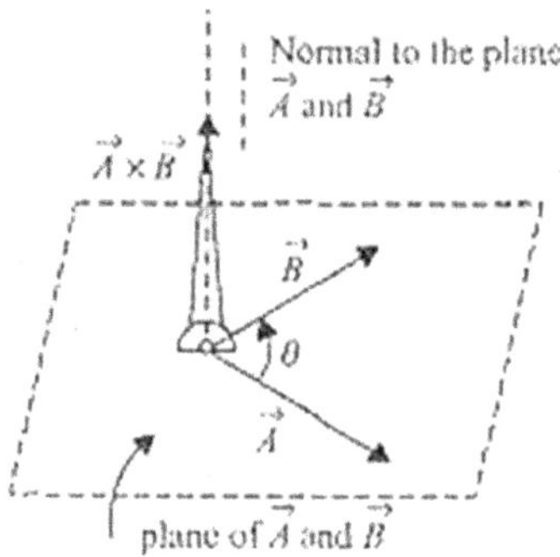

■ Properties of Cross Product :

[i] The cross product of two vectors does not obeys commutative law i.e. $(\vec{A} \times \vec{B}) \neq (\vec{B} \times \vec{A})$
Rather, $(\vec{A} \times \vec{B}) = -(\vec{B} \times \vec{A})$

[ii] Cross product is distributive. i.e. $\vec{A} \times (\vec{B} + \vec{C}) = (\vec{A} \times \vec{B}) + (\vec{A} \times \vec{C})$

[iii] If vectors $\vec{A}$ and $\vec{B}$ are parallel [$\theta = 0°$] then $\vec{A} \times \vec{B} = \vec{0}$

[iv] Cross product of two mutually perpendicular vectors is equal to the product of the magnitude of the given vectors, the direction being perpendicular to the plane of the given vectors.
If $\vec{A} \perp \vec{B}$ then $\theta = 90°$
$\therefore |\vec{A} \times \vec{B}| = |\vec{A}|\,|\vec{B}| \sin 90° = |\vec{A}|\,|\vec{B}|$

[v] Vector product is associative; i.e. $(m\vec{A}) \times \vec{B} = \vec{A} \times (m\vec{B}) = m(\vec{A} \times \vec{B})$

[vi] If two vectors are represented by the adjacent sides of a parallelogram, then the magnitude of their cross product will give the area of the parallelogram.

Proof :

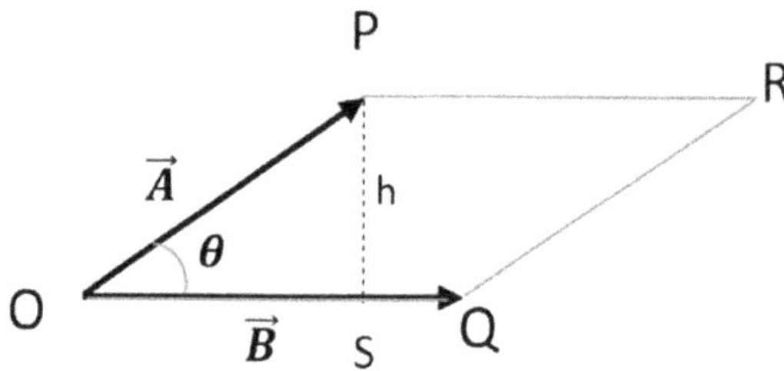

Let us consider, two vectors $\vec{A}$ and $\vec{B}$ are represented by the two adjacent sides OP and OQ respectively in figure.
Now, $|\vec{A} \times \vec{B}| = |\vec{A}|\,|\vec{B}| \sin\theta$
= OP. OQ $\sin\theta$
= base × height of parallelogram
= area of parallelogram

■ Examples of Cross Product :

(i) Torque : $\vec{\tau} = \vec{r} \times \vec{F}$
[Where, $\vec{r}$ = position vector and $\vec{F}$ = applied force]

(ii) Linear velocity : $\vec{v} = \vec{\omega} \times \vec{r}$
[Where, $\vec{\omega}$ = angular velocity and $\vec{r}$ = position vector or radius vector]

(iii) Angular momentum : $\vec{L} = \vec{r} \times \vec{P}$
[Where, $\vec{P}$ = linear momentum and $\vec{r}$ = position vector or radius vector]

(iv) Tangential acceleration $\overrightarrow{a_T} = \vec{\alpha} \times \vec{r}$
[Where, $\vec{\alpha}$ = angular acceleration and and $\vec{r}$ = position vector or radius vector]

(3) Vector Algebra – II (with co-ordinate representation)

(3.1) Representation of Vector by its Coordinates

(a) Taking the Initial Point of the Vector as Origin :

A vector that determines the position of a point with respect to the origin is called the position vector for that point.

Two dimensional representation :

A point P with co-ordinate (x, y) is in two dimensional space and point O is the origin, then

(i) The **vector representation** of the position vector of the point P : $\vec{r} = x\,\hat{\imath} + y\,\hat{\jmath}$

(ii) **Magnitude** of the Position Vector : $|\vec{r}| = \sqrt{x^2 + y^2}$

(iii) **Direction :** If $\vec{r}$ makes angles θ with x-axis then $\tan\theta = \frac{y}{x}$ or, $\theta = \tan^{-1}\frac{y}{x}$

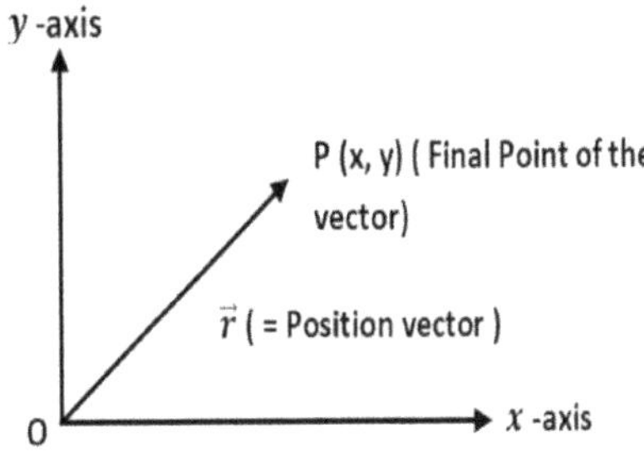

(origin or initial Point of the vector)

Three dimensional representation :

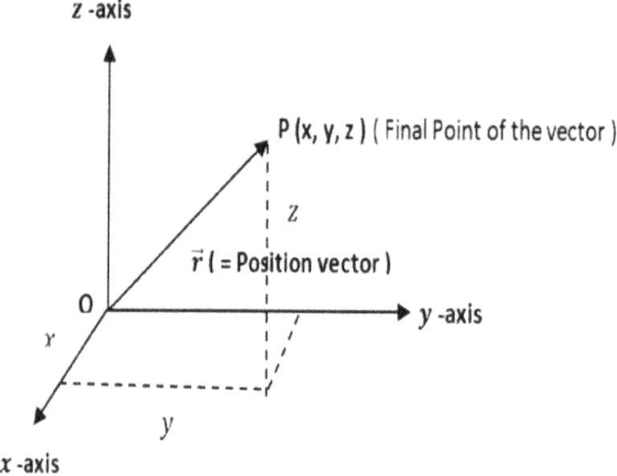

A point P with co-ordinate (x, y, z) is in two dimensional space and point O is the origin, then

(i) The **vector representation** of the position vector of the point P : $\vec{r} = x\,\hat{\imath} + y\,\hat{\jmath} + z\,\hat{k}$

(ii) **Magnitude** of the Position Vector : $|\vec{r}| = \sqrt{x^2 + y^2 + z^2}$

(iii) **Direction :** If $\vec{r}$ makes angles α, β and γ with x, y and z axes respectively then, directional cosine of $\vec{r}$ are :

$\cos\alpha = \frac{x}{r}$,

$\cos\beta = \frac{y}{r}$

and $\cos\gamma = \frac{z}{r}$ → Direction Cosine

(b) Taking Any Arbitrary Point as Origin :

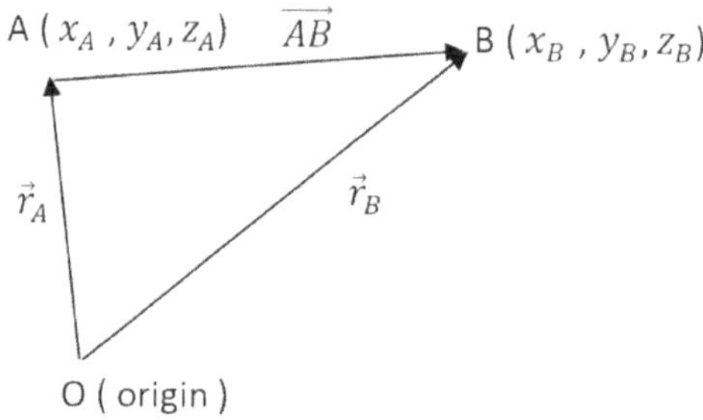

The coordinate of the two points A and B are given by (x_A, y_A, z_A) and (x_B, y_B, z_B)

Therefore the position vectors of the point A and B are given by $\vec{r_A} = x_A\,\hat{\imath} + y_A\,\hat{\jmath} + z_A\,\hat{k}$

and, $\vec{r_B} = x_B\,\hat{\imath} + y_B\,\hat{\jmath} + z_B\,\hat{k}$

Form the figure, we get, $\vec{r_B} = \vec{r_A} + \overrightarrow{AB}$

or, $\overrightarrow{AB} = \vec{r_B} - \vec{r_A}$

or, $\overrightarrow{AB} = (x_B\hat{\imath} + y_B\,\hat{\jmath} + z_B\hat{k}) - (x_A\,\hat{\imath} + y_A\,\hat{\jmath} + z_A\,\hat{k})$

$\therefore\ \overrightarrow{AB} = (x_B - x_A)\hat{\imath} + (y_B - y_A)\hat{\jmath} + (z_B - z_A)\,\hat{k}$

The magnitude of the vector : $|\overrightarrow{AB}| = \sqrt{(x_B - x_A)^2 + (y_B - y_A)^2 + (z_B - z_A)^2}$

(3.2) Resultant Calculation :

Let us consider, $\vec{A} = A_x\hat{i} + A_y\hat{j} + A_z\hat{k}$
and $\vec{B} = B_x\hat{i} + B_y\hat{j} + B_z\hat{k}$

$\therefore \vec{R} = \vec{A} + \vec{B}$

$= (A_x + B_x)\,\hat{i} + (A_y + B_y)\,\hat{j} + (A_z + B_z)\hat{k}$

$|\vec{R}| = \sqrt{(A_x + B_x)^2 + (A_y + B_y)^2 + (A_z + B_z)^2}$

$\therefore \vec{C} = \vec{A} - \vec{B}$

$= (A_x - B_x)\,\hat{i} + (A_y - B_y)\,\hat{j} + (A_z - B_z)\hat{k}$

$|\vec{C}| = \sqrt{(A_x - B_x)^2 + (A_y - B_y)^2 + (A_z - B_z)^2}$

(3.3) Resolution and Components of a Vector

If $\vec{A} = A_x\hat{i} + A_y\hat{j} + A_z\hat{k}$, then the quantities A_x, A_y and A_z are called x-, y- and z-components of the vector $\vec{A}$.

As described earlier a position vector $\vec{r}$ can be expressed as $\vec{r} = x\,\hat{i} + y\,\hat{j} + z\,\hat{k}$, where x, y and z are the components of $\vec{r}$ along x, y and z axes respectively.

(3.4) Multiplication Of Vectors

[A] Scalar (or Dot) Product :

Definition : If the vectors $\vec{A}$ and $\vec{B}$ are inclined at an angle θ, then $\vec{A}\,.\,\vec{B} = |\vec{A}|\,|\vec{B}|\cos\theta$

Scalar Product of unit vectors : (i) $\hat{i}\,.\,\hat{i} = 1.\,1.\,\cos 0° = 1$
(ii) $\hat{j}\,.\,\hat{j} = 1$
(iii) $\hat{k}\,.\,\hat{k} = 1$
(iv) $\hat{i}\,.\,\hat{j} = 1\,.\,1\,.\cos 90° = 0 = \hat{j}\,.\,\hat{i}$
(v) $\hat{j}\,.\,\hat{k} = 0 = \hat{k}\,.\,\hat{j}$
(vi) $\hat{k}\,.\,\hat{i} = 0 = \hat{i}\,.\,\hat{k}$

Now, Let us consider, $\vec{A} = A_x\hat{i} + A_y\hat{j} + A_z\hat{k}$ and $\vec{B} = B_x\hat{i} + B_y\hat{j} + B_z\hat{k}$

$\therefore \vec{A}\,.\,\vec{B} = (A_xB_x)\,(\hat{i}.\hat{i}) + (A_yB_y)\,(\hat{j}.\hat{j}) + (A_zB_z)\,(\hat{k}.\hat{k})$
$= (A_x\,B_x) + (A_y\,B_y) + (A_z\,B_z)$

To find angle: Let us consider, $\vec{A} = A_x\hat{i} + A_y\hat{j} + A_z\hat{k}$ and $\vec{B} = B_x\hat{i} + B_y\hat{j} + B_z\hat{k}$
$\therefore \vec{A}\,.\,\vec{B} = A_x\,B_x + A_yB_y + A_z\,B_z$
$|\vec{A}| = \sqrt{A_x^2 + A_y^2 + A_z^2}$
$|\vec{B}| = \sqrt{B_x^2 + B_y^2 + B_z^2}$
If α be the angle between two vectors, $\vec{A}\,.\,\vec{B} = |\vec{A}|\,|\vec{B}|\cos\alpha$

$$\text{or, } \cos\alpha = \frac{\vec{A}\,.\,\vec{B}}{|\vec{A}|\,|\vec{B}|}$$

$$\therefore \cos\alpha = \frac{A_x B_x + A_y B_y + A_z B_z}{\sqrt{A_x^2 + A_y^2 + A_z^2}\ \sqrt{B_x^2 + B_y^2 + B_z^2}}$$

[B] Vector (or Cross) Product :

If the vectors $\vec{A}$ and $\vec{B}$ are inclined at an angle θ, then $\vec{A} \times \vec{B} = |\vec{A}|\,|\vec{B}| \sin\theta\ \hat{n}$

Cross product of unit vectors : $\hat{\imath} \times \hat{\imath} = (1.1. \sin 0°)\,\hat{n} = 0$
$\hat{\jmath} \times \hat{\jmath} = (1.1. \sin 0°)\,\hat{n} = 0$
$\hat{k} \times \hat{k} = (1.1. \sin 0°)\,\hat{n} = 0$

$\hat{\imath} \times \hat{\jmath} = (1.1. \sin 90°)\,\hat{k} = \hat{k}$
$\hat{\jmath} \times \hat{k} = (1.1. \sin 90°)\,\hat{\imath} = \hat{\imath}$
$\hat{k} \times \hat{\imath} = (1.1. \sin 90°)\,\hat{\jmath} = \hat{\jmath}$

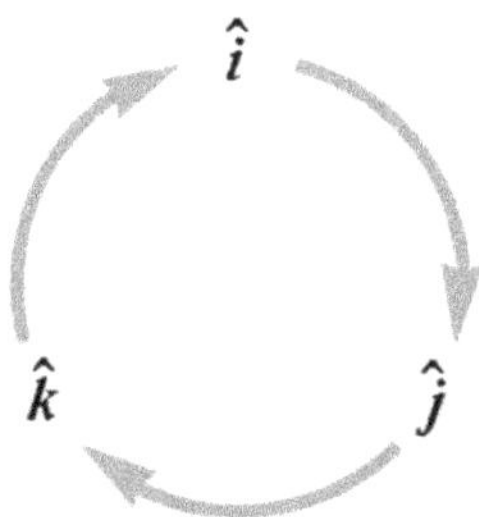

Let us consider, $\vec{A} = A_x\hat{\imath} + A_y\hat{\jmath} + A_z\hat{k}$
$\vec{B} = B_x\hat{\imath} + B_y\hat{\jmath} + B_z\hat{k}$

$\therefore \vec{A} \times \vec{B} = (A_x\hat{\imath} + A_y\hat{\jmath} + A_z\hat{k}) \times (B_x\hat{\imath} + B_y\hat{\jmath} + B_z\hat{k})$
$= A_x B_x (\hat{\imath} \times \hat{\imath}) + A_x B_y (\hat{\imath} \times \hat{\jmath}) + A_x B_z (\hat{\imath} \times \hat{k}) + A_y B_x (\hat{\jmath} \times \hat{\imath}) + A_y B_y (\hat{\jmath} \times \hat{\jmath}) + A_y B_z (\hat{\jmath} \times \hat{k}) + A_z B_x (\hat{k} \times \hat{\imath}) + A_z B_y (\hat{k} \times \hat{\jmath}) + A_z B_z (\hat{k} \times \hat{k})$
$= A_x B_y\,\hat{k} - A_x B_z\,\hat{\jmath} - A_y B_x\,\hat{k} + A_y B_z\,\hat{\imath} + A_z B_x\,\hat{\jmath} - A_z B_y\,\hat{\imath}$
$= (A_y B_z - A_z B_y)\,\hat{\imath} + (A_z B_x - A_x B_z)\,\hat{\jmath} + (A_x B_y - A_y B_x)\,\hat{k}$

$$= \begin{vmatrix} \hat{\imath} & \hat{\jmath} & \hat{k} \\ A_x & A_y & A_z \\ B_x & B_y & B_z \end{vmatrix}$$

[c] Scalar Triple Product : $\vec{\mathbf{A}}\,.\,(\vec{\mathbf{B}} \times \vec{\mathbf{C}})$

Let us consider, $\vec{A} = A_x\hat{\imath} + A_y\hat{\jmath} + A_z\hat{k}$
$\vec{B} = B_x\hat{\imath} + B_y\hat{\jmath} + B_z\hat{k}$
$\vec{C} = C_x\hat{\imath} + C_y\hat{\jmath} + C_z\hat{k}$

$$\therefore \vec{A}\,.\,(\vec{B} \times \vec{C}) = \begin{vmatrix} A_x & A_y & A_z \\ B_x & B_y & B_z \\ C_x & C_y & C_z \end{vmatrix}$$

Solved Examples & Exercise

Group – A : Vector Algebra – I (Without Coordinate Representation)

Basic Concepts of Vector

Question : Is current electricity a vector quantity?

Answer : Current Electricity is a scalar quantity. (because it does not obey the rules of vector mathematics)

Question : Is a vector necessarily changed if it is rotated through an angle?

Answer : A vector can be changed by changing its magnitude and direction. So, If we rotate a vector through an angle, its direction changes and we can say that the vector has changed.

Try Yourself

(1) A quantity has both magnitude and direction. Is it necessarily a vector?
(2) Is current electricity a vector quantity?
(3) Is finite rotation a vector quantity?
(4) Is infinitesimally small rotation a vector quantity?
(5) What is the effect on the dimensions of a vector if it is multiplied by a non-dimensional scalar?

On Resultant Calculation

Question : Can you add two vectors representing physical quantities having different dimensions?

Answer : No, we cannot add two vectors representing physical quantities of different dimensions.

Question : What is the maximum and minimum possible magnitude of resultant of two vectors having magnitudes 3 and 5 ?

Answer : The maximum magnitude of resultant of two vectors having magnitudes 3 and 5 is 8 and the minimum magnitude of resultant of these two vectors is 2.

Try Yourself

(6) Why vectors cannot be added algebraically?
(7) Fifty vectors, each of magnitude 10 units, are represented by the sides of a polygon, all taken in the same order. What will be the resultant?
[Ans : Zero]

Problem : Show that : $|\vec{A} + \vec{B}| \leq |\vec{A}| + |\vec{B}|$

Solution : $|\vec{A} + \vec{B}| = (|\vec{A}|^2 + |\vec{B}|^2 + 2|\vec{A}|\,|\vec{B}|\cos\theta)^{\frac{1}{2}}$

The maximum value of $\cos\theta$ is + 1

$\therefore |\vec{A} + \vec{B}| \leq (|\vec{A}|^2 + |\vec{B}|^2 + 2|\vec{A}|\,|\vec{B}|)^{\frac{1}{2}}$

or, $|\vec{A} + \vec{B}| \leq [(|\vec{A}| + |\vec{B}|)^2]^{\frac{1}{2}}$

$\therefore |\vec{A} + \vec{B}| \leq |\vec{A}| + |\vec{B}|$

Problem : Show that : $|\vec{A} + \vec{B}| \geq \big||\vec{A}| - |\vec{B}|\big|$

Solution : $|\vec{A} + \vec{B}| = (|\vec{A}|^2 + |\vec{B}|^2 + 2|\vec{A}|\,|\vec{B}|\cos\theta)^{\frac{1}{2}}$

The minimum value of $\cos\theta$ is – 1

$\therefore |\vec{A} + \vec{B}| \geq (|\vec{A}|^2 + |\vec{B}|^2 - 2|\vec{A}|\,|\vec{B}|)^{\frac{1}{2}}$

or, $|\vec{A} + \vec{B}| \geq [\,\big||\vec{A}| - |\vec{B}|\big|^2\,]^{\frac{1}{2}}$

$\therefore |\vec{A} + \vec{B}| \geq \big||\vec{A}| - |\vec{B}|\big|$

Try Yourself

(8) For what angle between $\vec{A}$ and $\vec{B}$, the value of $\vec{A} + \vec{B}$ is maximum?
[Ans : 0°]

(9) Under what condition $|\vec{A} + \vec{B}| = |\vec{A}| + |\vec{B}|$ holds good?
[Ans : 0°]

(10) Under what condition $|\vec{A} + \vec{B}| = |\vec{A}| - |\vec{B}|$ holds good?
[Ans : 180°]

Problem : If $\vec{A} + \vec{B} = \vec{C}$ and $A^2 + B^2 = C^2$, find the angle between $\vec{A}$ and $\vec{B}$.

Solution : Let us consider, the angle between $\vec{A}$ and $\vec{B}$ is θ
Since, $\vec{A} + \vec{B} = \vec{C}$
$\therefore C^2 = A^2 + B^2 + 2\,A\,B\cos\theta$
Again, $A^2 + B^2 = C^2$
$\therefore C^2 = C^2 + 2\,A\,B\cos\theta$
or, $2\,A\,B\cos\theta = 0$
or, $\cos\theta = 0 = \cos 90°$
$\therefore \theta = 90°$

Try Yourself

(11) If $\vec{A} + \vec{B} = \vec{C}$ and A + B = C, find the angle between $\vec{A}$ and $\vec{B}$.
[Ans : 0°]

Problem : Can two vectors of same magnitude have resultant equal to either of them? Explain.

Solution : Let us consider, the magnitude of each vector is x and the angle between the vectors is θ. According to the problem, the magnitude of the resultant is also x.
Then, $x^2 = x^2 + x^2 + 2\,x\,x\cos\theta$
or, $x^2 = 2x^2(1 + \cos\theta)$
or, $1 + \cos\theta = \frac{1}{2}$

or, $\cos\theta = -\frac{1}{2} = \cos 120°$

$\therefore \theta = 120°$

Two vectors of same magnitude can have resultant equal to either of them when they makes an angle of 120° to each other.

Try Yourself

(12) In which conditions will the resultant of two vectors having equal magnitude be (1) $\sqrt{2}$ times the magnitude of any vector and (2) $\sqrt{3}$ times the magnitude of any vector ?
[Ans : (1) 90° (2) 60°]

Problem : Two forces of magnitudes P and Q acting at a point at an angle θ have their resultant (2n+1) $\sqrt{P^2 + Q^2}$ and when at an angle $(90° - \theta)$, the resultant is (2n – 1) $\sqrt{P^2 + Q^2}$. Show that $\tan\theta = \frac{n-1}{n+1}$.

Solution : In first case,

$\{(2n+1)\sqrt{P^2 + Q^2}\}^2 = P^2 + Q^2 + 2PQ\cos\theta$

or, $2PQ\cos\theta = (2n+1)^2 (P^2 + Q^2) - (P^2 + Q^2)$

or, $2PQ\cos\theta = (P^2 + Q^2)\{(2n+1)^2 - 1\}$

or, $2PQ\cos\theta = (P^2 + Q^2)(2n + 1 + 1)(2n + 1 - 1)$

or, $2PQ\cos\theta = (P^2 + Q^2)\ 2n(2n+2)$

or, $2PQ\cos\theta = (P^2 + Q^2)\ 4n(n+1)$ ....(1)

In second case, $\{(2n-1)\sqrt{P^2 + Q^2}\}^2 = P^2 + Q^2 + 2PQ\cos(90 - \theta)$

or, $2PQ\sin\theta = (2n-1)^2 (P^2 + Q^2) - (P^2 + Q^2)$

or, $2PQ\sin\theta = (P^2 + Q^2)\{(2n-1)^2 - 1\}$

or, $2PQ\sin\theta = (P^2 + Q^2)(2n - 1 + 1)(2n - 1 - 1)$

or, $2PQ\sin\theta = (P^2 + Q^2)\ 2n(2n-2)$

or, $2PQ\sin\theta = (P^2 + Q^2)\ 4n(n-1)$ ....(2)

Dividing (2) by (1), we get, $\tan\theta = \frac{n-1}{n+1}$

Try Yourself

(13) Two vectors having magnitudes of 2P and P are inclined to each other at such an angle that if the first vector is doubled, the value of the resultant increases by three times. What is the angle between the two vectors?
[Ans : 180°]

(14) Magnitude of the resultant of two vectors which have equal magnitudes and which act at right angles to each other is 1414. Calculate the magnitude of each vector.
[Ans : 1000]

(15) Two vectors whose magnitudes are in the ratio of 3:5 give a resultant of magnitude 35. If the angle of inclination be 60°; calculate the magnitude if each vector.

On Subtraction of Vectors

Problem : If unit vectors $\hat{A}$ and $\hat{B}$ are inclined at an angle θ, then prove that $|\hat{A} - \hat{B}| = 2 \sin\frac{\theta}{2}$.

Solution : L.H.S. = $|\hat{A} - \hat{B}|$

$= \sqrt{1^2 + 1^2 + 2.1.1\cos\theta}$

$= \sqrt{2(1 + \cos\theta)}$

$= \sqrt{2.2\sin^2\frac{\theta}{2}}$

$= 2 \text{ Sin}\frac{\theta}{2}$ = R.H.S. (proved)

Try Yourself

---

(16) If $\vec{C} = \vec{a} - \vec{b}$, show that, $C^2 = a^2 + b^2 - 2ab\cos\theta$ where θ is the angle between $\vec{a}$ and $\vec{b}$

(17) The sum and difference of two vectors are equal in magnitude. What conclusion do you draw from this?
[Ans : $\theta = 90°$]

On Resolution and Components of a Vector

Problem : A vector ($\vec{A}$) having magnitude 30 is inclined to the y-axis at an angle of 60°. Find the components of the vector along x and y axes respectively.

Solution : Here, A = 30 and the vector is inclined to the y-axis with an angle of 60° then,

$A_y = A\cos\theta$

= 30 cos 60°

= 15

and $A_x = A\cos\theta$

= 30 sin 60°

$= 30 . \frac{\sqrt{3}}{2}$

$= 15\sqrt{3}$

Try Yourself

---

(18) A vector of magnitude 10 units makes an angle of 30° with the horizontal. Find its horizontal and vertical components.
[Ans : $5\sqrt{3}$ unit and 5 unit]

(19) A vector has a magnitude of 15 units and make an angle of 60° with the positive x-axis. Find its x and y components.
[Ans : $15\sqrt{3}$ unit and 15 unit]

On Dot Product of Vectors

Question : Can you multiply two vectors representing physical quantities having different dimensions?

Answer : Yes, we can multiply two vectors representing physical quantities with different dimensions.

Question : What is the scalar product of two mutually perpendicular vectors?

Answer : The Scalar product of two mutually perpendicular vectors is zero. [$\vec{A}\cdot\vec{B} = |\vec{A}|\,|\vec{B}|\cos 90° = 0$]

Problem : Show that : $|\vec{A} + \vec{B}|^2 - |\vec{A} - \vec{B}|^2 = 4\vec{A}\cdot\vec{B}$

Solution : L.H.S. = $|\vec{A} + \vec{B}|^2 - |\vec{A} - \vec{B}|^2$

$= (\vec{A} + \vec{B})\cdot(\vec{A} + \vec{B}) - (\vec{A} - \vec{B})\cdot(\vec{A} - \vec{B})$

$= \vec{A}\cdot\vec{A} + \vec{A}\cdot\vec{B} + \vec{B}\cdot\vec{A} + \vec{B}\cdot\vec{B} - \vec{A}\cdot\vec{A} + \vec{A}\cdot\vec{B} + \vec{B}\cdot\vec{A} - \vec{B}\cdot\vec{B}$

$= \vec{A}\cdot\vec{B} + \vec{B}\cdot\vec{A} + \vec{A}\cdot\vec{B} + \vec{B}\cdot\vec{A}$

$= 4\vec{A}\cdot\vec{B}$ [$\because \vec{A}\cdot\vec{B} = \vec{B}\cdot\vec{A}$]

= R.H.S. (proved)

Try Yourself

(20) What is the scalar product of two mutually perpendicular vectors?
[Ans : 0]

(21) If $(\vec{A} + \vec{B})\cdot(\vec{A} - \vec{B}) = 0$, then what is the relation between $\vec{A}$ and $\vec{B}$?
[Ans : A = B]

(22) If $(\vec{A}\cdot\vec{B})^2 = A^2B^2$ then what is the relation between $\vec{A}$ and $\vec{B}$?
[Ans : They are parallel]

(23) If unit vectors $\hat{A}$ and $\hat{B}$ are inclined at an angle θ, then prove that $|\hat{A} - \hat{B}| = 2\sin\frac{\theta}{2}$.

(24) Show that component of $\vec{b}$ along $\vec{a}$ can be written as $\frac{(\vec{b}\cdot\vec{a})\,\vec{a}}{a^2}$.

(25) Show that : $(\vec{A} + 2\vec{B})\cdot(2\vec{A} - 3\vec{B}) = 2A^2 + AB\cos\theta - 6B^2$

On Vector Product of Vectors

Question : What is the vector product of two parallel vectors?

Answer : If two vectors $\vec{A}$ and $\vec{B}$ are parallel [θ = 0°] then $\vec{A} \times \vec{B} = \vec{0}$

Question : Is $\vec{A} \times \vec{B}$ equal to $\vec{B} \times \vec{A}$?

Answer : The magnitude of $(\vec{A} \times \vec{B})$ is equal to $(\vec{B} \times \vec{A})$, but the direction of these two vectors are opposite. Therefore, $(\vec{A} \times \vec{B})$ is not equal to $(\vec{B} \times \vec{A})$.

Question : What is the angle between $\vec{A} + \vec{B}$ and $\vec{A} \times \vec{B}$?

Answer : The angle between $(\vec{A} + \vec{B})$ and $(\vec{A} \times \vec{B})$ is 90°.

Try Yourself

(26) What is the vector product of two mutually perpendicular vectors
[Ans : 0]

(27) What is the angle between $\vec{A}$ and $\vec{A} \times \vec{B}$?
[Ans : 90°]

(28) What is the angle between $\vec{A} - \vec{B}$ and $\vec{A} \times \vec{B}$?
[Ans : 90 °]

(29) Show that $(\vec{A} + \vec{B}) \times (\vec{A} - \vec{B}) = 2(\vec{B} \times \vec{A})$

On Scalar & Vector Product of Vectors

Question : If $|\vec{x} \times \vec{y}| = |\vec{x}.\vec{y}|$ and θ be the angle between them, find the value of θ.

Solution : Given, $|\vec{x} \times \vec{y}| = |\vec{x}.\vec{y}|$

or, $x\, y \sin\theta = x\, y \cos\theta$

or, $\tan\theta = 1 = \tan 45°$

$\therefore \theta = 45°$

Problem : If $|\vec{A} \times \vec{B}| = \sqrt{3}\, \vec{A}.\vec{B}$, then calculate $|\vec{A} + \vec{B}|$.

Solution : Given, $|\vec{A} \times \vec{B}| = \sqrt{3}\,\vec{A}.\vec{B}$

or, $A\, B \sin\theta = \sqrt{3}\, A\, B \cos\theta$

or, $\tan\theta = \sqrt{3} = \tan 60°$

$\therefore \theta = 60°$

Now, $|\vec{A} + \vec{B}| = \sqrt{A^2 + B^2 + 2\,A\,B\,cos\,60°}$

$= \sqrt{A^2 + B^2 + 2\,A\,B\,\frac{1}{2}}$

$= \sqrt{A^2 + B^2 + A\,B}$

Try Yourself

---

(30) Calculate the value of the product $(\vec{B} \times \vec{A}).\vec{A}$; when the angle between the vectors $\vec{B}$ and $\vec{A}$ is θ.
[Ans : 0]

(31) If the ratio of the magnitude of the cross product and dot product be $\frac{1}{\sqrt{3}}$, then find the angle between the two vectors.
[Ans : 30°]

(32) Show that $|\vec{A} \times \vec{B}|^2 + |\vec{A}.\vec{B}|^2 = A^2B^2$

On Triple Products of Vectors

Question : Three sides of a rectangular parallelepiped are $\vec{A}$, $\vec{B}$ and $\vec{C}$ respectively. What is its volume?

Answer : If three sides of a rectangular parallelepiped are $\vec{A}$, $\vec{B}$ and $\vec{C}$ respectively, then its volume is :

$$V = \vec{A}\,.\,(\vec{B} \times \vec{C})$$

Question : What is the condition for the three vectors $\vec{A}$, $\vec{B}$ and $\vec{C}$ to be coplanar?

Answer : The condition for the three vectors $\vec{A}$, $\vec{B}$ and $\vec{C}$ to be coplanar is : $\vec{A}\,.\,(\vec{B} \times \vec{C}) = 0$

Problem : Prove that : $\vec{A} \times (\vec{B} \times \vec{C}) + \vec{B} \times (\vec{C} \times \vec{A}) + \vec{C} \times (\vec{A} \times \vec{B}) = 0$

Solution : $\vec{A} \times (\vec{B} \times \vec{C}) = \vec{B}(\vec{A}.\vec{C}) - \vec{C}(\vec{A}.\vec{B})$

$\vec{B} \times (\vec{C} \times \vec{A}) = \vec{C}(\vec{B}.\vec{A}) - \vec{A}(\vec{B}.\vec{C})$

$\vec{C} \times (\vec{A} \times \vec{B}) = \vec{A}(\vec{C}.\vec{B}) - \vec{B}(\vec{C}.\vec{A})$

$\therefore \vec{A} \times (\vec{B} \times \vec{C}) + \vec{B} \times (\vec{C} \times \vec{A}) + \vec{C} \times (\vec{A} \times \vec{B}) = 0$

Group – B : Vector Algebra – II (With Coordinate Representation)

On Representation of Vector by its Coordinates

Problem : Find the magnitude and direction of the position vector $3\,\hat{\imath} + 4\,\hat{\jmath}$. What are the co-ordinates of its end point?

Solution : Given, $\vec{r} = 3\,\hat{\imath} + 4\,\hat{\jmath}$

$\therefore$ Magnitude of the vector : $|\vec{r}| = \sqrt{(3)^2 + (4)^2}$

$= \sqrt{9 + 16}$

$= 5$ unit

If the position vector makes an angle θ with the x-axis then, $\tan\theta = \frac{4}{3}$

$\therefore \theta = \tan^{-1}\left(\frac{4}{3}\right)$

The co-ordinates of its end point is (3,4)

Try Yourself

(33) Two vectors are given as $\vec{A} = 2\,\hat{\imath} + 3\,\hat{\jmath} + 4\,\hat{k}$ and $\vec{B} = 3\,\hat{\imath} + 2\,\hat{\jmath} - 4\,\hat{k}$. Which one of two is larger in magnitude? Justify your answer.

(34) Position coordinates of the end point of a vector $\overrightarrow{OP}$ is (4, 3, – 5). Express the vector in terms of its co-ordinates and find its absolute value.

(35) Find the angle subtended by the vector $\vec{A} = 4\,\hat{\imath} + 3\,\hat{\jmath} + 12\,\hat{k}$ with the x-axis.

(36) Find the directional cosine of $5\,\hat{\imath} + 2\,\hat{\jmath} + 4\,\hat{k}$.

(37) If $\vec{A} = 0.8\,\hat{\imath} - C\,\hat{\jmath} + 0.6\,\hat{k}$ and $|\vec{A}| = 2$, then find the value of C.

On Unit Vector

Problem : Find the magnitude of the vector $\vec{A} = \hat{\imath} - 2\,\hat{\jmath} + 3\,\hat{k}$. Also find the unit vector in the direction of $\vec{A}$.

Solution : Given, $\vec{A} = \hat{\imath} - 2\,\hat{\jmath} + 3\,\hat{k}$

$\therefore$ Magnitude of the vector : $|\vec{A}| = \sqrt{(1)^2 + (-2)^2 + (3)^2}$

$= \sqrt{1 + 4 + 9} = \sqrt{14}$ unit

The unit vector in the direction of $\vec{A}$ is given by, $\hat{A} = \frac{\vec{A}}{|\vec{A}|}$

or, $\hat{A} = \frac{\hat{\imath} - 2\,\hat{\jmath} + 3\,\hat{k}}{\sqrt{14}}$

$\therefore \hat{A} = \frac{1}{\sqrt{14}}\hat{\imath} - \frac{2}{\sqrt{14}}\hat{\jmath} + \frac{3}{\sqrt{14}}\hat{k}$

Try Yourself

(38) Find the unit vector of $3\hat{\imath} + 4\,\hat{\jmath} - \hat{k}$.

(39) What is the value of m in $\frac{1}{2}\hat{I} + m\,\hat{\jmath} + \frac{1}{2}\,\hat{K}$ to be unit vector ?

On Resultant Calculation & Vector Subtraction

Problem : Given: $\vec{A}$ = $\hat{i} - 2\hat{j} - 3\hat{k}$ and $\vec{B}$ = $4\hat{i} - 2\hat{j} + 6\hat{k}$. Calculate the angle made by ($\vec{A} + \vec{B}$) with x-axis?

Solution : Given, $\vec{A} = \hat{i} - 2\hat{j} - 3\hat{k}$
and $\vec{B} = 4\hat{i} - 2\hat{j} + 6\hat{k}$

$\therefore \vec{A} + \vec{B} = (\hat{i} - 2\hat{j} - 3\hat{k}) + (4\hat{i} - 2\hat{j} + 6\hat{k}) = 5\hat{i} - 4\hat{j} + 3\hat{k}$

If ($\vec{A} + \vec{B}$) vector makes an angle θ with x-axis then $\cos\theta = \frac{5}{\sqrt{25+16+9}} = \frac{5}{5\sqrt{2}} = \frac{1}{\sqrt{2}}$

$\therefore \theta = 45°$

Problem : The (x, y, z) coordinates of two points A and B are given respectively as $(0, 3, -1)$ and $(-2, 6, 4)$. Write down the displacement vector from A to B.

Solution :

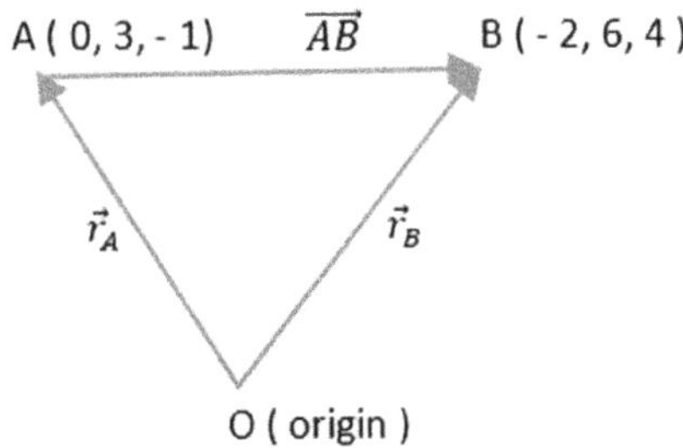

The coordinates of the two points A and B are given by $(0, 3, -1)$ and $(-2, 6, 4)$.

Therefore the position vectors of the point A and B are given by $\vec{r_A} = 0\hat{i} + 3\hat{j} - \hat{k}$ and, $\vec{r_B} = -2\hat{i} + 6\hat{j} + 4\hat{k}$

Form the figure, we get, $\vec{r_B} = \vec{r_A} + \overrightarrow{AB}$

or, $\overrightarrow{AB} = \vec{r_B} - \vec{r_A}$

or, $\overrightarrow{AB} = (-2\hat{i} + 6\hat{j} + 4\hat{k}) - (0\hat{i} + 3\hat{j} - \hat{k})$

$\therefore \overrightarrow{AB} = -2\hat{i} + 3\hat{j} + 5\hat{k}$

Question : What is the magnitude of component of $9\hat{i} - 7\hat{j} + 13.9\hat{k}$ along X axis?

Answer : The magnitude of component of $9\hat{i} - 7\hat{j} + 13.9\hat{k}$ along X axis is 9 unit.

Try Yourself

(40) Given: $\vec{A} = 3\hat{i} + 2\hat{j}$ and $\vec{B} = 3\hat{j} + 4\hat{k}$. Calculate the magnitude of the resultant.

(41) If $\vec{A} = 2\hat{\imath} + \hat{\jmath}$, $\vec{B} = 3\hat{\jmath} - \hat{k}$ and $\vec{C} = 6\hat{\imath} - 2\hat{\jmath}$, find value of $\vec{A} - 3\vec{B} + 3\vec{C}$.

(42) Determine that vector when added to the resultant of $\vec{A} = 3\hat{\imath} - 5\hat{\jmath} + 7\hat{k}$ and $\vec{B} = 2\hat{\imath} - 4\hat{\jmath} + 3\hat{k}$ gives unit vector along y direction.

(43) A vector $\vec{F} = 4\hat{\imath} + 3\hat{\jmath} - 2\hat{k}$ is given. What is the magnitude of the y-component of the vector ?

On Dot Product of Vectors

Problem : What is the dot product of $-2\hat{\imath} + 3\hat{\jmath} + 2\hat{k}$ and $\hat{\imath} + 2\hat{\jmath} - 4\hat{k}$?

Solution : Given, $\vec{A} = -2\hat{\imath} + 3\hat{\jmath} + 2\hat{k}$

and $\vec{B} = \hat{\imath} + 2\hat{\jmath} - 4\hat{k}$

$\therefore \vec{A} . \vec{B} = (-2\hat{\imath} + 3\hat{\jmath} + 2\hat{k}).(\hat{\imath} + 2\hat{\jmath} - 4\hat{k})$

$= -2 + 6 - 8 = -4$

Problem : What is the angle between the following pairs of vectors : $\vec{A} = \hat{\imath} + 2\hat{\jmath} - \hat{k}$ and $\vec{B} = \hat{\imath} + \hat{\jmath} - 2\hat{k}$

Solution : Given, $\vec{A} = \hat{\imath} + 2\hat{\jmath} - \hat{k}$

and $\vec{B} = \hat{\imath} + \hat{\jmath} - 2\hat{k}$

$\therefore \vec{A} . \vec{B} = (\hat{\imath} + 2\hat{\jmath} - \hat{k}).(\hat{\imath} + \hat{\jmath} - 2\hat{k})$

$= 1 + 2 + 2 = 5$

Again, $|\vec{A}| = \sqrt{(1)^2 + (2)^2 + (-1)^2} = \sqrt{6}$

and $|\vec{B}| = \sqrt{(1)^2 + (1)^2 + (-2)^2} = \sqrt{6}$

If θ be the angle between the two vectors then $\cos\theta = \frac{\vec{A}.\vec{B}}{|\vec{A}|\,|\vec{B}|}$

or, $\cos\theta = \frac{5}{\sqrt{6}\,\sqrt{6}} = \frac{5}{6}$

$\therefore \theta = \cos^{-1}\frac{5}{6}$

Problem : Prove that the vectors $2\hat{\imath} - 3\hat{\jmath} + \hat{k}$ and $\hat{\imath} + \hat{\jmath} + \hat{k}$ are perpendicular to each other.

Solution : Given, $\vec{A} = 2\hat{\imath} - 3\hat{\jmath} + \hat{k}$

and $\vec{B} = \hat{\imath} + \hat{\jmath} + \hat{k}$

$\therefore \vec{A} . \vec{B} = (2\hat{\imath} - 3\hat{\jmath} + \hat{k}).(\hat{\imath} + \hat{\jmath} + \hat{k})$

$= 2 - 3 + 1 = 0$

Since $\vec{A} . \vec{B} = 0$, therefore, the given vectors are mutually perpendicular.

Problem : Two vectors $5\hat{\imath} + 7\hat{\jmath} - 3\hat{k}$ and $2\hat{\imath} + 2\hat{\jmath} - c\hat{k}$ are mutually perpendicular. What is the value of c?

Solution : Given, $\vec{A} = 5\hat{\imath} + 7\hat{\jmath} - 3\hat{k}$

and $\vec{B} = 2\hat{\imath} + 2\hat{\jmath} - c\hat{k}$

$\therefore \vec{A}.\vec{B} = (5\hat{\imath} + 7\hat{\jmath} - 3\hat{k}).(2\hat{\imath} + 2\hat{\jmath} - c\hat{k})$

$= 10 + 14 + 3c$

$= 24 + 3c$

According to the problem, the given vectors are mutually perpendicular.

Therefore, $\vec{A}.\vec{B} = 0$

or, $24 + 3c = 0$

$\therefore c = -8$

Problem : Given: $\vec{P} = 2\hat{\imath} + 3\hat{\jmath}$ and $\vec{Q} = \hat{\imath} + \hat{\jmath}$. What is the vector component of $\vec{P}$ in the direction of $\vec{Q}$?

Solution : Given, $\vec{P} = 2\hat{\imath} + 3\hat{\jmath}$ and $\vec{Q} = \hat{\imath} + \hat{\jmath}$

The vector component of $\vec{P}$ in the direction of $\vec{Q}$ is given by $(\vec{P}.\vec{Q})\frac{\vec{Q}}{Q^2}$

$\therefore \vec{P}.\vec{Q} = (2\hat{\imath} + 3\hat{\jmath}).(\hat{\imath} + \hat{\jmath})$

$= 2 + 3 = 5$

Again, $Q = \sqrt{1^2 + 1^2} = \sqrt{2}$

$\therefore$ The vector component of $\vec{P}$ in the direction of $\vec{Q}$ is given by : $5\frac{(\hat{\imath} + \hat{\jmath})}{2} = \frac{5}{2}\hat{\imath} + \frac{5}{2}\hat{\jmath}$

Try Yourself

---

(44) If $\vec{A} = \hat{\imath} + \hat{k}$ and $\vec{B} = \hat{\jmath} + \hat{k}$, then calculate the value of $\vec{A}.\vec{B}$.

(45) What is the angle between the following pair of vectors : $\vec{A} = \hat{\imath} + \hat{\jmath} - 2\hat{k}$ and $\vec{B} = -\hat{\imath} + 2\hat{\jmath} - \hat{k}$

(46) What is the angle between the following pair of vectors : $\vec{A} = 2\hat{\imath} + 3\hat{\jmath}$ and $\vec{B} = -3\hat{\imath} + 2\hat{\jmath}$

(47) Prove that the vectors $\hat{\imath} + 2\hat{\jmath} + 3\hat{k}$ and $2\hat{\imath} - \hat{\jmath}$ are perpendicular to each other.

(48) Prove that the vectors $\vec{P} = 2\hat{\imath} + 3\hat{\jmath}$ and $\vec{Q} = 6\hat{\imath} - 4\hat{\jmath}$ are perpendicular to each other.

(49) What is the value of a so that the vector $a\hat{\imath} - 2\hat{\jmath} + \hat{k}$ may be perpendicular to vector $2a\hat{\imath} + a\hat{\jmath} - 4\hat{k}$?

(50) Find the vector projection of $5\hat{\imath} - 2\hat{\jmath} + \hat{k}$ along the vector $3\hat{\imath} - 2\hat{\jmath} + 4\hat{k}$.

On Vector Product of Vectors

Problem : If $\vec{A} = 2\hat{\imath} - 3\hat{\jmath} - \hat{k}$ and $\vec{B} = \hat{\imath} + 4\hat{\jmath} - 2\hat{k}$, find $\vec{A} \times \vec{B}$.

Solution : Given, $\vec{A} = 2\hat{\imath} - 3\hat{\jmath} - \hat{k}$

and $\vec{B} = \hat{\imath} + 4\hat{\jmath} - 2\hat{k}$

$$\therefore \vec{A} \times \vec{B} = \begin{vmatrix} \hat{\imath} & \hat{\jmath} & \hat{k} \\ 2 & -3 & -1 \\ 1 & 4 & -2 \end{vmatrix}$$

$= (6 + 4)\hat{\imath} - (-4 + 1)\hat{\jmath} + (8 + 3)\hat{k}$

$= 10\hat{\imath} + 3\hat{\jmath} + 11\hat{k}$

Show that the vectors $\vec{A} = 3\hat{\imath} + 6\hat{\jmath} + 9\hat{k}$ and $\vec{B} = \hat{\imath} + 2\hat{\jmath} + 3\hat{k}$ are parallel.

O9mSolution : Given, $\vec{A} = 3\,\hat{\imath} + 6\,\hat{\jmath} + 9\,\hat{k}$

and $\vec{B} = \hat{\imath} + 2\,\hat{\jmath} + 3\,\hat{k}$

Given vectors are parallel, if $\vec{A} \times \vec{B} = \vec{0}$

Now, $\vec{A} \times \vec{B} = \begin{vmatrix} \hat{\imath} & \hat{\jmath} & \hat{k} \\ 3 & 6 & 9 \\ 1 & 2 & 3 \end{vmatrix}$

$= (18 - 18)\,\hat{\imath} - (9 - 9)\hat{\jmath} + (6 - 6)\hat{k}$

$= \vec{0}$

Since, $\vec{A} \times \vec{B} = \vec{0}$, therefore the vectors $\vec{A}$ and $\vec{B}$ are parallel to each other.

Problem : Determine a unit vector which is perpendicular to both the vectors $2\,\hat{\imath} + \hat{\jmath} + \hat{k}$ and $\hat{\imath} - \hat{\jmath} + 2\hat{k}$.

Solution : Given, $\vec{A} = 2\,\hat{\imath} + \hat{\jmath} + \hat{k}$

and $\vec{B} = \hat{\imath} - \hat{\jmath} + 2\hat{k}$

We know that vector ($\vec{A} \times \vec{B}$) is perpendicular to both $\vec{A}$ and $\vec{B}$ then, $\hat{n} = \frac{\vec{A} \times \vec{B}}{|\vec{A} \times \vec{B}|}$

Now, $\vec{A} \times \vec{B} = \begin{vmatrix} \hat{\imath} & \hat{\jmath} & \hat{k} \\ 2 & 1 & 1 \\ 1 & -1 & 2 \end{vmatrix}$

$= (2 + 1)\,\hat{\imath} - (4 - 1)\hat{\jmath} + (-2 - 1)\hat{k}$

$= 3\,\hat{\imath} - 3\hat{\jmath} - 3\hat{k}$

Also, $|\vec{A} \times \vec{B}| = \sqrt{(3)^2 + (-3)^2 + (-3)^2} = 3\sqrt{3}$

$\therefore \hat{n} = \frac{\vec{A} \times \vec{B}}{|\vec{A} \times \vec{B}|}$

or, $\hat{n} = \frac{3\,\hat{\imath} - 3\hat{\jmath} - 3\hat{k}}{3\sqrt{3}}$

$\therefore \hat{n} = \frac{1}{\sqrt{3}}\,\hat{\imath} - \frac{1}{\sqrt{3}}\hat{\jmath} - \frac{1}{\sqrt{3}}\hat{k}$

Try Yourself

---

(51) Two vectors $\vec{A} = \hat{\imath}\cos\theta + \hat{\jmath}\sin\theta$ and $\vec{B} = -\,\hat{\imath}\sin\theta + \hat{\jmath}\cos\theta$, then calculate $\vec{A} \,.\, \vec{B}$ and $\vec{A} \times \vec{B}$.

(52) Prove that the vectors $2\,\hat{\imath} - 3\,\hat{\jmath} - \hat{k}$ and $-6\,\hat{\imath} + 9\,\hat{\jmath} + 3\,\hat{k}$ are parallel.

(53) Determine a unit vector which is perpendicular to both the vectors $\hat{\imath} + \hat{\jmath} + \hat{k}$ and $\hat{\imath} - \hat{\jmath} + 2\hat{k}$.

On Triple Products of Vectors

Problem : If $\vec{A} = \hat{\imath} - 2\,\hat{\jmath} - 3\,\hat{k}$, $\vec{B} = 2\,\hat{\imath} + \hat{\jmath} - \hat{k}$ and $\vec{C} = \hat{\imath} + 3\,\hat{\jmath} - 2\,\hat{k}$, find the value of $\vec{A} \,.\, (\vec{B} \times \vec{C})$.

Solution : Given, $\vec{A} = \hat{\imath} - 2\,\hat{\jmath} - 3\,\hat{k}$

$\vec{B} = 2\,\hat{\imath} + \hat{\jmath} - \hat{k}$

and $\vec{C} = \hat{\imath} + 3\,\hat{\jmath} - 2\,\hat{k}$

Now, $\vec{A}\cdot(\vec{B}\times\vec{C}) = \begin{vmatrix}1 & -2 & -3\\ 2 & 1 & -1\\ 1 & 3 & -2\end{vmatrix}$

$= 1(-2+3) + 2(-4+1) - 3(6-1)$

$= 1 - 6 - 15 = -20$

Problem : Three vectors are expressed by $2\hat{i} + 3\hat{j} + 4\hat{k}$, $5\hat{i} - 6\hat{j} + 7\hat{k}$ and $\hat{i} + 2\hat{j} + 3\hat{k}$ respectively. Examine if they are coplanar.

Solution : Given, $\vec{A} = 2\hat{i} + 3\hat{j} + 4\hat{k}$

$\vec{B} = 5\hat{i} - 6\hat{j} + 7\hat{k}$

and $\vec{C} = \hat{i} + 2\hat{j} + 3\hat{k}$

If these vectors are coplanar, then $\vec{A}\cdot(\vec{B}\times\vec{C})$ must be zero.

Now, $\vec{A}\cdot(\vec{B}\times\vec{C}) = \begin{vmatrix}2 & 3 & 4\\ 5 & -6 & 7\\ 1 & 2 & 3\end{vmatrix}$

$= 2(-18-14) - 3(15-7) + 4(10+6)$

$= -64 - 24 + 64 = -24$

Since, $\vec{A}\cdot(\vec{B}\times\vec{C}) \neq 0$, these vectors are not coplanar.

Problem : For what value of x are three vectors $2\hat{i} + 3\hat{j} + 4\hat{k}$, $5\hat{j} + 10\hat{k}$ and $x\hat{i} + 2\hat{j} + 3\hat{k}$ coplanar?

Solution : Given, $\vec{A} = 2\hat{i} + 3\hat{j} + 4\hat{k}$

$\vec{B} = 5\hat{j} + 10\hat{k}$

and $\vec{C} = x\hat{i} + 2\hat{j} + 3\hat{k}$

Now, $\vec{A}\cdot(\vec{B}\times\vec{C}) = \begin{vmatrix}2 & 3 & 4\\ 0 & 5 & 10\\ x & 2 & 3\end{vmatrix}$

$= 2(15-20) - 3(0-10x) + 4(0-5x)$

$= -10 + 30x - 20x$

$= -10 + 10x$

Since, these vectors are coplanar, $\vec{A}\cdot(\vec{B}\times\vec{C})$ must be zero.

$\therefore -10 + 10x = 0$

or, $x = 1$

Try Yourself

---

(54) If $\vec{A} = \hat{i} - 3\hat{j} - 3\hat{k}$, $\vec{B} = \hat{i} + 3\hat{j} - \hat{k}$ and $\vec{C} = \hat{i} + 3\hat{j} - 2\hat{k}$, find the value of $\vec{A}\cdot(\vec{B}\times\vec{C})$.

(55) Three vectors are expressed by $2\hat{i} + 3\hat{j} + 4\hat{k}$, $5\hat{j} + 10\hat{k}$ and $\hat{i} + 2\hat{j} + 3\hat{k}$ respectively. Examine if they are coplanar.

(56) For what value of C three vectors $2\hat{i} + 3\hat{j} + 4\hat{k}$, $5\hat{j} + 10\hat{k}$ and $C\hat{i} + 2\hat{j} + 3\hat{k}$ are coplanar?

(57) Find λ such that $2\hat{i} - \hat{j} + \hat{k}$, $\hat{i} + 2\hat{j} - 3\hat{k}$ and $3\hat{i} + \lambda\hat{j} + 5\hat{k}$ are coplanar.

Group – C : Applications of Vector Mathematics in Physics

Applications of Resultant Calculation in Physics

▫ To find the net force acting on a body :

Problem : Find the magnitude of the resultant of two forces, one 6 N due east and the other 8 N due north.

Solution : Given, F_1 = 6 N
F_2 = 8 N
and the angle between the two forces are 90°
Therefore, the magnitude of the resultant is given by F = $\sqrt{6^2 + 8^2 + 2 \,.\, 6 . 8 \cos 90°}$ N
or, F = $\sqrt{36 + 64}$ N
∴ F = 10 N

Try Yourself

(58) What is the maximum and minimum possible resultant of two forces 2 N and 5 N?
(59) The maximum and minimum values of the resultant of two forces are 15 N and 7 N. If the value of each force be increased by 1N and they act at an angle 90° to each other, find the magnitude and direction of their resultant.
(60) The value of the resultant of two mutually perpendicular forces is 80 dyne. The resultant makes an angle 60° with one of the forces. Find the magnitudes of the forces.
(61) Magnitude of the resultant of two forces which have equal magnitudes and which act at right angles to each other is 1414 dyne. Calculate the magnitude of each force?

▫ River and Boat Problem :

(i) Crossing in shortest distance : To cross the river over shortest distance (or, cross the river straight) the boat should go upstream making an angle θ with the shortest distance.

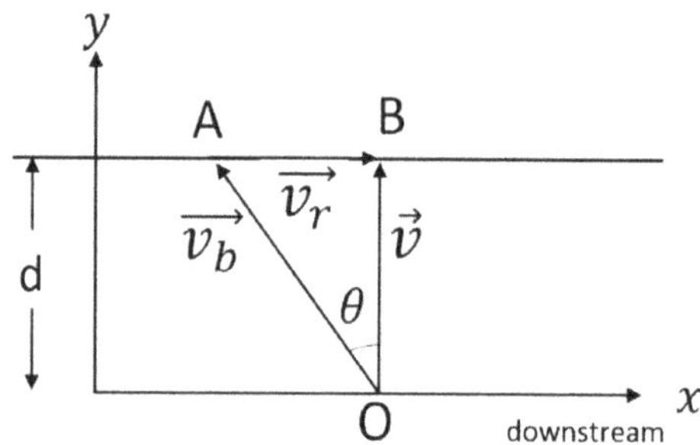

- **Condition to cancel drift :** Sin $\theta = \frac{v_r}{v_b}$ or, tan $\theta = \frac{v_r}{\sqrt{{v_b}^2 - {v_r}^2}}$

- **Effective velocity across the river :** $v_{br} = \sqrt{{v_b}^2 - {v_r}^2}$

- **Time taken to cross the river** : t = $\frac{width\ of\ the\ river}{\sqrt{{v_b}^2 - {v_r}^2}}$

(ii) Crossing in shortest time : To cross the river in possible shortest time the boat should go straight and the boat will reach the opposite bank at a distance (say x)

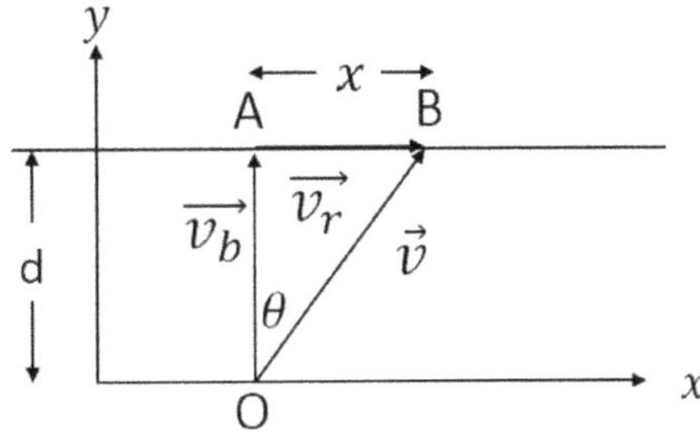

- **Resultant velocity :** $v_{br} = \sqrt{{v_b}^2 + {v_r}^2}$

- **Angle of resultant path (downstream) :** tan $\theta = \frac{v_r}{v_b} = \frac{x}{d}$

- **Time to cross the river :** t = $\frac{width\ of\ the\ river}{v_b}$

- **Drift :** $x = v_r\ t = \frac{v_r}{v_b}(\ width\ of\ the\ river\ )$

Try Yourself

(62) A boat can move at 5 m s^{-1} in still water. The river is 100 m wide and flows at 3 m s^{-1}.
(a) How long does the boat take to cross the river ?
(b) How far downstream does it drift ?
(c) What is the resultant velocity ?

(63) A river is 120 m wide and flows at 4 m s^{-1}. A swimmer can swim at 6 m s^{-1} in still water. Find
(a) At What angle with upstream must the swimmer swim to land directly opposite ?
(b) How much time will it take to cross the river ?
(c) What is the swimmer's effective velocity across the river ?

Applications of Subtraction of vectors in Physics

▫ To determine change in velocity (and acceleration) :

Problem : A car is travelling towards east at 10 m s^{-1}. The car took 10 s to change its direction of motion to north and continues with the same velocity. Find the magnitude and direction of the average acceleration of the car.

Solution : According to the problem, initial velocity v_i = 10 ms^{-1}, along east and
final velocity v_f = 10 ms^{-1}, along north

∴ Change in Velocity $\Delta\vec{v} = \vec{v}_f - \vec{v}_i = \vec{v}_f + (-\vec{v}_i)$

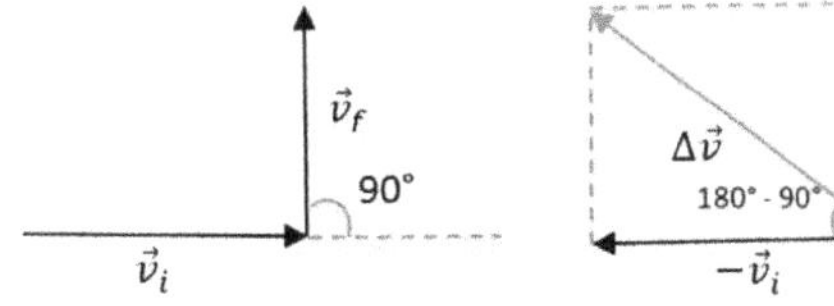

Magnitude of change in velocity $\Delta v = \sqrt{10^2 + 10^2 + 2.10.\,10\cos(180° - 90°)}$ ms^{-1}

$= \sqrt{200}\ ms^{-1}$

$= 10\sqrt{2}\ ms^{-1}$

∴ Average acceleration of the car $a = \frac{\Delta v}{\Delta t}$

$= \frac{10\sqrt{2}}{10}\ ms^{-2} = \sqrt{2}\ ms^{-2}$

If the average acceleration makes an angle α with north, then, $\tan\alpha = \frac{10\sin(180° - 90°)}{10 + 10\cos(180° - 90°)}$

$= \frac{10}{10} = 1 = \tan 45°$

i.e. the direction of the acceleration is north-west.

Try Yourself

---

(64) Two velocity vectors with magnitude and directions of 3 ms^{-1} towards north and 4 ms^{-1} towards east, are named as $\overrightarrow{v_1}$ and $\overrightarrow{v_2}$ respectively. Find the difference $\overrightarrow{v_1} - \overrightarrow{v_2}$.

◘ To find relative velocity :

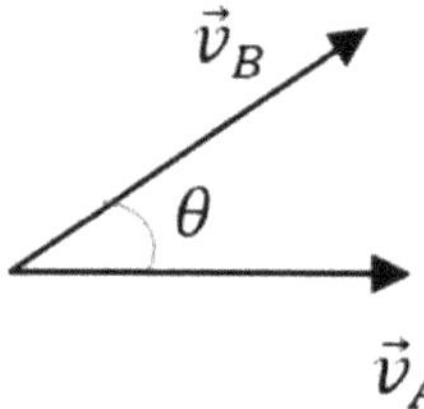

When two objects are in motion, the relative velocity of object A with respect to object B is the time rate of change of position of A with respect to object B.

If two objects A and B are moving with velocity and w.r.t. the ground then

(i) relative velocity of A w.r.t. B : $\vec{v}_{AB}$ or, $\vec{v}_{relative} = \overrightarrow{v_A} - \overrightarrow{v_B}$

$= \overrightarrow{v_A} + (-\overrightarrow{v_B})$

[The relative velocity of object A w.r.t. object B is equal to the vector addition of velocity vector of A and the negative velocity vector of B]

and (ii) relative velocity of B w.r.t. A : $\vec{v}_{BA}$ or, $\vec{v}_{relative} = \overrightarrow{v_B} - \overrightarrow{v_A}$

$= \overrightarrow{v_B} + (-\overrightarrow{v_A})$

Relative motion in 1D :

(1) If two objects are moving in the same direction, the magnitude of relative velocity of one object with respect to another is equal to the difference in magnitude of two velocities.

$\vec{v}_B$ $\quad$ $-\vec{v}_B$

$\vec{v}_A$ $\quad$ $\vec{v}_A$

Two objects A and B are moving with velocities v_A and v_B respectively in the same direction. The magnitude of the relative velocity of A w.r.t. B is $\boldsymbol{v_{AB} = v_A - v_B}$

(2) If two objects are moving in the opposite direction, the magnitude of relative velocity of one object with respect to another is equal to the sum of magnitude of their velocities.

$\vec{v}_B$ $\quad\rightarrow\quad$ $-\vec{v}_B$

$\vec{v}_A$ $\qquad\qquad$ $\vec{v}_A$

Two objects A and B are moving with velocities v_A and v_B respectively in the opposite direction. The magnitude of the relative velocity of A w.r.t. B is $\boldsymbol{v_{AB} = v_A + v_B}$

Problem : A train moves northwards with speed 80 km $\mathbf{h^{-1}}$, while a car moves towards east with a speed of 60 km $\mathbf{h^{-1}}$. What is the velocity of the train w.r.t. the driver of the car ?

Solution : Step - 1 : Mathematical vector form

Let us consider, the velocity of the train in $\vec{v}_t$ and velocity of the car is $\vec{v}_c$

∴ The relative velocity of the train w.r.t. the car is given by : $\vec{v}_{relative} = \vec{v}_t - \vec{v}_c$

$$= \vec{v}_t + (-\vec{v}_c)$$

Step - 2 : Figure

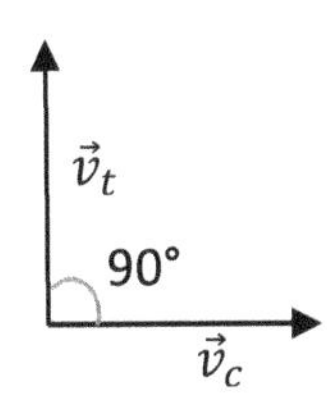

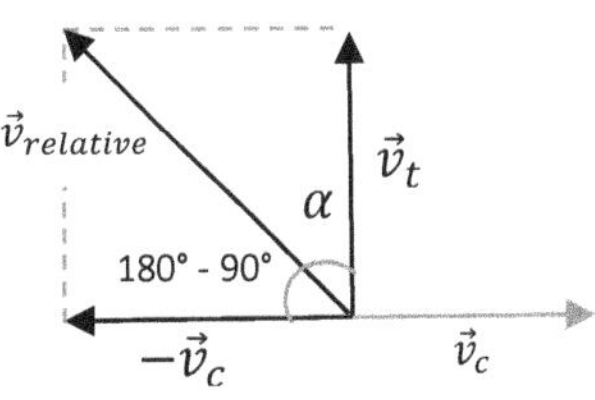

Step : 3 Resultant Calculation (magnitude and direction)

Magnitude of the relative velocity : $\Delta v = \sqrt{80^2 + 60^2 + 2.80.60\cos(180° - 90°)}$ kms^{-1}

$$= \sqrt{10000} \text{ kms}^{-1}$$

$$= 10 \text{ kms}^{-1}$$

If the relative velocity makes an angle α with north, then, $\tan\alpha = \dfrac{60\sin(180° - 90°)}{80 + 60\cos(180° - 90°)}$

$$\text{or, } \tan\alpha = \frac{80}{60} = \frac{4}{3}$$

$$\text{i.e. } \alpha = \tan^{-1}\left(\frac{4}{3}\right)$$

Try Yourself

(65) Two airplanes take off from the same airport at the same time. Plane A is flying at 300 km h^{-1} towards the north-east and plane B is flying at 250 km h^{-1} towards the north-west. What is the velocity of plane A relative to plane B ?

▫ To compute displacement from position vectors :

Problem : A particle is displaced from position (3, 5) to another position (5, −6) under the action of a force. Find the displacement of the particle.

Solution :

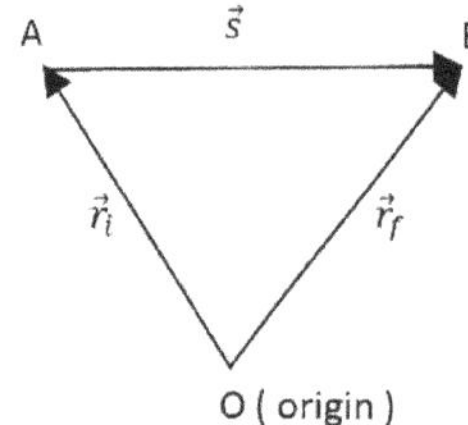

According to the problem, Initial and the final position coordinates of the particle is given by (3, 5) and (5, −6) respectively.

Therefore, Initial Position vector : $\vec{r_i} = 3\,\hat{\imath} + 5\,\hat{\jmath}$

and final position vector $\vec{r_f} = 5\,\hat{\imath} - 6\,\hat{\jmath}$

Form the figure, we get, $\vec{r_f} = \vec{r_i} + \vec{s}$ [where, $\vec{s}$ = displacement of the particle]

or, $\vec{s} = \vec{r_f} - \vec{r_i}$

or, $\vec{s} = (5\,\hat{\imath} - 6\,\hat{\jmath}) - (3\,\hat{\imath} + 5\,\hat{\jmath})$

$\therefore \vec{s} = 2\hat{\imath} - 11\hat{\jmath}$

Applications of Resolution and components of vector in Physics

Problem : A force of 30 dyne is inclined to the y-axis at an angle of 60°. Find the components of the force along x and y axes respectively.

Solution : Here, F = 30 dyne and the force is inclined to the y-axis with an angle of 60° then,

$F_y = F\cos\theta$

$= 30\cos 60°$

$= 15$ dyne

and $F_x = F\cos\theta$

$= 30\sin 60°$

$= 30 \cdot \frac{\sqrt{3}}{2}$

$= 15\sqrt{3}$ dyne

Problem : A velocity of 10 ms^{-1} has its Y component $5\sqrt{2}$ ms^{-1}. Calculate its X-component.

Solution : Here, v = 10 ms^{-1}

and $v_y = 5\sqrt{2}\ ms^{-1}$

If the velocity vector makes an angle θ with the x -axis then, $v_y = v \sin\theta$

or, $10 \sin\theta = 5\sqrt{2}$

or, $\sin\theta = \frac{1}{\sqrt{2}} = \sin 45°$

$\therefore \theta = 45°$

Hence the magnitude of the x-component is given by : $v_x = v \sin 45°$

or, $v_x = 10 . \frac{1}{\sqrt{2}}$

$\therefore v_x = 5\sqrt{2}\ ms^{-1}$

Try Yourself

---

(66) A force of 20 N is inclined at 30° to the X axis. Calculate its X and Y components.

(67) An aeroplane takes off at an angle 60° to the horizontal. If the velocity of the plane is 150 km h^{-1}. Calculate the horizontal and vertical component of velocity.

(68) A worker pushes a crate along the floor by a force of 10 N that points downwards at an angle of 45° below the horizontal. Find the horizontal and vertical components of force.

(69) Two billiard balls are rolling on a flat table. One has the velocity components $V_x = 1\ ms^{-1}$, $V_y = \sqrt{3}\ ms^{-1}$ and the other has $V'_x = 2\ ms^{-1}$, $V'_y = 2\ ms^{-1}$. If both the balls start moving from the same point; what is the angle between their paths?

(70) A force vector has components 6 N in the x-direction and 8 N in the y-direction. Find the magnitude and direction of the force.

Applications of Dot Product in Physics

▫ To calculate work done by a force :

Problem : A force $\vec{F} = \hat{i} + 5\hat{j} + 7\hat{k}$ acts on a particle and displaces it through $\vec{S} = 6\hat{i} + 9\hat{k}$. Calculate the work done if the force is in newton and distance is in metre.

Solution : Given, Force $\vec{F} = (\hat{i} + 5\hat{j} + 7\hat{k})$ N

and displacement $\vec{S} = 6\hat{i} + 9\hat{k}$

Work done W = $\vec{F} . \vec{S}$

$= (\hat{i} + 5\hat{j} + 7\hat{k}) . (6\hat{i} + 9\hat{k})$ J

= (6 + 63) J

= 69 J

Problem : A particle is displaced from position $2\hat{i} - \hat{j} + \hat{k}$ to another position $3\hat{i} + 2\hat{j} - 2\hat{k}$ under the action of force $2\hat{i} + \hat{j} - \hat{k}$. Find the work done by the force in an arbitrary unit.

Solution : Given, Initial Position vector : $\vec{r_i} = 2\hat{i} - \hat{j} + \hat{k}$

and final position vector $\vec{r_f} = 3\hat{i} + 2\hat{j} - 2\hat{k}$

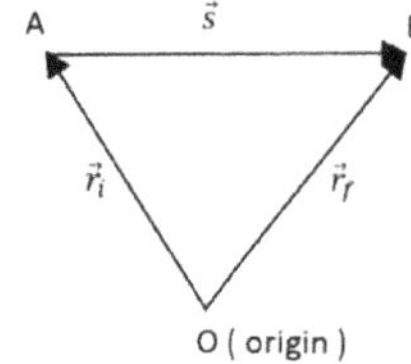

Form the figure, we get, $\vec{r_f} = \vec{r_i} + \vec{s}$

or, $\vec{s} = \vec{r_f} - \vec{r_i}$

or, $\vec{s} = (3\hat{\imath} + 2\hat{\jmath} - 2\hat{k}) - (2\hat{\imath} - \hat{\jmath} + \hat{k})$

$\therefore \vec{s} = \hat{\imath} + 3\hat{\jmath} - 3\hat{k}$

Therefore the work done by the force is given by W = $\vec{F} \cdot \vec{s}$

$= (2\hat{\imath} + \hat{\jmath} - \hat{k}).(\hat{\imath} + 3\hat{\jmath} - 3\hat{k})$
$= 2 + 3 + 3 = 8$ unit

Try Yourself

(71) A force $\vec{F} = (\hat{\imath} + 5\hat{\jmath} + 7\hat{k})$ N acts on a particle and displaces it through $\vec{S} = (6\hat{\imath} + 5\hat{\jmath} - 9\hat{k})$ m. Calculate the work done by the force.

(72) A particle moves from position $3\hat{\imath} + 2\hat{\jmath} + 6\hat{k}$ to $14\hat{\imath} + 13\hat{\jmath} + 9\hat{k}$ due to uniform force of $4\hat{\imath} + \hat{\jmath} + 3\hat{k}$ N. Find the work done if displacement is in metre.

(73) Two forces $\vec{F_1} = \hat{\imath} - \hat{\jmath} + \hat{k}$ and $\vec{F_2} = -\hat{\imath} + \hat{\jmath} + 2\hat{k}$ act on a particle while displacing it from the point P (1, 1, 1) to Q (−1, 2, 3). Calculate the work done by the net force.

◘ To compute power :

Problem : A force $\vec{F} = (2\hat{\imath} + 4\hat{\jmath})$ N displaces the body by $\vec{s} = (3\hat{\jmath} + 5\hat{k})$ m in 2 s. Calculate the power generated in this case.

Solution : Given, $\vec{F} = (2\hat{\imath} + 4\hat{\jmath})$ N

and $\vec{s} = (3\hat{\jmath} + 5\hat{k})$ m

$\therefore$ Work done W = $\vec{F} \cdot \vec{s}$

$= (2\hat{\imath} + 4\hat{\jmath}).(3\hat{\jmath} + 5\hat{k})$

$= 12$ J

$\therefore$ Power generated in this case is given by: P = $\frac{W}{t} = \frac{12}{2} = 6$ watt

Try Yourself

(74) A particle is moving with velocity $\vec{v} = \hat{\imath} - 2\hat{\jmath} + \hat{k}$ when force $\vec{F} = -2\hat{\imath} + \hat{\jmath} + 5\hat{k}$ is acting on particle. Calculate the power delivered in this case.

Problem : Velocity and acceleration of a charged particle moving perpendicular to the direction of a magnetic field at a given instant of time are $\vec{v} = 2\hat{\imath} + c\hat{\jmath}$ and $\vec{a} = 3\hat{\imath} + 4\hat{\jmath}$ respectively. Calculate the value of c.

Solution : When a charged particle is moving perpendicular to the direction of a magnetic field , it follows a circular path. That's why the velocity and acceleration is perpendicular to each other.

Given, $\vec{v} = 2\hat{\imath} + c\hat{\jmath}$

and $\vec{a} = 3\hat{\imath} + 4\hat{\jmath}$

$\therefore \vec{v}\,.\,\vec{a} = (2\hat{\imath} + c\hat{\jmath}).(3\hat{\imath} + 4\hat{\jmath})$

$= 6 + 4c$

Since, $\vec{v}\,.\,\vec{a} = 0$

or, $6 + 4c = 0$

$\therefore c = -\frac{3}{2}$

Applications of Cross Product in Physics

▫ To calculate the area of a parallelogram :

Problem : The adjacent sides of a parallelogram is represented by vectors $\vec{A} = \hat{\imath} + \hat{\jmath} + \hat{k}$ and $\vec{B} = 2\hat{\imath} - \hat{\jmath} - \hat{k}$. Calculate the area of the parallelogram.

Solution : Given, $\vec{A} = \hat{\imath} + \hat{\jmath} + \hat{k}$ and $\vec{B} = 2\hat{\imath} - \hat{\jmath} - \hat{k}$.

We know that, if the adjacent sides of parallelogram represented by vectors $\vec{A}$ and $\vec{B}$, then area of the parallelogram is given by ($\vec{A} \times \vec{B}$)

$$\text{Now, } \vec{A} \times \vec{B} = \begin{vmatrix} \hat{\imath} & \hat{\jmath} & \hat{k} \\ 1 & 1 & 1 \\ 2 & -1 & -1 \end{vmatrix}$$

$$= (-1+1)\,\hat{\imath} - (-1-2)\hat{\jmath} + (-1-2)\hat{k}$$

$$= -2\hat{\imath} + 3\hat{\jmath} - 3\hat{k}$$

Try Yourself

---

(75) Calculate the area of the parallelogram when adjacent sides are given by the vectors $\vec{A} = \hat{\imath} + 2\hat{\jmath} + 3\hat{k}$ and $\vec{B} = 2\hat{\imath} - 3\hat{\jmath} + \hat{k}$.

(76) Calculate the area of the triangle determined by the vectors $\vec{A} = 3\hat{\imath} + 4\hat{\jmath}$ and $\vec{B} = -3\hat{\imath} + 7\hat{\jmath}$.

▫ To calculate torque produced by a force :

Problem : Find the torque of a force $\vec{F} = 7\hat{\imath} + 3\hat{\jmath} + \hat{k}$ acting at the point $\vec{r} = -3\hat{\imath} + \hat{\jmath} + 5\hat{k}$

Solution : Given, Force : $\vec{F} = 7\hat{\imath} + 3\hat{\jmath} + \hat{k}$

and position vector $\vec{r} = -3\hat{\imath} + \hat{\jmath} + 5\hat{k}$

$\therefore$ Torque about the origin is given by : $\vec{\tau} = \vec{r} \times \vec{F}$

$$= \begin{vmatrix} \hat{\imath} & \hat{\jmath} & \hat{k} \\ -3 & 1 & 5 \\ 7 & 3 & 1 \end{vmatrix}$$

$$= (1-15)\,\hat{\imath} - (-3-35)\hat{\jmath} + (-9-7)\hat{k}$$

$$= -14\hat{\imath} + 38\hat{\jmath} - 16\hat{k}$$

Try Yourself

(77) Calculate the torque of a force $\vec{F} = 2\,\hat{i} - 3\,\hat{j} + 4\,\hat{k}$ N acting at a point $\vec{r} = 3\,\hat{i} + 2\,\hat{j} + 3\,\hat{k}$ meter about origin

▫ To find the angular momentum of a particle :

Problem : A particle of mass m = 2 kg is moving in space. At a certain instant, its position vector relative to the origin is $\vec{r} = 3\,\hat{i} + 2\,\hat{j} + \hat{k}$ (in m) and its velocity vector is $\vec{v} = 2\,\hat{i} - \hat{j} + 4\,\hat{k}$ (in m s^{-1}).
(a) Find the linear momentum of the particle.
(b) Find the angular momentum of the particle about the origin.

Solution : Given, mass (m) = 2 kg
and velocity : $\vec{v} = 2\,\hat{i} - \hat{j} + 4\,\hat{k}$ m s^{-1}
(a) Linear momentum : $\vec{P} = m\vec{v}$
$= 2\,(2\,\hat{i} - \hat{j} + 4\,\hat{k})$ kg m s^{-1}
$= 4\,\hat{i} - 2\,\hat{j} + 8\,\hat{k}$ kg m s^{-1}

(b) Also given, position vector relative to the origin $\vec{r} = 3\,\hat{i} + 2\,\hat{j} + \hat{k}$ m
∴ Angular momentum of the particle about the origin : $\vec{L} = \vec{r} \times \vec{P}$

$$= \begin{vmatrix} \hat{i} & \hat{j} & \hat{k} \\ 3 & 2 & 1 \\ 4 & -2 & 8 \end{vmatrix}$$

$= (16 + 2)\,\hat{i} - (24 - 4\,)\hat{j} + (-\,6 - 8\,)\hat{k}$
$= 18\,\hat{i} - 20\,\hat{j} - 14\,\hat{k}$

Try Yourself

(78) Given position vector $\vec{r} = \hat{i} + \hat{j} + \hat{k}$ and linear momentum $\vec{P} = \hat{i} - \hat{j} + 2\hat{k}$. Calculate the angular momentum.

Applications of Differentiation of Vector in Physics

▫ To find velocity from displacement :

Problem : The position vector of an object at time t is given by $\vec{r} = 4\,t^2\,\hat{i} - 5\,t\,\hat{j}$. Find its velocity at time t = 2s.

Solution : Given, Position vector : $\vec{r} = 4\,t^2\,\hat{i} - 5\,t\,\hat{j}$

∴ Velocity of the object : $\vec{v} = \frac{d\vec{r}}{dt}$
$= \frac{d}{dt}\,[\,4\,t^2\,\hat{i} - 5\,t\,\hat{j}]$
$= 8t\,\hat{i} - 5\,\hat{j}$
∴ Velocity of the object at t = 2 s is $\vec{v} = 16\,\hat{i} - 5\,\hat{j}$

Try Yourself

(79) The position vector of a particle is $\vec{r} = (a\cos\omega t)\,\hat{i} + (a\sin\omega t)\,\hat{j}$. State the direction of the velocity of the particle.

▫ To find acceleration from velocity :

Problem : A particle moves in the plane such that its velocity as a function of time t is given by $\vec{v} = (3t^2 + 2)\,\hat{i} - 4t\,\hat{j}$. Find the instantaneous acceleration vector of the particle at t = 2s. Also find the magnitude of the acceleration at that instant.

Solution : Given, Velocity : $\vec{v} = (3t^2 + 2)\,\hat{i} - 4t\,\hat{j}$

∴ Instantaneous acceleration of the particle : $\vec{a} = \frac{d\vec{v}}{dt}$

$$= \frac{d}{dt}[(3t^2 + 2)\hat{i} - 4t\hat{j}]$$

$$= 6t\,\hat{i} - 4\,\hat{j}$$

∴ Acceleration of the particle at t = 2 s is $\vec{a} = 12\,\hat{i} - 4\,\hat{j}$

Magnitude of acceleration at that instant is given by $a = \sqrt{(12)^2 + (-4)^2}$ unit

$= \sqrt{160}$ unit = 12.65 unit

Try Yourself

---

(80) A particle moves in a plane such that its velocity $\vec{v} = (4t + 1)\,\hat{i} + (6t^2 - 3t)\,\hat{j}$. Determine the instantaneous acceleration at t = 3s.

▫ To find force from linear momentum :

Problem : A particle moves in the x-y plane under the influence of a force such that its linear momentum is $\vec{p} = A[\hat{i}\cos(kt) - \hat{j}\sin(kt)]$ where A and k are constants. Find the angle between the force and momentum.

Solution : Given, Linear momentum : $\vec{p} = A[\hat{i}\cos(kt) - \hat{j}\sin(kt)]$

Force $\vec{F} = \frac{d\vec{p}}{dt}$

$$= \frac{d}{dt}[\hat{i}A\cos(kt) - \hat{j}A\sin(kt)]$$

$$= -Ak\cos(kt)\,\hat{i} - Ak\sin(kt)\,\hat{j}$$

Now, $\vec{p}.\vec{F} = [\hat{i}A\cos(kt) - \hat{j}A\sin(kt)].[-Ak\cos(kt)\,\hat{i} - Ak\sin(kt)\,\hat{j}]$

$$= -A^2k\cos^2(kt) + A^2k\sin^2(kt)$$

$$= 0$$

Try Yourself

---

(81) A particle of mass 3 kg moves along a straight line such that its velocity at time t s is given by $\vec{v}(t) = (2t^2 + 1)\,\hat{i}$. Find the expression for the net force $\vec{F}(t)$ acting on the particle as a function of time.

MCQ – 2 : Vector

Physics
MCQ | | Class – XI

Vector

Topic : Basic Concepts of Vector

Important Points

Important Definitions :

- A **vector quantity** has both a magnitude and a direction and obeys the laws of vector mathematics.

Important Facts :

- If a vector is displaced parallel to itself it does not change.
- If a vector is rotated through an angle other than multiple of 2π (or, 360º) it changes.
- If the frame of reference is translated or rotated the vector does not change (though its component may change).
- Angle between two vectors means smaller of the two angles between the vectors when they are placed tail to tail by displacing either of the two vectors parallel to itself. (i.e. $0 \leq \theta \leq \pi$)
- $\vec{A} = \vec{B}$ implies that

(a) they have same magnitude

(b) they are in same direction

(c) they are same in nature

(1) Which of the following is a vector?
(a) Current
(b) Time
(c) Acceleration
(d) Volume

(2) The vector quantity among the following is
(a) Mass
(b) Time
(c) Distance
(d) Displacement

(3) Identify the vector quantity among the following
(a) Heat
(b) Energy
(c) Distance
(d) Angular momentum

(4) The change in a vector may occur due to
(a) Rotation of frame of reference
(b) Translation of frame of reference
(c) Rotation of vector
(d) Both (a) and (c)

(5) A vector is not changed if
(a) it is displaced parallel to itself
(b) it is rotated through an arbitrary angle
(c) it is cross-multiplied by a unit vector
(d) it is multiplied by an arbitrary scalar

(6) A displacement vector is
(a) Change in position
(b) Velocity
(c) Scalar
(d) Distance without direction

(7) Unit vector does not have any
(a) Direction
(b) Magnitude
(c) Unit
(d) All of these

(8) Which of the following represents a unit vector?
(a) $\frac{|\vec{A}|}{\vec{A}}$
(b) $\frac{\vec{A}}{|\vec{A}|}$
(c) $\frac{\vec{A}}{\vec{A}}$
(d) $\frac{|\vec{A}|}{|\vec{A}|}$

(9) Let θ be the angle between vectors $\vec{A}$ and $\vec{B}$ which of the following figures correctly represents the angle θ
(a)

(b)

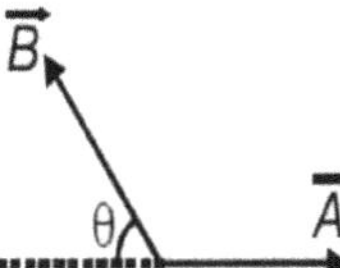

(c)

(d)

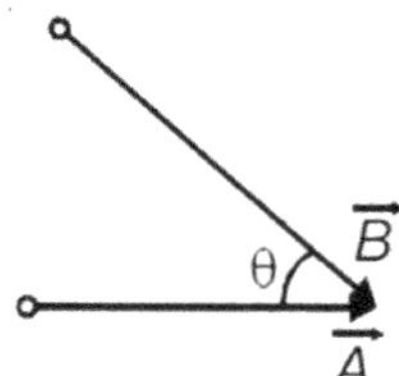

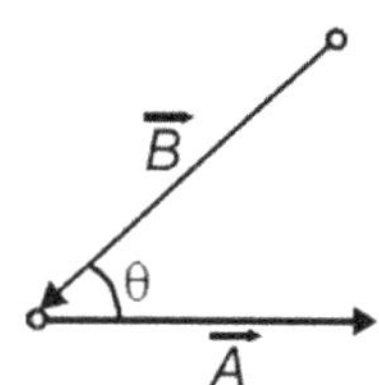

(10) $\vec{A}$ is a vector of magnitude 2.7 units due east. What is the magnitude and direction of vector 4 $\vec{A}$?
(a) 4 units due east
(b) 4 units due west
(c) 2.7 units due east
(d) 10.8 units due east

Representation of Vector by Co-ordinates

(11) The magnitude of vector $\hat{\imath} + \hat{\jmath}$ is
(a) 2
(b) 0
(c) $\sqrt{2}$
(d) 4

(12) The vector $\overrightarrow{OA}$, where O is origin is given by $\overrightarrow{OA} = 2\,\hat{\imath} + 2\,\hat{\jmath}$. Now it is rotated by 45° anticlockwise about O. What will be the new vector?
(a) $2\sqrt{2}\,\hat{\jmath}$
(b) $2\,\hat{\jmath}$
(c) $2\sqrt{2}\,\hat{\imath}$
(d) $2\,\hat{\imath}$

(13) A particle starting from the origin (0,0) moves in a straight line in the (x, y) plane, its coordinates at a later time are ($\sqrt{3}$, 3). The path of the particle makes with the x axis an angle of
(a) 0°
(b) 45°
(c) 30°
(d) 60°

(14) If a unit vector is represented by $0.5\,\hat{\imath} + 0.8\,\hat{\jmath} + C\,\hat{k}$, the value of C is
(a) $\sqrt{0.11}$
(b) 1
(c) $\sqrt{0.01}$
(d) 0.39

(15) The angle between the z-axis and the vector $\hat{\imath} + \hat{\jmath} + \sqrt{2}\,\hat{k}$ is
(a) 30°
(b) 45°
(c) 60°
(d) 90°

(16) The direction cosines of $\hat{\imath} + \hat{\jmath} + \hat{k}$ are
(a) 1,1,1
(b) 2,2,2
(c) $\frac{1}{\sqrt{2}}, \frac{1}{\sqrt{2}}, \frac{1}{\sqrt{2}}$
(d) $\frac{1}{\sqrt{3}}, \frac{1}{\sqrt{3}}, \frac{1}{\sqrt{3}}$

Answer

Vector

Topic : Basic Concepts of Vector

(1)	(c)	(5)	(a)	(9)	(c)	(13)	(c)
(2)	(d)	(6)	(a)	(10)	(d)	(14)	(a)
(3)	(d)	(7)	(c)	(11)	(c)	(15)	(b)
(4)	(d)	(8)	(b)	(12)	(a)	(16)	(d)

Physics MCQ | | Class – XI

Vector

Topic : Resultant Calculation of Vectors

Without Co-ordinate Representation

 # Important Points

The magnitude of the resultant of two vectors :

$$|\vec{R}| = \sqrt{|\vec{A}|^2 + |\vec{B}|^2 + 2\,|\vec{A}|\,|\vec{B}|\,\cos\theta}$$

The direction of the resultant : If the resultant makes an angle α with vector $\vec{A}$ then

$$\tan\alpha = \frac{|\vec{B}|\sin\theta}{|\vec{A}| + |\vec{B}|\cos\theta}$$

Where, θ is the angle between the two vectors

(1) $\vec{A} + \vec{B}$ can also be written as
(a) $\vec{B} + \vec{A}$
(b) $\vec{B} - \vec{A}$
(c) $\vec{A} - \vec{B}$
(d) $\vec{B} \cdot \vec{A}$

(2) The resultant of $\vec{P}$ and $\vec{Q}$ makes an angle α with $\vec{P}$ and β with $\vec{Q}$, then
(a) α is always less than β
(b) $\alpha < \beta$ if $P < Q$
(c) $\alpha < \beta$ if $P > Q$
(d) $\alpha < \beta$ if $P = Q$

(3) A vector is added to an equal and opposite vector of similar nature, forms a
(a) Unit vector
(b) Position vector
(c) Null vector
(d) Displacement vector

(4) If the magnitude of vectors $\vec{A}$, $\vec{B}$ and $\vec{C}$ are 12, 5 and 13 unit respectively and $\vec{A} + \vec{B} = \vec{C}$. then angle between $\vec{A}$ and $\vec{B}$ will be
(a) $\frac{\pi}{2}$
(b) $\frac{\pi}{4}$
(c) π
(d) 0

(5) Two vectors each of magnitude A have a resultant of same magnitude A. The angle between the two vectors is
(a) 30°
(b) 60°
(c) 120°
(d) 150°

(6) If $|\vec{A} + \vec{B}| = |\vec{A}| = |\vec{B}|$ then angle between $\vec{A}$ and $\vec{B}$ will be
(a) 0°
(b) 90°
(c) 120°
(d) 180°

(7) If $\vec{P} + \vec{Q} = \vec{R}$ and $|\vec{P}| = |\vec{Q}| = |\vec{R}|$ then angle between $\vec{P}$ and $\vec{Q}$ will be
(a) 30°
(b) 60°
(c) 90°
(d) 120°

(8) If the angle between two vectors $\vec{P}$ and $\vec{Q}$ is 120°, its resultant $\vec{R}$
(a) $|\vec{R}| = |\vec{P} - \vec{Q}|$
(b) $|\vec{R}| < |\vec{P} - \vec{Q}|$
(c) $|\vec{R}| > |\vec{P} - \vec{Q}|$
(d) $|\vec{R}| = |\vec{P} + \vec{Q}|$

(9) If $\vec{A} = \vec{B} + \vec{C}$ and the vales of $\vec{A}$, $\vec{B}$ and $\vec{C}$ are 13, 12 and 5 respectively, then the angle between $\vec{A}$ and $\vec{C}$ will be
(a) $\cos^{-1}\frac{5}{13}$
(b) $\cos^{-1}(\frac{13}{12})$
(c) $\frac{\pi}{2}$
(d) $\sin^{-1}(-\frac{5}{12})$

(10) The resultant of $\vec{P}$ and $\vec{Q}$ is perpendicular to $\vec{P}$. What is the angle between $\vec{P}$ and $\vec{Q}$?
(a) $\cos^{-1}\frac{P}{Q}$
(b) $\cos^{-1}(-\frac{P}{Q})$
(c) $\sin^{-1}\frac{P}{Q}$
(d) $\sin^{-1}(-\frac{P}{Q})$

(11) The resultant of two vectors at an angle 150° is 10 units and is perpendicular to one vector. The magnitude of the smaller vector is

(a) 10 units

(b) $10\sqrt{3}$ units

(c) $10\sqrt{2}$ units

(d) $5\sqrt{3}$ units

Answer

Vector

Topic : Resultant Calculation of Vectors

(1)	(a)	**(4)**	(a)	**(7)**	(d)	**(10)**	(b)
(2)	(c)	**(5)**	(c)	**(8)**	(c)	**(11)**	(b)
(3)	(c)	**(6)**	(c)	**(9)**	(a)		

Physics MCQ || Class – XI

Vector

Topic : Subtraction and Resolution of Vectors

 # Important Points

The subtraction of a vector $\vec{B}$ from vector $\vec{A}$ is defined as the addition of vector $-\vec{B}$ to vector $\vec{A}$.

$$\vec{C} = \vec{A} - \vec{B} = \vec{A} + (-\vec{B})$$

(1) If $|\vec{A} - \vec{B}| = A + B$ then the angle between $\vec{A}$ and $\vec{B}$ is
(a) 0°
(b) 90°
(c) 270°
(d) 180°

(2) If the sum of two unit vectors is also a unit vector, then magnitude of their difference and angle between the two given unit vectors is (a) $\sqrt{3}$, 60°
(b) $\sqrt{3}$, 120°
(c) $\sqrt{2}$, 60°
(d) $\sqrt{2}$, 120°

(3) The unit vectors $\hat{a}$ and $\hat{b}$ are inclined at an angle θ, then the value of $|\hat{a} - \hat{b}|$
(a) $2 \sin\frac{\theta}{2}$
(b) $2 \cos\frac{\theta}{2}$
(c) $2 \tan\frac{\theta}{2}$
(d) None of these

(4) If A = B then the angle between $\vec{A} + \vec{B}$ and $\vec{A} - \vec{B}$ is
(a) 0°
(b) 90°
(c) 45°
(d) 60°

 # Important Points

On Resolution and Components of a Vector

If the components ($\vec{a}$ and $\vec{b}$) of vector $\vec{R}$ makes an angle α and β with with the vector $\vec{R}$, then the magnitude of the components are

$$a = \frac{\sin\beta}{\sin(\alpha+\beta)} R \text{ and } b = \frac{\sin\alpha}{\sin(\alpha+\beta)} R$$

(5) The maximum number of rectangular components in which a vector can be resolved in a plane, is
(a) Four
(b) Two
(c) One
(d) Infinite

(6) What is the magnitude of component of $9\hat{i} - 7\hat{j} + 13.9\hat{k}$ along X axis?
(a) 9
(b) 7
(c) 13.9
(d) 29.9

(7) What is the magnitude of component of $9\hat{i} + 13.9\hat{k}$ along Y axis?
(a) 9
(b) 4.9
(c) 13.9
(d) 0

Answer

Vector

Topic : Subtraction of Vectors

(1)	(d)	**(3)**	(a)	**(5)**	(b)	**(7)**	(d)
(2)	(b)	**(4)**	(b)	**(6)**	(a)		

Physics
MCQ || Class – XI

Vector

Topic : Multiplication of Vectors

Without Co-ordinate Representation

Important Points

Two vectors, when multiplied may produce either a scalar or a vector. Accordingly they are called scalar or dot product and vector or cross product.

Scalar Product (or, dot product) : If the vectors $\vec{A}$ and $\vec{B}$ are inclined at an angle θ, then

$$\vec{A} . \vec{B} = |\vec{A}|\,|\vec{B}| \cos\theta$$

Vector Product (or, cross product) : If the vectors $\vec{A}$ and $\vec{B}$ are inclined at an angle θ, then

$$\vec{A} \times \vec{B} = |\vec{A}|\,|\vec{B}| \sin\theta\,\hat{n}$$

(1) The vectors are perpendicular if
(a) $\vec{A} . \vec{B} = 0$
(b) $\vec{A} \times \vec{B} = 0$
(c) $\vec{A} . \vec{B} = 1$
(d) $\vec{A} . \vec{B} = AB$

(2) When $\vec{A} . \vec{B} = -|\vec{A}|\,|\vec{B}|$, then
(a) $\vec{A}$ and $\vec{B}$ are perpendicular to each other
(b) $\vec{A}$ and $\vec{B}$ act in the same direction
(c) $\vec{A}$ and $\vec{B}$ act in the opposite direction
(d) $\vec{A}$ and $\vec{B}$ can act in any direction

(3) A vector, $\vec{A}$ points vertically upwards and $\vec{B}$ towards north. The vector product $\vec{A} \times \vec{B}$ is
(a) zero
(b) along east
(c) along west
(d) vertically downward

(4) A vector, $\vec{A}$ points towards North and vector $\vec{B}$ points upwards. Then $\vec{A} \times \vec{B}$ points towards
(a) East
(b) West
(c) North
(d) South

(5) For two vectors $\vec{A}$ and $\vec{B}$ making an angle θ, which of the following relations is correct ?
(a) $\vec{A} \times \vec{B} = \vec{B} \times \vec{A}$
(b) $\vec{A} \times \vec{B} = AB \sin\theta$
(c) $\vec{A} \times \vec{B} = AB \cos\theta$
(d) $\vec{A} \times \vec{B} = -\vec{B} \times \vec{A}$

(6) If resultant of two vectors having magnitude 3 and 4 is 5. The magnitude of their cross product is
(a) 12
(b) 15
(c) 20
(d) Zero

(7) The resultant of two vectors having magnitude 2 and 3 is 1. What is their cross product?
(a) 6
(b) 3
(c) 1
(d) 0

(8) If $\sqrt{3}\,|\vec{A} \times \vec{B}| = \vec{A} . \vec{B}$, the value of $|\vec{A} + \vec{B}|$ is
(a) $[A^2 + B^2 + AB]^{\frac{1}{2}}$
(b) $[A^2 + B^2 + \sqrt{3}AB]^{\frac{1}{2}}$
(c) $[A^2 + B^2 - AB]^{\frac{1}{2}}$
(d) $[A^2 + B^2]^{\frac{1}{2}}$

(9) $|\vec{A} \times \vec{B}| = \vec{A} . \vec{B}$, then angle between $\vec{A}$ and $\vec{B}$ will be
(a) 30°
(b) 60°
(c) 45°
(d) 90°

(10) The angle between vectors ($\vec{A} \times \vec{B}$) and ($\vec{B} \times \vec{A}$) is
(a) 0°
(b) 90°
(c) 120°
(d) 180°

(11) The vector product of two vectors $\vec{A}$ and $\vec{B}$ is zero. The scalar product of $\vec{A}$ and ($\vec{A} + \vec{B}$) will be

(a) Zero
(b) AB
(c) A^2
(d) A^2 + AB

(12) If $\vec{A} + \vec{B} + \vec{C} = \vec{0}$ then $\vec{A} \times \vec{B}$ is
(a) $\vec{C} \times \vec{B}$
(b) $\vec{B} \times \vec{C}$
(c) $\vec{A} \times \vec{C}$
(d) zero

(13) If the angle between the vectors $\vec{A}$ and $\vec{B}$ is θ, The value of the product of ($\vec{B} \times \vec{A}$). $\vec{A}$ is equal to
(a) $BA^2 \sin\theta$
(b) $BA^2 \sin\theta \cos\theta$
(c) $BA^2 \cos\theta$
(d) zero

(14) Angle between $\vec{A}$ and $\vec{B}$ is θ, then $\vec{A}$. ($\vec{B} \times \vec{A}$) is equal to
(a) $BA^2 \sin\theta$
(b) $BA^2 \cos\theta$
(c) BA^2
(d) zero

(15) Three vectors satisfy the relation $\vec{A} . \vec{B} = \mathbf{0}$ and $\vec{A} . \vec{C} = \vec{0}$ then $\vec{A}$ is parallel to
(a) $\vec{C}$
(b) $\vec{B}$
(c) $\vec{B} \times \vec{C}$
(d) $\vec{B} . \vec{C}$

(16) Which of the following is correct relation between an arbitrary vector $\vec{A}$ and null vector $\vec{0}$?
(a) $\vec{A} + \vec{0} + \vec{A} \times \vec{0} = \vec{A}$
(b) $\vec{A} + \vec{0} + \vec{A} \times \vec{0} \neq \vec{A}$
(c) $\vec{A} + \vec{0} + \vec{A} \times \vec{0} = \vec{0}$
(d) None of these

With Co-ordinate Representation

Dot Product of Vectors

(17) The angle between the vectors $3\hat{\imath} + 4\hat{\jmath} + 5\hat{k}$ and $3\hat{\imath} + 4\hat{\jmath} - 5\hat{k}$ i
(a) 0°
(b) 90°
(c) 30°
(d) 60°

(18) If a vector $2\hat{\imath} + 3\hat{\jmath} + 8\hat{k}$ is perpendicular to the vector $4\hat{\imath} - 4\hat{\jmath} + \alpha\hat{k}$, then the value of α is
(a) $\frac{1}{2}$
(b) $-\frac{1}{4}$
(c) 1
(d) −1

(19) When vector $\hat{n} = a\ \hat{\imath} + b\ \hat{\jmath}$ is perpendicular to ($\hat{\imath} + \hat{\jmath}$), then a and b ar
(a) 0, 1
(b) −2, 0
(c) $-\frac{1}{\sqrt{2}}, \frac{1}{\sqrt{2}}$
(d) 0, −2

(20) Vector which is perpendicular to $a \cos\theta\, \hat{\imath} + b \sin\theta\, \hat{\jmath}$ is
(a) $b \sin\theta\, \hat{\imath} - a \cos\theta\, \hat{\jmath}$
(b) $\frac{1}{a} \sin\theta\, \hat{\imath} - \frac{1}{b} \cos\theta\, \hat{\jmath}$
(c) $5\hat{k}$
(d) All of these

(21) What is the component of $3\hat{\imath} + 4\hat{\jmath}$ along $\hat{\imath} + \hat{\jmath}$
(a) $\frac{1}{2}(\hat{\imath} + \hat{\jmath})$
(b) $\frac{3}{2}(\hat{\imath} + \hat{\jmath})$
(c) $\frac{5}{2}(\hat{\imath} + \hat{\jmath})$
(d) $\frac{7}{2}(\hat{\imath} + \hat{\jmath})$

(22) The projection of the vector $\vec{a} = 2\hat{\imath} - 3\hat{\jmath} + 6\hat{k}$ on the vector $\vec{b} = \hat{\imath} + 2\hat{\jmath} + 2\hat{k}$ is
(a) $\frac{7}{8}$
(b) $\frac{7}{3}$
(c) $\frac{9}{7}$
(d) $\frac{8}{3}$

(23) Two vector $\vec{a} = 3\hat{\imath} + 8\hat{\jmath} - 2\hat{k}$ and $\vec{b} = 6\hat{\imath} + 16\hat{\jmath} + x\hat{k}$ are such that the component of $\vec{b}$ perpendicular to $\vec{a}$ is zero, then the value of x will be
(a) 8
(b) −4
(c) −8
(d) +4

Cross Product of Vectors

(24) Let $\vec{a} = 2\hat{\imath} - 3\hat{\jmath} + 4\hat{k}$ and $\vec{b} = 4\hat{\imath} + \hat{\jmath} + 2\hat{k}$ then $|\vec{a} \times \vec{b}|$ is equal to
(a) 440
(b) $2\sqrt{110}$
(c) $\sqrt{220}$
(d) $4\sqrt{65}$

(25) A unit vector which is perpendicular to both the vectors $2\hat{i} + \hat{j} + \hat{k}$ and $\hat{i} - \hat{j} + 2\hat{k}$ is

(a) $\frac{1}{\sqrt{3}}\hat{i} + \frac{1}{\sqrt{3}}\hat{j} + \frac{1}{\sqrt{3}}\hat{k}$

(b) $-\frac{1}{\sqrt{3}}\hat{i} - \frac{1}{\sqrt{3}}\hat{j} - \frac{1}{\sqrt{3}}\hat{k}$

(c) $\frac{1}{\sqrt{3}}\hat{i} - \frac{1}{\sqrt{3}}\hat{j} - \frac{1}{\sqrt{3}}\hat{k}$

(d) None of these

Triple Product of Vectors

(26) If $\vec{A} = \hat{i} - 2\hat{j} - 3\hat{k}$, $\vec{B} = 2\hat{i} + \hat{j} - \hat{k}$ and $\vec{C} = \hat{i} + 3\hat{j} - 2\hat{k}$, then the value of $\vec{A} \cdot (\vec{B} \times \vec{C})$ is

(a) – 20

(b) 0

(c) 20

(d) – 4

(27) For what value of C are three vectors $2\hat{i} + 3\hat{j} + 4\hat{k}$, $5\hat{j} + 10\hat{k}$ and $C\hat{i} + 2\hat{j} + 3\hat{k}$ coplanar?

(a) – 1

(b) 0

(c) 1

(d) – 6

(28) Find λ such that $2\hat{i} - \hat{j} + \hat{k}$, $\hat{i} + 2\hat{j} - 3\hat{k}$ and $3\hat{i} + \lambda\hat{j} + 5\hat{k}$ are coplanar.

(a) – 4

(b) 0

(c) 4

(d) – 6

Answer

Vector

Topic : Multiplication of Vectors

(1)	(a)	**(7)**	(d)	**(13)**	(d)	**(19)**	(c)	**(25)**	(a)
(2)	(c)	**(8)**	(b)	**(14)**	(d)	**(20)**	(d)	**(26)**	(a)
(3)	(c)	**(9)**	(c)	**(15)**	(c)	**(21)**	(d)	**(27)**	(c)
(4)	(a)	**(10)**	(d)	**(16)**	(a)	**(22)**	()	**(28)**	(a)
(5)	(d)	**(11)**	(d)	**(17)**	(b)	**(23)**	()		
(6)	(a)	**(12)**	(b)	**(18)**	(a)	**(24)**	(b)		

Physics
MCQ || Class – XI

Vector

Topic : Applications of Vector Mathematics in Physics

Applications of Resultant Calculation

Displacement calculation

(1) A body moves 6 m north, 8 m east and 10 m vertically upwards, the resultant displacement from its initial position is
(a) $10\sqrt{2}$ m
(b) $\frac{10}{2}$ m
(c) 10 m
(d) 20 m

Resultant force calculation

(2) Two forces of 10 N and 6 N act upon a body. The direction of the forces are unknown. The resultant force on the body may be
(a) 15 N
(b) 3 N
(c) 2 N
(d) 17 N

(3) Two forces of magnitude 8 N and 15 N respectively act at a point. If the resultant force is 17 N, the angle between the force has to be
(a) 45°
(b) 60°
(c) 90°
(d) 30°

(4) Two equal forces (P each) act at a point inclined to each other at an angle of 120°. The magnitude of their resultant is
(a) $\frac{P}{2}$
(b) $\frac{P}{4}$
(c) P
(d) 2P

(5) Maximum and minimum magnitudes of the resultant of two vectors of magnitudes P and Q are in the ratio 3 : 1, which of the following relations is true?
(a) P = 2Q
(b) P = Q
(c) PQ = 1
(d) None of these

(6) The resultant of two forces 3P and 2P is R. If the first force is doubled, then the resultant is also doubled. The angle between the two forces is
(a) 0°
(b) 90°
(c) 120°
(d) 180°

(7) The square of resultant of two equal forces is three times their product. Angle between the forces is
(a) $\frac{\pi}{2}$
(b) $\frac{\pi}{4}$
(c) π
(d) $\frac{\pi}{3}$

(8) Two forces are such that the sum of their magnitudes is 18 N and their resultant is perpendicular to the smaller force and magnitude of resultant is 12. Then the magnitudes of the forces are
(a) 12 N, 6 N
(b) 13 N, 5 N
(c) 10 N, 8 N
(d) 16 N, 2 N

(9) The resultant of two forces, one double the other in magnitude, is perpendicular to the smaller of the two forces. The angle between the two forces is
(a) 60°
(b) 120°
(c) 150°
(d) 90°

(10) A body is at rest under the action of three forces, two of which are $\vec{F_1} = 4\,\hat{i}$, $\vec{F_2} = 6\,\hat{j}$; then third force is
(a) $4\,\hat{i} + 6\,\hat{j}$
(b) $4\,\hat{i} - 6\,\hat{j}$
(c) $-4\,\hat{i} + 6\,\hat{j}$
(d) $-4\,\hat{i} - 6\,\hat{j}$

River-boat problem

(11) A person aiming to reach exactly opposite point on the bank of a stream is swimming with a speed of 0.5 m s^{-1} at an angle of 120° with the direction of flow of water. The speed of water in stream is
(a) 0.25 m s^{-1}
(b) 0.5 m s^{-1}

(c) 1.0 m s^{-1}
(d) 0.433 m s^{-1}

(12) A person, reaches a point directly opposite on the other bank of a flowing river, while swimming at a speed of 5 m s^{-1} at an angle of 120° with flow. The speed of the flow must be
(a) 2.5 m s^{-1}
(b) 3 m s^{-1}
(c) 4 m s^{-1}
(d) 1.5 m s^{-1}

(13) A boat is sent across a river with a velocity of 8 km h^{-1}. If the resultant velocity of the boat is 10 km h^{-1}, then velocity of the river is
(a) 8 km h^{-1}
(b) 10 km h^{-1}
(c) 12.8 km s^{-1}
(d) 6 km h^{-1}

(14) The speed of a boat is 5 km h^{-1} in still water. It crosses a river of width 1.0 km along the shortest possible path in 15 minute. The velocity of the river water (in km h^{-1}) is
(a) 3
(b) 1
(c) 4
(d) 5

(15) The rowing speed of a man relative to water is 5 km h^{-1} and the speed of water flow is 3 km h^{-1}. At what angle to the river flow should be head if he wants to reach a point on the other bank, directly opposite to starting point ?
(a) 127°
(b) 143°
(c) 120°
(d) 150°

(16) A river is flowing from West to East at a speed of 8 m per min. A man on the south bank of the river, capable of swimming at 20 m min^{-1} in still water, wants to swim across the river in the shortest time. He should swim in a direction
(a) due North
(b) 30° East of North
(c) 30° West of North
(d) 60° East of North

Applications of Subtraction of Vectors

To determine Change in Velocity

(17) The vector sum of two forces is perpendicular to their vector differences. In that case, the forces
(a) Cannot be predicted
(b) are not equal to each other in magnitude
(c) are equal to each other in magnitude
(d) are equal to each other

(18) A particle is moving in a circle of radius r having centre O, with a constant speed v. The magnitude of change in velocity in moving from A to B is

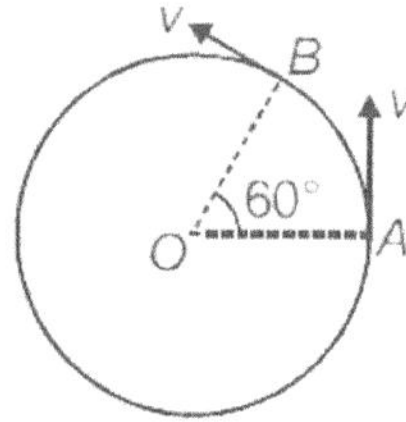

(a) 2v
(b) 0
(c) $\sqrt{3}$v
(d) v

(19) A particle is moving on a circular path with constant speed v. It moves between two points A and B, which subtends an angle 60° at the centre of circle. The change in magnitude of its velocity during motion from A to B are respectively
(a) 2v
(b) 0
(c) $\sqrt{3}$v
(d) v

(20) Two forces of equal magnitude act at a point making an angle θ with each other. If the direction of one of the forces is reversed, the direction of the resultant will turn through
(a) $\frac{\pi}{2}$
(b) $\frac{\pi}{4}$
(c) π
(d) 0

(21) A body is moving with velocity 30 m s^{-1} towards east. After 10 s its velocity becomes 40 m s^{-1} towards north. The average acceleration of the body is
(a) 5 m s^{-2}
(b)1 m s^{-2}
(c) 7 m s^{-2}
(d) $\sqrt{7}$ m s^{-2}

Relative Velocity in 1 D

(22) Two objects A and B are moving with velocities v_A and v_B respectively in the same direction. The magnitude of relative velocity of A w.r.t. B is
(a) $v_A - v_B$
(b) $v_A + v_B$

(c) $v_B - v_A$
(d) $\frac{v_A}{v_B}$

(23) Two objects A and B are moving in opposite directions with velocities v_A and v_B respectively. The magnitude of relative velocity of A w.r.t. B is
(a) $v_A - v_B$
(b) $v_A + v_B$
(c) $v_B.v_A$
(d) $\frac{v_A}{v_B}$

(24) Two cars are moving along a straight line in opposite direction with the same speed v. The relative velocity of two cars w.r.t. each other is
(a) $2v$
(b) v
(c) zero
(d) $\frac{v}{2}$

(25) The relative velocity of two objects A and B is 10 m s^{-1}. If the velocity of the object A is 40 m s^{-1} then the velocity with which B is moving is (assume both objects are moving in same direction)
(a) 10 m s^{-1}
(b) 40 m s^{-1}
(c) 30 m s^{-1}
(d) 15 m s^{-1}

(26) Two trains are moving in a straight line in the same direction with a speed of 80 km h^{-1}. the relative velocity of one train w.r.t. other is
(a) 80 kmh^{-1}
(b) 40 km h^{-1}
(c) zero
(d) 160 km h^{-1}

(27) A boat takes two hours to travel 8 km down and 8 km up the river when the water is still. How much time will the boat take to make the same trip when the river starts flowing at 4 km h^{-1}?
(a) 2 h
(b) 2 h 40 minute
(c) 3 h
(d) 3 h 40 minute

(28) A boat covers certain distance between two spots in a river taking t_1 h going downstream and t_2 h going upstream. What time will be taken by boat to cover same distance in still water?
(a) $\frac{t_1 + t_2}{2}$
(b) $2 (t_1 + t_2)$
(c) $\frac{2\ t_1\ t_2}{t_1 + t_2}$
(d) $\sqrt{t_1\ t_2}$

(29) A train of 150 m length is going towards North at a speed of 10 m s^{-1}. A bird is flying at 5 m s^{-1} parallel to the track towards South. The time taken by the bird to cross the train is
(a) 10 s
(b) 15 s
(c) 30 s
(d) 12 s

(30) Two trains each of length 100 m moving parallel towards each other at speed 72 km h^{-1} and 36 km h^{-1} respectively. In how much time will they cross each other?
(a) 6.6 s
(b) 5 s
(c) 8 s
(d) 10 s

(31) Two bodies starts moving from same point along a straight line with velocities 6 m s^{-1} and 10 m s^{-1} simultaneously. After what time their separation becomes 40 m?
(a) 6 s
(b) 8 s
(c) 12 s
(d) 10 s

(32) Two cars are moving in the same direction with a speed of 30 km h^{-1}. They are separated from each other by 5 km. Third car moving in the opposite direction meets the two cars after an interval of 4 minutes. The speed of the third car is
(a) 30 km h^{-1}
(b) 25 km h^{-1}
(c) 40 km h^{-1}
(d) 45 km h^{-1}

Relative Velocity in 2D

(33) Ram moves in east direction at a speed of 6 m s^{-1} and Shyam moves 30° east of north at a speed of 6 m s^{-1}. the magnitude of their relative velocity is
(a) 3 ms^{-1}
(b) 6 ms^{-1}
(c) $6\sqrt{3}$ ms^{-1}
(d) $6\sqrt{2}$ ms^{-1}

(34) A bus appears to go with a speed of 24 km h^{-1} to a car driver, driving at the rate 7 km h^{-1} northwards. If the bus actually travels in east direction, its speed is

(a) 24 km h^{-1}
(b) 23 km h^{-1}
(c) 26 km h^{-1}
(d) 30 km h^{-1}

(35) Figure shows two ships moving in x-y plane with velocities V_A and V_B. The ships move such that B always remains north of A. The ratio $\frac{V_A}{V_B}$ is equal to

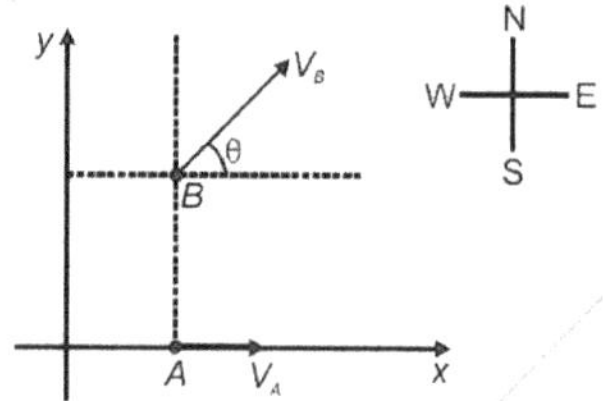

(a) sin θ
(b) cos θ
(c) sec θ
(d) cosec θ

(36) A train moving towards East and a car is along North, both with same speed. The observed direction of car to the passenger in train is
(a) East-North direction
(b) West-North direction
(c) South-East direction
(d) None of these

(37) A particle (A) moves due North at 3 km h^{-1} and another particle (B) moves due West at 4 km h^{-1}. The relative velocity of A w.r.t. B is (tan 37° = $\frac{3}{4}$)
(a) 5 km h^{-1}, 37° North of East
(b) 5 km h^{-1}, 37° East of North
(c) $5\sqrt{2}$ km h^{-1}, 53° North of East
(d) $5\sqrt{2}$ km h^{-1}, 53° East of North

(38) A ship A moving due North with speed v observes that another ship B is moving due west with same speed v. The actual velocity of B is
(a) $\sqrt{2}\,v$ towards South-West
(b) $\sqrt{2}\,v$ towards North-West
(c) $\sqrt{2}\,v$ towards South-East
(d) v towards North-East

(39) A car P moves along north with velocity 30 km h^{-1} and another car Q moves along east with velocity 40 km h^{-1}. The relative velocity of P w.r.t. Q is
(a) 50 km h^{-1} North-East
(b) 50 km h^{-1} North-West
(c) 50 km h^{-1} at an angle $\tan^{-1}\frac{3}{4}$ North of West
(d) 50 km h^{-1} at an angle $\tan^{-1}\frac{4}{3}$ West of North

To compute displacement from position vector

(40) If a particle moves from point P (2, 3, 5) to point Q (3, 4, 5). Its displacement vector will be
(a) $\hat{i} + \hat{j} + 10\,\hat{k}$
(b) $\hat{i} + \hat{j} + \hat{k}$
(c) $\hat{i} + \hat{j}$
(d) $2\,\hat{i} + 4\,\hat{j} + 6\,\hat{k}$

(41) The position vector of a moving particle at time t is $\vec{r} = t^3\,\hat{i} - 4\,t^2\,\hat{j} + 4\,\hat{k}$. Its displacement during the time interval t = 1 s to t = 2 s is
(a) $7\,\hat{i} + 12\,\hat{j}$
(b) $7\,\hat{i} - 12\,\hat{j}$
(c) $12\,\hat{i} + 7\,\hat{j}$
(d) $12\,\hat{i} - 7\,\hat{j}$

Rainfall

(42) A car with a vertically windshield moves in a rain storm at a speed of 40 km h^{-1}. The rain drops fall vertically with a constant speed of 20 m s^{-1}. The angle at which rain drops strike the windshield is
(a) $\tan^{-1}\frac{5}{9}$
(b) $\tan^{-1}\frac{9}{5}$
(c) $\tan^{-1}\frac{3}{2}$
(d) $\tan^{-1}\frac{2}{3}$

(43) A man is walking on road with velocity 3 km h^{-1} suddenly rain starts falling. Velocity of rain is 10 km h^{-1} in vertically downward direction, the relative velocity of the rain with respect to man is
(a) $\sqrt{13}$ km h^{-1}
(b) $\sqrt{7}$ km h^{-1}
(c) $\sqrt{109}$ km h^{-1}
(d) 13 km h^{-1}

(44) Rain drops are falling with velocity ($2\,\hat{\imath} - 4\,\hat{\jmath}$) m s^{-1}. What should be the velocity of man so rain drops hit him with speed 5 m s^{-1}
(a) $-\,\hat{\imath}$

(b) $5\hat{\imath}$

(c) $2\hat{\imath}$

(d) Both (a) and (b)

(45) A man standing on a road has to hold his umbrella at 30° with the vertical to keep the rain away. He throws the umbrella and starts running at 10 km h^{-1}. He finds that raindrops are hitting his head vertically
(a) $10\sqrt{3}$ km h^{-1}
(b) 20 km h^{-1}
(c) $\frac{20}{\sqrt{3}}$ km s^{-1}
(d) $\frac{10}{\sqrt{3}}$ km h^{-1}

(46) A stationary man observes that the rain id falling vertically downward. When he starts running with a velocity of 12 km h^{-1}, he observes that the rain is falling at an angle 60° with the vertical. The actual velocity of rain is
(a) $12\sqrt{3}$ km h^{-1}
(b) $6\sqrt{3}$ km h^{-1}
(c) $4\sqrt{3}$km s^{-1}
(d) $2\sqrt{3}$ km h^{-1}

(47) A boy is running on the plane road with velocity v with a long hollow tube in his hand. The water is falling vertically downwards with velocity u. At what angle to the vertical, he must inclined the tube so that the water drops enter it without touching its sides ?
(a) $\tan^{-1}\left(\frac{v}{u}\right)$
(b) $\sin^{-1}\left(\frac{v}{u}\right)$
(c) $\tan^{-1}\left(\frac{u}{v}\right)$
(d) $\cos^{-1}\left(\frac{v}{u}\right)$

Applications of Components of Vector

(48) Which one of the following pair cannot be the rectangular components of force vector of 10 N?
(a) 6 N & 8 N
(b) 7 N & $\sqrt{51}$ N
(c) $6\sqrt{2}$ N & $2\sqrt{7}$ N
(d) 9 N & 1 N

(49) A displacement vector of magnitude 4 makes an angle 30° with the x-axis. Its rectangular components in x-y plane are
(a) $2\sqrt{3}$, 2
(b) $4\sqrt{3}$, 4
(c) $\frac{2}{\sqrt{3}}$, 2
(d) $\frac{4}{\sqrt{3}}$, 4

Applications of Dot product of Vectors

(50) The velocity and acceleration vectors of charged particle moving perpendicular to the direction of a magnetic field at a given instant of time are $\vec{v} = 2\,\hat{\imath} + c\hat{\jmath}$ and $\vec{a} = 3\,\hat{\imath} + 4\,\hat{\jmath}$ respectively. Then the value of c is
(a) 3
(b) 1.5
(c) – 1.5
(d) – 3

(51) A particle is moving with velocity $\vec{v} = \hat{\imath} - 2\hat{\jmath} + \hat{k}$ when force $\vec{F} = -2\hat{\imath} + \hat{\jmath} + 5\hat{k}$ is acting on particle. Then the power delivered is
(a) 2 units
(b) 3 units
(c) 1 unit
(d) 5 units

(52) A force $\vec{F} = (2\hat{\imath} + 4\hat{\jmath})$ N displaces the body by $\vec{s} = (3\hat{\jmath} + 5\hat{k})$ m in 2 s. The power generated in this case is
(a) 2 W
(b) 3 W
(c) 6 W
(d) 5 W

(53) Two forces $\vec{F}_1 = \hat{\imath} - \hat{\jmath} + \hat{k}$ and $\vec{F}_2 = -\hat{\imath} + \hat{\jmath} + 2\hat{k}$ act on a particle while displacing it from the point P (1, 1, 1) to Q (−1, 2, 3). The work done by the net force is
(a) – 6 units
(b) 10 units
(c) 1 unit
(d) – 1 unit

Applications of Cross Product of Vectors

(54) Find the torque of a force $\vec{F} = -3\hat{\imath} + \hat{\jmath} + 5\hat{k}$ acting at the point $\vec{r} = 7\hat{\imath} + 3\hat{\jmath} + \hat{k}$
(a) $-21\hat{\imath} + 3\hat{\jmath} + 5\hat{k}$
(b) $-14\hat{\imath} + 3\hat{\jmath} + 16\hat{k}$
(c) $4\hat{\imath} + 4\hat{\jmath} + 6\hat{k}$
(d) $14\hat{\imath} - 38\hat{\jmath} + 16\hat{k}$

(55) What is the value of linear velocity, if $\vec{\omega} = 3\hat{\imath} - 4\hat{\jmath} + \hat{k}$ and $\vec{r} = 5\hat{\imath} - 6\hat{\jmath} + 6\hat{k}$
(a) $6\hat{\imath} + 2\hat{\jmath} - 3\hat{k}$
(b) $-18\hat{\imath} - 13\hat{\jmath} + 2\hat{k}$
(c) $4\hat{\imath} - 13\hat{\jmath} + 6\hat{k}$
(d) $6\hat{\imath} - 2\hat{\jmath} + 8\hat{k}$

Applications of Differentiation of Vector

(56) The position vector of a particle is $\vec{r} = (a\cos\omega t)\,\hat{\imath} + (a\sin\omega t)\,\hat{\jmath}$. The velocity of the particle is
(a) directed towards the origin
(b) directed away from the origin
(c) parallel to the position vector

(d) perpendicular to the position vector

(57) The position vector $\vec{r}$ of a particle is given by $\vec{r} = (A \sin \omega t)\ \hat{\imath} + (A \cos \omega t)\ \hat{\jmath}$. If $\vec{v}$ is the velocity of the particle then $\vec{v} \cdot \vec{r}$ =
(a) zero
(b) A^2
(c) $A^2\ sin^2\ \omega t$
(d) $A^2\ cos^2\ \omega t$

(58) The position vector of an object at any time t is given by $3\ t^2\ \hat{\imath} + 6t\ \hat{\jmath} + \hat{k}$. Its velocity along y-axis has the magnitude
(a) 6t
(b) 6
(c) 0
(d) 9

Answer

Vector

Topic : Applications of Vector Mathematics in Physics

Q	Ans	Q	Ans	Q	Ans	Q	Ans	Q	Ans
(1)	(a)	**(13)**	(d)	**(25)**	(a)	**(37)**	(b)	**(49)**	(a)
(2)	(a)	**(14)**	(c)	**(26)**	(d)	**(38)**	(a)	**(50)**	(c)
(3)	(c)	**(15)**	(c)	**(27)**	(b)	**(39)**	(a)	**(51)**	(c)
(4)	(c)	**(16)**	(a)	**(28)**	(a)	**(40)**	(c)	**(52)**	(a)
(5)	(a)	**(17)**	(c)	**(29)**	(a)	**(41)**	(b)	**(53)**	(b)
(6)	(c)	**(18)**	(d)	**(30)**	(b)	**(42)**	(d)	**(54)**	(d)
(7)	(d)	**(19)**	(b)	**(31)**	(a)	**(43)**	(c)	**(55)**	(b)
(8)	(b)	**(20)**	(a)	**(32)**	(d)	**(44)**	(d)	**(56)**	(d)
(9)	(b)	**(21)**	(a)	**(33)**	(d)	**(45)**	(a)	**(57)**	(a)
(10)	(d)	**(22)**	(a)	**(34)**	(c)	**(46)**	(a)	**(58)**	(b)
(11)	(c)	**(23)**	(a)	**(35)**	(c)	**(47)**	(a)		
(12)	(d)	**(24)**	(a)	**(36)**	(b)	**(48)**	(d)		

Mechanics - I

Kinematics	
1	**Discussion on Rest & Motion**
2	**Graphical Representation of Motion**

(1) Discussion on Rest & Motion

(1) Rest & Motion	(2) Coordinate System
(3) Frame of Reference	(4) Types of Motion
(5) Position and Change in Position	(6) Concepts of Acceleration
(7) Equations of Uniformly Accelerated Motion in 1D	(8) Motion with variable acceleration

(1) Rest and Motion

(1) Rest :

A particle is said to be at rest if it does not change its position with respect to the surrounding.
Ex : The white board in the classroom is at rest with respect to the classroom.

(2) Motion :

A particle is said to be in motion if it changes its position with respect to the surrounding.
Ex : When we walk, run or ride a bike we are in motion w.r.t. the ground.

(3) Rest and Motion are relative :

Rest and motion depends upon the observer. In one situation an object may be at rest to an observer, whereas the same object may be in motion to another observer.
Ex : The driver of a moving car is in motion with respect to an observer standing on the ground whereas, the same driver is at rest with respect to the man (observer) in the passenger seat.

(4) Point Object :

While studying the motion of an object, sometimes, its dimensions are of no importance. That's why we consider it as point object or particle. It is only a mathematical idealisation.

Therefore, in mechanics, a particle is a geometrical mass point or a material body of negligible dimensions.

(2) Coordinate System

(5) Co-ordinate system :

In geometry, a co-ordinate system is a reference system where number or co-ordinates are used to determine the position of a point or other geometrical element in space.

(5.1) One dimensional Cartesian system :

At any instant of time, the position of a particle in a one dimensional Cartesian system is described by a single co-ordinate x.

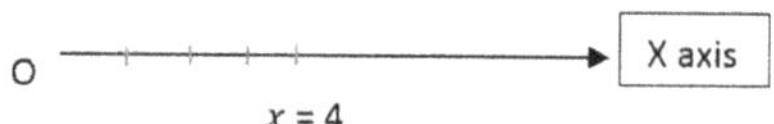

(5.2) Two dimensional Cartesian system :

At any instant of time, the position of a particle in a two dimensional Cartesian system is described by two co-ordinates x and y. They are given as (x, y).

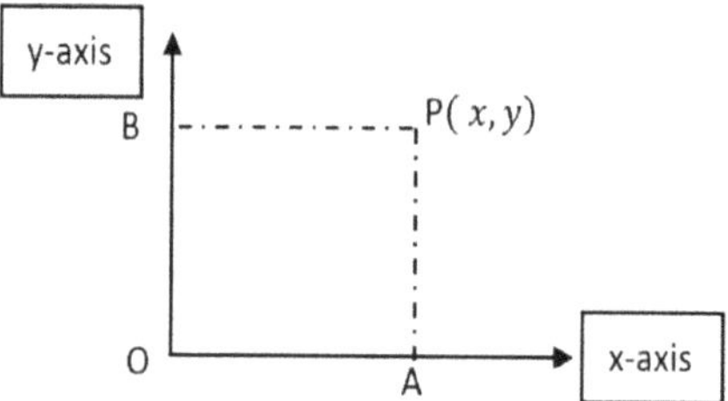

(5.3) Polar co-ordinate System :

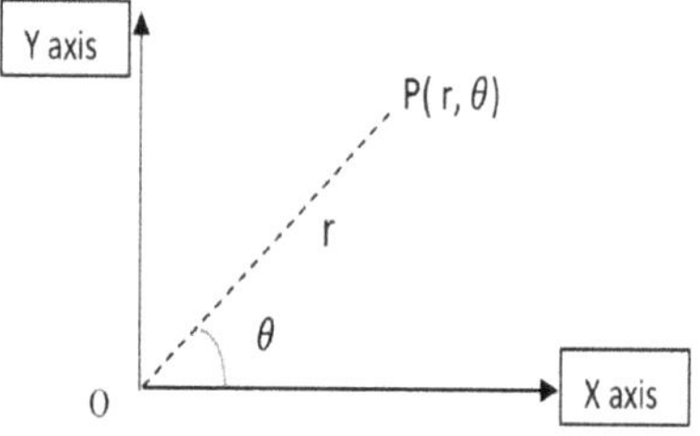

At any instant of time, the position of a particle in a polar co-ordinate system is described by a straight line distance from a reference point (typically the origin or the centre of rotation) and an angle from a reference direction (often counter clockwise from the positive x-axis). These are referred to as the radial and angular coordinates (r, θ).

(5.4) Relation between cartesian and Polar co-ordinate System :

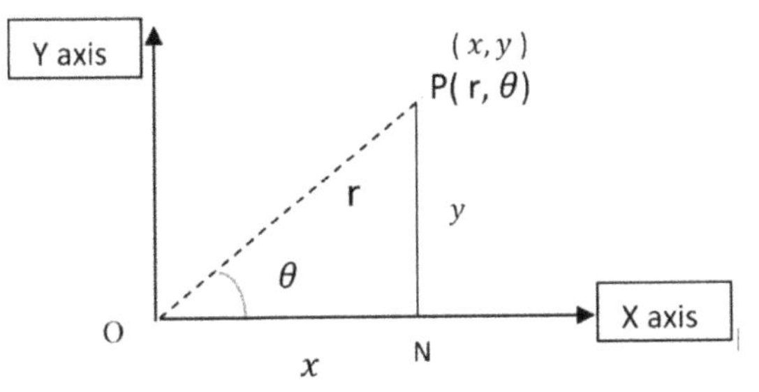

(i) $x = r \cos \theta$

(ii) $y = r \sin \theta$

(iii) $r = \sqrt{x^2 + y^2}$

(iv) $\theta = \tan^{-1}\frac{y}{x}$

(5.5) Three dimensional Cartesian co-ordinate system :

At any instant of time, the position of a particle in a three dimensional Cartesian system is described by three co-ordinates x, y and z. They are given as (x, y, z).

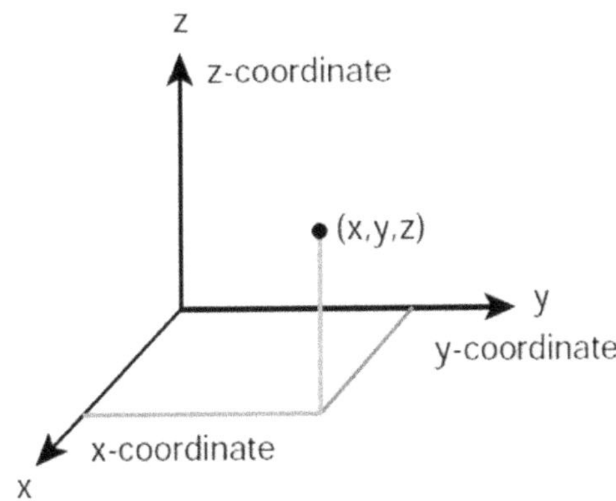

(5.6) Spherical co-ordinate system :

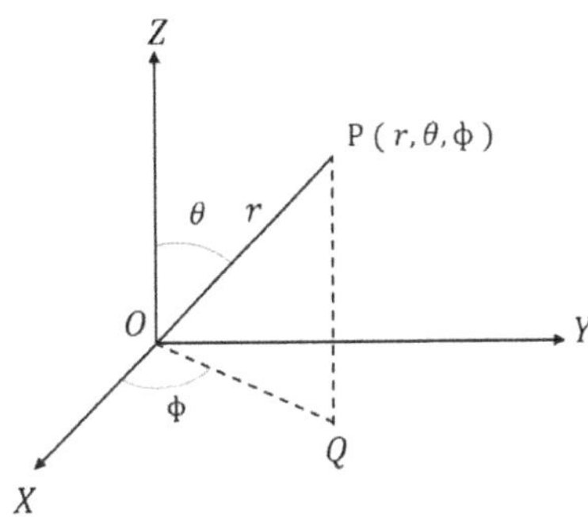

(5.7) Relation between Cartesian and spherical co-ordinate system :

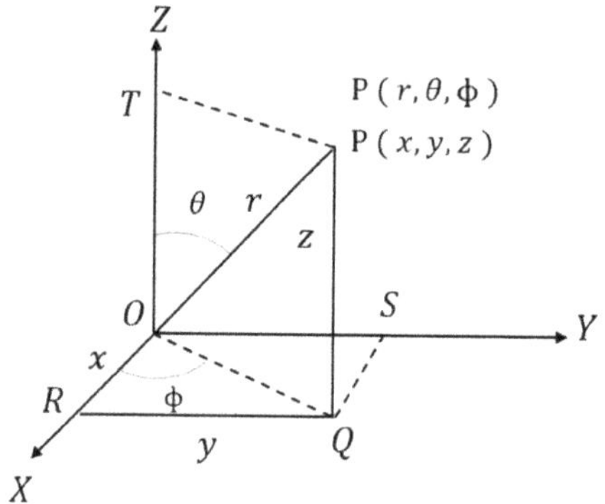

$x = r \sin \theta \cos \Phi$
$y = r \sin \theta \sin \Phi$
$z = r \cos \theta$

(6) Reference body :

A reference body is an object with respect to which the state of rest or motion of an object or particle is described.

If the position of a particle changes w.r.t. the reference body, the particle is in a state of motion and if the position of a particle does not change w.r.t. the reference body, the particle is in a state of rest.

(3) Frame of Reference

(7) Frame of reference :

A frame in which an observer is situated and makes his observations is known as his 'Frame of reference'. A frame of reference is associated with a co-ordinate system and a clock to measure the position and time of events happening in space.

(8) Types of frame of reference :

Frame of reference are of two types:
(a) Inertial frame of reference or, unaccelerated frame of reference or Newtonian frame of reference or Galilean frame of reference.
(b) Non-inertial frame of reference.

(8.1) Inertial frame of reference :

A frame of reference which is at rest or which is moving with a uniform velocity along a straight line is called an inertial frame of reference.

Ideally no inertial frame exist in universe. For practical purpose a frame of reference may be considered as inertial if it's acceleration is negligible with respect to the acceleration of the object to be observed.

Example : The lift at rest, lift moving (up or down) with constant velocity, car moving with constant velocity on a straight road may be considered as an inertial frame of reference. A distant Star may be considered as an inertial frame.

(8.3) Non inertial frame of reference :

A frame of reference which is moving with an acceleration is called an inertial frame of reference.

Example : Car moving in uniform circular motion, lift which is moving upward or downward with some acceleration, plane which is taking off.

(9) Newton's laws of motion holds good in inertial frame of reference. To write the force equation in a non-inertial frame of reference we must have to consider the pseudo force.

(4) Types of Motion

(10) Classification of Motion on the basis of Motion of Particles :

(a) Linear Motion : In linear motion, the particle move from one point to another in either a straight line or a curved path.
Linear motion is divided as follow :
(i) Rectilinear Motion : The path of the motion is straight line
(ii) Curvilinear Motion : The path of the motion is curved.
Example : An person running on a straight track.

(b) Circular Motion : In circular motion, the particle moves along a circular path.
Example : (i) Motion of satellites around planets
(ii) Motion of a car turning to a curved road

(c) Rotational Motion : When a body turns (or spins) about a fixed axis, it is called rotational motion.
Example : Motion of a giant wheel

(d) Periodic Motion : A motion that repeats itself after equal intervals of time is known as periodic motion.
Example : (i) A moving Pendulum
(ii) Hands of Working clock

(11) Classification of Motion on the basis of Positional Reference coordinates of Particles :

(a) One Dimensional Motion : Motion of a particle in a straight line is called one dimensional motion. In one dimensional motion only one coordinate of the position of the particle changes with time.
Example : (I) Motion of car on a straight road.

(ii) Motion of freely falling body.

(b) Two Dimensional Motion : Motion of a particle in a plane is called two dimensional motion. In two dimensional motion two coordinates of the position of a particle changes with.
Example : (i) Motion of car on a circular turn
(ii) Motion of billiards ball.

(c) Three Dimensional Motion : Motion of particle in a space is called three dimensional motion. In three dimensional motion all three coordinates of the position of the particles change with time.
Example : (i) Motion of flying kite.
(ii) Motion of flying insect.

(5) Position and Change in Position

(12) To define the change in position we have two physical quantities : (a) Distance
(b) Displacement

	Distance	Displacement
Definition	Distance is the actual path traversed by the particle during the course of motion.	Displacement is the vector drawn from the initial position of the particle to its final position.
Nature of the quantity	Scalar	Vector
Dimensional formula	[L]	[L]
Unit	m (SI unit)	m (SI unit)

(13) Expression for the displacement and distance in 1D motion :

$(x = 0\,, t = 0)$ (x_1, t_1) (x_2, t_2)

O (origin) P Q

If x_1 and x_2 be the position of a point object at times t_1 and t_2, then distance : $x = x_2 - x_1$
and displacement : $\vec{x} = (x_2 - x_1)\,\hat{\imath}$

Note : In one dimensional motion, distance and magnitude of displacement is equal.

(14) Expression for the displacement in 2D motion :

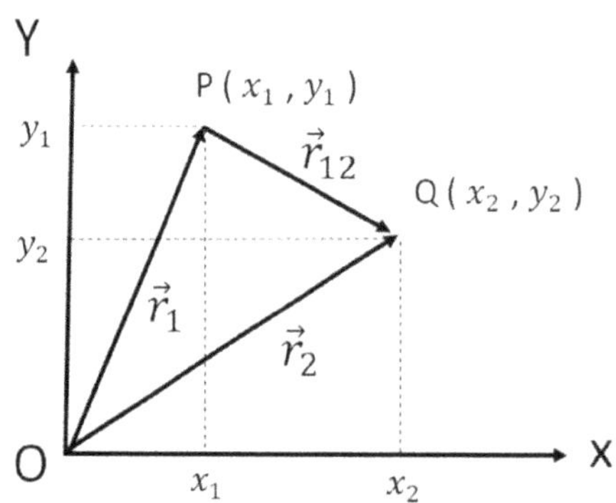

Let us consider, a particle located initially at point P having position vector $\vec{r}_1$. In time interval Δt the particle is moved to the point Q having position vector $\vec{r}_2$.

Displacement of the particle is given by : $\overrightarrow{PQ} = \vec{r}_{12}$ (or $\Delta\vec{r}$) $= \vec{r}_2 - \vec{r}_1$

$$= (x_2\,\hat{\imath} + y_2\hat{\jmath}) - (x_1\hat{\imath} + y_1\hat{\jmath})$$
$$= (x_2 - x_1)\,\hat{\imath} + (y_2 - y_1)\,\hat{\jmath}$$
$$= \Delta x\,\hat{\imath} + \Delta y\,\hat{\jmath}$$

If we take $\Delta t \rightarrow 0$, displacement of the particle takes the form $d\vec{r} = dx\hat{\imath} + dy\,\hat{\jmath} \Longrightarrow$ differential displacement vector

(15) Displacement is a vector quantity. That's why displacement of an object in a given time can be both positive and negative. But distance does not have direction. That's why distance covered by the object in a given time is always positive.

(16) In one dimensional motion, distance and magnitude of displacement is equal, but in two dimensional motion, distance is less than the magnitude of the displacement.
Thus, Distance ≥ | Displacement |

or, $\frac{Distance}{|Displacement\,|} \geq 1$

(17) The displacement of a particle between two points is a unique path, which can take the particle from its initial position to final position. But it does not tell exactly how the object actually moved between those two points.

(18) Distinction between Distance and Displacement :

Distance	Displacement
(i) Distance is the path length traversed by an object in certain time.	(i) Displacement is the vector drawn from the initial position of the particle to its final position.
(ii) It has only the magnitude, that's why it is a scalar quantity.	(ii) It has both magnitude and direction that's why it is a vector quantity.
(iii) It depends on the path followed by the object.	(iii) It does not depend on the path followed by the object.
(iv) Distance is always positive.	(iv) Displacement can be positive or negative depending upon the direction.
(v) Distance can be more than or equal to the magnitude of displacement.	(v) Magnitude of displacement can be less than or equal to the distance, but can never be greater than the distance.

(19) Speed (v):

Definition : The time rate of covering the distance by an object is called speed.

$$\text{Speed } (v) = \frac{\text{Distance}}{Time}$$

Nature of the quantity : Scalar

Dimensional formula : [LT^{-1}]

Unit : m s^{-1} (SI unit)

(20) Instantaneous speed :

It is the speed of a particle at any instant of time.
It is equal to the limiting value of the average speed of the particle in small time interval taken around that instant, when the time interval approaches zero.

$$\therefore\ v = \lim_{\Delta t \to 0} \frac{\Delta x}{\Delta t} = \frac{dx}{dt}$$

(21) Velocity ($\vec{v}$) :

Definition : The time rate of displacement of an object is called velocity of the object.

$$\text{Velocity } (\vec{v}) = \frac{\text{Displacement}}{Time}$$

Nature of the quantity : Vector

Dimensional formula : [LT^{-1}]

Unit : m s^{-1} (SI unit)

(22) Instantaneous velocity :

It is the velocity of a particle at any instant of time.
It is equal to the limiting value of the average velocity of the particle in small time interval taken around that instant, when the time interval approaches zero.

$$\therefore\ \vec{v} = \lim_{\Delta t \to 0} \frac{\Delta \vec{x}}{\Delta t} = \frac{d\vec{x}}{dt}$$

(23) Representation of speed & velocity in 1D

$(x = 0, t = 0)$ (x_1, t_1) (x_2, t_2)

O (origin) P Q

If x_1 and x_2 be the position of a point object at times t_1 and t_2, then the average speed (from t_1 and t_2) is given by : $v_{av} = \frac{x_2 - x_1}{t_2 - t_1} = \frac{\Delta x}{\Delta t}$

and average velocity : $\vec{v}_{av} = \frac{(x_2 - x_1)\hat{\imath}}{t_2 - t_1} = \frac{\Delta x}{\Delta t}\hat{\imath}$

Velocity of an object can be both positive (moving towards right of the origin of position axis), zero (at rest) and negative (moving towards left of the origin of position axis). But speed of an object can only positive and zero.[Speed ≥ 0]
If we take $\Delta t \to 0$, we get instantaneous speed (or, velocity). Therefore,

instantaneous speed : $v = \lim_{\Delta t \to 0} \frac{\Delta x}{\Delta t} = \frac{dx}{dt}$

and instantaneous velocity : $\vec{v} = \lim_{\Delta t \to 0} \frac{\Delta x}{\Delta t}\,\hat{\imath} = \frac{dx}{dt}\,\hat{\imath}$

Mathematically,
(i) *Instantaneous speed of a particle is equal to the first order derivative of its distance w.r.t. time* and
(ii) *Instantaneous velocity of a particle is equal to the first order derivative of its displacement w.r.t. time.*

Again, average velocity : $v_{av} = \frac{x_2 - x_1}{t_2 - t_1}$

or, $x_2 - x_1 = v_{av}(t_2 - t_1)$

$\therefore x_2 = x_1 + v_{av}(t_2 - t_1) \Rightarrow$ **Position – Time Relation**

(24) Representation of Speed & Velocity in 2D

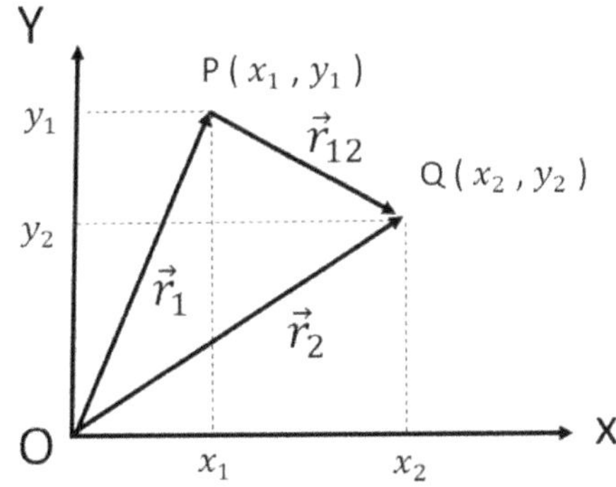

Let us consider, a particle located initially at point P having position vector $\vec{r}_1$. In time interval Δt the particle is moved to the point Q having position vector $\vec{r}_2$.

Displacement of the particle is given by : $\overrightarrow{PQ} = \vec{r}_{12}$ (or $\Delta\vec{r}$) $= \vec{r}_2 - \vec{r}_1$

$$= (x_2\,\hat{\imath} + y_2\hat{\jmath}) - (x_1\hat{\imath} + y_1\hat{\jmath})$$
$$= (x_2 - x_1)\,\hat{\imath} + (y_2 - y_1)\,\hat{\jmath}$$
$$= \Delta x\,\hat{\imath} + \Delta y\,\hat{\jmath}$$

If the particle takes Δt time for this displacement then, average velocity [It is defined as ratio of the displacement vector to the corresponding time interval] of the particle is given by :

$$\vec{v}_{av} = \frac{\Delta\vec{r}}{\Delta t}$$
$$= \frac{\Delta x\,\hat{\imath} + \Delta y\,\hat{\jmath}}{\Delta t}$$
$$= \frac{\Delta x}{\Delta t}\,\hat{\imath} + \frac{\Delta y}{\Delta t}\,\hat{\jmath}$$
$$= (v_{av})_x\,\hat{\imath} + (v_{av})_y\,\hat{\jmath}$$

Where, $(v_{av})_x$ = x component of the average velocity and $(v_{av})_y$ = y component of the average velocity
If we take $\Delta t \to 0$, displacement of the particle takes the form $d\vec{r} = dx\,\hat{\imath} + dy\,\hat{\jmath}$

If we take $\Delta t \to 0$, we get instantaneous velocity (or, simply velocity). Therefore, instantaneous velocity :

$$\vec{v} = \lim_{\Delta t \to 0} \frac{\Delta \vec{r}}{\Delta t}$$
$$= \frac{d\vec{r}}{dt}$$
$$= \frac{dx}{dt}\,\hat{\imath} + \frac{dy}{dt}\,\hat{\jmath}$$
$$= v_x\,\hat{\imath} + v_y\,\hat{\jmath}$$

Where, $v_x = \frac{dx}{dt}$ = x component of the velocity and $v_y = \frac{dy}{dt}$ = y component of the velocity

In this situation, the magnitude of velocity is called speed and is given by $|\vec{v}| = \sqrt{v_x^2 + v_y^2}$

(25) Uniform speed or constant speed :

When a particle covers equal distances in equal intervals of time, (no matter how small the intervals are) then it is said to be moving with uniform speed.

(26) Non-uniform speed or variable speed :

When a particle covers unequal distances in equal intervals of time, then it is said to be moving with non-uniform speed.

(27) Uniform velocity :

When a particle covers equal displacement in equal intervals of time, then it is said to be moving with uniform velocity.
Or, A particle is said to be moving with uniform velocity of constant velocity if the magnitude and direction of the velocity do not change with time.

(28) Variable Velocity or non-uniform velocity :

A particle is said to be moving with variable velocity if magnitude of the velocity changes or direction of motion changes or both changes with time.

(29) When a moving particle returns to its initial point :

(a) Displacement is zero.
(b) Average velocity is zero.
(c) Distance is NOT zero.
(d) Average Speed is NOT zero.

(30) Facts about uniform velocity :

(a) It is on a straight line path and always in the same direction.
(b) Magnitude of velocity is constant and it is equal to speed.
(c) Average velocity is equal to instantaneous velocity.
(d) Since velocity remains constant, acceleration is zero.
(e) Magnitude of displacement is equal to the actual distance travelled by the particle.
(f) Resultant force or net force acting on the particle is zero.

(31) Distinction between speed and velocity :

Speed	Velocity
(i) It is the distance travelled by a particle per unit time in any direction.	(i) The time rate of displacement of an object is called velocity of the particle.
(ii) It has only the magnitude, that's why it is a scalar quantity.	(ii) It has both magnitude and direction that's why it is a vector quantity.
(iii) Speed of a moving particle is always positive.	(iii) Velocity can be positive or negative depending upon the direction of motion.

(6) Concepts of Acceleration

(32) Non-Uniform Motion

An object is said to be moving with non-uniform motion if its velocity changes with time.
In non-uniform motion, velocity of a particle changes and the particle is said to be possessed acceleration.

(33) Acceleration ($\vec{a}$)

Definition : The time rate of change of velocity of an object is called acceleration of the object.

$$\text{Acceleration } (\vec{a}) = \frac{\textbf{Change in Velocity}}{Time}$$

Nature of the quantity : It is a vector quantity. Its direction is same as that of **change in velocity** (not of the velocity)

Dimensional formula : $[\mathrm{LT}^{-2}]$

Unit : $\mathrm{m\ s}^{-2}$ (SI unit)

(34) Possible Ways of Velocity Change

(a) When only direction of velocity changes, acceleration is perpendicular to velocity.
Ex : Uniform circular motion
(b) When only magnitude of velocity changes, acceleration is parallel or anti-parallel to velocity.
Ex : Motion under gravity
(c) When both magnitude and direction of velocity changes, acceleration has two components one is perpendicular to velocity and another parallel or anti-parallel to velocity
Ex : Projectile motion

(35) Average acceleration :

For an object moving with variable velocity, the average acceleration is defined by the ratio of the total change in velocity to the time taken to undergo this change.

$$\therefore \vec{a}_{av} = \frac{\Delta\vec{v}}{\Delta t}$$

(36) Instantaneous acceleration :

Instantaneous acceleration is the acceleration at any instant of time.
It is equal to the limiting value of the average acceleration of the particle in small time interval taken around that instant, when the time interval approaches zero.

$$\therefore \vec{a} = \lim_{\Delta t \to 0} \frac{\Delta\vec{v}}{\Delta t} = \frac{d\vec{v}}{dt}$$

(37) Representation of acceleration in 1D

$(x = 0, t = 0)$ (v_1, t_1) (v_2, t_2)

O (origin) P Q

While dealing the motion between the points P and Q,
Change in velocity $= v_2 - v_1 = \Delta v$
and time $= t_2 - t_1 = \Delta t$
Therefore, average acceleration $a_{av} = \frac{\Delta v}{\Delta t}$

If we take $\Delta t \to 0$, we get instantaneous acceleration.
Therefore, instantaneous acceleration : $a = \lim_{\Delta t \to 0} \frac{\Delta v}{\Delta t} = \frac{dv}{dt}$

Mathematically, ***Instantaneous acceleration of a particle is equal to the first order derivative of its velocity w.r.t. time or second order derivative of position w.r.t. time.***

(38) Representation of acceleration in 2D

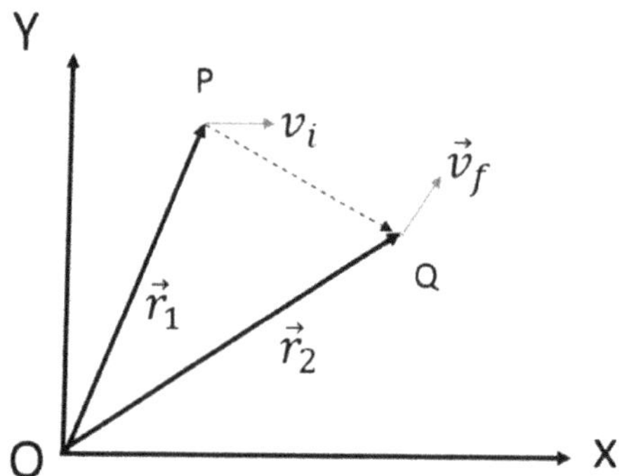

Let us consider, the velocity of the particle at P and Q be $\vec{v}_1$ and $\vec{v}_2$ respectively.
Change in velocity of the particle is given by: $\Delta\vec{v} = \vec{v}_2 - \vec{v}_1$

or, $\Delta\vec{v} = (v_{x2}\,\hat{i} + v_{y2}\hat{j}) - (v_{x1}\hat{i} + v_{y1}\hat{j})$

or, $\Delta\vec{v} = (v_{x2} - v_{x1})\,\hat{i} + (v_{y2} - v_{y1})\,\hat{j}$

or, $\Delta\vec{v} = \Delta v_x\,\hat{i} + v_y\,\hat{j}$

If the particle takes Δt time for this change then, average acceleration [It is defined as ratio of the change in velocity to the corresponding time interval] of the particle is given by :

$\vec{a}_{av} = \frac{\Delta \vec{v}}{\Delta t}$

or, $\vec{a}_{av} = \frac{\Delta v_x \hat{\imath} + v_y \hat{\jmath}}{\Delta t}$

or, $\vec{a}_{av} = \frac{\Delta v_x}{\Delta t} \hat{\imath} + \frac{\Delta v_y}{\Delta t} \hat{\jmath}$

or, $\vec{a}_{av} = (a_{av})_x \hat{\imath} + (a_{av})_y \hat{\jmath}$

Where, $(a_{av})_x$ = x component of the average acceleration and $(a_{av})_y$ = y component of the average acceleration

For $\Delta t \rightarrow 0$, we get instantaneous acceleration (or, simply acceleration).

Therefore, instantaneous acceleration $\vec{a} = \lim_{\Delta t \to 0} \frac{\Delta \vec{v}}{\Delta t}$

or, $\vec{a} = \frac{d\vec{v}}{dt}$

or, $\vec{a} = \frac{dv_x}{dt} \hat{\imath} + \frac{dv_y}{dt} \hat{\jmath}$

or, $\vec{a} = a_x \hat{\imath} + a_y \hat{\jmath}$

Where, $a_x = \frac{dv_x}{dt}$ = x component of the acceleration and $a_y = \frac{dv_y}{dt}$ = y component of the acceleration

The magnitude of acceleration is given by $a = \sqrt{a_x^2 + a_y^2}$

(39) If the velocity of a particle increases, the acceleration is said to positive. If the velocity of the particle decreases w.r.t. time the acceleration is said to be negative and it is referred as retardation or deceleration. Decreasing acceleration is **NOT** called retardation.

(40) Uniform acceleration :

The acceleration is said to be uniform or constant when equal changes in velocity takes place in equal intervals of time.

(41) Non-uniform acceleration Or Variable Acceleration :

The acceleration is said to be non-uniform or variable when change in velocity is not same in the same intervals of time.

(42) For motion in one dimension, the velocity and acceleration are always along the same line either in same direction (for accelerated motion) or in opposite direction (for decelerated motion).
But for motion in two or three dimensions, the angle between velocity and acceleration vector may have any value between 0° to 180°.

(43) The rate of change of acceleration with time can be defined but it is not important to mechanics. It is because, the basic laws of motion involve only acceleration and the quantity- the rate of change of acceleration is not required at all. Galileo and Newton discovered that to understand and explain motion, it is enough to define velocity (rate of change of position) and acceleration (rate of change of velocity).

(7) Equations of Uniformly Accelerated Motion in 1D

[1] Acceleration (a) = constant

[2] Velocity –time relation : $v_f = v_i + at$

[3] Position – time relation : $s = v_i t + \frac{1}{2} a t^2$

[4] Velocity – displacement relation : $v_f{}^2 = v_i{}^2 + 2a\,s$

[5] Displacement in the tth second of motion : $s_t = v_i + \frac{1}{2}a\,(2t - 1)$

[These equations are **NOT** to be used in the case of **variable acceleration**]

v_i = initial velocity
a = uniform acceleration
s = distance travelled in time t
v_f = final velocity
s_t = distance covered during t^th^ second of motion

PROOF:

Proof of $v_f = v_i + at$:

Let us consider, the initial velocity of a particle is v_i and its velocity after time t is v_f. (Where, $v_f > v_i$)

∴ Change in velocity in time t = $v_f - v_i$

∴ Rate of change of velocity with time

$$= \frac{v_f - v_i}{t}$$

By definition,

Acceleration (a) = Rate of change in velocity

or, $a = \frac{v_f - v_i}{t}$

or, $v_f - v_i = at$

∴ $v_f = v_i + at$

Proof of $s = v_i t + \frac{1}{2}a\,t^2$:

Let us consider, the initial velocity of a particle is v_i and its velocity after time t is v_f. (Where, $v_f > v_i$)
We know that, $v_f = v_i + at$
Where, a = acceleration of the particle

The average velocity of the particle for the time t = $\frac{v_f + v_i}{2}$

∴ Distance travelled by the particle in time t is given by :

s = Average velocity × Time

$= \frac{v_f + v_i}{2} \times t$

Putting $v_f = v_i + a\,t$ we get,

$s = \frac{v_i + at + v_i}{2} \times t$

∴ $s = v_i t + \frac{1}{2}a\,t^2$

Proof of $v_f{}^2 = v_i{}^2 + 2\,a\,s$:

Let us consider, the initial velocity of a particle is v_i and its velocity after time t is v_f. (Where, $v_f > v_i$)
We know that, $v_f = v_i + at$
Where, a = acceleration of the particle

Squaring both sides, we get

$v_f{}^2 = (v_i + at)^2$

or, $v_f{}^2 = v_i{}^2 + 2\,v_i\,at + a^2 t^2$

or, $v_f{}^2 = v_i{}^2 + 2\,a\,(v_i t + \frac{1}{2}a\,t^2)$

∴ $v_f{}^2 = v_i{}^2 + 2\,a\,s$

Proof of $s_t = v_i + \frac{1}{2}a\,(2t - 1)$:

Let us consider, the initial velocity of a particle is v_i and its velocity after time t is v_f. (Where, $v_f > v_i$)

Distance travelled by the particle in time t is given by $s = v_i t + \frac{1}{2} a t^2$
Where, a = acceleration of the particle

But the distance covered during t^{th} second of motion is given by

S_t = Distance covered in t second – Distance covered in (t – 1) second

$= v_i t + \frac{1}{2} a t^2 - [v_i (t-1) + \frac{1}{2} a (t-1)^2]$

$= v_i t + \frac{1}{2} a t^2 - v_i t + v_i - \frac{1}{2} a (t^2 - 2t + 1)$

$= v_i t + \frac{1}{2} a t^2 - v_i t + v_i - \frac{1}{2} a t^2 + at - \frac{1}{2} a$

$= v_i + at - \frac{1}{2} a$

$= v_i + \frac{1}{2} a (2t - 1)$

Points to Remember

(1) If a body starts from rest and moves with uniform acceleration then distance covered by the body in t s is proportional to t^2 (i.e. $s \propto t^2$). So the ratio of distance covered in 1 s, 2 s and 3 s is $1^2 : 2^2 : 3^2$ or 1 : 4 : 9.

Proof : The distance covered during t second of motion is given by $s = v_i t + \frac{1}{2} a t^2$
If a body starts from rest, then $v_i = 0$

Therefore, the distance covered in 1 s, 2 s and 3 s are respectively

$s_1 = 0 + \frac{1}{2} a (1)^2 = \frac{1}{2} a$

$s_2 = 0 + \frac{1}{2} a (2)^2 = \frac{4}{2} a$

and $s_3 = 0 + \frac{1}{2} a (3)^2 = \frac{9}{2} a$

$\therefore s_1 : s_2 : s_3 = \frac{1}{2} a : \frac{4}{2} a : \frac{9}{2} a = 1 : 4 : 9$

(2) If a body starts from rest and moves with uniform acceleration then distance covered by the body in t^{th} s is proportional to (2t – 1) [i.e. $s_t \propto (2t - 1)$] So the ratio of distance covered in I s, II s and III s is 1 : 3 : 5.

Proof : The distance covered during t^{th} second of motion is given by :

$$s_t = v_i + \frac{1}{2} a (2t - 1)$$

If a body starts from rest, then $v_i = 0$

Therefore, the distance covered in 1st s, 2nd s and 3rd s are respectively

$s_1 = 0 + \frac{1}{2} a (2 - 1) = \frac{1}{2} a$

$s_2 = 0 + \frac{1}{2} a (2 \times 2 - 1) = \frac{3}{2} a$

and $s_3 = 0 + \frac{1}{2} a (2 \times 3 - 1) = \frac{5}{2} a$

$\therefore s_1 : s_2 : s_3 = \frac{1}{2} a : \frac{3}{2} a : \frac{5}{2} a = 1 : 3 : 5$

(3) Stopping Distance of Vehicles :

When breaks are applied to a moving vehicles, the distance it travels before stopping is called stopping distance. Stopping distance is an important factor for road safety. It depends upon the initial velocity and breaking capacity, or deceleration ' a ' that is caused by the breaking.
Stopping distance is an important factor considered in setting speed limits, for example in school zones.

A body moving with a velocity v is stopped by application of brakes after covering a distance s.

From $v_f{}^2 = v_i{}^2 + 2 a s$ we get

$0 = v^2 - 2 a s$

or, $s = \frac{v^2}{2a}$

$\therefore s \propto v^2$ [since a = constant]

If the same body moves with velocity nv and same braking force is applied on it then it will come to rest after covering a distance of n^2s. So we can say that if v becomes n times then s becomes n^2 times that of previous value.

(8) Motion with Variable Acceleration

When acceleration of particle is not uniform or constant, we go for basic equations of velocity and acceleration, i.e. (1) Velocity : $\vec{v} = \frac{d\vec{r}}{dt}$

(2) Acceleration : $\vec{a} = \frac{d\vec{v}}{dt}$

Problems of non-uniform accelerated motion can be solved either by differentiation or integration (with some boundary conditions)

$$\textbf{Displacement} \xrightarrow{differentiation} \textbf{Velocity} \xrightarrow{differentiation} \textbf{Acceleration}$$

$$\textbf{Acceleration} \xrightarrow{integration} \textbf{Velocity} \xrightarrow{integration} \textbf{Displacement}$$

For one dimensional motion, If acceleration is a function of time then, a = f(t)

$$\text{or, } \frac{dv}{dt} = f(t)$$

$$\text{or, } dv = f(t)\,dt$$

$$\therefore v = \int_{t_1}^{t_2} f(t)dt$$

If acceleration is a function of distance, then $a = f(x)$

$$\text{or, } v\frac{dv}{dx} = f(x)$$

$$\text{or, } v\,dv = f(x)\,dx$$

$$\therefore \int_{v_1}^{v_2} v\,dv = \int_{t_1}^{t_2} f(x)dx$$

If acceleration is a function of velocity, $a = f(v)$ then $t = \int_u^v \frac{dv}{f(v)}$ and $x = x_0 + \int_u^v \frac{v dv}{f(v)}$

Questions & Answers : Discussion on Rest & Motion

Question : When does a cyclist appear to be stationary with respect to another cyclist ?

Answer : A cyclist appears to be stationary w.r.t. another cyclist when both cyclist have the same velocity, i.e., the same speed and direction.

Question : State in the following cases, whether the motion is one, two or three dimensional:
(I) a kite flying on a windy day
(ii) a speeding car on a long straight highway
(iii) a carrom coin rebounding from the side of the board
(iv) an insect crawling on a globe
and (v) a planet revolving around its star

Answer : (i) Three dimensional
(ii) One dimensional
(iii) Two dimensional
(iv) Two dimensional
(v) Two dimensional

Question : Can the earth be regarded as point object when it is describing its yearly journey around the sun ?

Answer : Yes, the earth can be regarded as a point object when describing its yearly journey around the sun because size of the earth is much smaller than the distance from the sun.

Question : Name the physical quantity that essentially varies as a body moves.

Answer : The physical quantity that essentially varies as a body moves is its position.

Question : **What does the odometer of an automobile measure ?**

Answer : The odometer of an automobile measures the total distance travelled by the vehicle.

Question : When is the magnitude of displacement equal to the distance?

Answer : The magnitude of displacement is equal to distance if the motion of the body is in a fixed direction.

Question : Can displacement be zero even if distance is not zero ? Give one example to explain your answer.

Answer : Yes, displacement can be zero even when the distance is not zero, especially when the body returns to the starting point.
For example, when a body is thrown vertically upwards from a point A on the ground, after sometime it comes back to the same point A. The displacement of the body is zero, but the distance travelled by it is not zero.

Question : Can speed of a body be negative ?

Answer : No, speed of a body can never be negative because speed is defined as the distance travelled per unit time and distance can never be negative.

Question : What does the speedometer of a car measure ?

Answer : The speedometer of a car measures the instantaneous speed.

Question : **When is the instantaneous speed same as the average speed ?**

Answer : The instantaneous speed is equal to the average speed when the body moves with uniform speed, i.e. the speed does not change with time.

Question : Which quantity speed or velocity gives the direction of motion of the body ?

Answer : Velocity gives the direction of motion of a body because it is a vector quantity, having both magnitude and direction whereas speed is a scalar quantity and it has no direction.

Question : What does the path of an object look like when it is in uniform motion?

Answer : When an object is in uniform motion, it moves with constant speed in a straight line, so its path is a straight line.

Question : When is the average speed of an object equal to the magnitude of its average velocity ? Give reason also.

Answer : The average speed of an object equal to the magnitude of its average velocity when an object moves along a straight line without changing its direction, i.e. when the total distance travelled is equal to the displacement.

Question :What is the numerical ratio of average velocity to average speed of an object when it is moving along a straight path ?

Solution : The numerical ratio of average velocity to average speed is 1 when the object is moving along a straight path.

Question : Give an example of motion in which average velocity is zero, but the average speed is not zero.

Answer : When a body returns to its starting point, its average velocity is zero (since displacement = 0), but its average speed is not zero (since distance $\neq 0$).
For example, a boy walks one complete round on a circular track, its average velocity is zero but average speed is not zero.

Question : Can a body have a constant speed but a varying velocity?

Answer : Yes, when a body moves along a circular path with uniform angular speed, it possesses constant speed but a varying velocity.

Question : Can a particle in one dimensional motion have zero speed and non-zero velocity ?

Answer : No, a particle in one-dimensional motion cannot have zero speed and nonzero velocity. If the speed is zero, the velocity will be necessarily zero.

Question : Under what condition is the average velocity is equal to the instantaneous velocity ?

Answer : When an object moves with constant velocity, its average velocity over any time interval is equal to the instantaneous velocity.

Question : When a stone is thrown vertically upwards its velocity is continuously decreases. Why ?

Answer : When a stone is thrown vertically upwards its velocity is continuously decreases because gravity acts downwards, opposing the upward motion and causing a constant downward acceleration.

Question : Can a body have zero velocity and still be accelerating ?
Or, Give example : An object with a constant acceleration but with zero velocity

Answer : Yes, A body can have acceleration and zero velocity at a particular instant.
For example, a body thrown vertically upwards has zero velocity at its highest point but has acceleration equal to the acceleration due to gravity.

Question : Can an object have an eastward velocity while experiencing a westward acceleration ?

Answer : Yes, an object can have an eastward velocity while experiencing a westward acceleration.
For example, a pendulum oscillating in east-west direction will have eastward velocity and westward acceleration in half cycle of its oscillation.

Question : Can the direction of velocity of an object change, when acceleration is constant ?

Answer : Yes, the direction of velocity of an object change, even if acceleration is constant.
For example, an object thrown vertically upwards, the direction of velocity changes during its rise and fall, but acceleration acts always downwards and remains constant.

Question : Is it possible for an object to be accelerated without speeding up or slowing down ? If so, give an example?

Answer : Yes, an object can be accelerated without changing its speed, as long as its direction of motion changes.
For example, an object in uniform circular motion is accelerating but its speed neither decreases nor increases.

Question : Is the direction of acceleration same as the direction of velocity ?

Answer : The direction of acceleration is not necessarily same as the direction of velocity. If the velocity increases, acceleration acts in the direction of velocity and if velocity decreases, acceleration acts in the opposite direction of velocity.

Question : Which of the two velocity and acceleration, gives the direction of motion of the body?

Answer : It is the velocity and not the acceleration, which gives the direction of motion of the body. When a body is projected upward, both its direction of motion and velocity are in upward direction but the acceleration is in the downward direction.

Give an example : An object moving in a certain direction with acceleration in the perpendicular direction

Answer : When an object moves in a circular path with constant speed, the velocity of the object is always tangent to the circular path but the acceleration is always directed toward the centre of the circle along the radius. So, the acceleration is perpendicular to the velocity at every point on the path.

Question : Is it possible for an object to move with acceleration but have uniform velocity ? If yes, give an example.

Answer : No, it is not possible for an object to have acceleration and uniform velocity at the same time.

Exercise | | Subjective Questions — Kinematics

(1) When a body is said to be at rest ? (1)

(2) When a body is said to be in motion ? (1)

(3) When does a cyclist appear to be stationary with respect to another cyclist ? (1)

(4) State in the following cases, whether the motion is one, two or three dimensional: (2)
(i) a kite flying on a windy day
(ii) a speeding car on a long straight highway
(iii) a carrom coin rebounding from the side of the board
(iv) an insect crawling on a globe
and (v) a planet revolving around its star

(5) Can the earth be regarded as point object when it is describing its yearly journey around the sun ? (1)

(6) Name the physical quantity that essentially varies as a body moves. (1)

(7) What does the odometer of an automobile measure ? (1)

(8) Name the device that is fitted in automobile to show the distance travelled by them. (1)

(9) Define displacement. State its unit. (2)

(10) When is the magnitude of displacement equal to the distance ? (1)

(11) An object has moved through a distance. Can it have zero displacement ? If yes, support your answer with an example. (2)

(12) Which of the following is true for displacement ?
(a) It cannot be zero.
(b) Its magnitude is greater than the distance travelled by the object.

(13) Define speed. Mention its dimensional formula. (2)

(14) Can speed of a body be negative ? (1)

(15) What does the speedometer of a car measure ? (1)

(16) When is the instantaneous speed same as the average speed ? (1)

(17) Define velocity. State its unit. (2)

(18) Which quantity speed or velocity gives the direction of motion of the body ? (1)
Or, Which of the two velocity and acceleration, gives the direction of motion of the body?
Or, Which of the quantity, velocity or acceleration determines the direction of motion ? (1)

(19) What does the path of an object look like when it is in uniform motion? (1)

(20) Under what condition(s) is the magnitude of the average velocity of an object equal to its average speed.

Or, When is the average speed of an object equal to the magnitude of its average velocity ? Give reason also. (1)

(21) What is the numerical ratio of average velocity to average speed of an object when it is moving along a straight path ? (1)

(22) Give an example of motion in which average velocity is zero, but the average speed is not zero. (1)

(23) Can a body have a constant speed but a varying velocity? (1)

(24) Can a particle in one dimensional motion have zero speed and non-zero velocity ? (1)

(25) Under what condition is the average velocity is equal to the instantaneous velocity ? (1)

(26) When a stone is thrown vertically upwards its velocity is continuously decreases. Why ? (1)

(27) Distinguish between speed and velocity. (2)

(28) Define acceleration. State its SI unit. (2)

(29) Name the physical quantity whose SI units are given below : $\mathrm{m\ s^{-1}}$ and $\mathrm{m\ s^{-2}}$ (1)

(30) When will you say a body is in (a) uniform acceleration and (b) non-uniform acceleration? (2)

(31) Can a body have zero velocity and still be accelerating ?

(32) Can an object have an eastward velocity while experiencing a westward acceleration ?

(33) Can the direction of velocity of an object change, when acceleration is constant ?

(34) Is it possible for an object to be accelerated without speeding up or slowing down ? If so, give an example?

(35) Is the direction of acceleration same as the direction of velocity ?

(36) Define the term acceleration due to gravity. State its average value ? (2)

(37) State the type of motion shown by a freely falling stone. (1)

(38) State which of the following situations are possible and give an example for each of these.
(a) An object with a constant acceleration but with zero velocity
(b) An object moving in a certain direction with acceleration in the perpendicular direction
(c) An object moving with acceleration but with uniform speed.

(39) Write the three equations of uniformly accelerated motion. Give the meaning of symbol which occurs in them. (2)

(40) Derive the formula : $v = u + at$, where the symbols have usual meanings. (2)

(41) For constant acceleration derive the formula : $s = ut + \frac{1}{2}at^2$, where the symbols have usual meanings.

(42) Derive the following equation of motion : $v^2 = u^2 + 2\,a\,s$, where the symbols have their usual meanings. (2)

Solved Examples & Exercise : Discussion on Rest & Motion

On Distance & Displacement in 1D

Problem : The position of a particle going along a straight line is x = 30 m at 10.25 am and x = 45 m at 10.30 am. Find the displacement between 10.25 am to 10.30 am.

Solution : Here, x_1 = 30 m and x_2 = 45 m

Hence, Displacement (r) = $x_2 - x_1$ = (45 – 30) m = 15 m

Try Yourself

---

(1) A car moves 120 m due east and then 30 m due west. (a) What is the distance covered by the car ? (b) What is its displacement ?

On Distance & Displacement in 2D

Problem : A Jogger jogs along one length and breadth of a rectangle park. If the dimension of the park are 100 m × 80 m, then find the distance and displacement of the jogger.

Solution : The distance travelled by the jogger (d) = (100 + 80) m = 180 m

Displacement of the jogger (r) = $\sqrt{100^2 + 80^2}$ m

= $\sqrt{100^2 + 80^2}$ m = 20 $\sqrt{41}$ m

Try Yourself

---

(2) A person walks along the sides of a square field. Each of the side is 100 m long. What is the maximum magnitude of displacement of the person in any time interval.

(3) A body moves in a circular path of radius 20 m. If it complete two and half revolutions along the circular path then find distance and displacement of the body.

(4) The x and y components of a position vector $\vec{r}$ have numerical values 3 and 4 respectively. Find the magnitude and direction of $\vec{r}$.

(5) An object moves from positions (6, 8) to (12, 11) in the x-y plane. Find the magnitude and direction of displacement.

On Average speed & Average velocity in 1D

Problem : A train is running with a uniform velocity 6 m s^{-1}. How far will it go in 10 minutes?

Solution : Here, v = 6 m s^{-1}
and time t = 10 min = 600 s

Hence, s = vt

= 6 × 600 m

= 3600 m = 3.6 km

Try Yourself

---

(6) If a particle is at x_1 = 10 m at t_1 = 2 s and at x_2 = 6 m at t_2 = 4 s, find its displacement and average velocity for this time interval.

(7) A man runs 200 m in first 25 s and then turns back and runs 100 m in next 15 s towards the starting point. Find out his average velocity and his average speed.

(8) A body travels a distance x_1 with velocity v_1 and a distance x_2 with velocity v_2 in the same direction. What is the average velocity of the body?

Problem : A bicyclist is travelling along a straight road for the first half time with speed v_1 and for the second half time with speed v_2. What is the average speed of the bicyclist ?

Solution : Let us consider, the total time be $2t$.

∴ Total distance travelled by the bicyclist (d) = $v_1 t + v_2 t = t\,(v_1 + v_2)$

Hence, the average speed $v_{av} = \frac{t\,(v_1+v_2)}{2t} = \frac{v_1+v_2}{2}$

Try Yourself

---

(9) A person travels along a straight road for the first $\frac{t}{3}$ time with a speed v_1 and for next $\frac{2t}{3}$ time with a speed v_2 Then calculate the mean speed of the person.

Problem : A person travels along a straight road due east for the first half distance with speed v_1 and second half distance with speed v_2. What is the average speed of the person?

Solution : Let us consider, $2x$ be the total distance travelled by the person.

∴ Total time taken t = $\frac{x}{v_1} + \frac{x}{v_2} = x\,(\frac{v_1+v_2}{v_1 v_2})$

Hence, the average speed $v_{av} = \frac{2x}{x\,(\frac{v_1+v_2}{v_1 v_2})} = \frac{2\,v_1 v_2}{v_1+v_2}$

Try Yourself

---

(10) A motor car travels half the distance between two paces with a speed of 40 km h^{-1} and the next half with a speed of 60 km h^{-1}. What is the average speed of the car ?

(11) A particle travels equal distances d each at speeds v_1, v_2, v_3 and v_n respectively; then find average speed of the particle.

(12) A particle moves along x-axis with speed 6 m s^{-1} for the first half distance of a journey and the second half distance with a speed 3 m s^{-1}. Calculate the average speed in the total journey.

(13) A particle traversed half the distance with a velocity v_0. The remaining part of the distance was covered with a velocity v_1 for half the time and with a velocity v_2 for the other half of the time. Find the mean velocity of the particle over the while time of motion.

On Average speed & Average velocity in 2D

Problem : The position of an object changes from $\vec{r_1}$ = (2 î + ĵ) m to $\vec{r_2}$ = (4 î + 3 ĵ) m in 2 s. Finds its average velocity.

Solution : Initial position vector $\vec{r_1}$ = (2 î + ĵ) m

and final position vector $\vec{r_2}$ = (4 î + 3 ĵ) m

∴ Displacement of the object $\vec{r} = \vec{r_2} - \vec{r_1}$

$= [(4\hat{i} + 3\hat{j}) - (2\hat{i} + \hat{j})]$ m

$= 2\hat{i} + 2\hat{j} = 2 (\hat{i} + \hat{j})$ m

Now the velocity of the object : $\vec{v} = \frac{2 (\hat{i} + \hat{j})}{2}$

$= (\hat{i} + \hat{j}) \text{ m s}^{-1}$

Try Yourself

(14) The position of an object changes from $\vec{r_1} = (5\hat{i} + \hat{j})$ m to $\vec{r_2} = (3\hat{i} + 4\hat{j})$ m in 2 s. Find the magnitude of its average velocity.

(15) A particle moves in xy plane from positions (2 m, 4 m) to (6 m, 8 m) in 2 s. Find the magnitude and direction of average velocity.

On Instantaneous Speed, Instantaneous Velocity and Instantaneous Acceleration (1D)

Problem : The position of a particle moving along x axis is given by s = (2 t + 3 t^2) m. Calculate the instantaneous velocity of the particle at t = 2 s.

Solution : Given, s = (2 t + 3 t^2) m

Instantaneous velocity : $v = \frac{ds}{dt}$

$= \frac{d}{dt} (2t + 3t^2)$

$= 2 + 6t$

∴ Instantaneous velocity of the particle at t = 2 s is given by : v = 2 + 6 × 2 = 14 m s^{-1}

Try Yourself

(16) The position of a ball dropped from rest a cliff is given by x = 16 t^2, where, x is in meters measured downwards from the original position at t = 0 and t is in seconds. Find the velocity at some time t_0.

(17) Find the acceleration of the particle when displacement equation is 3s = 9t + $5t^2$.

(18) The position of a particle moving along x axis is given by x = (2 – t + 3 t^2) m. Calculate the instantaneous velocity of the particle at t = 2 s.

(19) The distance travelled by an object along a straight line in time t is given by s = 3 – 4t + $5t^2$. Find the initial velocity of the object.

(20) A particle moves in a straight line and its position x at time t is given by x^2 = 2 + t. Calculate the acceleration of the particle.

(21) The position x of particle moving along x-axis varies with time t as x = A sin (ωt) where A and ω are positive constants. Find out the acceleration a of particle in terms of its position (x).

Problem : The displacement-time equation of a moving particle is given by $\sqrt{x}$ = 2t + 3. What is the nature of the motion of the particle.

Solution : Given, $\sqrt{x}$ = 2t + 3

or, x = $4t^2$ + 12t + 9

∴ Velocity of the particle : $v = \frac{dx}{dt}$

$= \frac{d}{dt}(4t^2 + 12t + 9)$

$= 8t + 12$

Again, the acceleration of the particle : $a = \frac{dv}{dt}$

$= \frac{d}{dt}(8t + 12) = 8$

Therefore, the acceleration of the particle is uniform.

Try Yourself

(22) The displacement-time equation of a moving particle is given by $x = 3 - 4t + 5t^2$. What is the nature of the motion of the particle.

(23) Suppose the distance travelled by a particle is directly proportional to the square of the time. State the nature of the acceleration of the particle.

Problem : A particle is moving along X-axis and its position with time is given as x (t) = 8 t – 3 t^2. Where, x is in meter and t is in second.

(a) Find the average velocity between time interval $t = 0$ and $t = 1$ s.

(b) Find the instantaneous velocity at time t = 2 s.

Solution : Given, $x(t) = (8t - 3t^2)$ m

(a) $x|_{t=0} = 0$ and $x|_{t=1\,s} = 5$ m

∴ Average velocity $v_{av} = \frac{5-0}{1-0} = 5$ m s^{-1}

(b) Instantaneous velocity : $v = \frac{dx}{dt}$

$= \frac{d}{dt}(8t - 3t^2)$

$= 8 - 6t$

∴ Instantaneous velocity of the particle at t = 2 s is given by $v = 8 - 6 \cdot 2 = -4$ m s^{-1}

Try Yourself

(24) The motion of a particle along a straight line is described by the function $x = a + bt^2$, a = 8.5 m and b = 2.5 m s^{-2} and t is in second.
(a) Find the instantaneous velocity at time t = 2 s.
(b) Find the average velocity between time interval $t = 2$ s and $t = 4$ s.

(25) The motion of a particle along a straight line is described by the function $x = (2t - 3)^2$ where, x is in metres and t is in second.
(a) Find the position, velocity and acceleration at t = 2 s.
(b) Find velocity of the particle at origin.

Problem : The position of a particle moving a long x-axis is given by x = 10t - 2 t^2. When does the particle come to rest?

Solution : Given, $x = 10t - 2t^2$

∴ Velocity : $v = \frac{dx}{dt}$

$= \frac{d}{dt}(10t - 2t^2)$

$= 10 - 4t$

When the particle come to rest, v = 0

or, $10 - 4t = 0$

or, $t = \frac{10}{4} = 2.5$ s

Try Yourself

---

(26) The position of a particle moving a long x-axis is given by $x = 12t - 5t^2$. When does the particle come to rest?

(27) The motion of a particle along a straight line is described by the function $t = \sqrt{x} + 3$. Calculate the displacement of the particle when its velocity is zero?

Problem : The equation of motion of a particle is $x = at^2 + bt + c$, where, a, b and c are three constants. Prove that $4a(x - c) = v^2 - b^2$; v is the velocity of the particle.

Solution : Given, $x = at^2 + bt + c$

Velocity : $v = \frac{dx}{dt}$

$= \frac{d}{dt}(at^2 + bt + c)$

$= 2at + b$

Squaring, $v^2 = 4a^2t^2 + 4abt + b^2$

or, $v^2 - b^2 = 4a(at^2 - bt)$

or, $v^2 - b^2 = 4a(x - c)$ [$\because x = at^2 + bt + c$]

∴ **$4a(x - c) = v^2 - b^2$ (Proved)**

On Instantaneous Speed, Instantaneous Velocity and Instantaneous Acceleration (2D)

Problem : The position vector of an object at any time t is given by $3t^2\,\hat{i} + 6t\,\hat{j}$. Find its velocity along y axis.

Solution : Given, $\vec{r} = 3t^2\,\hat{\imath} + 6t\,\hat{\jmath}$

∴ Velocity of the object $\vec{v} = \frac{d\vec{r}}{dt}$

$= \frac{d}{dt}[3t^2\,\hat{\imath} + 6t\,\hat{\jmath}]$

$= 6t\,\hat{\imath} + 6\,\hat{\jmath}$

∴ The magnitude of the velocity of the object is 6 unit.

Try Yourself

---

(28) The coordinates of a moving particle at any instant t are given by $x = Ct^2$ and $y = Bt^2$. Find the speed of the particle.

(29) The height y and distance x along the horizontal for a body projected in the x-y plane are given by $y = 8t - 5t^2$ and $x = 6t$. What is the initial speed of projection ?

(30) The position vector of an object at any time t is given by $\vec{r} = (4t^2\,\hat{i} + 2t\,\hat{j})$ m and t is in second. Find its acceleration.

(31) The position co-ordinates of a particle at time t is $(3t^2, 5t)$. Find the acceleration of the particle at t = 3 s.

On Equations of Motion (1D)

Problem : A motor car running with a velocity 30 km h^{-1} applied brakes and became stationary in 5 s. What retardation was produced ?

Solution : Given, Initial velocity (v_i) = 30 km h^{-1} = $30 \times \frac{5}{18}$ m s^{-1} = $\frac{50}{6}$ m s^{-1}

Final velocity (v_f) = 0

and time (t) = 5 s

From $v_f = v_i + at$ we get, $0 = \frac{50}{6} + (-a)(5)$

or, $5a = \frac{50}{6}$

$\therefore a = \frac{10}{6} = 1.67$ ms^{-2}

Problem : An object is moving with uniform acceleration. Its velocity after 5 s in 25 ms^{-1} and after 8 s, it is 34 ms^{-1}. Find the distance travelled by the object in 12th second.

Solution : Let us consider, Initial velocity (v_i) = u cm s^{-1} and its acceleration = a cm s^{-2}

In first case, From $v_f = v_i + a\,t$ we get, 25 = u + $5a$ ......(1)

In second case, From $v_f = v_i + a\,t$ we get, 34 = u + $8\,a$ ....(2)

Subtracting (1) from (2), we get $3\,a = 9$

$\therefore a = 3$

Putting $a = 3$ in equation (1), we get, 25 = u + 15

$\therefore$ u = 10

Now, from $s_t = v_i + \frac{1}{2}a(2t-1)$ we get, $s_{12} = 10 + \frac{1}{2}3\{(2)(12) - 1\} = 44.5$

$\therefore$ The distance travelled by the object in 12th second is 44.5 m.

Problem : A particle describes 25 cm in 5th second and 33 cm in 7th second of its motion. Calculate the initial velocity and the acceleration of the particle.

Solution : Let us consider, Initial velocity (v_i) = u cm s^{-1} and its acceleration = a cm s^{-2}

From $s_t = v_i + \frac{1}{2}a(2t-1)$ we get, $25 = u + \frac{1}{2}a\{(2)(5) - 1\} = u + \frac{9}{2}a$ ......(1)

and $33 = u + \frac{1}{2}a\{(2)(7) - 1\} = u + \frac{13}{2}a$ ....(2)

Subtracting (1) from (2), $\left(\frac{13}{2} - \frac{9}{2}\right)a = 8$

or, 2 a = 8

$\therefore a = 4$

Putting a = 4 in equation (1), we get, 25 = u + 18

$\therefore$ u = 7

Hence, the initial velocity of the particle is 7 cm s^{-1} and its acceleration = 4 cm s^{-2}.

Try Yourself

(32) An electron travelling with a speed of 5 × 10^3 m s^{-1} passes through an electric field with an acceleration of 10^{12} m s^{-2}. How long will it take for the electron to double its speed?

(33) A particle starts moving with velocity 5.0 m s^{-1} along the positive x-direction and it accelerates uniformly at the rate of 1.00 m s^{-2}.
(i) How much time does it take to acquire the velocity of 25 m s^{-1} ?
(ii) How much distance will it travel in acquiring the velocity of 25 m s^{-1}?
(iii) How much distance will it travel in the first 6 s ?

(34) Derive an expression for stopping distance of a car in terms of initial velocity v_0 and acceleration a.

(35) A car travelling at a speed of 30 km/h is brought to rest in a distance of 8 m by applying brakes. If the same car is moving at a speed of 60 km/h then how much distance will it travel before stopping with same brakes ?

(36) A bullet after entering a wooden block at rest covers 30 cm inside it and loses half of its velocity after how much further distance will it cover to rest ?

(37) A body travels 200 cm in the first two second and 220 cm in the next four second. What will be the velocity at the end of seventh second from start?

(38) A body describes 10 metre in the third second of motion and 28 metre in the sixth second. What distance will be covered by the body in the seventh second of motion?

(39) A particle starts moving with acceleration 2 ms^{-2}. Calculate the distance travelled by it in 5th half second.

On Equations of Motion (2D)

Problem : A particle has initial velocity of $3\,\hat{i} + 4\,\hat{j}$ and an acceleration of $0.4\,\hat{i} + 0.3\,\hat{j}$. Find its speed after 10 s.

Solution : Given, Initial velocity $\vec{v}_i = 3\,\hat{i} + 4\,\hat{j}$

Acceleration $\vec{a} = 0.4\,\hat{i} + 0.3\,\hat{j}$

and time (t) = 10 s

let us consider, the final velocity of the particle is $\vec{v}_f$

From $\vec{v}_f = \vec{v}_i + \vec{a}\,t$ we get, $\vec{v}_f = (3\,\hat{i} + 4\,\hat{j}) + (0.4\,\hat{i} + 0.3\,\hat{j}) \times 10$

$= (3\,\hat{i} + 4\,\hat{j}) + (4\,\hat{i} + 3\,\hat{j})$

$= (7\,\hat{i} + 7\,\hat{j})$

Try Yourself

(40) A body lying initially at point (2, 5) starts moving with a constant acceleration of $3\hat{i}$. Find the final position co-ordinate after 4 s.

(41) The initial position of an object at rest is given by $3\,\hat{i} + 4\,\hat{j}$ .It moves with constant acceleration and reaches to the position $6\,\hat{i} + 9\,\hat{j}$ after 5 s. What is its acceleration ?

On Variable Acceleration (1D)

N.P. based on Differentiation (Displacement → Velocity → Acceleration)

Problem : The displacement of a particle is proportional to cube of the time of travel. What is the nature of the acceleration.

Solution : According to the problem, $x \propto t^3$

or, $x = k\,t^3$ [where, k = proportional constant]

∴ Velocity of the particle : $v = \frac{dx}{dt}$

$= \frac{d}{dt}\,(k\,t^3)$

$= 3\,k\,t^2$

Again, acceleration of the particle : $a = \frac{dv}{dt}$

or, $a = \frac{d}{dt}\,(3\,k\,t^2)$

$\therefore a = 6\,k\,t$

Therefore, the acceleration of the particle is non-uniform.

Problem : A particle moves along a straight line OX. At a time t (in second) the distance x (in meters) of the particle from O is given by $x = 40 + 12\,t - t^3$. How long would the particle travel before coming to rest.

Solution : Given, $x = 40 + 12\,t - t^3$

∴ Velocity : $v = \frac{dx}{dt}$

$= \frac{d}{dt}\,(40 + 12\,t - t^3)$

$= 12 - 3\,t^2$

When the particle come to rest, v = 0

or, $12 - 3\,t^2 = 0$

$\therefore t = \sqrt{4} = 2$ s

Now, at t = 2 s, the position of the particle : $x = 40 + 12\,(2) - 2^3 = 56$ m

And at t = 0, the position of the particle was : $x = 40$ m

∴ The particle would travel (56 – 40) m = 16 m before coming to rest.

Try Yourself

(42) The position of a particle is given by $x = (3t - 5\,t^2 + t^3)$ m where, t is in second. Find the velocity and acceleration of the particle as a function of time.

(43) A body is moving with variable acceleration (a) along a straight line. What will be the average velocity of the body in time interval t_1 and t_2.

(44) The displacement travelled by a body is given to proportional to the cube of time elapsed. Comment on the acceleration of the body.

(45) The position x of a particle varies with time as $x = (at^2 - bt^3)$. At what time instant the acceleration will be zero?

(46) Suppose the velocity of the particle is given by the equation : $v = (2 + 4t^2)$ m / s.
(a) Find the average acceleration between time interval $t_1 = 2$ s and $t_2 = 4$ s.
(b) Find the instantaneous acceleration at time t = 2 s.

(47) A particle is moving along X-axis and its position with time is given as $x(t) = 2t^3 - 3t^2 + 1$.
(a) At what time instant is its velocity zero.
(b) What is the velocity when it passes through origin ?

(48) A particle moves along a straight line OX. At a time t (in second) the distance x (in meters) of the particle from O is given by $x = 40 + 12t - t^3$. How long would the particle travel before coming to rest.

(49) The position of a particle moving along x axis given by $x(t) = (-2t^3 + 3t^2 + 5)$ m . What is its acceleration when its velocity becomes zero?

(50) The position x of a particle with respect to time t along x-axis is given by $x = (-t^3 + 9t^2)$, where x is in metres and t in seconds. What will be the position of this particle when it achieves maximum speed along the positive x-direction?

(51) The motion of a particle along a straight line is described by equation $x = 8 + 12t - 2t^3$, where x is in metre and t in second. Find out the retardation of the particle when its velocity becomes zero.

(52) Displacement time equation of a particle moving along x-axis is $x = 20 + t^3 - 12$
(a) Find position and velocity of particle at time t = 0.
(b) State whether the motion is uniformly accelerated or not.
(c) Find position of the particle when velocity is zero.

(53) The velocity of an object is changing with time and relation is given by the following equation : $v = 2t + 3t^2$. Calculate the position of the object from the origin at t = 2s. Assume particle to be at origin at t = 0.

N.P. Based on Integration (Acceleration → Velocity → Displacement)

Type – 1 : v = f (t)

Problem : The velocity of an object is changing with time and relation is given by the following equation : $v = (3t^2 + 4t)$ m s^{-1}. Calculate the position of the object from the origin at t = 2 s. Assume particle to be at origin at t = 0.

Solution : Given, Velocity $v = 3t^2 + 4t$

$$\text{or, } \frac{dx}{dt} = 3t^2 + 4t$$

$$\text{or, } dx = (3t^2 + 4t)\,dt$$

Integrating, $\int_0^x dx = \int_0^2 (3t^2 + 4t)dt$

$$\text{or, } [x]_0^x = \left[3\frac{t^3}{3} + 4\frac{t^2}{2}\right]_0^2$$

$$\text{or, } x = 2^3 + 2 \times 2^2$$

$$\therefore x = 8 + 8 = 16$$

∴ Position of the object is at x = 16 m from the origin at t = 2 s .

Try Yourself

(54) The initial velocity of the particle is u and the acceleration at time t is kt, k being a constant. What will be its velocity at time t.

(55) The acceleration of a particle is increasing linearly with time t as bt. The particle starts from origin with an initial velocity v_0. What distance will be covered by the particle in time t?

(56) The initial velocity of a particle is u (at t = 0) and the acceleration a is given by $\alpha\, t^{\frac{3}{2}}$. Find out the velocity of the particle at time t.

(57) The relation between the acceleration and time for an object is given below : $a(t) = 3t - 4t^2$ Calculate the velocity with which the object is moving at t = 1 s (At t = 0, v = 0)

Type – 2 : a = f (x)

Problem : The initial velocity of a particle moving along x-axis is u (at t = 0 and x = 0) and its acceleration a is given by $a = kx$. Derive the correct equation between its velocity (v) and position (x) ?

Solution : According to the problem, acceleration : $a = k\,x$

$$\text{or, } v\frac{dv}{dx} = k\,x$$

$$\text{or, } v\,dv = k\,x\,dx$$

Integrating, $\int_u^v v\,dv = k\int_0^x x\,dx$

$$\text{or, } \left[\frac{v^2}{2}\right]_u^v = k\left[\frac{x^2}{2}\right]_0^x$$

$$\text{or, } \frac{v^2}{2} - \frac{u^2}{2} = k\frac{x^2}{2}$$

$$\text{or, } v^2 - u^2 = k\,x^2$$

$$\therefore v^2 = u^2 + k\,x^2$$

The correct equation between its velocity (v) and position (x) is : $v^2 = u^2 + k\,x^2$

Try Yourself

(58) The initial velocity of a particle moving along x-axis is u (at t = 0 and x = 0) and its acceleration a is given by $a = kx$. Derive the correct equation between its velocity (v) and position (x) ?

(59) A particle moves according to the law $a = -$ k y. Find the velocity as a function of distance y where v_0 is the initial velocity and a is the acceleration.

On Variable Acceleration (2D)

Try Yourself

(60) The coordinates of a moving particle at any instant t are given by $x = 5t^2$ and y = $3t^3$. Find the acceleration of the particle.

(61) A particle moves along the positive branch of the curve y = $\frac{x^2}{2}$, where x = $\frac{t^2}{2}$, x and y are measured in m and t in s. Find the velocity of the particle at t = 2 s.

(62) Position vector of a particle is $\vec{r} = a\cos\omega t\,\hat{\imath} + a\sin\omega t\,\hat{\jmath}$. What is the angle between its velocity and position vector ?

MCQ – 3 : Discussion on Rest & Motion

Physics MCQ | | Class – XI	Kinematics
	Topic : On Displacement in 1D and 2D

(1) The motion of a train on a straight track is an example of ….. motion.
(a) Two-dimensional motion
(b) Three dimensional motion
(c) One dimensional motion
(d) All of the above

(2) The SI unit of displacement is
(a) cm
(b) milli-meter
(c) nm
(d) m

(3) If a body starts its motion from one point A to B and comes back to the same point after a certain time interval, the displacement is

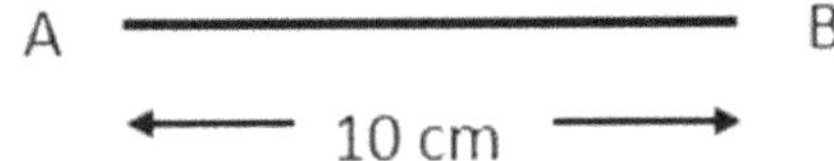

(a) 10
(b) 20
(c) 0
(d) 15

(4) The position of a particle moving along x-axis at time t is given by $x = (2 + 8t - 4t^2)$ m. The distance travelled by particle in time interval t = 0 to t = 2 s is
(a) 0
(b) 8
(c) 12
(d) 16

(5) The position of a body moving along x-axis at time t is given by $x = (6 - 4t + t^2)$ m. The distance travelled by body in time interval t = 0 to t = 3 s is
(a) 5 m
(b) 7 m
(c) 4 m
(d) 3 m

(6) The numerical ratio of displacement to the distance covered is always
(a) Less than one
(b) Equal to one
(c) Equal to or less than one
(d) Equal to or greater than one

(7) A car moves with speed 60 km h^{-1} for 1 hour in east direction and with same speed for 30 min in south direction. The displacement of car from initial position is
(a) 60 km
(b) $30\sqrt{3}$ km
(c) $30\sqrt{5}$ km
(d) $60\sqrt{2}$ km

(8) A man goes 10 m towards North, then 20 m towards east then displacement is
(a) 22.4 m
(b) 25 m
(c) 25.5 m
(d) 30 m

(9) The displacement of a particle from point having position vector $2\hat{i} + 4\hat{j}$ to another point having position vector $5\hat{i} + 1\hat{j}$ is
(a) 3 units
(b) $3\sqrt{2}$ units
(c) 5 units
(d) $5\sqrt{3}$ units

(10) A particle starting from the origin (0,0) moves in a straight line in (x,y) plane. Its coordinates at a later time are $(\sqrt{3}, 3)$. The path of the particle makes with the x-axis an angle of
(a) 0°
(b) 30°
(c) 60°
(d) 45°

(11) An object moves from position (6,8) to (12, 10) in the x-y plane. Magnitude and direction of displacement is
(a) $\sqrt{40}$ and 18.43°
(b) $\sqrt{40}$ and 71.56°
(c) 10 and 53°
(d) $\sqrt{224}$ and 53°

(12) The position vector of a particle is given by $\vec{r} = (t^2 - 1)\hat{i} + (2t)\hat{j}$. The locus of the particle in the x-y plane is
(a) Straight line
(b) Circle
(c) Parabola

(d) Ellipse

(13) A particle moves in x-y plane according to rule $x = a \sin \omega t$ and $y = a \cos \omega t$. The particle follows
(a) an elliptical path
(b) a circular path
(c) a parabolic path
(d) a straight line path inclined equally to x- and y axis

(14) A particle is moving with velocity $\vec{v} = k\,(y\,\hat{\imath} + x\,\hat{\jmath})$, where, k is a constant. The general equation for its path is
(a) $y^2 = x^2$ + constant
(b) $y = x^2$ + constant
(c) $y^2 = x$ + constant
(d) xy = constant

Answer	**Kinematics**
	Topic : Displacement in 1D and 2D

(1)	**(a)**	**(4)**	**(b)**	**(7)**	**(c)**	**(10)**	**(c)**	**(13)**	**(b)**
(2)	**(d)**	**(5)**	**(a)**	**(8)**	**(a)**	**(11)**	**(a)**	**(14)**	**(a)**
(3)	**(c)**	**(6)**	**(c)**	**(9)**	**(b)**	**(12)**	**(c)**		

Physics MCQ || Class – XI	Kinematics
	Topic : Average Speed and Average Velocity in 1 D

(1) If magnitude of average speed and average velocity over a time interval are same, then
(a) The particle must move with zero acceleration
(b) The particle must move with non-zero acceleration
(c) The particle must be at rest
(d) The particle must move in a straight line without turning back.

(2) A body whose speed in a particular direction is constant
(a) must be accelerating
(b) must be retarding
(c) has a constant velocity in that direction
(d) all the above

(3) A car moves form x to y with a uniform speed v_u and returns to x with a uniform speed v_d . The average speed for his round trip is
(a) $\frac{v_u - v_d}{2}$
(b) $\frac{2\, v_u\, v_d}{v_u + v_d}$
(c) $\sqrt{v_u v_d}$
(d) $\frac{v_d + v_u}{v_d\, v_u}$

(4) A person completes half of its his journey with speed v_1 and rest half with speed v_2. The average speed of the person is
(a) $v = \frac{v_1 + v_2}{2}$
(b) $v = \frac{2\, v_1\, v_2}{v_1 + v_2}$
(c) $v = \frac{v_1\, v_2}{v_1 + v_2}$
(d) $v = \sqrt{v_1 v_2}$

(5) A person travelling in a straight line moves with a constant velocity v_1 for a certain distance v_2 for next equal distance. The average velocity v is given by the relation
(a) $\frac{1}{v} = \frac{1}{v_1} + \frac{1}{v_2}$
(b) $\frac{2}{v} = \frac{1}{v_1} + \frac{1}{v_2}$
(c) $\frac{v}{2} = \frac{v_1 + v_2}{2}$
(d) $v = \sqrt{v_1 v_2}$

(6) If a car covers $\frac{2}{5}$ th of the total distance with v_1 speed and $\frac{3}{5}$th distance with v_2 then average speed is
(a) $\frac{1}{2}\sqrt{v_1 v_2}$
(b) $\frac{v_1 + v_2}{2}$
(c) $\frac{2 v_1 v_2}{v_1 + v_2}$
(d) $\frac{5 v_1 v_2}{3 v_1 + 2 v_2}$

(7) A particle moves along x axis with speed 6 m s^{-1} for the first half distance of a journey and the second half distance with a speed 3 m s^{-1} . The average speed in the total journey is
(a) 5 ms^{-1}
(b) 4.5 ms^{-1}
(c) 4 m s^{-1}
(d) 2 ms^{-1}

(8) A car moving on a straight road covers one third of the distance with 20 km h^{-1} and the rest with 60 km h^{-1}. The average speed is
(a) 40 km h^{-1}
(b) 80 km h^{-1}
(c) $46\frac{2}{3}$ km h^{-1}
(d) 36 km h^{-1}

(9) A car covers the first half of the distance between two places at 40 km h^{-1} and other half at 60 km h^{-1}. The average speed of the car is
(a) 40 km h^{-1}
(b) 48 km h^{-1}
(c) 50 km h^{-1}
(d) 60 km h^{-1}

(10) A car moves a distance 200 m. It covers the first-half of the distance at speed 40 km h^{-1} and the second half of distance at speed v km h^{-1}. The average speed is 48 km h^{-1}. Find the value of v
(a) 56 km h^{-1}
(b) 60 km h^{-1}
(c) 50 km h^{-1}
(d) 48 km h^{-1}

(11) A bus travelling the first one-third distance at speed of 10 km h^{-1}, the next one-

third at 20 km h^{-1} and the last one third at 60 km h^{-1}. The average speed of the bus is
(a) 9 km h^{-1}
(b) 16 km h^{-1}
(c) 18 km h^{-1}
(d) 48 km h^{-1}

(12) A train has a speed of 60 km h^{-1} for the first one hour and 40 km h^{-1} for the next half hour. Its average speed in km h^{-1} is
(a) 50
(b) 53.33
(c) 48
(d) 70

(13) A person travels along a straight road for the first $\frac{t}{3}$ time with a speed v_1 and for next $\frac{2t}{3}$ time with a speed v_2. Then the mean speed v is given by
(a) $v = \frac{v_1 + 2v_2}{3}$
(b) $\frac{1}{v} = \frac{1}{3v_1} + \frac{2}{3v_2}$
(c) $v = \frac{1}{3}\sqrt{2v_1v_2}$
(d) $v = \sqrt{\frac{3v_2}{2v_1}}$

(14) A particle travels half of the distance of straight journey with a speed 6 m s^{-1}. The remaining part of the distance is covered with speed 2 m s^{-1} for half of the time of remaining journey and with speed 4 m s^{-1} for the other half time. The average speed of the particle is
(a) 3 ms^{-1}
(b) 4 ms^{-1}
(c) $\frac{3}{4}$ m s^{-1}
(d) 5 ms^{-1}

(15) A man walks on a straight road from his home to a market 2.5 km away with a speed of 5 km h^{-1}. Finding the market closed, he instantly turns and walks back home with a speed of 7.5 km h^{-1}. The average speed of the man over the interval of time 0 to 40 min. is equal to
(a) 5 km h^{-1}
(b) $\frac{25}{4}$ km h^{-1}
(c) $\frac{30}{4}$ km h^{-1}
(d) $\frac{45}{8}$ km h^{-1}

(16) Preeti reached the metro station and found that the escalator is not working. She walked up the stationary escalator in time t_1. On other day, if she remains stationary on the moving escalator, then the escalator takes her up in time t_2. The time taken by her to walk up on the moving escalator will be

(a) $\frac{t_1 + t_2}{2}$

(b) $\frac{t_1 t_2}{t_2 - t_1}$

(c) $\frac{t_1 t_2}{t_2 + t_1}$

(d) $t_1 - t_2$

Answer	Kinematics
	Topic : Average Speed and Average Velocity in 1 D

1.	(d)	5.	(b)	9.	(b)	13.	(a)
2.	(c)	6.	(d)	10.	(b)	14.	(b)
3.	(b)	7.	(c)	11.	(c)	15.	(d)
4.	(b)	8.	(d)	12.	(b)	16.	(c)

Physics MCQ || Class – XI	Kinematics
	Topic : Average Speed and Average Velocity in 2 D

(1) A particle moves in east direction with 15 m s^{-1} for 2 s then moves in northward with 5 m s^{-1} for 8 s. The average speed of the particle is
(a) 1 m s^{-1}
(b) 5 m s^{-1}
(c) 7 m s^{-1}
(d) 10 m s^{-1}

(2) A car moves towards north at a speed of 54 km h^{-1} for 1 hr. Then it moves eastward with same speed for same duration. The average speed and velocity of a car for complete journey is
(a) 54 km h^{-1}, 0
(b) 15 m s^{-1}, $\frac{15}{\sqrt{2}}$ m s^{-1}
(c) 0,0
(d) 0, $\frac{54}{\sqrt{2}}$ km h^{-1}

(3) A particle is moving such that its position coordinates (x, y) are (2m, 3m) at time t = 0, (6m, 7 m) at time t = 2 s and (13 m, 14 m) at time t = 5 s. Average velocity $\overrightarrow{v_{av}}$ from t = 0 to t = 5 s
(a) $\frac{1}{5}(13\hat{i} + 14\hat{j})$
(b) $\frac{7}{3}(\hat{i} + \hat{j})$
(c) $2(\hat{i} + \hat{j})$
(d) $\frac{11}{5}(\hat{i} + \hat{j})$

(4) A particle moves in x-y plane from positions (2m, 4m) to (6m, 8 m) in 2 s. Magnitude and direction of average velocity is
(a) $\sqrt{2}$ m s^{-1} and 45°
(b) $2\sqrt{2}$ and 45°
(c) $4\sqrt{2}$ and 30°
(d) $2\sqrt{2}$ and 60°

(5) A particle moves along the positive branch of the curve $y = \frac{x^2}{2}$ where, $x = \frac{t^2}{2}$, x and y are measured in meters and t in second. At t = 2 s, the velocity of the particle is
(a) $2\hat{i} - 4\hat{j}$ m s^{-1}
(b) $4\hat{i} + 2\hat{j}$ m s^{-1}
(c) $2\hat{i} + 4\hat{j}$ m s^{-1}
(d) $4\hat{i} - 2\hat{j}$ m s^{-1}

Answer	Kinematics
	Topic : Average Speed and Average Velocity in 2 D

1.	(c)	2.	(b)	3.	(d)	4.	(b)	5.	(c)

Physics MCQ || Class – XI	Kinematics
	Topic : Basic Concepts of Acceleration

(1) If the velocity of an object is increasing and changing at a uniform rate then the acceleration of the object is
(a) Positive
(b) Zero
(c) Negative
(d) Not defined

(2) A particle moves with velocity v_1 for time t_1 and v_2 for time t_2 along straight line. The magnitude of its average acceleration is
(a) $\frac{v_2 - v_1}{t_1 - t_2}$
(b) $\frac{v_2 - v_1}{t_1 + t_2}$
(c) $\frac{v_2 - v_1}{t_2 - t_1}$
(d) $\frac{v_1 + v_2}{t_1 - t_2}$

(3) A car accelerated from initial position and then returned at initial point, then
(a) Velocity is zero but speed increases
(b) Speed is zero but velocity increases
(c) Both speed and velocity increase
(d) Both speed and velocity decrease

(4) A body in one dimensional motion has zero speed at an instant. At that instant, it must have
(a) zero velocity
(b) zero acceleration
(c) non-zero velocity
(d) non zero acceleration

(5) If a body is moving with constant speed, then its acceleration
(a) must be zero
(b) may be variable
(c) may be uniform
(d) both (b) and (c)

(6) If a particle is moving along straight line with increasing speed, then
(a) its acceleration is negative
(b) its acceleration may be decreasing
(c) its acceleration is positive
(d) both (b) and (c)

(7) An object is moving with variable speed, then
(a) Its velocity may be constant
(b) Its velocity must be variable
(c) Its acceleration may be zero
(d) Its velocity must be constant

(8) When the velocity of a body is variable, then
(a) Its speed may be constant
(b) Its acceleration may be constant
(c) Its average acceleration may be constant
(d) All of these

(9) Acceleration of a particle changes when
(a) direction of velocity changes
(b) magnitude of velocity changes
(c) Both (a) and (b)
(d) speed changes

(10) If a particle moves with an acceleration, then which of the following can remain constant ?
(a) Both speed and velocity
(b) Neither speed nor velocity
(c) Only the velocity
(d) Only the speed

(11) At any instant, the velocity and acceleration of a particle moving along a straight line are v and a. The speed of the particle is increasing
(a) $v > 0, a > 0$
(b) $v < 0, a > 0$
(c) $v > 0, a < 0$
(d) $v > 0, a = 0$

(12) If v is the velocity of a body moving along x axis then acceleration of body is
(a) $\frac{dV}{dx}$
(b) $v\frac{dV}{dx}$
(c) $x\frac{du}{dx}$
(d) $v\frac{dx}{du}$

(13) A body is moving with variable acceleration (a) along a straight line. The average acceleration of the body in time interval t_1 and t_2 is

(a) $\frac{a(t_2 + t_1)}{2}$

(b) $\frac{a(t_2 - t_1)}{2}$

(c) $\frac{\int_{t_1}^{t_2} a\,dt}{t_2 + t_1}$

(d) $\frac{\int_{t_1}^{t_2} a\,dt}{t_2 - t_1}$

Answer	Kinematics
	Topic : Basic Concepts of Acceleration

1.	**(a)**	**4.**	**(a)**	**7.**	**(b)**	**10.**	**(b)**	**13.**	**(d)**
2.	**(b)**	**5.**	**(b)**	**8.**	**(d)**	**11.**	**(a)**		
3.	**(a)**	**6.**	**(b)**	**9.**	**(c)**	**12.**	**(b)**		

Physics

MCQ | | Class – XI

Kinematics

Topic :Instantaneous Speed & Instantaneous Velocity in 1D

(1) The motion of a particle is described by the equation $x = a + bt^2$ where, a = 15 cm and b = 3 cm. Its instantaneous velocity at time 3 s will be
(a) 36 cm s^{-1}
(b) 18 cm s^{-1}
(c) 16 cm s^{-1}
(d) 32 cm s^{-1}

(2) The displacement of a body is given by 2s = gt^2, where g is a constant. The velocity of the body at any time t is
(a) g t
(b) $\frac{gt}{2}$
(c) $\frac{gt^2}{2}$
(d) $\frac{gt^3}{2}$

(3) Two cars P and Q start from a point at the same time in a straight line and their positions are represented by $x_P(t) = at + bt^2$ and $x_Q(t) = ft - t^2$. At what time do the cars have the same velocity ?
(a) $\frac{a-f}{1+b}$
(b) $\frac{a+f}{2(b-1)}$
(c) $\frac{a+f}{2(1+b)}$
(d) $\frac{f-a}{2(1+b)}$

(4) The displacement S of a particle is S = $8t^2 + 3t - 5$ m. The initial velocity of the particle is
(a) 3 ms^{-1}
(b) 16 ms^{-1}
(c) 15 ms^{-1}
(d) 2 ms^{-1}

(5) The distance travelled by an object along a straight line in time t is given by $3 - 4t + 5t^2$, the initial velocity of the object is
(a) 3 unit
(b) - 3 unit
(c) 4 unit
(d) −4 unit

(6) The position of a particle moving along x-axis is given by x = ($10t - 2t^2$). Then the time (t) at which it will momently come to rest is
(a) 0
(b) 2.5 s
(c) 5 s
(d) 10 s

(7) The displacement x (in m) of a body varies with time t (in s) as, $x = -2t^2 + 20t + 3$. How long does the body take to come to rest?
(a) 15 s
(b) 2.5 s
(c) 5 s
(d) 10 s

(8) The relation $3t = \sqrt{3x} + 6$ describes the displacement of a particle in one direction where x is in metres and t in second. The displacement, when velocity is zero, is
(a) 24 m
(b) 12 m
(c) 5 m
(d) zero

(9) The displacement x (in meter) of a particle of mass m (in kg) moving in one dimension under the action of a force, is related to time t (in second) as $t = \sqrt{x} + 3$. The displacement of the particle when its velocity is zero, will be
(a) 2 m
(b) 4 m
(c) 0 m
(d) 6 m

(10) The displacement x of a particle varies with time t as $x = a\,e^{-\alpha t} + b\,e^{\beta t}$, where a, b, α and β are positive constants. The velocity of the particle will
(a) Go on decreasing with time
(b) Be independent of β
(c) Drop to zero when α and β
(d) Go on increasing with time

(11) A particle moving in a straight line has velocity and displacement equation is $v = 4\sqrt{1+S}$, where v is in ms^{-1} and s is in m. The initial velocity of the particle is
(a) 4 ms^{-1}
(b) 16 ms^{-1}
(c) 2 ms^{-1}
(d) zero

(12) The displacement x of a particle moving in one dimension under a constant acceleration is related to time t as $t = \sqrt{x} + 3$. The displacements of the particle when its velocity is zero will be
(a) 0
(b) 3 ms^{-1}
(c) $\sqrt{3}$ ms^{-1}
(d) $\frac{1}{3}$ ms^{-1}

(13) A particle located at x = 0 at time t = 0. Starts moving along the positive x-direction with a velocity v that varies as $v = a\sqrt{x}$. The displacement of the particle varies with time as
(a) t^3
(b) t^2
(c) t
(d) $t^{\frac{1}{2}}$

(14) A particle located at x = 0 at time t = 0, starts moving along the positive x-direction with a velocity v varies as $v = \alpha \sqrt{x}$ then velocity of particle varies with time as (α is a constant)
(a) $v \propto t$
(b) $v \propto t^2$
(c) $v \propto \sqrt{t}$
(d) v = constant

(15) The position x of a particle with respect to time t along x-axis is given by $x = 9t^2 - t^3$, where x is in metres and t in seconds. What will be the position of this particle when it achieves maximum speed along the positive x-direction?
(a) 24 m
(b) 32 m
(c) 54 m
(d) 81 m

(16) The displacement of a particle starting from rest (at t = 0) is given by $s = 6t^2 - t^3$. The time at which the particle will attain zero velocity again is
(a) 4 s
(b) 8 s
(c) 12 s
(d) 16 s

(17) A particle moves along a straight line OX. At a time t (in seconds) the distance x (in metres) of the particle from O is given by $x = 40 + 12t - t^3$. How long would the particle travel before coming to rest ?
(a) 24 m
(b) 40 m
(c) 56 m
(d) 16 m

(18) If the velocity of a particle is $v = At + Bt^2$ where, A and B are constants, then the distance travelled by it between 1 s and 2 s is
(a) 3A + 7 B
(b) $\frac{3}{2}A + \frac{7}{3}B$
(c) $\frac{A}{2} + \frac{B}{3}$
(d) $\frac{3}{2}A + 4B$

Answer	**Kinematics**
	Topic : Instantaneous Speed & Instantaneous Velocity in 1D

(1) (b)	(5) (d)	(9) (c)	(13) (b)	(17) (d)
(2) (a)	(6) (b)	(10) (d)	(14) (a)	(18) (b)
(3) (d)	(7) (c)	(11) (a)	(15) (c)	
(4) (a)	(8) (d)	(12) (a)	(16) (a)	

Physics MCQ || Class – XI	Kinematics
	Topic :Instantaneous Speed & Instantaneous Velocity in 2D

(1) A particle moves along the positive branch of the curve $y = \frac{x^2}{2}$ where, $x = \frac{t^2}{2}$, x and y are measured in meters and t in second. At t = 2 s, the velocity of the particle is
(a) $2\hat{i} - 4\hat{j}$ m s^{-1}
(b) $4\hat{i} + 2\hat{j}$ m s^{-1}
(c) $2\hat{i} + 4\hat{j}$ m s^{-1}
(d) $4\hat{i} - 2\hat{j}$ m s^{-1}

(2) At an instant t, the co-ordinate of a particle are $x = at^2$, $y = bt^2$ and z = 0. The magnitude of velocity of the particle at an instant is
(a) $t\sqrt{a^2 + b^2}$
(b) $\frac{v}{\sqrt{2}}$
(c) $\frac{v}{\sqrt{3}}$
(d) $2t\sqrt{a^2 + b^2}$

(3) The co-ordinates of a moving particle at any time t are given by $x = \alpha t^3$ and $y = \beta t^3$. The speed of the particle at time t is given by
(a) $3t\sqrt{\alpha^2 + \beta^2}$
(b) $3t^2\sqrt{\alpha^2 + \beta^2}$
(c) $t^2\sqrt{\alpha^2 + \beta^2}$
(d) $\sqrt{\alpha^2 + \beta^2}$

(4) The instantaneous co-ordinates of a particle are x = 6t m and $y = 4t^2$ m. The velocity of the particle at t = 1 s is
(a) 10 m s^{-1}
(b) 6 m s^{-1}
(c) 4 m s^{-1}
(d) 2 m s^{-1}

(5) The height y and distance x along the horizontal for a body projected in the x-y plane are given by $y = 8t - 5t^2$ and x = 6t. The initial speed of projection is
(a) 8 m s^{-1}
(b) 9 m s^{-1}
(c) 10 m s^{-1}
(d) $\frac{10}{3}$ m s^{-1}

(6) The position vector of a particle is $\vec{r} = (a\cos\omega t)\,\hat{i} + (a\sin\omega t)\,\hat{j}$. The velocity of the particle is
(a) directed towards the origin
(b) directed away from the origin
(c) parallel to the position vector
(d) perpendicular to the position vector

Answer	Kinematics
	Topic : Instantaneous Speed & Instantaneous Velocity in 2D

(1)	(c)	(3)	(b)	(5)	(c)
(2)	(d)	(4)	(a)	(6)	(d)

Physics

MCQ | | Class – XI

Kinematics

Topic : Instantaneous Acceleration in 1D

(1) If the displacement of a particle varies with time as $\sqrt{x}$ = t + 7, then
(a) velocity of the particle is inversely proportional to t
(b) velocity of the particle is proportional to t^2
(c) velocity of the particle is proportional to $\sqrt{t}$
(d) The particle moves with constant acceleration

(2) The displacement (x) of a particle moving in one dimension is related to time (t) by the equation $\sqrt{x}$ = t + 7. Which of the following is correct ? (where k is a constant)
(a) Velocity is inversely proportional to time
(b) Acceleration is proportional to time
(c) Acceleration is constant
(d) Acceleration is inversely proportional to time

(3) If for a particle position x ∝ t^2 then
(a) velocity is constant
(b) acceleration is constant
(c) acceleration is variable
(d) None of these

(4) The Velocity of a body depends on time according to the equation v = $\frac{t^2}{10}$ + 3. The body is undergoing
(a) uniform acceleration
(b) uniform retardation
(c) non-uniform acceleration
(d) Zero acceleration

(5) Which of the following relations representing displacement x(t) of a particle describes motion with constant acceleration ?
(a) x = 6 – $7t^{-2}$
(b) x = $3t^2 + 5\,t^3 + 7$
(c) x = $9t^2 + 8$
(d) x = $4t^{-2} + 3\,t^{-1}$

(6) The velocity v of a particle as a function of its position (x) is expressed as v = $\sqrt{C_1 - C_2x}$, where, C_1 and C_2 are positive constants. The acceleration of the particle is
(a) C_2
(b) $-\frac{C_2}{2}$
(c) $C_1 - C_2$
(d) $\frac{C_1+C_2}{2}$

(7) If x denotes displacement in time t and x = a cos t, then acceleration is
(a) a cos t
(b) – a cos t
(c) a sin t
(d) – a sin t

(8) The position x of particle moving along x-axis varies with time t as x = A sin ωt, where A and ω are positive constants. The acceleration a of particle varies with its position (x) as
(a) a = Ax
(b) $a = -\,\omega^2$x
(c) a = A ω x
(d) $a = -\,\omega^2$x A

(9) A body starts from origin and moves along x-axis so that its position at any instant is x = 4 t^2 – 12t, where, t is in second and V is in m s^{-1} . What is the acceleration of the particle
(a) 4 ms^{-2}
(b) 8 ms^{-2}
(c) 24 m s^{-2}
(d) 0 ms^{-2}

(10) The relation between position (x) and time (t) are given below for a particle moving along a straight line, which of the following equation represents uniformly accelerated motion? [where, α and β are positive constant]
(a) βx = αt + $\alpha\beta$
(b) αx = β + t
(c) x t = $\alpha\,\beta$
(d) αt = $\sqrt{\beta + x}$

(11) A particle of unit mass undergoes one-dimensional motion such that its velocity varies according to v(x) = $\beta\,x^{-2n}$. where β and n are constants and x is the position of the particle. The acceleration of the particle as a function of x, is given by
(a) –2n $\beta^2 x^{-4n+1}$
(b) –2n $\beta^2 x^{-2n-1}$
(c) –2n $\beta^2 x^{-4n-1}$
(d) –2 $\beta^2 x^{-2n+1}$

(12) The velocity v of a body moving along a straight line varies with time t as v = $2\,t^2\,e^{-t}$

where v is in m s^{-1} and t is in second. The acceleration of body is zero at t =
(a) 0
(b) 2 s
(c) 3 s
(d) Both (a) and (b)

(13) The relation between time and distance x is $t = \alpha x^2 + \beta x$, where, α and β are constants. The acceleration is
(a) $2\alpha v^2$
(b) $-2\alpha v^3$
(c) $2\beta v^3$
(d) $-2\alpha\beta v^2$

(14) A point moves in a straight line so that its displacement x at time t is given by $x^2 = t^2 + 1$. Its acceleration is
(a) $\frac{1}{x}$
(b) $\frac{1}{x^2}$
(c) $\frac{1}{x^3}$
(d) $-\frac{1}{x^3}$

(15) A point moves in a straight line and its position x at time t is given by $x^2 = t + 2$. Its acceleration is
(a) $-\frac{1}{4x^2}$
(b) $\frac{1}{x^2}$
(c) $-\frac{2}{x^3}$
(d) $-\frac{1}{4x^3}$

(16) In a straight line motion the distance travelled is proportional to the square root of the time taken. The acceleration of the particle is proportional to
(a) velocity
(b) v^2
(c) v^3
(d) $\sqrt{v}$

(17) A particle moves along X-axis as $x = 4(t-2) + a(t-2)^2$, which of the following is true ?
(a) The initial velocity of particle is 4
(b) The acceleration of particle is $2a$
(c) The particle is at origin at t = 0
(d) None of the above

(18) The displacement (x) of a particle depends on time t as $x = \alpha t^2 - \beta t^3$. Choose the incorrect statements from the following.
(a) The particle never returns to its starting point
(b) The particle comes to rest after time $\frac{2\alpha}{3\beta}$
(c) The initial velocity of the particle is zero
(d) The initial acceleration of the particle is zero

(19) Motion of a particle is given by equation $S = 3t^3 + 7t^2 + 1t + 5$ m. The value of acceleration of the particle at t = 1s is
(a) 10 ms^{-2}
(b) 32 ms^{-2}
(c) 23 ms^{-2}
(d) 16 ms^{-2}

(20) The displacement of a particle is represented by the following equation: $s = 3t^3 + 7t^2 + 5t + 8$. Where s is in metre and t in second. The acceleration of the particle at t = 1 s is
(a) 14 m s^{-2}
(b) 18 m s^{-2}
(c) 32 m s^{-2}
(d) zero

(21) The displacement of a particle moving in a straight line depends on time as : $x = \alpha t^3 + \beta t^2 + \gamma t + \delta$. The ratio of initial acceleration to its initial velocity depends
(a) Only on α and γ
(b) Only on β and γ
(c) Only on α and β
(d) Only on α

(22) The position x of a particle varies with time (t) as $x = at^2 - bt^3$. The acceleration will be zero at time t equal to
(a) zero
(b) $\frac{a}{3b}$
(c) $\frac{2a}{3b}$
(d) $\frac{a}{b}$

(23) The displacement of a particle is given by $y = a + bt + ct^2 - dt^4$. The initial velocity and acceleration are respectively
(a) b, – 4 d
(b) – b, 2c
(c) b, 2c
(d) 2c, – 4 d

(24) A particle moves along a straight line such that its displacement at any time t is given by $s = (t^3 - 6t^2 - 3t + 4)$ metres. The velocity when the acceleration is zero is
(a) 3 ms^{-1}
(b) – 15 m s^{-1}
(c) – 9 ms^{-1}
(d) 42 ms^{-1}

(25) The position of a particle moving along x-axis given by x = $-\ 2t^3 + 3t^2 + 5$ m. The acceleration of the particle at the instant its velocity becomes zero is
(a) 12 ms^{-2}
(b) – 12 m s^{-2}
(c) – 6 ms^{-2}
(d) zero

(26) The motion of a particle along a straight line is described by equation x = 8 + 12 t – t^3, where x is in meter and t in second. The retardation of the particle when its velocity become zero is
(a) 6 ms^{-2}
(b) 12 ms^{-2}
(c) 24 ms^{-2}
(d) Zero

(27) A particle moves a distance x in time t according to equation $x = (t + 5)^{-1}$. The acceleration of particle is proportional to
(a) $(velocity)^{\frac{3}{2}}$
(b) $(Distance)^2$
(c) $(Distance)^{-2}$
(d) $(velocity)^{\frac{2}{3}}$

(28) The velocity time relation of an electron starting from rest is given by v = k t where, k = 2 m s^{-2}. The distance traversed in first 3 s is
(a) 9 m
(b) 16 m
(c) 27 m
(d) 36 m

(29) A particle starts from rest having acceleration which depends on time as a = (3t + 4) ms^{-2}. The velocity of the particle at t = 2s is
(a) 10 m s^{-1}
(b) 14 m s^{-1}
(c) 12 m s^{-1}
(d) 16 m s^{-1}

(30) The acceleration a in m s^{-2}, of a particle is given by $a = 3t^2 +$ 2t + 2 where t is the time. If the particle starts out with a velocity v = 2 m s^{-1} at t =0, then the velocity at the end of 2 s is
(a) 12 m s^{-1}
(b) 14 m s^{-1}
(c) 16 m s^{-1}
(d) 18 m s^{-1}

(31) The initial velocity of a particle is u and the acceleration at the time t is kt, k being a constant. Then the velocity v at the time t is given by
(a) v = u
(b) v = u + kt
(c) v = u + k t^2
(d) v = u + $\frac{1}{2}$ k t^2

(32) The initial velocity of a particle is u (at t = 0) and its acceleration a is given by $a = \alpha\, t^{\frac{3}{2}}$. Which of the following relation is valid?
(a) v = u + $\alpha\, t^{\frac{3}{2}}$
(b) v = u + $\frac{3}{2}\alpha\, t^3$
(c) v = u + $\frac{2}{5}\alpha\, t^{\frac{5}{2}}$
(d) v = u + $\alpha\, t^{\frac{5}{2}}$

(33) The acceleration of a particle is increasing linearly with time t as bt. The particle starts from origin with an initial velocity v_0 . The distance travelled by the particle in time t will be
(a) v_0 t + $\frac{1}{3} b\, t^2$
(b) v_0 t + $\frac{1}{2} b\, t^2$
(c) v_0 t + $\frac{1}{6} b\, t^3$
(d) v_0 t + $\frac{1}{3} b\, t^3$

(34) The equation of motion of a particle in a medium is $\frac{dv}{dt} = -\,kv$ where, k = positive constant. If the initial velocity of the particle is u, then distance covered in time t is
(a) $\frac{u}{k}\ln(1 - kt)$
(b) $\frac{u}{k}(1 - e^{-kt})$
(c) $\ln\frac{ut}{k}$
(d) $\frac{u}{k}\, e^{-ukt}$

(35) The initial velocity of a particle moving along x-axis is u (at t = 0 and x = 0) and its acceleration a is given by a = kx. Which of the following equation is correct between its velocity (v) and position (x) ?

(a) $v^2 - u^2$ = 2 k x

(b) $v^2 = u^2$ + 2 k x^2

(c) $v^2 = u^2$ + k x^2

(d) $v^2 + u^2$ = 2 k x

(36) A particle moving along x-axis has acceleration f, at time t, given by f = $f_0\,(1 - \frac{t}{T})$. Where, f_0 and T are constants. The particle at t = 0 has zero velocity. In the time interval

between t = 0 and the instant when f = 0, the particle's velocity (v) is
(a) f_0 T
(b) $\frac{1}{2} f_0 T^2$
(c) $f_0 T^2$
(d) $\frac{1}{2} f_0 T$

(37) A particle located at x = 0 at time t = 0. Starts moving along the positive x-direction with a velocity v that varies as v = a$\sqrt{x}$. The displacement of the particle varies with time as
(a) t^3
(b) t^2
(c) t
(d) $t^{\frac{1}{2}}$

(38) A particle located at x = 0 at time t = 0, starts moving along the positive x-direction with a velocity v varies as v = α $\sqrt{x}$ then velocity of particle varies with time as (α is a constant)
(a) $v \propto t$
(b) $v \propto t^2$
(c) $v \propto \sqrt{t}$
(d) v = constant

Answer	**Kinematics**
	Topic : Instantaneous Acceleration in 1D

(1)	(d)	(9)	(b)	(17)	(b)	(25)	(c)	(33)	(c)
(2)	(c)	(10)	(d)	(18)	(a)	(26)	(b)	(34)	(b)
(3)	(b)	(11)	(c)	(19)	(c)	(27)	(a)	(35)	(c)
(4)	(c)	(12)	(d)	(20)	(c)	(28)	(a)	(36)	(d)
(5)	(c)	(13)	(b)	(21)	(b)	(29)	(b)	(37)	(b)
(6)	(b)	(14)	(c)	(22)	(b)	(30)	(d)	(38)	(a)
(7)	(b)	(15)	(d)	(23)	(c)	(31)	(d)		
(8)	(b)	(16)	(c)	(24)	(b)	(32)	(c)		

Physics MCQ | | Class – XI	Kinematics
	Topic : Instantaneous Acceleration in 2D

(1) The x and y coordinates of the particle at any time are x = 5t – $2t^2$ and y = 10 t respectively, where x and y are in meters and t in second. The acceleration of the particle at t = 2 s is
(a) 0
(b) 5 m s^{-2}
(c) – 4 m s^{-2}
(d) – 8 m s^{-2}

(2) The x and y coordinates of a particle at any time are given by $x = 7t + 4t^2$ and y = 5t respectively, where x and y are in meters and t in seconds. The acceleration of the particle at t = 5 s is
(a) 0
(b) 8 m s^{-2}
(c) 20 m s^{-2}
(d) 40 m s^{-2}

(3) A particle moves in an XY plane in such a way that its x and y co-ordinate vary with time according to x (t) = $t^3 - 32\,t$ and y (t) = $5t^2 + 12$. Find the acceleration of the particle, if t = 3 s
(a) $9\hat{\imath} + 5\,\hat{\jmath}$
(b) $18\hat{\imath} + 10\,\hat{\jmath}$
(c) $18\hat{\imath} - 5\,\hat{\jmath}$
(d) $-18\hat{\imath} + 10\,\hat{\jmath}$

(4) The co-ordinates of a moving particle at any time t are given by $x = 2t^3$, y = $3t^3$. Acceleration of the particle is given by
(a) t $\sqrt{468}$
(b) 234 t^2
(c) 468t
(d) t $\sqrt{234}$

(5) The position of a particle moving in the x-y plane at any time t is given by x (t) = $(3t^2 - 6t)$ m and y (t) = $(t^2 - 2t)$ m. Select the correct statement about the moving particle from the following
(a) The acceleration of the particle is zero at t = 0
(b) The velocity of the particle is zero at t = 0
(c) The velocity of the particle is zero at t = 1s
(d) The velocity and acceleration of the particle are zero

Answer	Kinematics
	Topic : Instantaneous Acceleration in 2D

(1) (c) | **(2)** (b) | **(3)** (b) | **(4)** (a) | **(5)** (c)

Physics MCQ || Class – XI	Kinematics
	Topic : Equations of Motion in 1D

(1) A particle starts moving with acceleration 2 m s^{-2}. Distance ravelled by it in 5th half second is
(a) 1.25 m
(b) 2.25 m
(c) 6.25 m
(d) 30.25 m

(2) A particle starts moving from rest state along a straight line under the action of a constant force and travel distance x in first 5 seconds. The distance travelled by it in next five seconds will be
(a) x
(b) 2 x
(c) 3 x
(d) 4 x

(3) A body starts from rest and moves with constant acceleration for t second. It travels a distance S_1 in first half of time and S_2 in the next half of time, then
(a) $S_2 = 3\,S_1$
(b) $S_2 = 4\,S_1$
(c) $S_2 = S_1$
(d) $S_2 = 2\,S_1$

(4) A particle starts its motion from rest under the action of a constant force. If the distance covered in first 10 s is S_1, and that covered in the first 20 seconds is S_2 then
(a) $S_2 = 3\,S_1$
(b) $S_2 = 4\,S_1$
(c) $S_2 = S_1$
(d) $S_2 = 2\,S_1$

(5) The distance travelled by a particle starting from rest and moving with an acceleration $\frac{4}{3}$ m s^{-2}, in the third second is
(a) $\frac{10}{3}$ m
(b) $\frac{19}{3}$ m
(c) 6 m
(d) 4 m

(6) A body starting from rest covers a distance of 9 m in the fifth second. The acceleration of the body is
(a) 2 ms^{-2}
(b) 0.2 ms^{-2}
(c) 1.8 m s^{-2}
(d) 4 ms^{-2}

(7) A body starts from rest and moves with uniform acceleration. The ratio of the distance covered in the nth second to the distance covered in n second is
(a) $\frac{2}{n} - \frac{1}{n^2}$
(b) $\frac{1}{n^2} - \frac{1}{n}$
(c) $\frac{1}{n} - \frac{1}{n^2}$
(d) $\frac{2}{n} - \frac{2}{n^2}$

(8) The two ends of a train moving with constant acceleration pass a certain point with velocities u and 3u. The velocity with which the middle point of the train passes the same point is
(a) 2 u
(b) $\frac{3}{2}$ u
(c) $\sqrt{5}$ u
(d) $\sqrt{10}$ u

(9) If a car at rest accelerates uniformly to a speed of 144 km h^{-1} in 20 s, it covers a distance of
(a) 1440 m
(b) 2980 m
(c) 20 m
(d) 400 m

(10) A particle moves in a straight line with a constant acceleration. It changes its velocity from 10 m s^{-1} to 20 m s^{-1} while passing through a distance 135 m in t second. The value of t is
(a) 9
(b) 10
(c) 1.8
(d) 12

(11) A train starts from rest from a station with acceleration 0.2 m s^{-2} on a straight track and then comes to rest after attaining maximum speed on another station due to retardation 0.4 m s^{-2}. If total time spent is half an hour, then distance between two stations is (neglect length of train)
(a) 216 km
(b) 512 km

(c) 728 km
(d) 1296 km

(12) A particle starts with initial speed u and retardation a to come to rest in time T. The time taken to cover first half of the total path travelled is
(a) $\frac{T}{\sqrt{2}}$
(b) $T\left(1 - \frac{1}{\sqrt{2}}\right)$
(c) $\frac{T}{2}$
(d) $\frac{3T}{4}$

(13) A car moving with speed v on a straight road can be stopped with a distance d on applying breaks. If the same car is moving with a speed 3v and breaks provide half retardation, then car will stop after travelling distance
(a) 6 d
(b) 3 d
(c) 9 d
(d) 18 d

(14) A car travelling at a speed of 30 km h^{-1} is brought to rest in a distance of 8 m by applying breaks. If the same car is moving at a speed of 60 km h^{-1} then it can be brought to rest with same brakes in
(a) 64 m
(b) 32 m
(c) 16 m
(d) 4 m

(15) On a foggy day, two drivers spot in front of each other when 80 m apart. They were travelling at 70 km h^{-1} and 60 km h^{-1}. Both apply brakes simultaneously which retard the cars at rate of 5 m s^{-2}. Which of the following statements is correct?
(a) the collision will be averted
(b) the collision will take place
(c) they will cross each other
(d) they will just collide

(16) Two cars A and B are moving in same direction with velocities 30 m s^{-1} and 20 m s^{-1}. When car A is at a distance d behind the car B, the driver of the car A applies breaks producing uniform retardation of 2 m s^{-2}. There will be no collision when
(a) d < 2.5 m
(b) d > 125 m
(c) d > 25 m
(d) d < 125 m

Answer	**Kinematics**
	Topic : Equations of Motion in 1D

(1)	(b)	(5)	(a)	(9)	(d)	(13)	(d)
(2)	(c)	(6)	(a)	(10)	(a)	(14)	(b)
(3)	(a)	(7)	(a)	(11)	(a)	(15)	(a)
(4)	(b)	(8)	(c)	(12)	(b)	(16)	(b)

Physics MCQ | | Class - XI	Kinematics
	Topic : Equations of Motion in 2D

(1) A particle has an initial velocity of $3\hat{\imath} + 4\hat{\jmath}$ and an acceleration of $0.4\hat{\imath} + 0.3\hat{\jmath}$. The magnitude of its velocity after 10 s is
(a) 7 units
(b) $7\sqrt{2}$ units
(c) 8.5 units
(d) 10 units

(2) A particle's velocity changes from $(2\hat{\imath} + 3\hat{\jmath})$ m s^{-1} to $(2\hat{\imath} - 3\hat{\jmath})$ m s^{-1} in 2 s. The acceleration in m s^{-2} is
(a) $\hat{\imath} + 5\hat{\jmath}$
(b) $\frac{\hat{\imath} + 5\hat{\jmath}}{2}$
(c) zero
(d) $-3\hat{\jmath}$

(3) A body lying initially at point (3, 7) starts moving with a constant acceleration of $4\hat{\imath}$. Its position after 3 s is given by the co-ordinate
(a) (7, 3)
(b) (7, 18)
(c) (21, 7)
(d) (3, 7)

(4) A particle is moving with velocity 30 m s^{-1} towards east. After 10 s its velocity becomes 40 m s^{-1} towards north. The average acceleration of the body is
(a) 5 m s^{-2}
(b) 1 m s^{-2}
(c) 7 m s^{-2}
(d) $\sqrt{7}$ m s^{-2}

Answer	Kinematics
	Topic : Equations of Motion in 2D

(1)	(b)	(2)	(d)	(3)	(c)	(4)	(a)

Sub-unit (3) : Graphical Representation of Straight Line Motion

(1) Displacement-Time Graph	(2) Velocity-Time Graph
(3) Acceleration-Time Graph	(4) Graphical Proof of Equations of Motion

Motion refers to the change in the position of a particle with time. A graph is a visual representation of the relation between two variable quantities. To describe the motion of a particle, we can use graph which show the dependence of one physical quantity on another quantity.

(i) Distance -time graph :

- This graph shows the **total distance** travelled by a particle over **time**.
- The graph never decreases, as distance travelled can't be negative.
- The slope of the distance-time graph represents the **speed** of the particle.
- The area under the distance-time graph does not have any specific significance.

(ii) Position-time graph or Displacement-time graph :

- This graph shows the **position** of a particle relative to a fixed reference point over **time**. It also shows how the particle's location changes over time, including direction changes.
- The slope of the displacement-time graph represents the **velocity** of the particle.
- The area under the distance-time graph does not have any specific significance.

(iii) Speed-time graph :

- This graph allows for direct reading of the **speed** at any given **time**.
- The slope of the speed-time graph represents the **acceleration** of the particle.
- The area under the speed-time graph represents the **distance** travelled.

(iv) Velocity-time graph :

- This graph allows for direct reading of the **velocity** at any given **time**.
- The slope of the velocity-time graph represents the **acceleration** of the particle.
- The area under the velocity-time graph represents the **displacement** travelled.

(v) Acceleration-time graph :

- This graph allows for direct reading of the **acceleration** at any given **time**.
- The slope of the acceleration-time graph represents the **jerk**, or the rate of change of acceleration.
- The area under the acceleration-time graph represents the **change in velocity**.

(1) Distance- Time Graph

In distance – time graph, distance of the particle is taken along Y axis and the time is taken along X axis.

• Distance time graph from different cases :

For Stationary object (or, zero speed)	For uniform motion	For nonuniform motion (or Increasing speed)	For nonuniform motion (or, decreasing speed)
Distance / Time	Distance / Time	Distance / Time	Distance / Time
A straight line parallel to time axis	A straight line having a constant slope	A curved line having increasing slope	A curved line having decreasing slope

Note : A negative slope in distance-time graph would mean the distance travelled is decreasing as time passes, which is impossible because distance can only increase or remain constant. If the graph plotted is a displacement-time graph (which shows the change in position with time), then a negative slope would be possible, indicating the object is moving towards its starting point.

• Calculation of speed from distance-time graph :

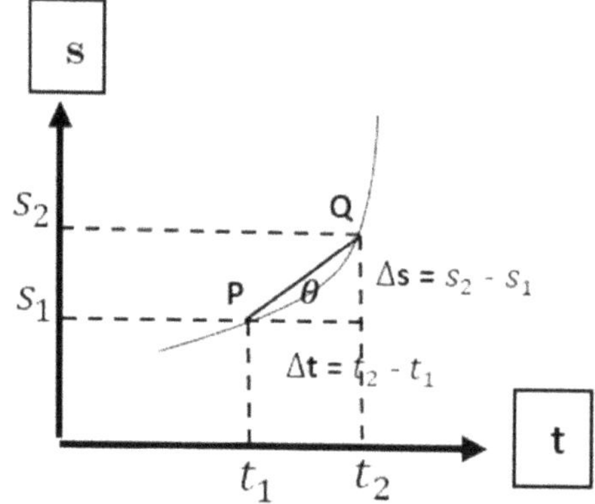

Let us consider, P and Q be the two points on the distance-time graph.

Slope of the line PQ (m) = tan θ

$$= \frac{\Delta s}{\Delta t} = \text{average speed}$$

i.e. The slope of straight line joining two points on the distance-time graph gives the **average speed** of the particle between those points or time interval.

When Δt approaches to zero, Q approaches to P. The cord PQ becomes a tangent line to the point P

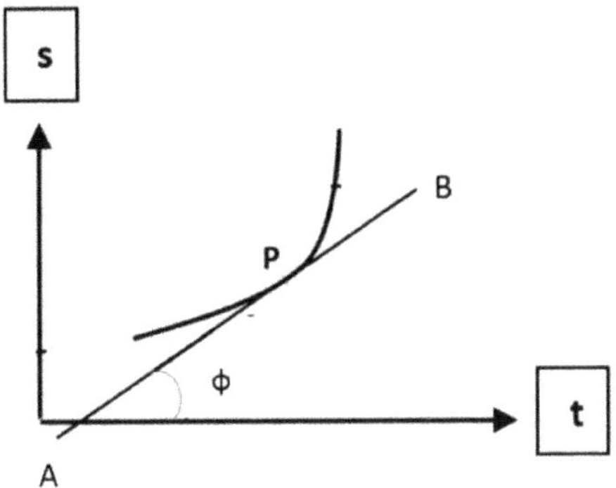

Now, Slope of the tangent AB = tan ϕ

$$= \lim_{\Delta t \to 0} \frac{\Delta s}{\Delta t}$$

$$= v \text{ (= Instantaneous speed)}$$

i.e. The slope of the tangent line at a point on the distance-time graph gives the value of **instantaneous speed** corresponding to that point or that instant.

(2) Displacement - Time Graph

In displacement – time graph, displacement of the particle is taken along Y axis and the time is taken along X axis. It is because time changes independently and displacement depends upon it.

• Displacement-time Graphs for Different Cases :

Particle is at rest (or Zero velocity i.e. Displacement is constant w.r.t. time)	
(a) When the particle in not at the origin:	**(b) When the particle is at the origin:**

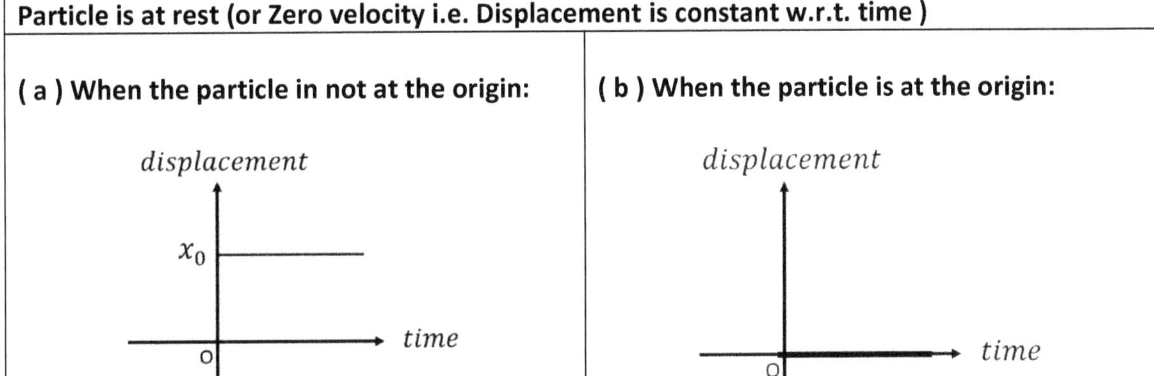

Explanation : θ = 0°
∴ Velocity (v) = tan θ = 0
In the first case initial displacement is x_0 and in the second case the initial displacement is zero.

Uniform motion (or zero acceleration)	
(a) Displacement is increasing w.r.t. time at constant rate or Constant positive velocity :	(b) Displacement is decreasing w.r.t. time at constant rate or Constant negative velocity :

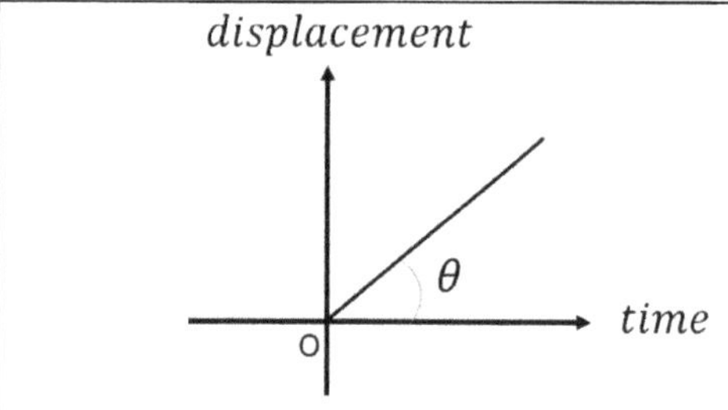	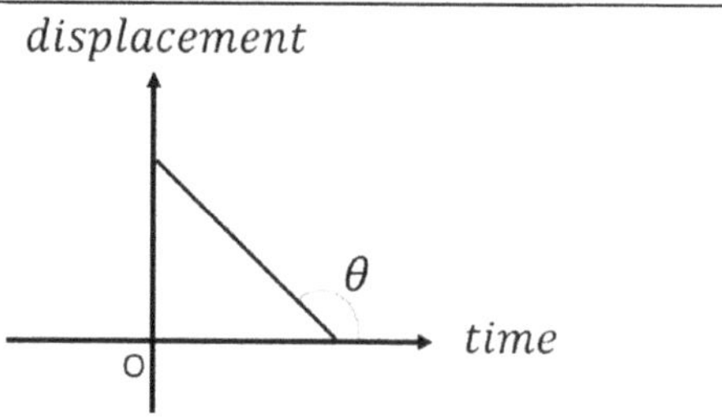
Explanation : θ = constant, [0° < θ < 90°] ∴ v (= tan θ) = (+ ve) constant	**Explanation :** θ = constant, [θ > 90°] ∴ v (= tan θ) = (− ve) constant

Uniform Accelerated Motion	**Uniformly retarded motion**
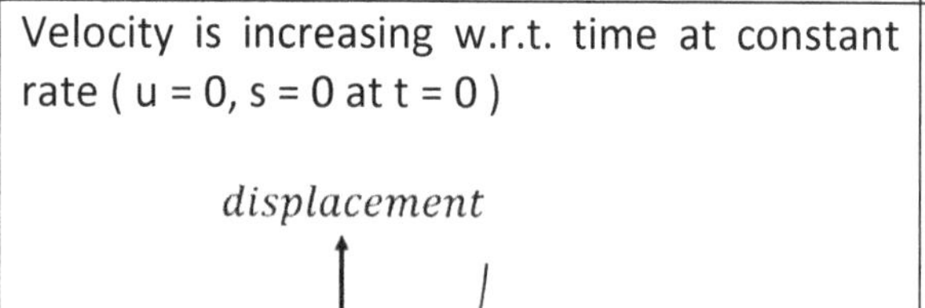 Velocity is increasing w.r.t. time at constant rate (u = 0, s = 0 at t = 0) displacement time O	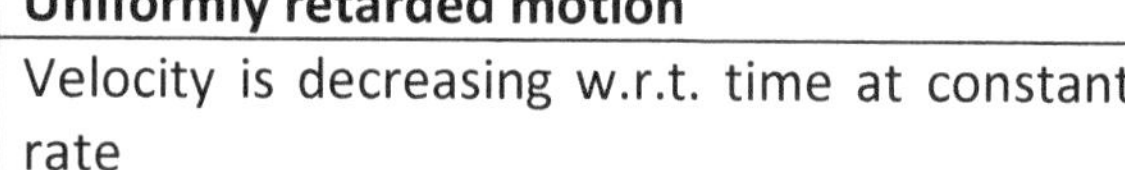 Velocity is decreasing w.r.t. time at constant rate 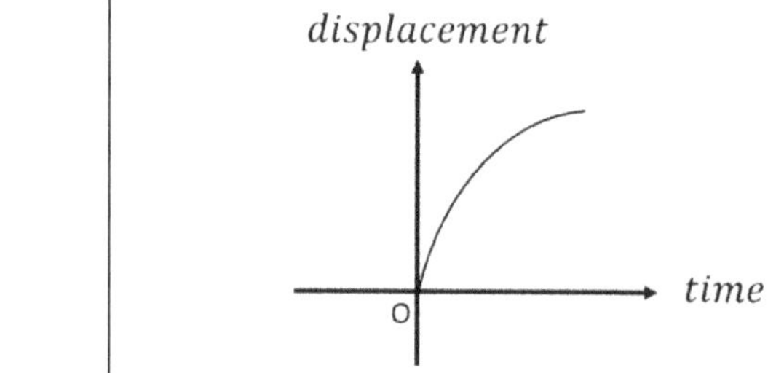
Explanation : θ = increasing ∴ v (= tan θ) is increasing. [In this situation, acceleration a is positive]	**Explanation :** θ = decreasing ∴ v (= tan θ) is decreasing. [In this situation, acceleration a is negative]

• If the displacement time graph is perpendicular to time axis, then it represents infinite velocity. Practically speaking, this is an **impossible situation**.

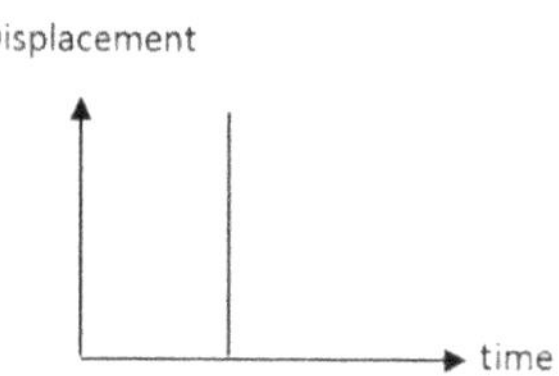

• Calculation of velocity from displacement-time graph :

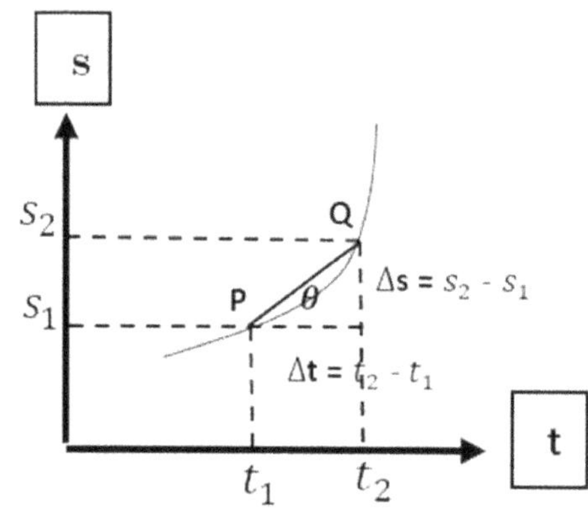

Let us consider, P and Q be the two points on the displacement-time graph.
Slope of the line PQ (m) = tan θ

$$= \frac{\Delta s}{\Delta t} = \text{average velocity}$$

i.e. The slope of straight line joining two points on the displacement-time graph gives the **average velocity** of the particle between those points or time interval.

When Δt approaches to zero, Q approaches to P. The cord PQ becomes a tangent line to the point P

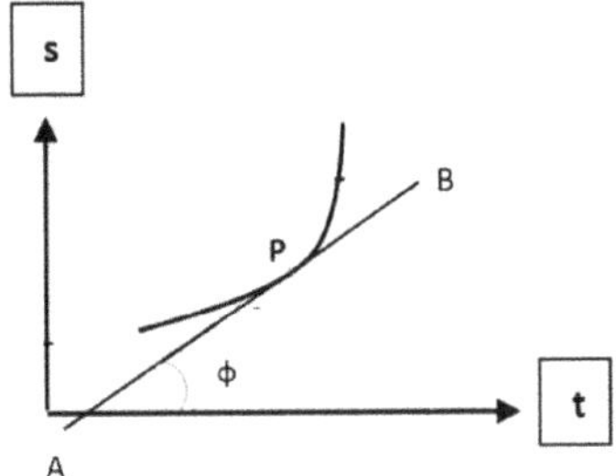

Now, Slope of the tangent AB = tan ϕ

$$= \lim_{\Delta t \to 0} \frac{\Delta s}{\Delta t}$$

$$= v \text{ (= Instantaneous velocity)}$$

i.e. The slope of the tangent line at a point on the displacement-time graph gives the value of **instantaneous velocity** corresponding to that point or that instant.

(3) Velocity - Time Graph

In velocity – time graph, velocity of the particle is taken along Y axis and the time is taken along X axis. It is because time changes independently and velocity depends upon it.

Velocity – Time Graph for Different Cases :

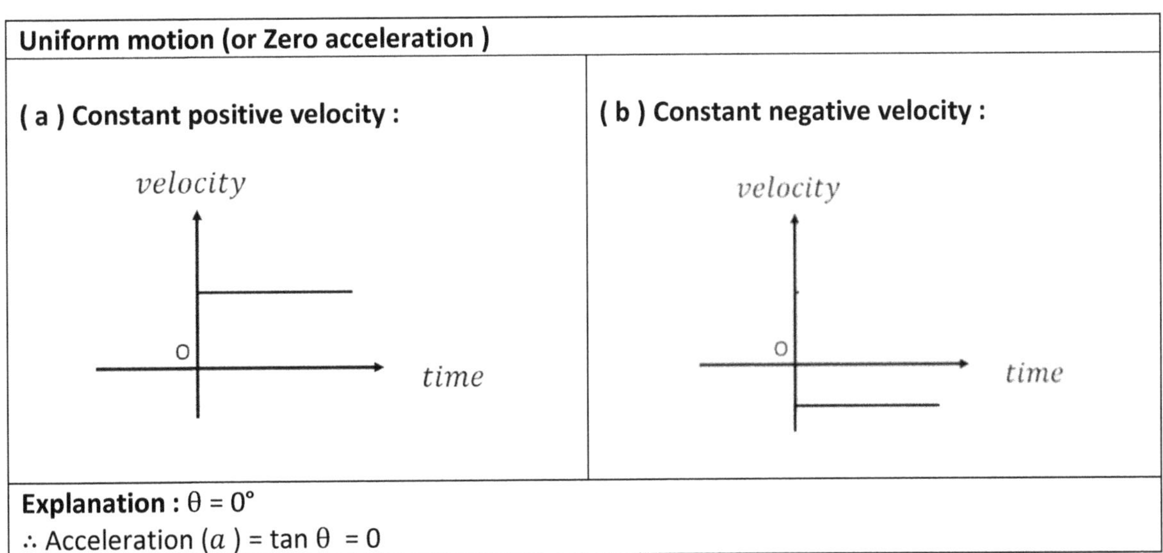

Uniformly accelerated motion (or constant acceleration)	
(a) Initial Velocity is zero (v_i = 0 at t = 0) 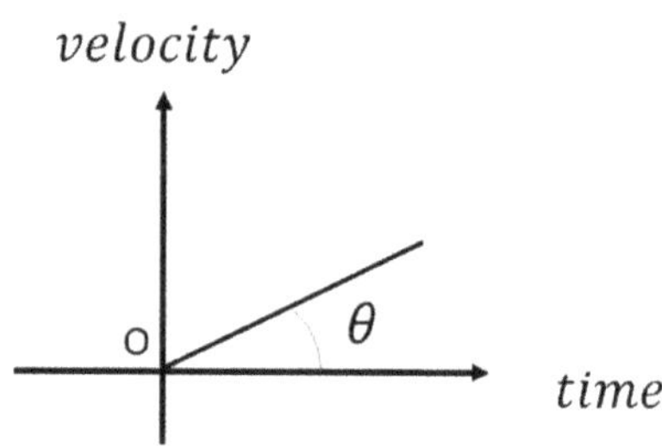 	**(b) Non-zero initial velocity ($v_i \neq$ 0 at t = 0):** 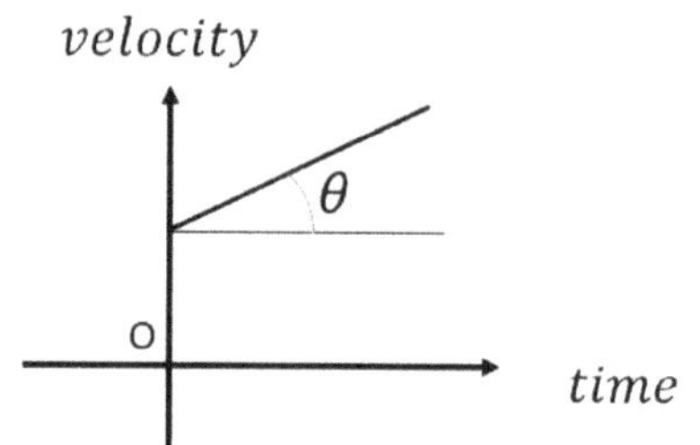
Explanation : θ = constant, [0° < θ < 90°] ∴ a (= tan θ) = (+ ve) constant i.e. Velocity is increasing w.r.t. time at constant rate	**Explanation :** θ = constant, [0° < θ < 90°] ∴ a (= tan θ) = (+ ve) constant

Uniformly retarded or decelerated motion or Uniformly negative acceleration	
(a) Initial Velocity is zero (v_i = 0 at t = 0) 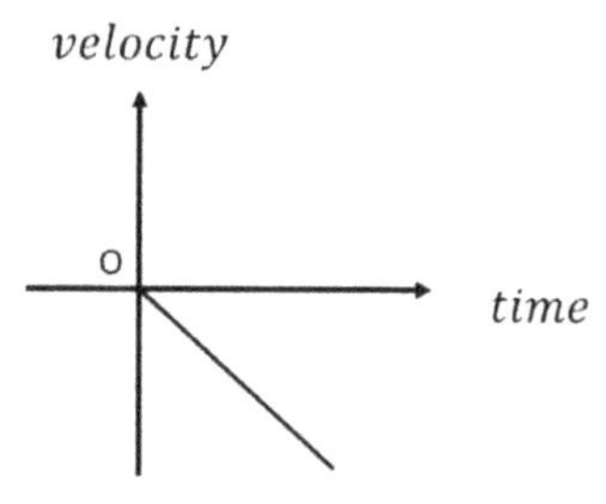 	**(b) Non-zero initial velocity ($v_i \neq$ 0 at t = 0):** 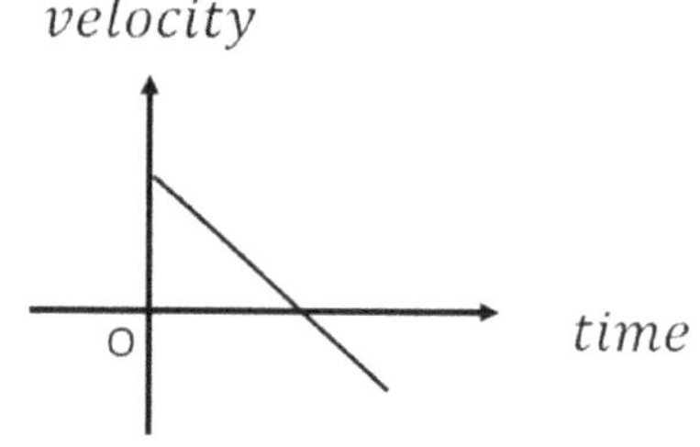
Explanation : θ = constant, [θ > 90°] ∴ a (= tan θ) = (– ve) constant i.e. Velocity is decreasing w.r.t. time at constant rate	

Non-uniformly accelerated motion	**Non-uniformly accelerated motion**
(a) Increasing acceleration	(b) Decreasing acceleration
Explanation : θ is increasing ∴ a (= tan θ) is increasing.	**Explanation :** θ is decreasing ∴ a (= tan θ) is decreasing.

• Velocity from velocity-time graph :

Velocity can be read from the graph.

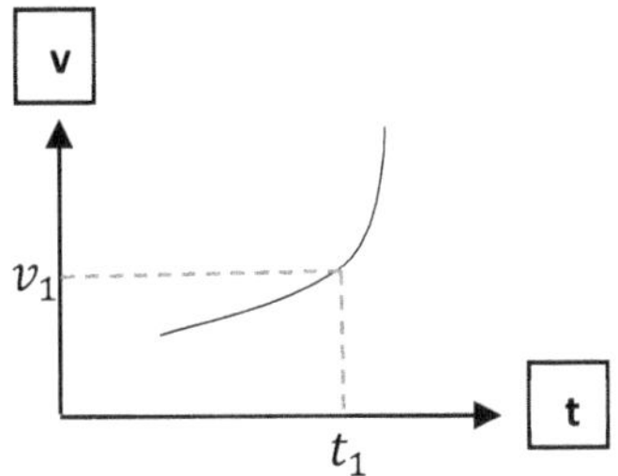

• Calculation of acceleration from velocity-time graph :

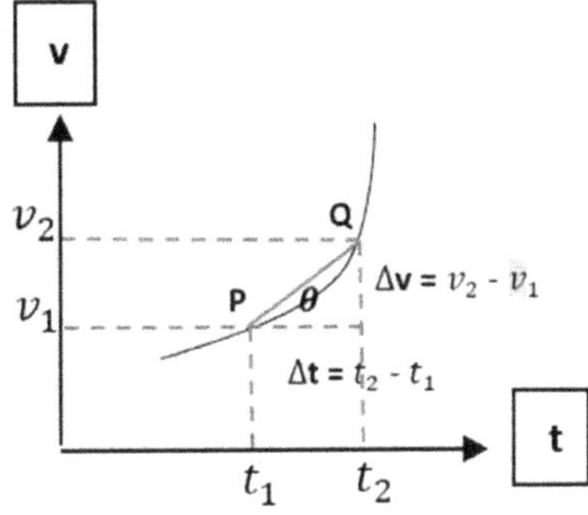

Let us consider, P and Q be the two points on the velocity-time graph.

Slope of the line PQ (m) = tan θ

$$= \frac{v_2 - v_1}{t_2 - t_1}$$

$$= \frac{\Delta v}{\Delta t} = a_{av} \text{ (= average acceleration)}$$

i.e. the slope of straight line joining two points on the velocity-time graph gives the **average acceleration** of the particle between those points or time interval.

When Δt approaches to zero, Q approaches to P. The cord PQ becomes a tangent line to the point P

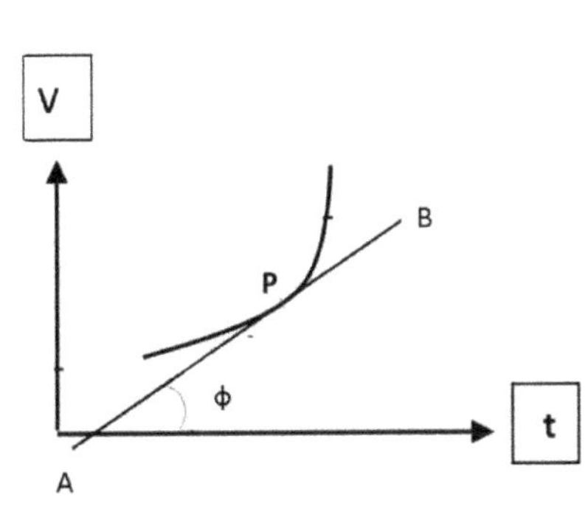

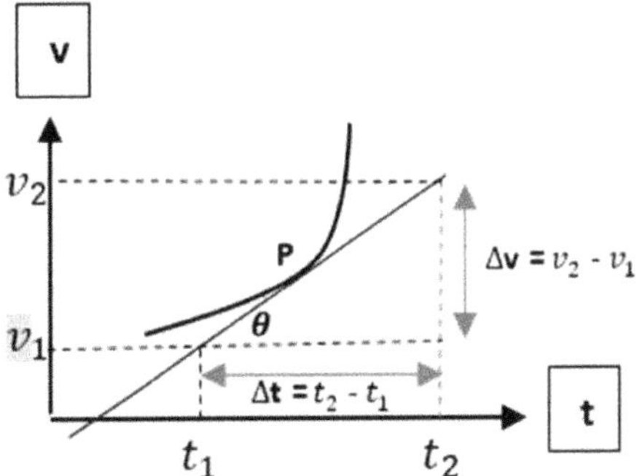

Now, Slope of the tangent AB = tan ϕ

$$= \lim_{\Delta t \to 0} \frac{\Delta v}{\Delta t}$$

$$= a \text{ (= Instantaneous acceleration)}$$

i.e. the slope of the tangent line at a point on the velocity-time graph gives the value of **instantaneous acceleration** corresponding to that point or that instant.

• Calculation of displacement from velocity-time graph :

The **area enclosed between the velocity-time graph and x axis (i.e. time axis) gives the displacement** of the particle.

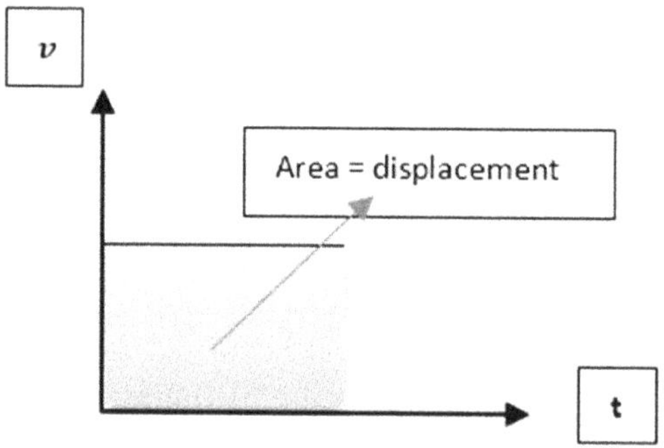

(3) Acceleration - Time Graph

In acceleration – time graph, velocity of the particle is taken along Y axis and the time is taken along X axis.

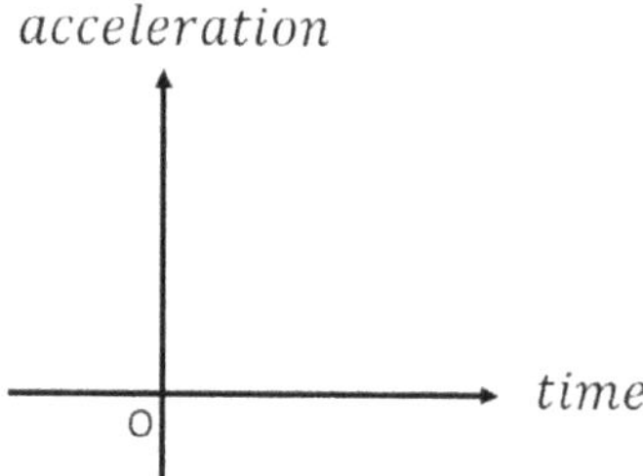

Acceleration –Time Graphs for Different Cases :

(i) Zero Acceleration :

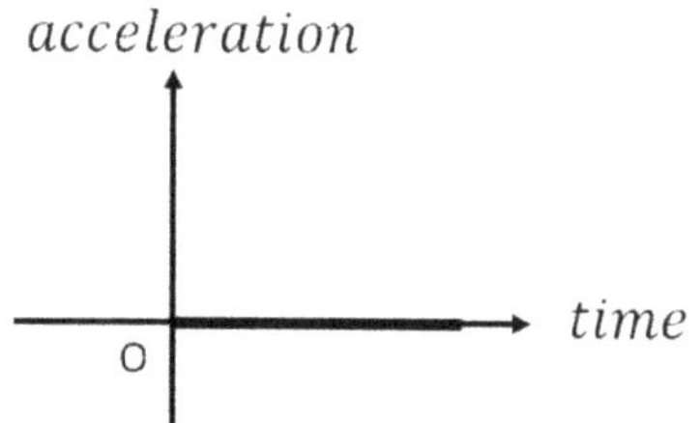

Explanation : a = 0

(ii) Uniform accelerated motion (constant positive acceleration)

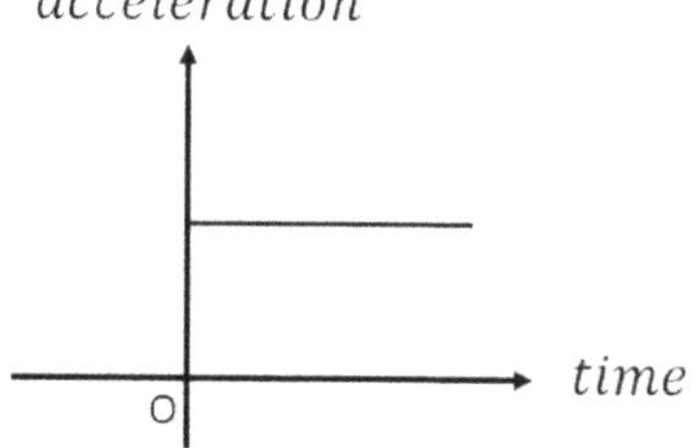

Explanation : a = constant

(iii) Uniform accelerated motion (constant negative acceleration)

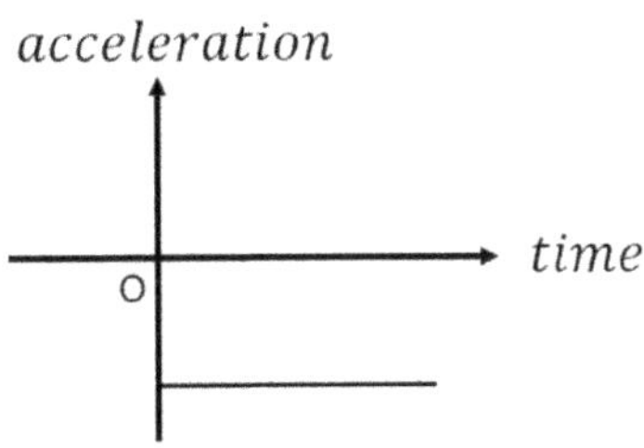

Explanation : a = constant

(iv) Non-uniformly accelerated motion

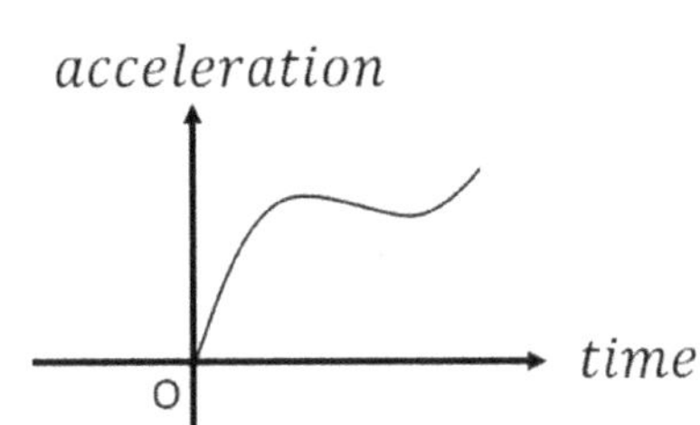

Explanation : a is variable

• Acceleration from acceleration-time graph :

Acceleration can be read from the graph.

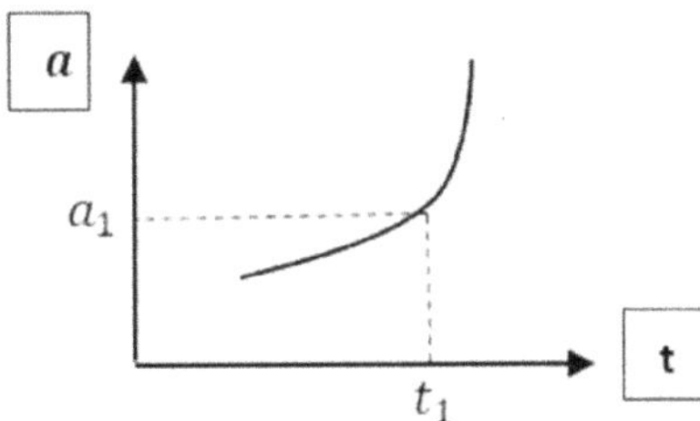

• Change in velocity from acceleration-time graph :

The **area enclosed between the acceleration-time graph and x axis (i.e. time axis) gives the change in velocity** of the particle.

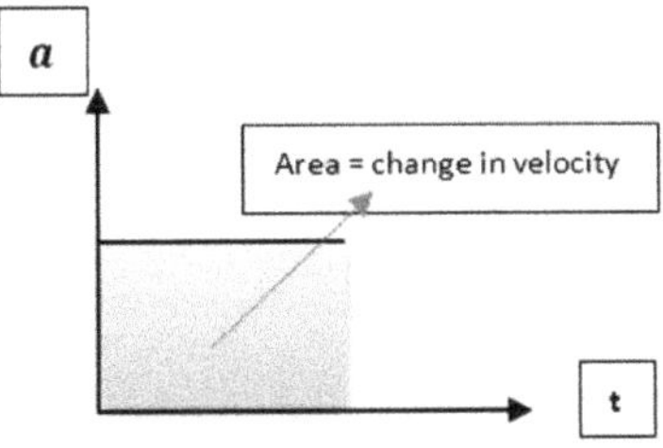

(4) Graphical Proof of the Equations of Motion :

(4.1) Proof of the equation $v_f = v_i + at$:

Let us consider a particle with initial velocity v_i and an acceleration a attains a final velocity v_f after time t.

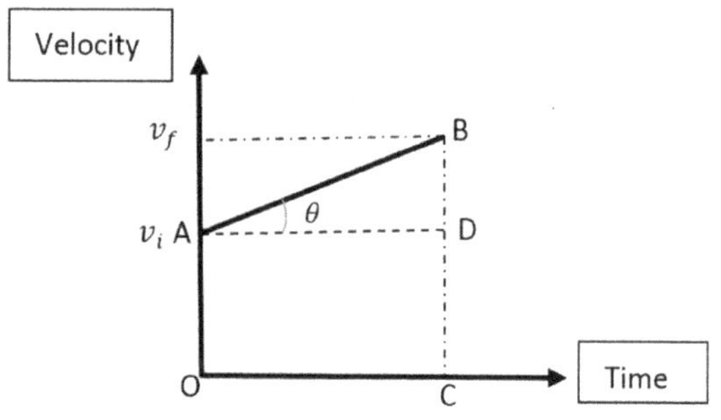

The velocity time graph of the particle is drawn by plotting time (t) along X axis and velocity (v) along Y axis. Since the particle is moving with uniform acceleration the line AB in the figure represents the motion.

According to the figure,
OA = initial velocity (v_i)
OC = time (t)
CB = final velocity (v_f)

Now, acceleration of the particle:
a = slope of AB
or, $a = \tan\theta$
or, $a = \frac{BD}{AD}$
or, $a = \frac{BC-DC}{OC} = \frac{v_f - v_i}{t}$
or, $v_f - v_i = at$
$\therefore v_f = v_i + at$

(4.2) Proof of the equation $s = v_i\, t + \frac{1}{2} a\, t^2$:

Let us consider a particle with initial velocity v_i and an acceleration a attains a final velocity v_f after time t.

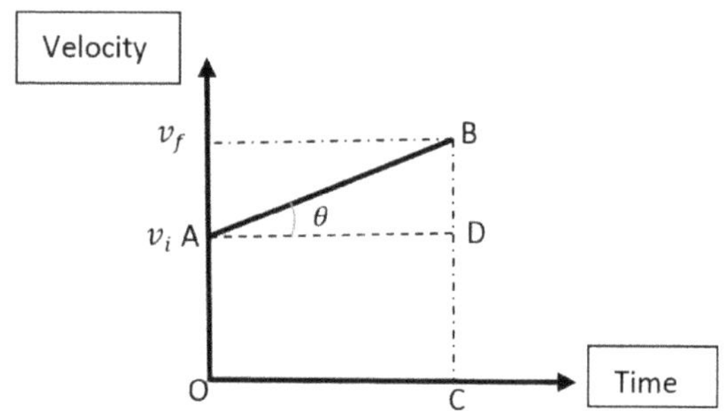

The velocity time graph of the particle is drawn by plotting time (t) along X axis and velocity (v) along Y axis. Since the particle is moving with uniform acceleration the line AB in the figure represents the motion.
According to the figure,
OA = initial velocity (v_i)
OC = time (t)
CB = final velocity (v_f)

Now, acceleration of the particle :

a = slope of AB
$= \tan\theta = \frac{BD}{AD}$

We know that the area enclosed between the velocity time graph and X axis (i.e. time axis) gives the displacement of the body.

Hence the distance covered by the particle in time t :
s = area of the trapezium AOCB
or, s = area of the rectangle AOCD + area of ΔABD
or, $s = AO \times OC + \frac{1}{2} AD \times BD$
or, $s = AO \times OC + \frac{1}{2} AD^2 \times \frac{BD}{AD}$
or, $s = v_i\, t + \frac{1}{2} t^2\, a$
$\therefore s = v_i\, t + \frac{1}{2} a\, t^2$

(4.3) Proof of the equation $v_f{}^2 = u^2 + 2\,a\,s$:

Let us consider a particle with initial velocity v_i and an acceleration a attains a final velocity v after time t.

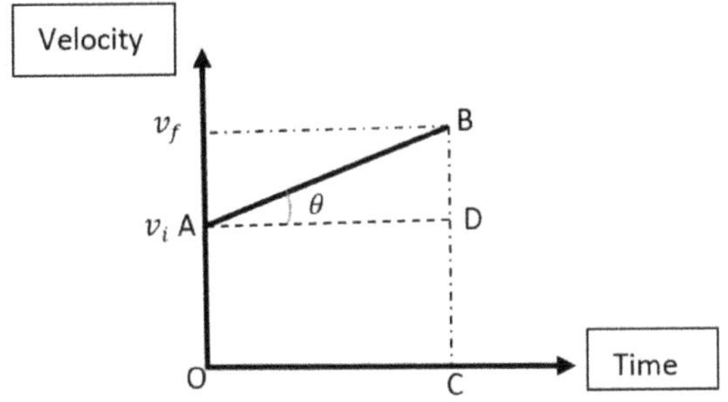

The velocity time graph of the particle is drawn by plotting time (t) along X axis and velocity (v) along Y axis. Since the particle is moving with uniform acceleration the line AB in the figure represents the motion. According to the figure,
OA = initial velocity (v_i)
OC = time (t)
CB = final velocity (v_f)

Now, acceleration of the particle :

a = slope of AB

= tan θ

$= \frac{BD}{AD} = \frac{BD}{OC}$

We know that the area enclosed between the velocity time graph and X axis (i.e. time axis) gives the displacement of the body.

Hence the distance covered by the particle in time t = s = area of the trapezium AOCB

or, $s = \frac{1}{2}(AO + BC) \times OC$

or, $s = \frac{1}{2}(AO + BC) \times \frac{BD}{a}$ $[\because a = \frac{BD}{OC}]$

or, $s = \frac{1}{2}(AO + BC) \times \frac{(BC - CD)}{a}$

or, $2as = (v_i + v_f)(v_f - v_i)$

or, $v_f^2 - v_i^2 = 2as$

$\therefore v_f^2 = v_i^2 + 2as$

(4.4) Proof of the equation $s_t = v_i + \frac{1}{2}a(2t - 1)$:

Let us consider a particle with initial velocity v_i and an acceleration a attains a final velocity v_f after time t.

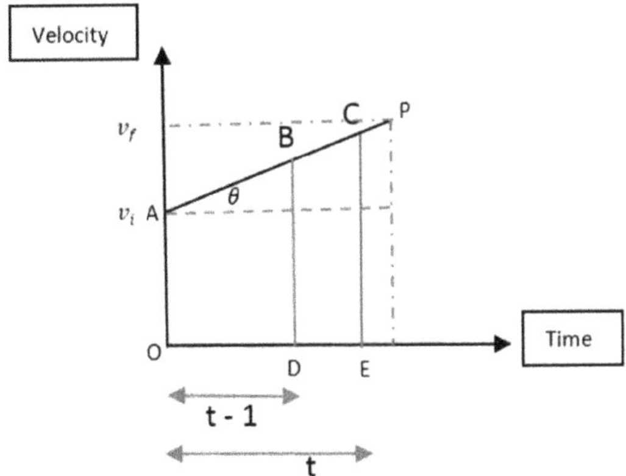

The velocity time graph of the particle is drawn by plotting time (t) along X axis and velocity (v) along Y axis. Since the particle is moving with uniform acceleration the line AP in the figure represents the motion. Hence, the equation of the straight line is

$$v_f = v_i + at\ .$$

The parts of this line AB and AC represent the motion of the particle in (t – 1) and t second respectively .

We know that the area enclosed between the velocity time graph and X axis (i.e. time axis) gives the displacement of the body.

∴ Displacement of the particle in t^{th} second

s_t = Area of the trapezium DBCE

$= \frac{1}{2}(BD + EC) \times DE$

According to the fig. DE = OE – OD

= t – (t – 1) = 1

BD = velocity in time (t-1)

$= v_i + a(t - 1)$

EC = velocity in time t

$= v_i + at$

$s_t = \frac{1}{2}[v_i + a(t - 1) + v_i + at] \times 1$

or, $s_t = \frac{1}{2}[v_i + a\ t - a + v_i + at]$

or, $s_t = \frac{1}{2}[2v_i + a(2t - 1)]$

$\therefore s_t = v_i + \frac{1}{2}a(2t - 1)$

Solved Examples & Exercise : Graphical Representation of Motion

Position – time graph

Type – 1 : Calculation of Distance or Displacement from Position-time Graph

Question : The position-time graph for a particle moving along a straight line is shown in the figure. What is the total distance travelled by it in time t = 0 to t = 10 s?

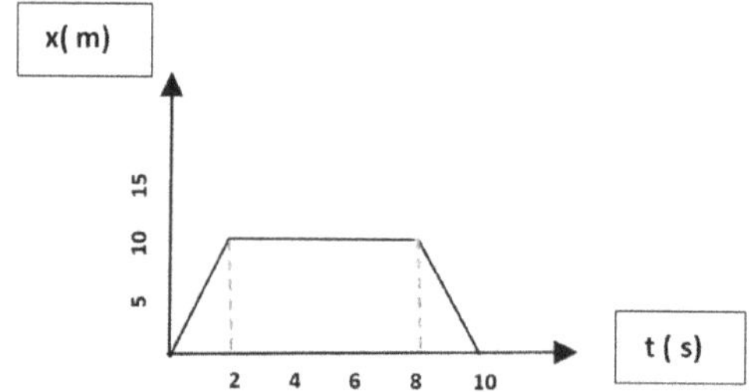

Answer : Distance travelled by the particle form t = 0 to t = 2s : S_1 = 10 m
Distance travelled by the particle form t = 2 s to t = 8 s : S_2 = 0 m
Distance travelled by the particle form t = 8 to t = 10 s : S_3 = 10 m
∴ The total distance travelled by it in time t = 0 to t = 10 s : S = 10 + 10 = 20 m

Type – 2 : Calculation of Average Speed or Velocity from Position-time Graph

Question : The position (x) of a particle moving along x-axis varies with time (t) as shown in figure. Find the average speed of particle in time interval t = 0 to t = 8 s.

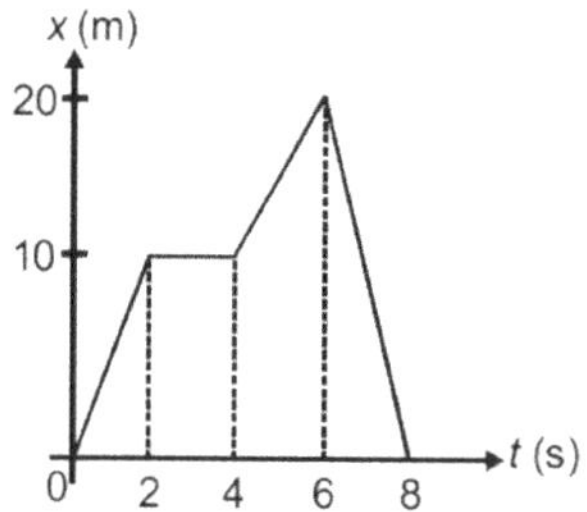

Answer : Distance travelled by the particle form t = 0 to t = 2s : S_1 = 10 m
Distance travelled by the particle form t = 2 s to t = 4 s : S_2 = 0 m
Distance travelled by the particle form t = 4 s to t = 6 s : S_3 = 10 m
Distance travelled by the particle form t = 6 s to t = 8 s : S_3 = 20 m
∴ The total distance travelled by it in time t = 0 to t = 8 s : s = (10 + 10 + 20) m = 40 m
∴ Average speed of the particle = $\frac{40}{8}$ = 5 m s^{-1}

Type – 3 : Finding the Nature of Velocity or Speed from Position-time graph

Question : What does the slope of displacement-time graph represent ?

Answer : Slope of displacement -time graph represents the velocity of the particle.

Question : Can x-t graph (position-time graph) have a negative slope ?

Answer : Yes, x-t graph can have a negative slope, when the velocity of the body is negative.

Question : The position-time graph of an object is given below. What is the velocity of the object?

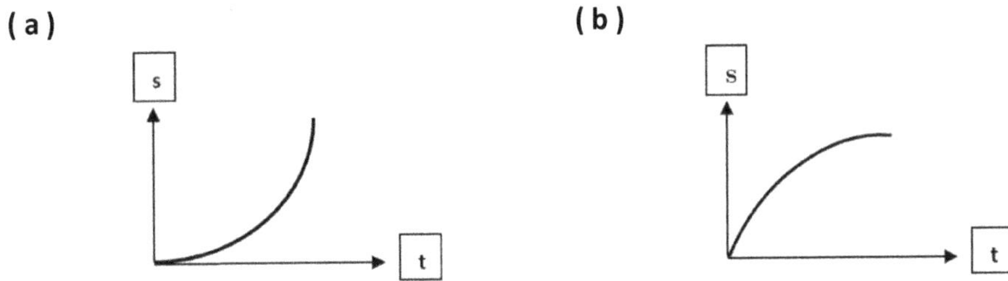

Answer : (a) The position-time graph in (a) represents accelerated motion because slope of the graph is increasing with time.

(b) The position time graph in (b) represents decelerated motion, because slope of the graph is decreasing with time.

Q : The displacement-time graph of two moving objects A and B are shown in the figure given below. Which of the object is moving with constant velocity ?

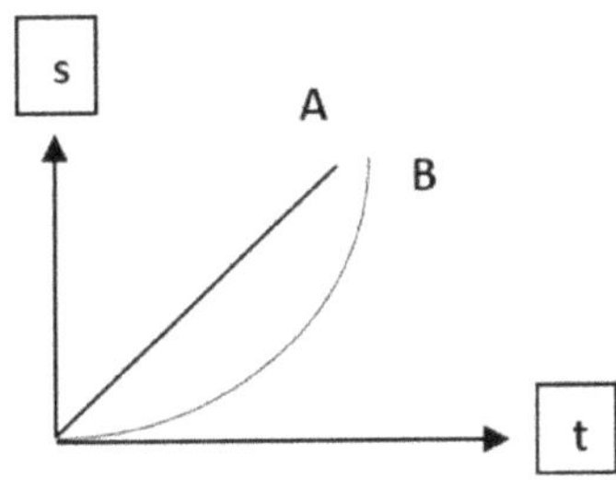

Answer : Since the slope of the displacement-time graph for the object A is constant, the object A is moving with constant velocity.

Question : The position-time graph of a moving particle is shown, At what point the instantaneous velocity of the particle is negative?

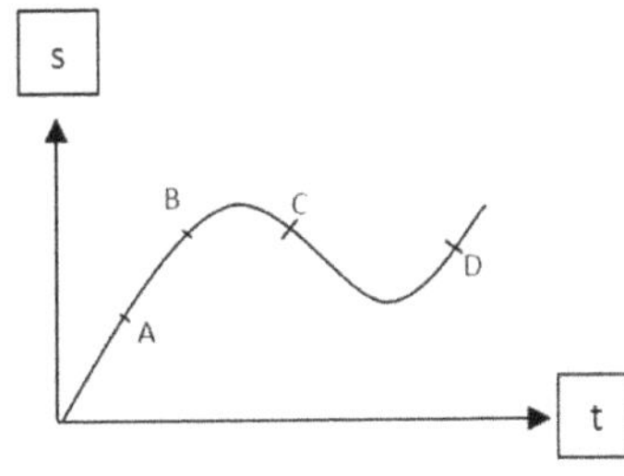

Answer : Since the slope of the position-time graph at the point C is negative, the velocity of the particle is negative at the point C.

Type – 4 : Drawing of Position -time Graph:

Question : Draw the position-time graph of an object moving with zero acceleration.

Answer : The position-time graph of an object moving with zero acceleration is shown below :

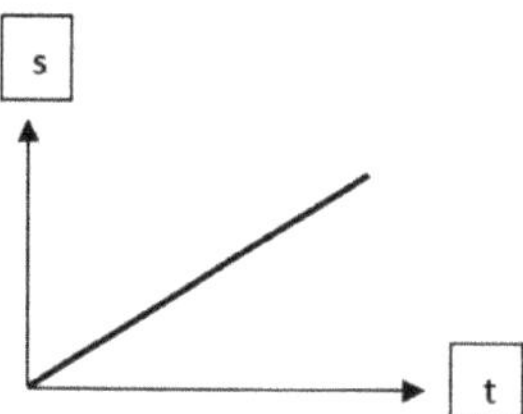

Question : Can position-time graph be a straight line parallel to position axis?

Answer : No, it is because, the x-t graph parallel to position axis indicates that the position of the object is changing at a given instant of time.

Type – 5 Calculation of Instantaneous Velocity or Speed

Q: The displacement-time graphs of two moving particles make angles of 30° and 60° with the X axis. Find the ratio of the velocities of the two particles.

Answer : The slope of the displacement-time graph of a particle is equal to the velocity of the particle. Now the velocity of the first particle : $v_1 = \tan 30° = \frac{1}{\sqrt{3}}$

and the velocity of the second particle : $v_2 = \tan 60° = \sqrt{3}$

$\therefore \frac{v_1}{v_2} = \frac{1}{\sqrt{3}} \times \frac{1}{\sqrt{3}} = \frac{1}{3}$

Q : The position-time graph of an object in uniform motion is given below. Calculate the velocity with which the object is moving?

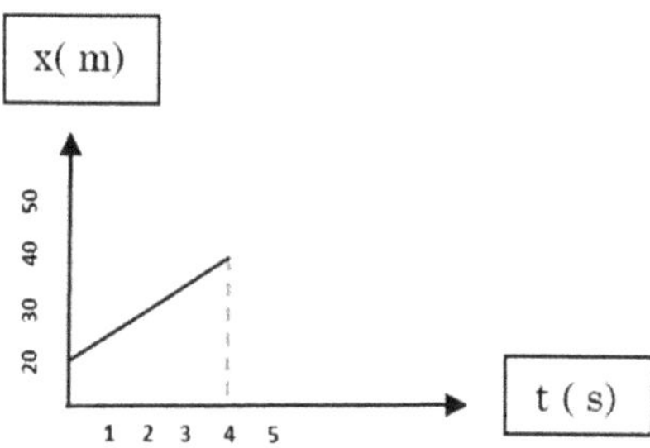

Answer :

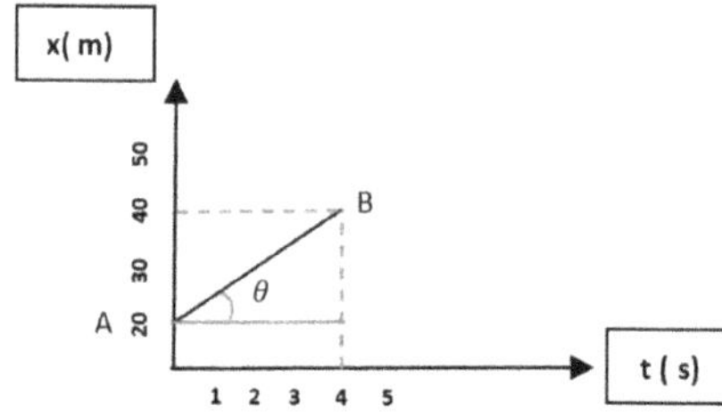

Velocity of the object (v) = slope of the line AB

$= \tan \theta$

$= \frac{40-20}{4-0}$

$= 5 \text{ m s}^{-1}$

Try Yourself

(1) What does the slope of displacement-time graph represent ?

(2) How can you find average velocity of a particle from displacement-time graph ?

(3) The position time graph of an object is given below. What is the velocity of the object?

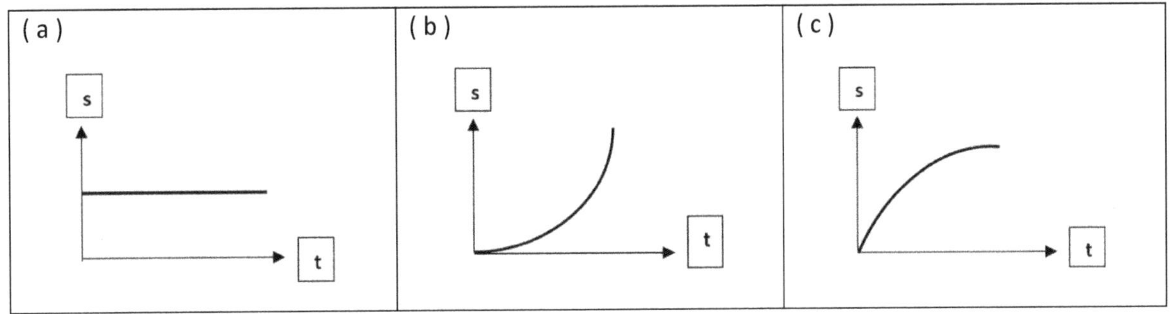

(4) Is the time variation of position, shown in the adjacent figure, observed in nature?

(5) A particle shows distance-time curve as given in the figure. At what point the instantaneous velocity is maximum?

(6) The position-time graph for a body moving along a straight line between O and A is shown in figure. During its motion between O and A, how many times body comes to rest?

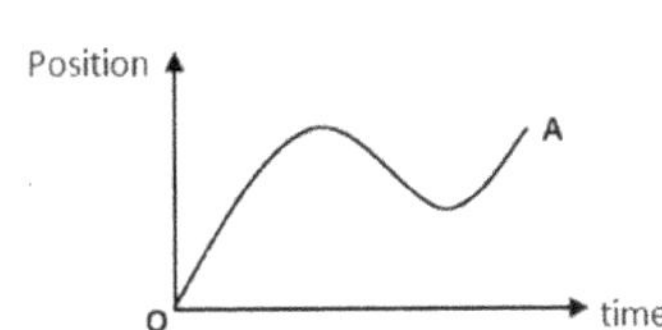

(7) Draw the position time graph of an object moving with zero acceleration.

(8) Draw the displacement-time graphs for the following : (a) accelerated motion, (b) retarded motion.

(9) The displacement-time graph for two particles A and B is as shown. Calculate the ratio of their velocities?

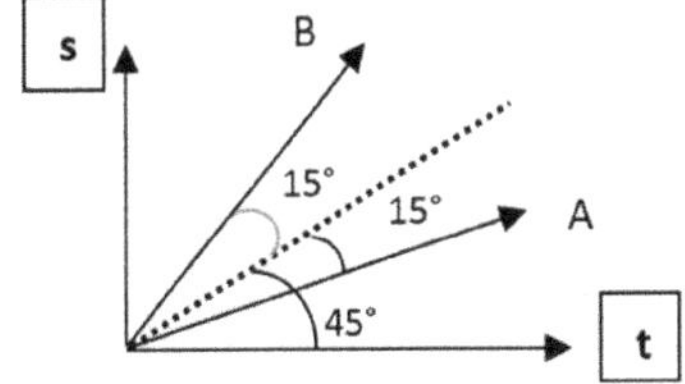

(10) Displacement–time graph of two particles shows in the figure. Is their relative velocity zero or constant?

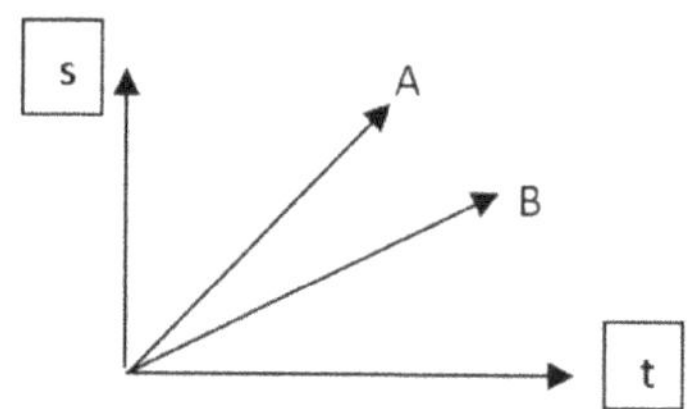

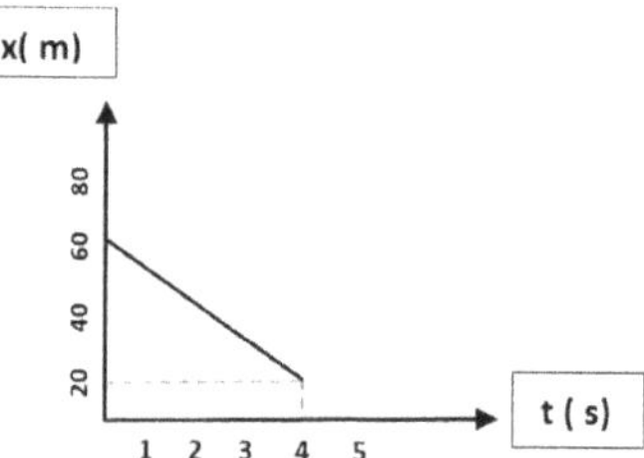

(11) The position -time graph of an object in uniform motion is given below. Calculate the velocity with which the object is moving?

(12) An object travels a distance of 25 m in first 5 seconds. From 5 s to 10 s, it moves constant velocity, then it moves 25 m to 0 in next 5 seconds.

(i) Draw the displacement-time graph.

(ii) Describe the motion of the object in each time interval.

(iii) What is the total distance travelled and net displacement ?

Speed – Time Graph and Velocity – Time Graph

Type – 6 : Calculation of Distance or Displacement from Velocity-time Graph :

Question : How can you determine the displacement from velocity-time graph of the motion?

Answer : The area enclosed by the velocity-time graph and time axis gives the displacement of the particle.

Question : The velocity-time graph of a body moving in straight line is given in the fig. Calculate the distance and displacement of the body in 5 s.

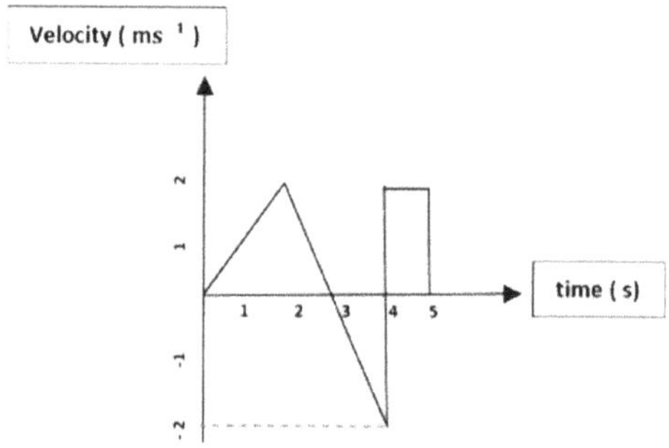

Answer : Distance travelled by body S = area under the speed-time graph

$$= \frac{1}{2} \times 3 \times 2 + \frac{1}{2} \times 1 \times 2 + 1 \times 2$$

$$= 3 + 1 + 2 = 6 \text{ m}$$

Displacement is positive from 0 to 3 s, negative from 3 s to 4 s and positive from 4 s to 5 s.

$\therefore$ Total displacement in 5 s is $S' = \frac{1}{2} \times 3 \times 2 - \frac{1}{2} \times 1 \times 2 + 1 \times 2$

$$= 3 - 1 + 2 = 5 \text{ m}$$

Type – 7 : Calculation of Average Velocity from Velocity-time Graph :

Question : The speed-time graph of a particle moving along a solid curves as shown below. Calculate the average speed travelled by the particle from t = 0 to t = 3 s.

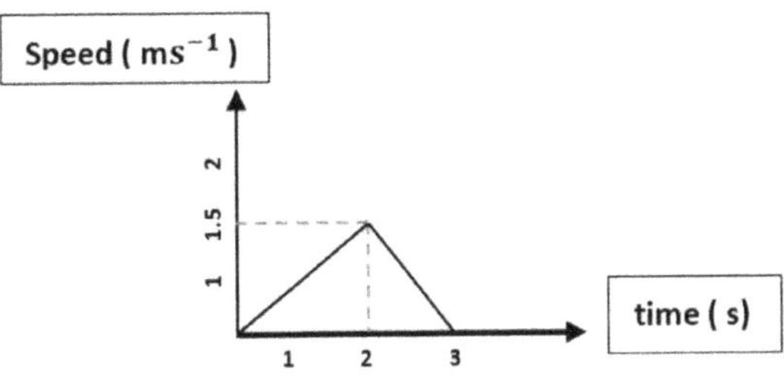

Answer : Distance travelled by the particle = area under the speed-time graph

$$= \frac{1}{2} \times 3 \times 1.5 \text{ m}$$

$$= 2.25 \text{ m}$$

∴ Average speed of the particle $v_{av} = \frac{2.25}{3} \text{ ms}^{-1} = 0.75 \text{ ms}^{-1}$

Type – 8 : Finding the Nature of Acceleration from Velocity-time Graph :

Question : How can you determine the average acceleration from velocity-time graph of the motion?

Answer : The slope of straight line joining two points on the velocity-time graph gives the **average acceleration** of the particle between those points or time interval.

Question : What do the following represent? [v = velocity and t = time]
(a) Slope of v-t graph
(b) Area of v-t graph

Answer : (a) Instantaneous acceleration

(b) change in velocity

Question : The Velocity-time graph of an object is given below. What is the acceleration of the object?

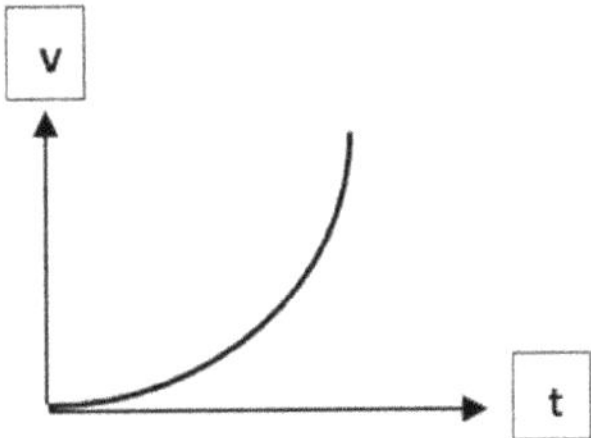

Answer : The velocity-time graph in the figure represents Increasing accelerated motion because slope of the graph is increasing with time.

Type – 9 : Calculation of Average / Instantaneous Acceleration

Q: The velocity time graph for two particles A and B is as follows. Calculate the ratio of their acceleration.

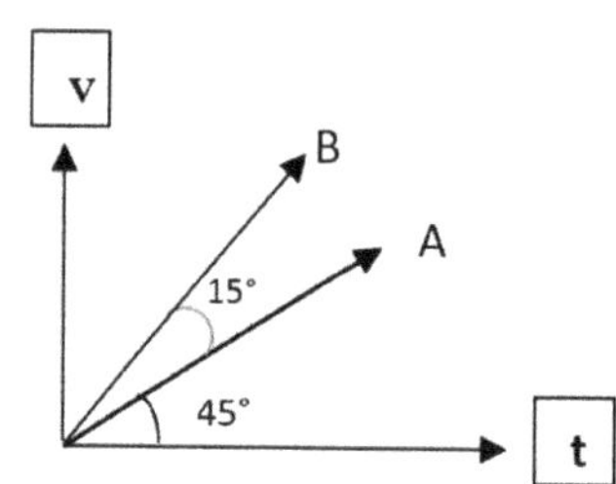

Answer : The slope of the acceleration-time graph of a particle is equal to the acceleration of the particle. Now the acceleration of the particle A : a_1 = tan $45°$ = 1

and the acceleration of the particle B : a_2 = tan $60°$ = $\sqrt{3}$

$\therefore \frac{a_1}{a_2} = 1 \times \frac{1}{\sqrt{3}} = \frac{1}{\sqrt{3}}$

Try Yourself

(13) How can you determine the displacement covered by a uniformly accelerated body from velocity-time graph of the motion?

(14) The velocity-time graph of a body moving in straight line is given in the fig. Calculate the displacement of the body in 10 s.

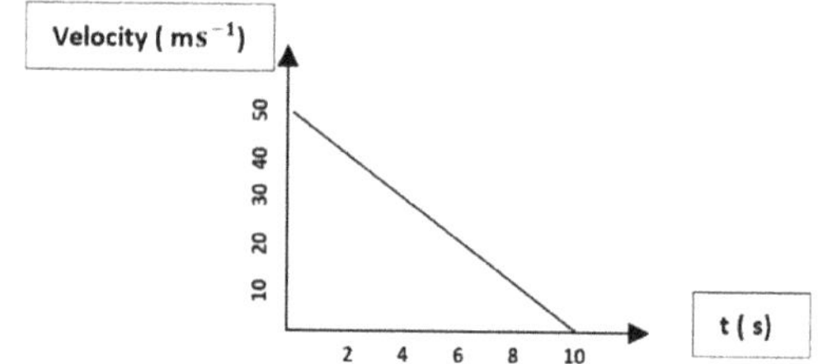

(15) The velocity-time graph of a body moving in straight line is given in the fig. Calculate the distance and the displacement of the body in 6 s.

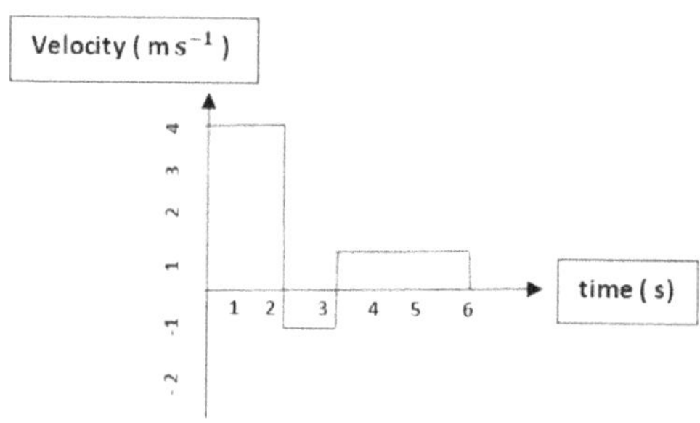

(16) The velocity-time graph of a body moving in straight line is given in the fig. Calculate the displacement of the body in 5 s.

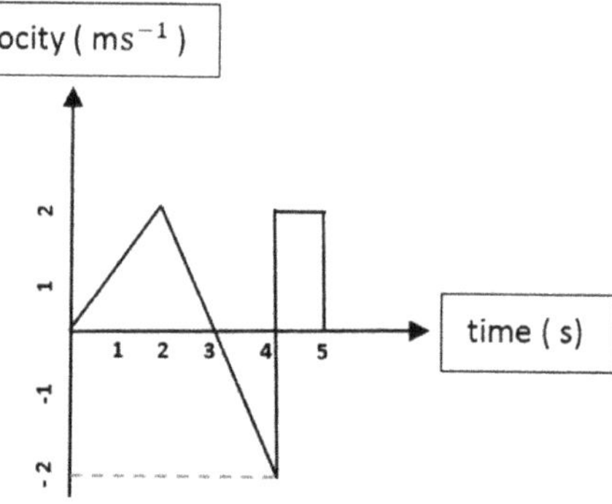

(17) The velocity-time graph of a body moving in straight line is given in the fig.
(i) Is the motion uniform ?
(ii) Does the body change its direction of motion ?
(iii) Find the distance covered from 0 to 4 s and from 4 s to 6 s.

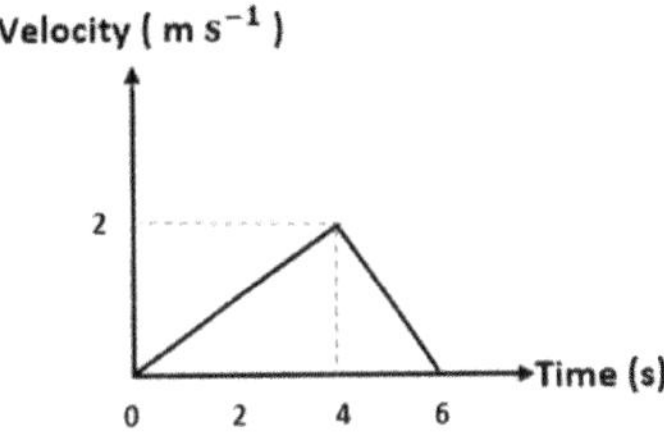

(18) The velocity-time graph of a body moving in straight line is given in the fig. Calculate the average velocity of the body.

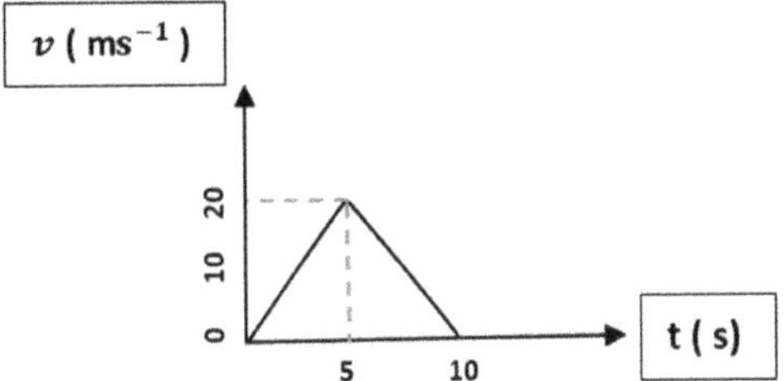

(19) What does the slope of velocity time graph represent ?
(20) Draw the velocity-time graphs for the following : (a) accelerated motion, (b) retarded motion.
(21) What is the velocity time graph for a body moving with uniform velocity?
(22) Establish the following relation graphically : (a) $s = ut + \frac{1}{2}at^2$;
(b) $v^2 = u^2 + 2as$
(23) Establish the following relation graphically : (a) $s_t = u + \frac{1}{2}a(2t - 1)$,(b) $s = \frac{1}{2}at^2$

(24) The speed-time graph of a particle moving along a solid curves as shown below. Calculate the distance travelled by the particle from t = 0 to t = 3 s.

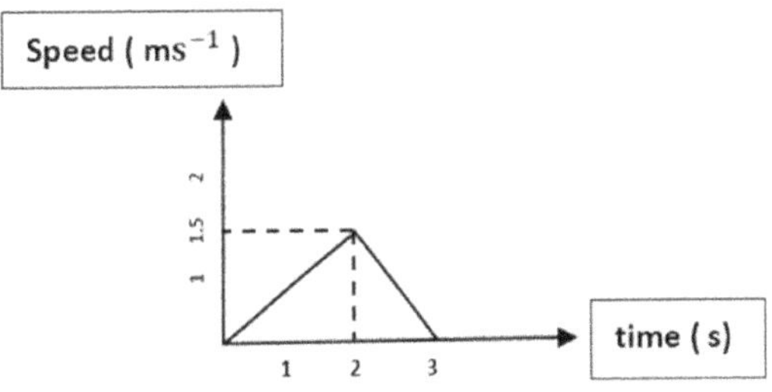

(25) The velocity-time graph of a moving particle is shown below. At what point the acceleration of the particle is negative ?

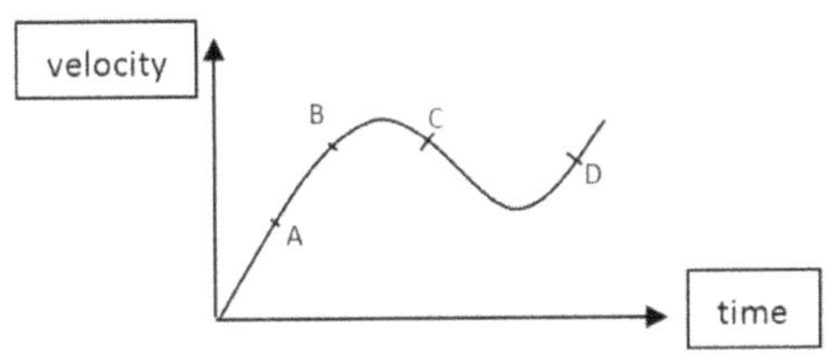

(26) The velocity-time graph of a body moving in straight line is given in the fig. Calculate the displacement of the body in 10 s.

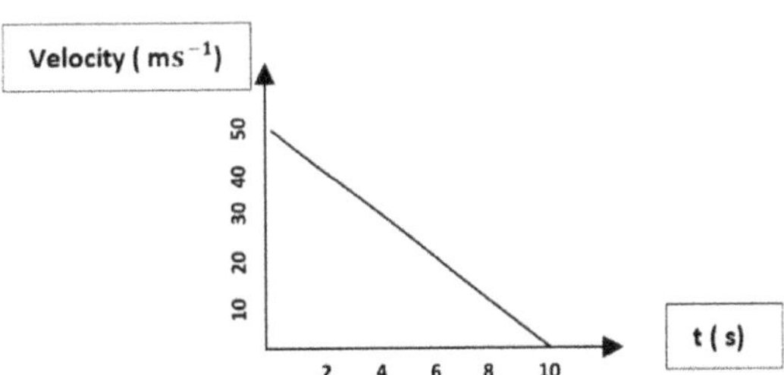

(27) Velocity–time graph of two particles shows in the figure. State the nature of their relative velocity.

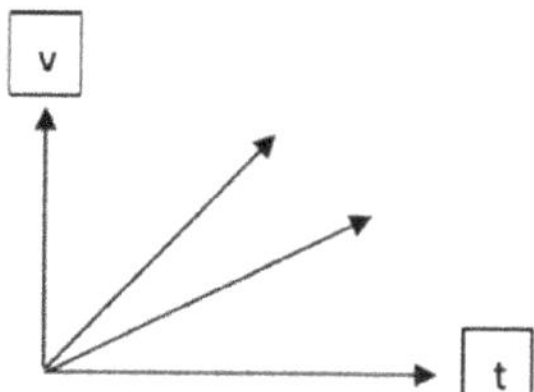

(28) A bus accelerates uniformly from rest to 15 m s^{-1} in 10 s. It maintains this speed for 20 s and then decelerates to rest in 5 s.
(a) Draw the velocity -time graph.
(b) Calculate : (i) acceleration during the first 10 s.
(ii) Total distance travelled by the bus.
(iii) retardation during the last 5 s.

(29) A car accelerates from rest at a constant rate α for some time, after which it decelerates at a constant rate β to come to rest. If the total time elapsed is t, evaluate (a) the maximum velocity reached and (b) the total distance travelled.

Acceleration-Time Graph

Type – 9 : Calculation of Change in Velocity from acceleration-time graph

Question : Acceleration–time graph of a particle moving in a straight line is shown in fig. The velocity of the particle at time t = 0 is 2 m/s. Find velocity at the end of fourth second.

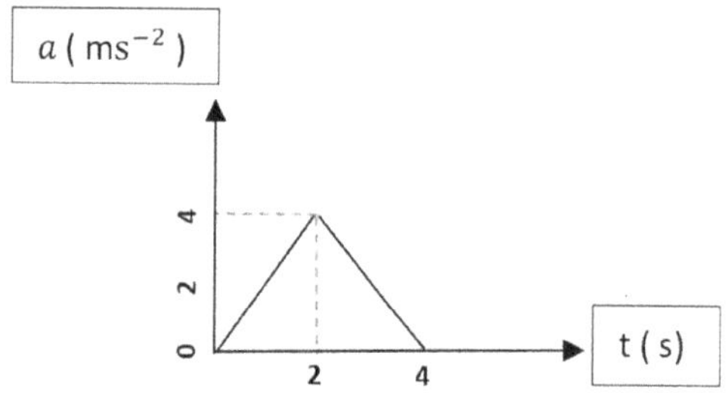

Answer : Change in velocity = area under the a-t graph

or, $v_f - v_i = \frac{1}{2} \times 4 \times 4$

or, $v_f - 2 = 8$

$\therefore v_f = 10$

∴ Final velocity at the end of fourth second is 10 m s^{-1}

(30) What does the area under acceleration-time graph represent?
(31) The position (x) of a particle moving along a straight line at time t is given by x = ($3t^2 - 5t + 2$) m. Find (1) velocity at t = 2 s (2) acceleration at t = 2 s and draw the corresponding velocity-time and acceleration–time graphs.

(32) A particle starts from rest at t = 0 and moves in a straight line with an acceleration as shown in the figure. Calculate the velocity of the particle at t = 3s.

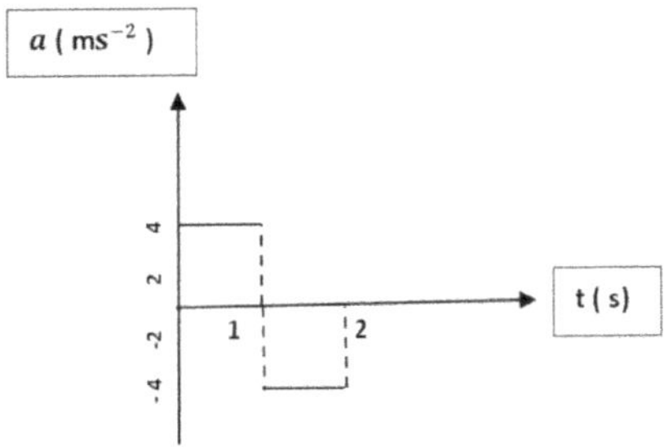

Type – 10 : Conversion of Graph

Problem : Acceleration-time graph of a moving object is shown in figure. Draw the velocity-time graph corresponding to this type of motion.

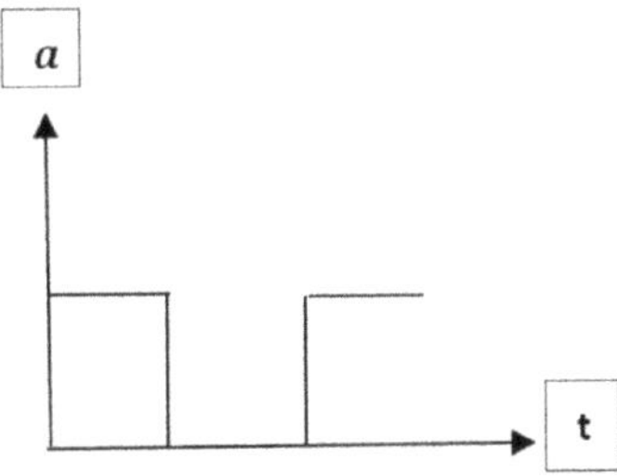

Solution : If we convert the given graph into velocity-time graph, it will be as shown below :

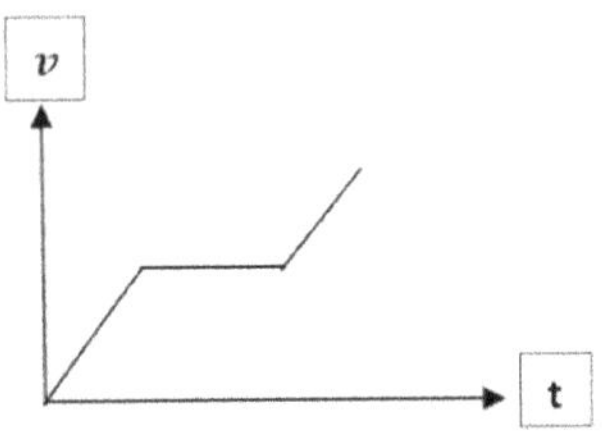

Try Yourself

(33) Displacement-time graph of any object is shown in the adjacent figure. Draw velocity-time graph for this motion.

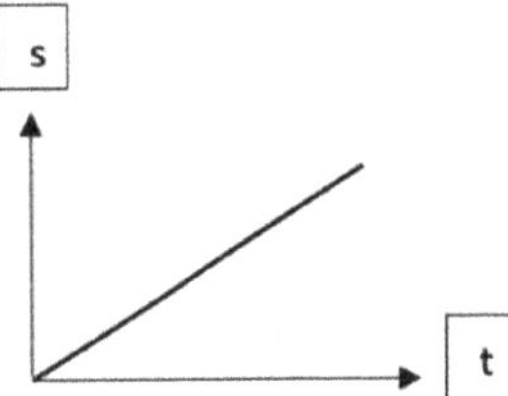

(34) A boy walks along a straight path to drop a letter in the letter box and cones back to the initial position. His displacement-time graph is as shown in the figure. Plot the velocity-time graph for the same.

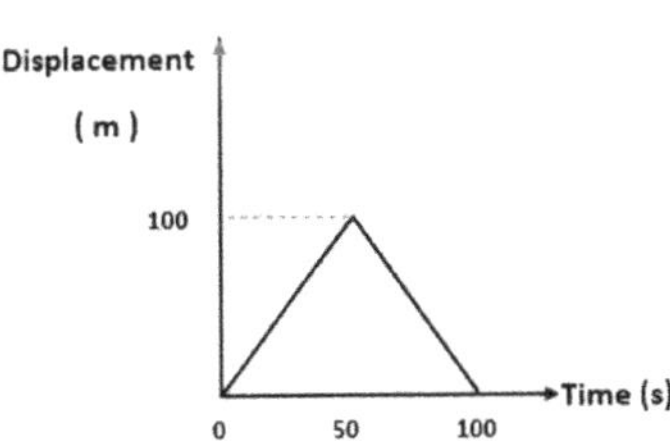

(35) A lift starts from rest. Its acceleration is plotted against time. When it comes to rest, calculate its displacement from starting point.

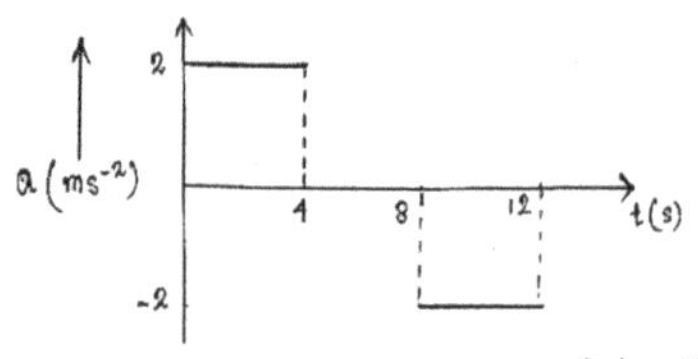

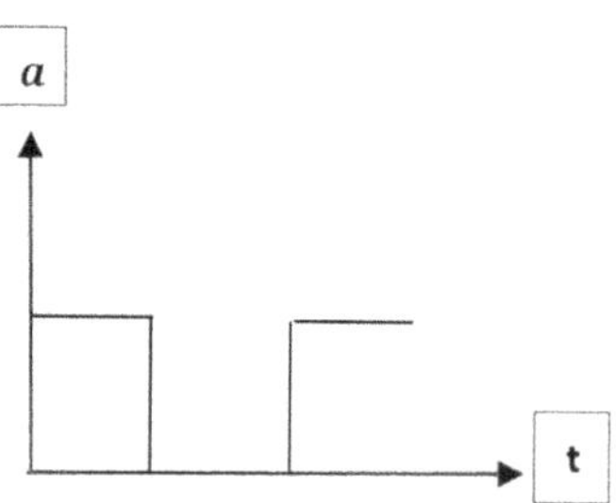

(36) Acceleration-time graph of a moving object is shown in figure. Draw the velocity-time graph and displacement-time graph corresponding to this type of motion.

MCQ – 4 : Graphical Representation of Straight Line Motion

Physics MCQ || Class – XI	Kinematics
	Topic : Distance-Time Graph & Displacement-Time Graph or Position-Time Graph

Important Points

Importance of Position-Time Graph :

- **Position or displacement** can be read from the graph.
- The slope of the straight line joining two points on the displacement-time graph gives the **average velocity** of the particle between those points or time interval.
- The slope of the tangent line at a point on the displacement-time graph gives the value of **instantaneous velocity** of that instant.

(1) If a particle moves with a constant speed, the distance-time graph is a
(a) Straight line
(b) Circle
(c) Stair like line
(d) Polygon

(2) The slope of distance-time graph gives
(a) Velocity
(b) Acceleration
(c) Speed
(d) Displacement

(3) The slope of displacement-time graph gives
(a) Velocity
(b) Acceleration
(c) Speed
(d) Displacement

Calculation of Displacement and Distance from s-t Graph :

(4) The position-time graph for a particle moving along a straight line is shown in figure. The total distance travelled by it in time t = 0 and t = 10 s is

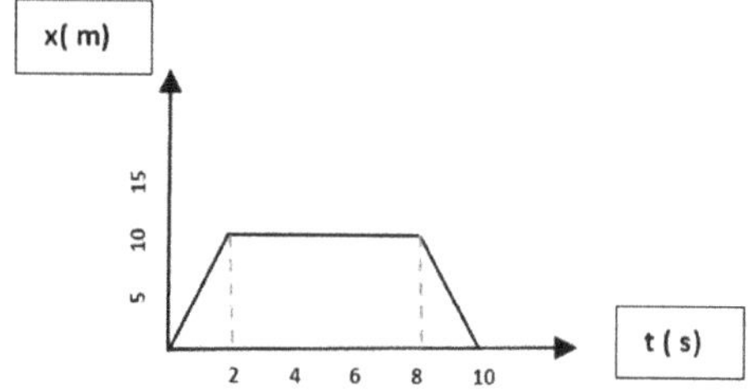

(a) zero
(b) 10 m
(c) 20 m
(d) 80 m

Calculation of Average Velocity or Speed from s-t Graph :

(5) Position-time graph of a particle moving along x-axis is shown in the figure. The average speed of particle in time interval t = 0 to t = 10 s is

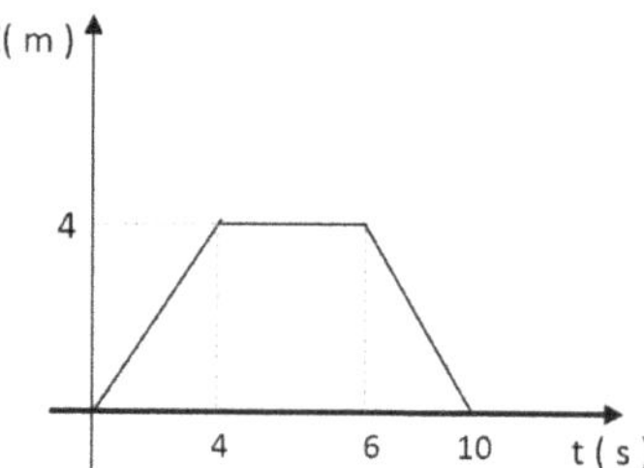

(a) 2 m s^{-1}
(b) $\frac{4}{5} \text{ m s}^{-1}$
(c) 1 m s^{-1}
(d) $\frac{5}{4} \text{ m s}^{-1}$

(6) The position (x) of a particle moving along x-axis varies with time (t) as shown in figure. The average speed of particle in time interval t = 0 to t = 8 s is

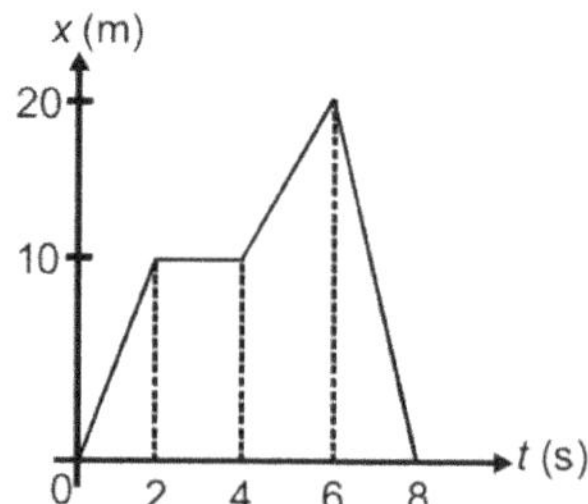

(a) zero

(b) 5 m s^{-1}
(c) 7.5 m s^{-1}
(d) 9.7 m s^{-1}

(7) The position (x) of a particle moving along x-axis varies with time (t) as shown in figure. The average speed of particle in time interval t = 0 to t = 8 s is

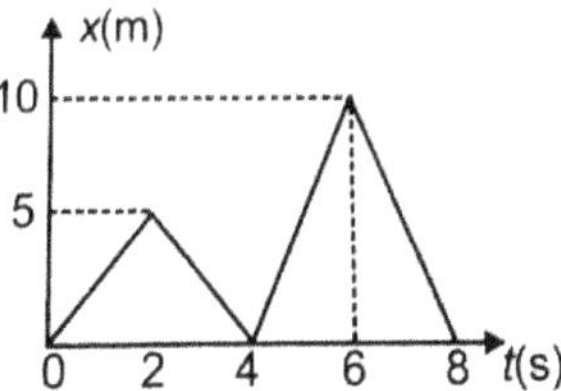

(a) zero
(b) 8 m s^{-1}
(c) 3.75 m s^{-1}
(d) 4.25 m s^{-1}

(8) Figure shows the graph of x-coordinate of a particle moving along x-axis as a function of time. Average velocity during t = 0 to 6 s and instantaneous velocity at t = 3 s respectively, will be

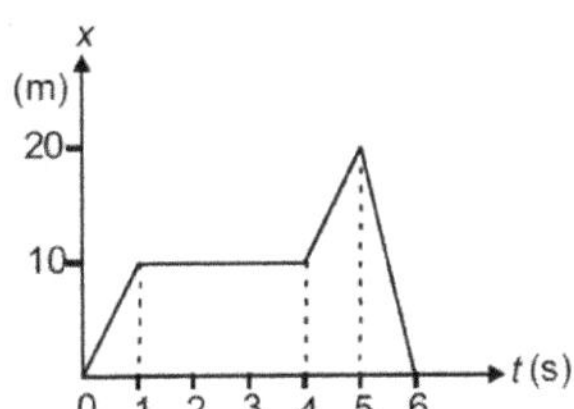

(a) 10 ms^{-1}, 0
(b) 60 ms^{-1} , 0
(c) 0, 0
(d) 0, 10 ms^{-1}

(9) Position-time graph for a particle is shown in figure. Starting from t = 0, at what time t, the average velocity is zero?

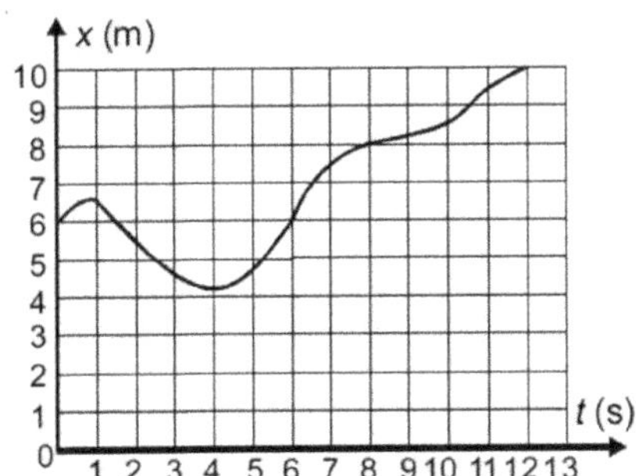

(a) 1 s
(b) 3 s
(c) 6 s
(d) 7 s

Finding the Nature of Velocity or Speed from s-t Graph

(10) The distance-time graph of a particle moving in a fixed direction is shown in figure. The object

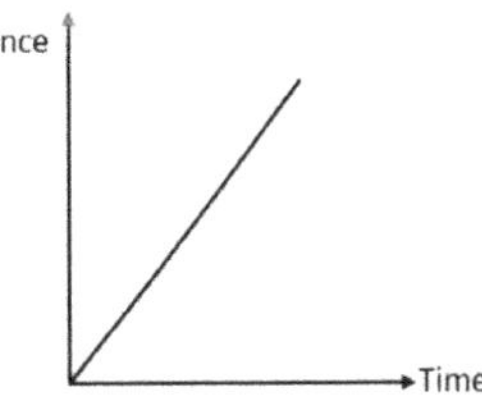

(a) is at rest
(b) moves with a constant velocity
(c) moves with a variable velocity
(d) moves with a constant acceleration

(11) The distance-time graph of a particle moving in a fixed direction is shown in figure. The object

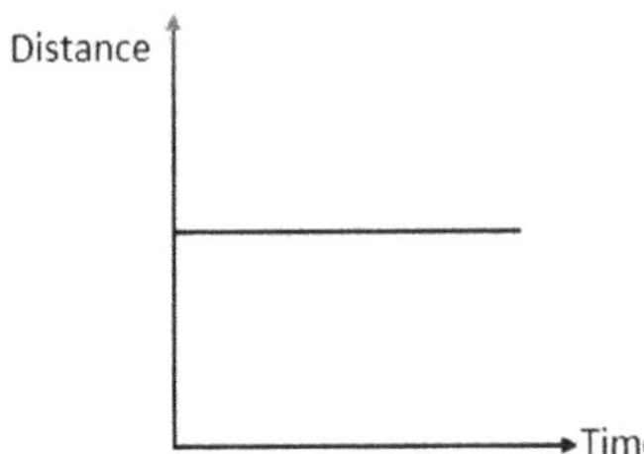

(a) is at rest
(b) moves with a constant velocity
(c) moves with a variable velocity
(d) moves with a constant acceleration

(12) The position-time graph for a body moving along a straight line between O and A is shown in figure. During its motion between O and A, how many times body comes to rest?

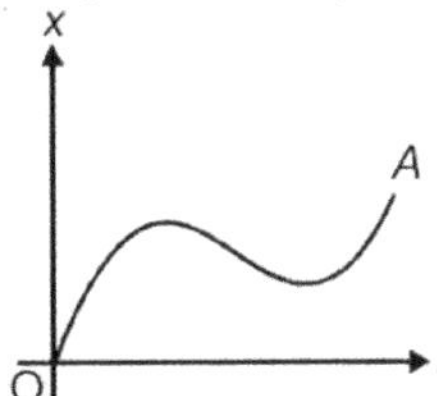

(a) zero
(b) one times
(c) two times
(d) three time

(13) The displacement-time graph of a moving particle is shown below. The instantaneous velocity of the particle is negative at that point

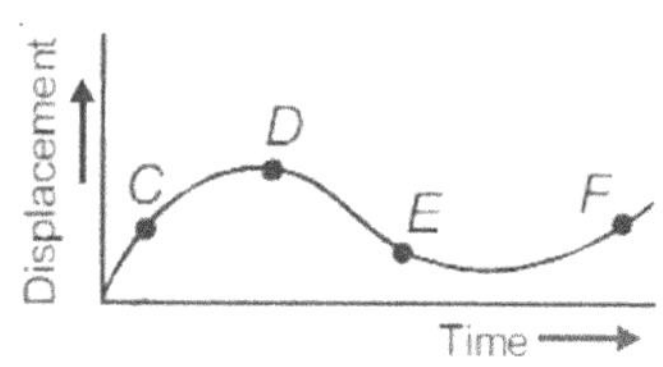

(a) E
(b) F
(c) C
(d) D

(14) A particle shows distance-time curve as shown in the figure. The maximum instantaneous velocity of the particle is around the point

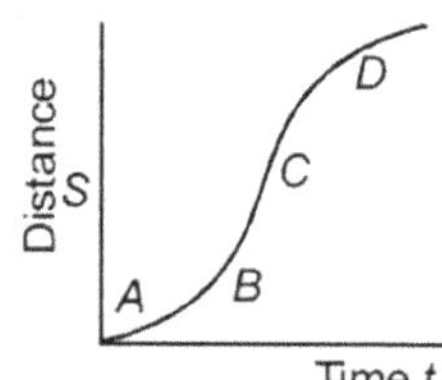

(a) A
(b) B
(c) C
(d) D

(15) The displacement-time graph of two moving objects A and B are shown in the figure given below. Which of the following is incorrect?

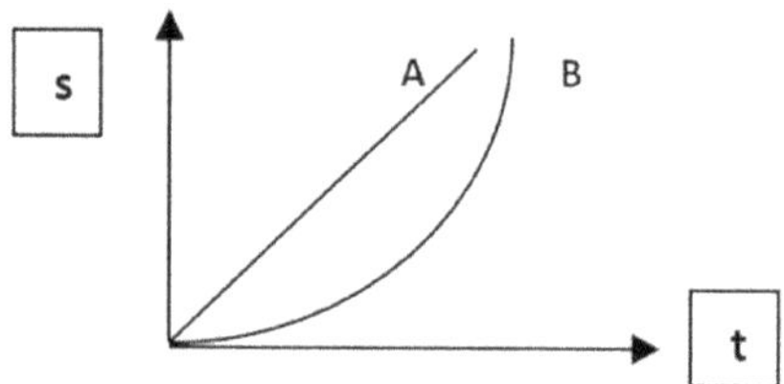

(a) A is moving with constant velocity
(b) B is moving with increasing velocity
(c) A is moving with non-zero constant acceleration
(d) Acceleration of B may be constant

(16) The position-time graph of an object in uniform motion is shown below, the velocity of object is

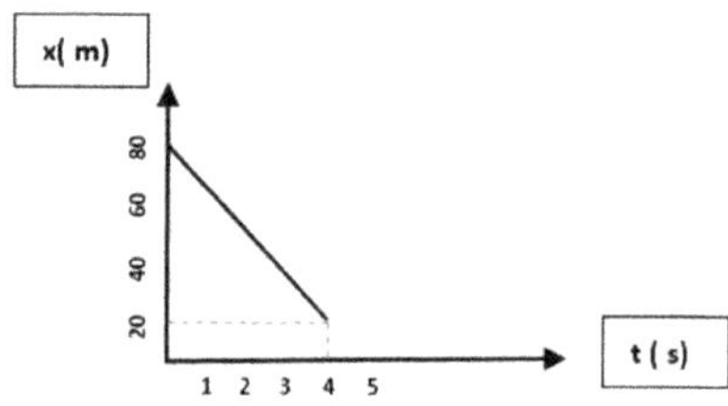

(a) zero
(b) Positive
(c) Negative
(d) None of these

(17) Which of the following graphs represent uniformly accelerated motion ?

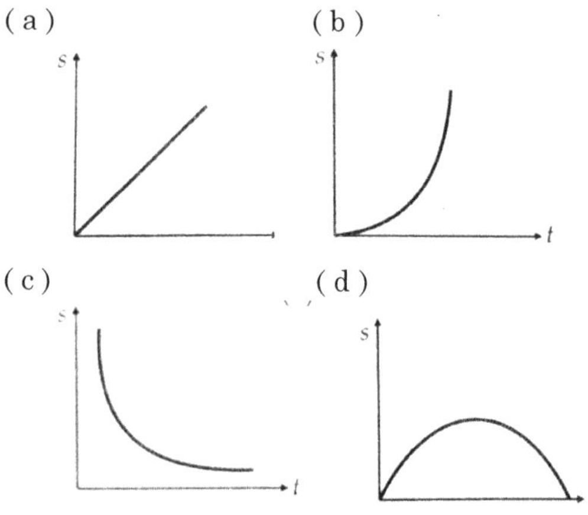

(18) Which one of the following graphs represents uniform motion ?

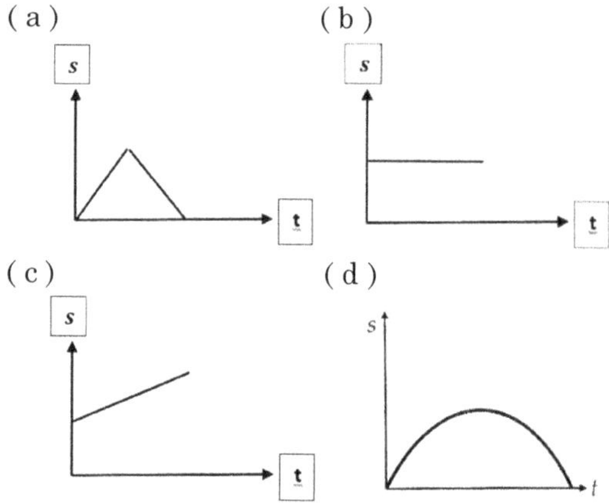

Calculation of Instantaneous Velocity or Speed from s-t Graph :

(19) From the displacement time graph, find out the velocity of the moving body

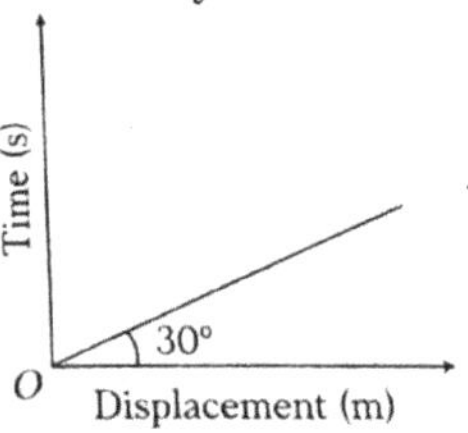

(a) $\frac{1}{\sqrt{3}}$ ms^{-1}
(b) 3 ms^{-1}
(c) $\sqrt{3}$ ms^{-1}

(d) $\frac{1}{3}$ ms^{-1}

(20) The displacement-time graphs of two moving particles make angles of 30° and 45° with the X axis. The ratio of the two velocities is
(a) $\sqrt{3}$: 1
(b) 1 : 1
(c) 1 : 2
(d) 1 : $\sqrt{3}$

(21) The position-time graphs of two cars A and B are straight lines making angles 30° and 60° with the time axis respectively. The ratio of velocities of A and B is
(a) $\sqrt{3}$: 1
(b) 1 : 3
(c) 3 : 1
(d) 1 : $\sqrt{3}$

(22) The displacement-time graph for two particles A and B is as follows. The ratio $\frac{V_A}{V_B}$

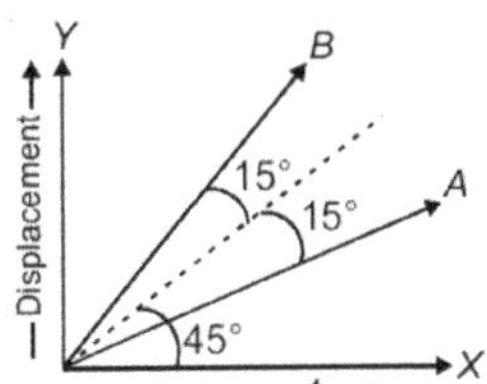

(a) $\sqrt{3}$: 1
(b) 1 : 3
(c) 1 : 2
(d) 1 : $\sqrt{3}$

(23) The ratio of velocity of two objects A and B is 1 : 3. If the position-time graph of object A is inclined to time axis at 30°, then the position-time graph of object is inclined to time axis at
(a) 0°
(b) 90°
(c) 30°
(d) 60°

Calculation of Average Acceleration after Finding the Velocity from s-t Graph

(24) The distance-time graph of a particle at time t makes angle 45° with the time axis. After one second, it makes angle 60° with the time axis. The average acceleration of the particle in this one second is
(a) $\sqrt{3} - 1$
(b) $\sqrt{3} + 1$
(c) $\sqrt{3}$
(d) 1

(25) The position (x) of a particle moving along x-axis varies with time (t) as shown in figure. The average acceleration of particle in time interval t = 0 to t = 8 s is

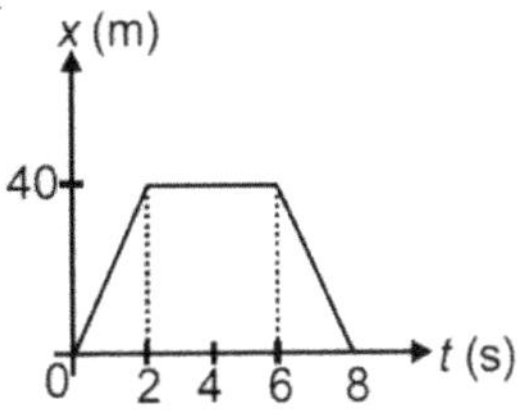

(a) 3 m s^{-2}
(b) – 5 m s^{-2}
(c) – 4 m s^{-2}
(d) 2.5 m s^{-2}

(26) The displacement (x) – time (t) graph of a particle is shown in figure. Which one of the following is correct ?

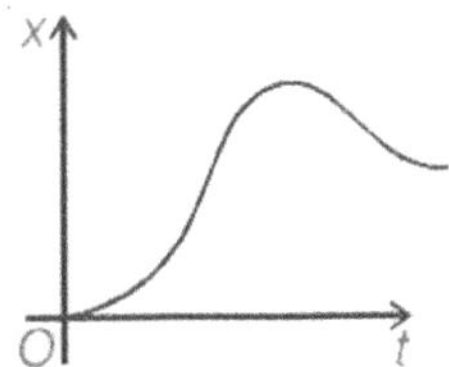

(a) Particle starts with zero velocity and variable acceleration
(b) Particle starts with non-zero velocity and variable acceleration
(c) Particle starts with zero velocity and uniform acceleration
(d) Particle starts with non-zero velocity and uniform acceleration

(27) Which one of the following time-displacement graph represents two moving objects P and Q with zero relative velocity?

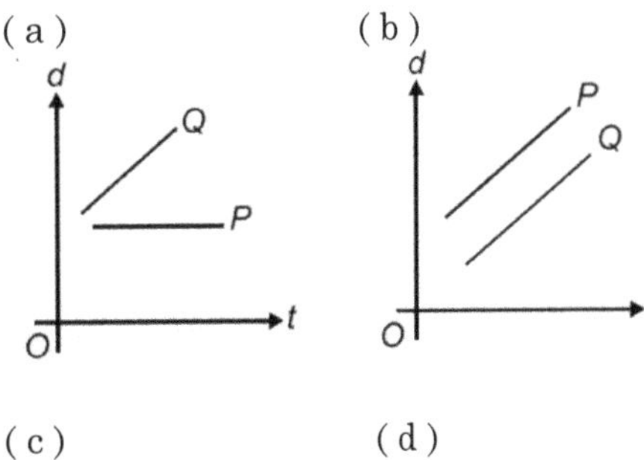

(c) (d)

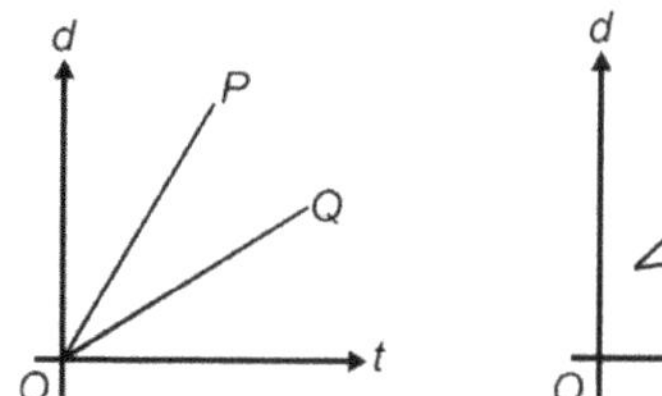

(28) Position time graph of a particle moving along x-axis straight line is shown which is in the form of semi-circle starting from t = 2 to t = 8 s. Select correct statement

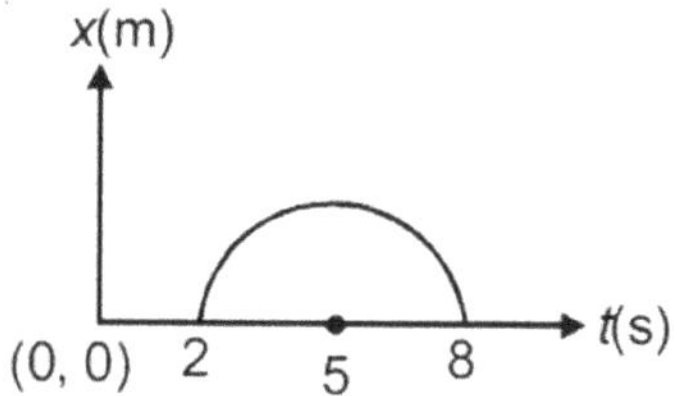

(a) Velocity of particle between t = 0 to t = 2 s is positive

(b) Velocity of particle is opposite to acceleration between t = 2 to t = 5 s

(c) Velocity of particle is opposite to acceleration between t = 5 to t = 8 s

(d) Acceleration of particle is positive between $t_1 = 2$ s to $t_2 = 5$ s while it is negative between $t_1 = 5$ s to $t_2 = 8$s

(29) The displacement (x) - time (t) graph of a particle is shown in figure. Which of the following is correct?

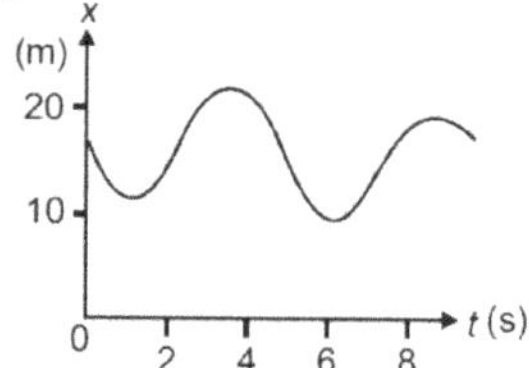

(a) The particle has come to rest 4 time

(b) The velocity at t = 8 s is negative

(c) The velocity remains positive for t = 2s to t = 6 s.

(d) The particle moves with a constant velocity.

Answer

Kinematics

Topic : Displacement-Time Graph or Position-Time Graph

(1)	(a)	(7)	(c)	(13)	(a)	(19)	(c)	(25)	(b)
(2)	(c)	(8)	(c)	(14)	(c)	(20)	(d)	(26)	(a)
(3)	(a)	(9)	(c)	(15)	(c)	(21)	(b)	(27)	(b)
(4)	(c)	(10)	(b)	(16)	(c)	(22)	(b)	(28)	(b)
(5)	(b)	(11)	(a)	(17)	(b)	(23)	(d)	(29)	(a)
(6)	(b)	(12)	(c)	(18)	(c)	(24)	(a)		

Physics MCQ | | Class – XI	Kinematics
	Topic : Speed-Time Graph and Velocity-Time Graph

Important Points

Importance of Velocity-Time Graph :

- **Velocity** can be read from the graph.
- The slope of the straight line joining two points on the displacement-time graph gives the **average acceleration** of the particle between those points or time interval.
- The slope of the tangent line at a point on the displacement-time graph gives the value of **instantaneous acceleration** of that instant.
- The area enclosed between the velocity time graph and x-axis (i.e. time axis) gives the **displacement** of the particle.

(1) The area under a speed-time graph is represented by the unit
(a) m^2
(b) m
(c) s
(d) s^2

(2) The acceleration of a moving body is found from the
(a) Area under velocity -time graph
(b) Area under displacement-time graph
(c) Slope of distance-time graph
(d) Slope of velocity-time graph

(3) The velocity -time graph of a body in motion is straight line to the time axis. The correct statement is
(a) velocity is uniform
(b) acceleration is uniform
(c) both velocity and acceleration are uniform
(d) neither velocity nor acceleration are uniform

(4) The x-t equation is given by $x = 2t + 1$. The corresponding v-t graph is
(a) A straight line passing through origin
(b) A straight line not passing through origin
(c) A parabola
(d) None of the above

Calculation of Displacement and Distance from v-t Graph :

(5) The area under the velocity-time graph of a moving particle between any two instants is a measure of its
(a) Velocity
(b) Acceleration
(c) Displacement
(d) Work done

(6) The speed-time graph of a particle moving along a solid curve is shown below. The distance traversed by the particle from t = 0 to t = 3 is

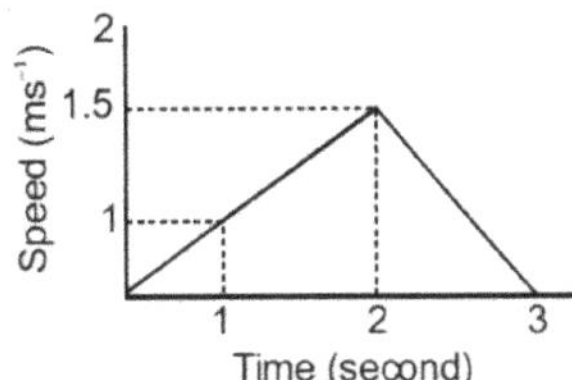

(a) $\frac{9}{2}$ m
(b) $\frac{9}{4}$ m
(c) $\frac{10}{3}$ m
(d) $\frac{10}{5}$ m

(7) The variation of velocity of particle moving along a straight line is illustrated in the figure. The distance travelled by the particle in 4 s is

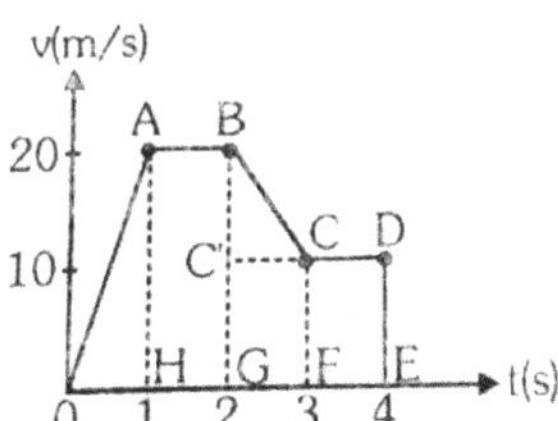

(a) 60 m
(b) 55 m
(c) 25 m
(d) 30 m

(8) The velocity-time graph of a particle moving along a straight line is shown in the figure given below. The displacement of the particle in 5 is

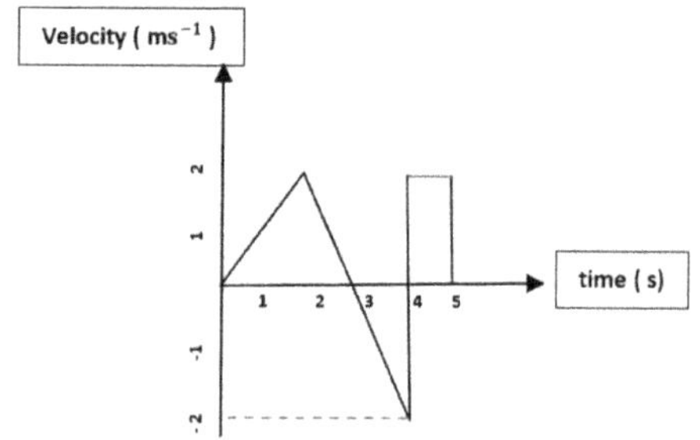

(a) 0.5 m
(b) 1 m
(c) 2 m
(d) 4 m

(9) The variation of velocity of a particle moving along a straight line is as shown in the figure given below. The distance travelled by the particle in 5 s is

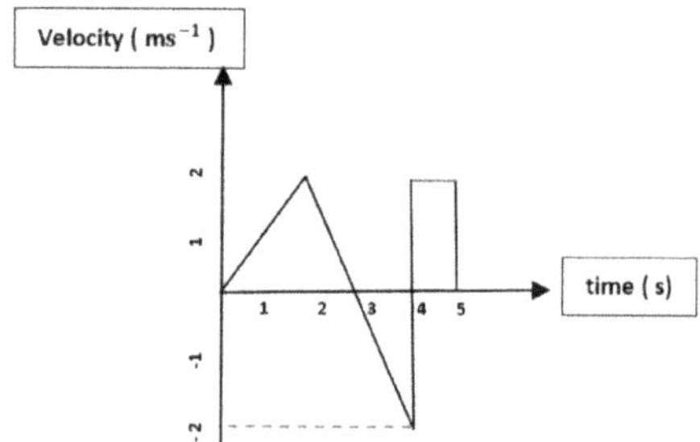

(a) 6 m
(b) 3 m
(c) 4 m
(d) 5 m

(10) The velocity-time graph for a moving object is shown in the figure. Total distance of the object during the time interval when there is non-zero acceleration and retardation is

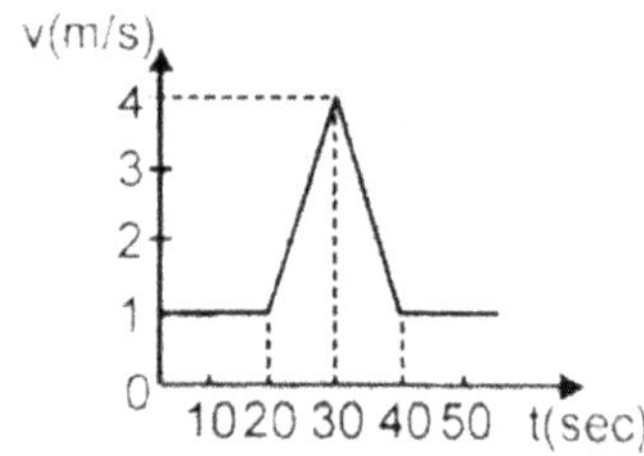

(a) 60 m
(b) 50 m
(c) 30 m
(d) 40 m

(11) The velocity-time graph of an ascending lift is shown in the figure. The height attained by the lift is

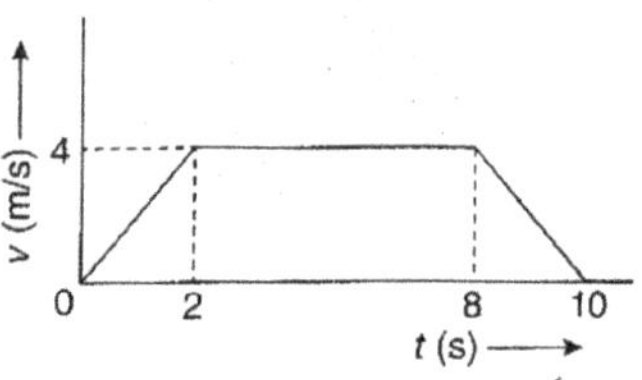

(a) 4 m
(b) 32 m
(c) 16 m
(d) 8 m

Calculation of Average Velocity from v-t Graph :

(12) The v-t plot of a moving object is shown in the figure. The average velocity of the object during the first 10 s is

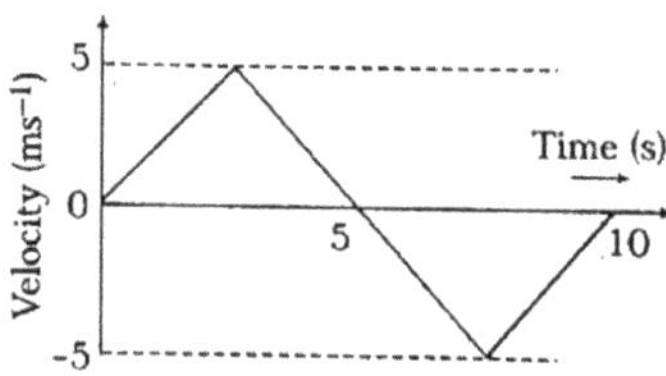

(a) zero
(b) 2.5 m s^{-1}
(c) 5 m s^{-1}
(d) 2 m s^{-1}

Calculation of Acceleration from v-t Graph :

(13) The graphs between velocity and time of particles A and B are given. The ratio of their acceleration $\frac{a_A}{a_B}$

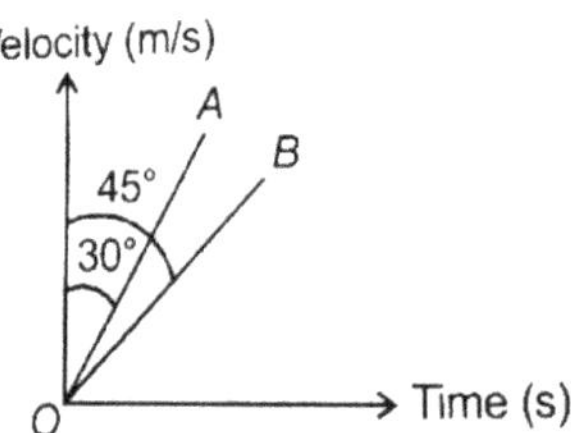

(a) $\frac{\sqrt{3}}{2}$
(b) $\frac{1}{\sqrt{3}}$
(c) $\sqrt{3}$
(d) $\frac{2}{\sqrt{3}}$

Calculation of Average Acceleration from v-t Graph :

(14) The velocity versus time graph of a body moving in a straight line as shown in the figure below

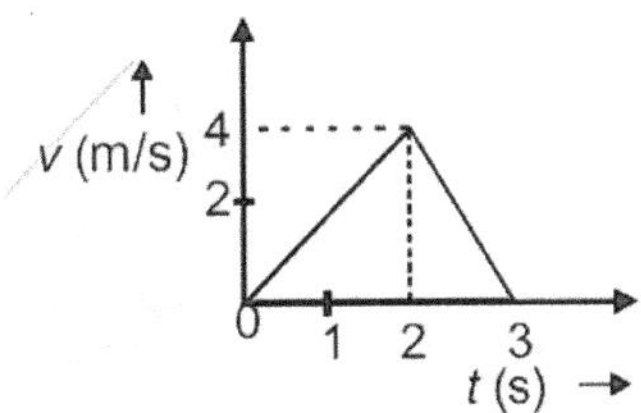

(a) the distance covered by the body in 0 to 2 s is 8 m
(b) the acceleration of the body in 0 to 2 s in 4 $m\ s^{-2}$
(c) the acceleration of the body in 2 to 3 s is 4 $m\ s^{-2}$
(d) the distance moved by the body during 0 to 3 s is 6 m.

(15) The speed-time graph for a body moving along a straight line is shown in figure. The average acceleration of body may be

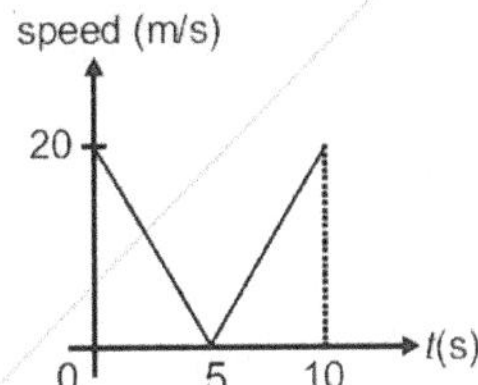

(a) 0
(b) 4 $m\ s^{-2}$
(c) – 4 $m\ s^{-2}$
(d) All of these

(16) The velocity-time graph of a body is shown in given figure. The maximum acceleration (in $m\ s^{-2}$) is

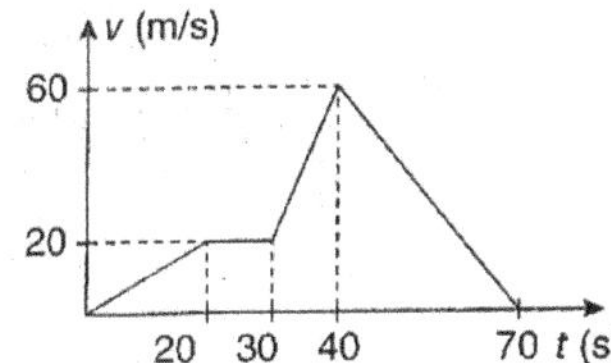

(a) 4
(b) 3
(c) 2
(d) 1

Finding the Nature of Acceleration from v-t Graph

(17) The velocity-time graph of a particle is not a straight line. Its acceleration is
(a) 0
(b) negative
(c) constant
(d) variable

(18) The speed-time graph for a body moving along a straight line is shown in figure. The body

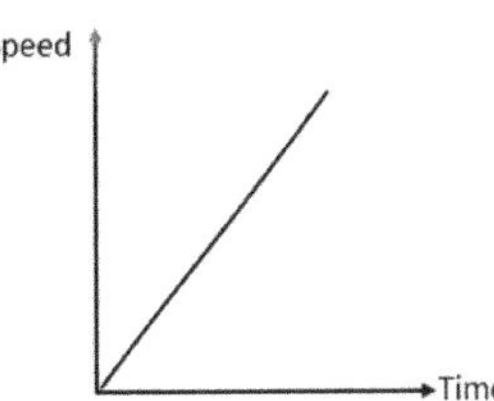

(a) is at rest
(b) moves with a constant speed
(c) moves with a constant velocity
(d) moves with a constant acceleration

(19) The speed-time graph of a particle moving in a fixed direction is shown in figure. The particle

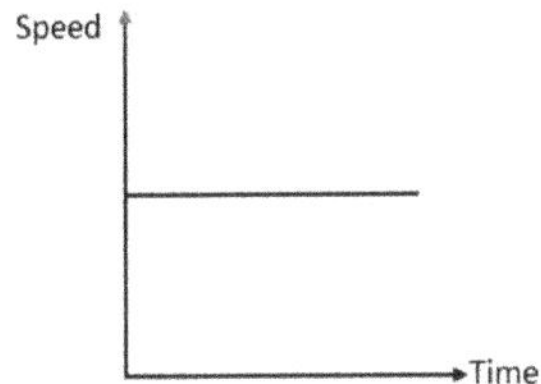

(a) is at rest
(b) moves with fluctuating speed
(c) moves with a constant speed
(d) moves with a nonzero acceleration

(20) Which of the following v-t graph represent uniform motion

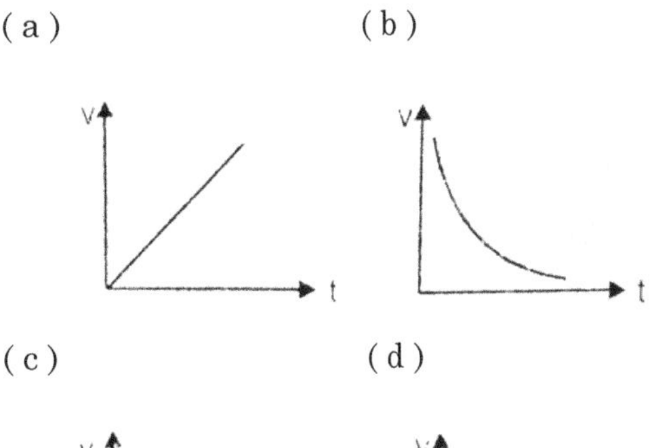

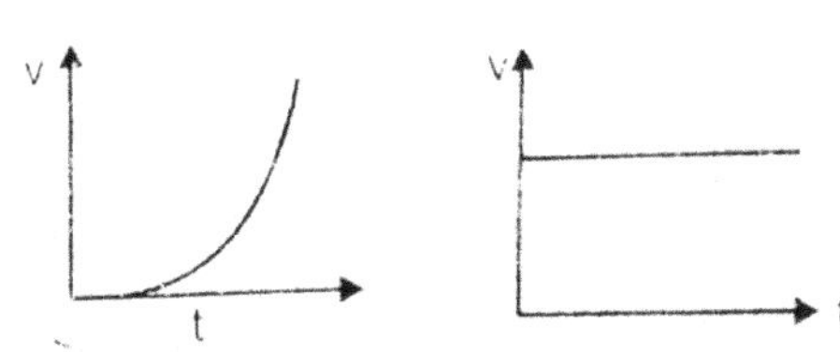

(21) A particle moves along x-axis in such a way that its co-ordinate varies with time according to the equation $x = 4 - 2t + t^2$. The speed of the particle will vary with time as

(a) (b) (c) (d)

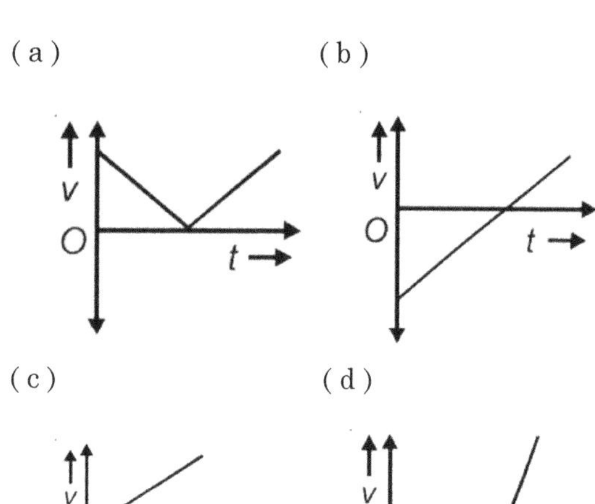

Impossible v-t Graph :

(22) Which of the following graph for a body moving along a straight line is possible?

(a) (b) (c) (d)

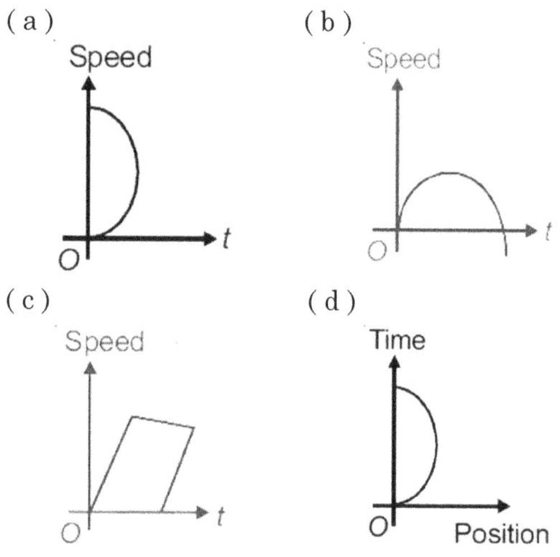

(23) Which of the following speed-time (v-t) graphs is physically not possible?

(a) (b)

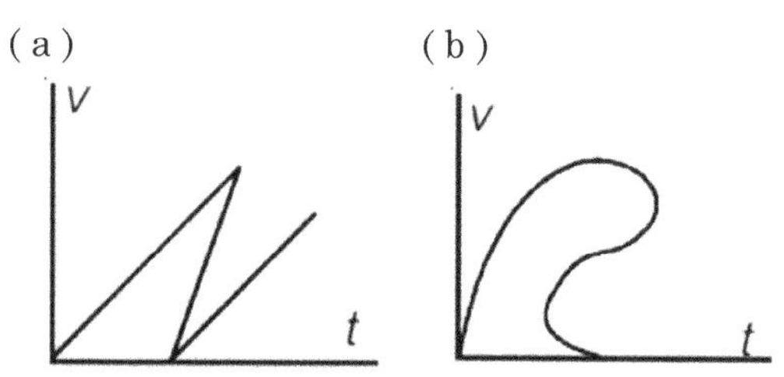

(c) (d) All of these

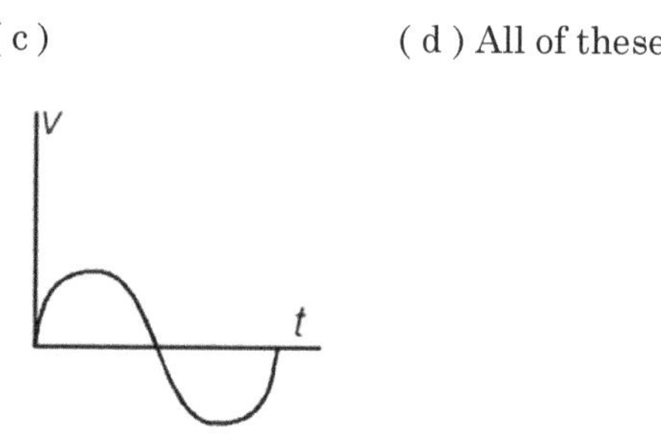

(24) Which of the following graph for a body moving along a straight line is not possible?

(a) (b) (c) (d)

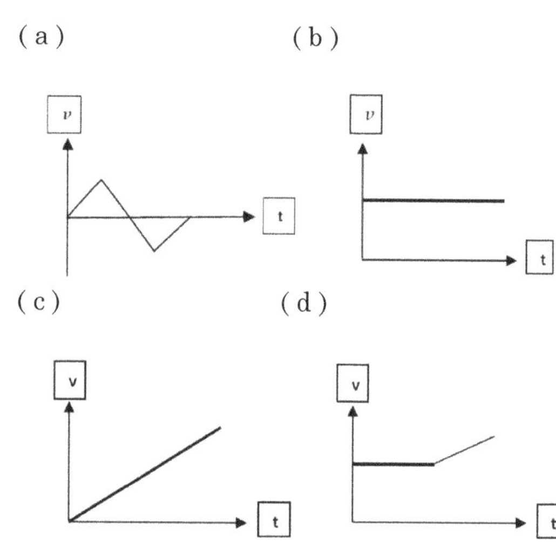

(25) Which of the following curves does not represent motion in one dimension ?

(a) (b) (c) (d)

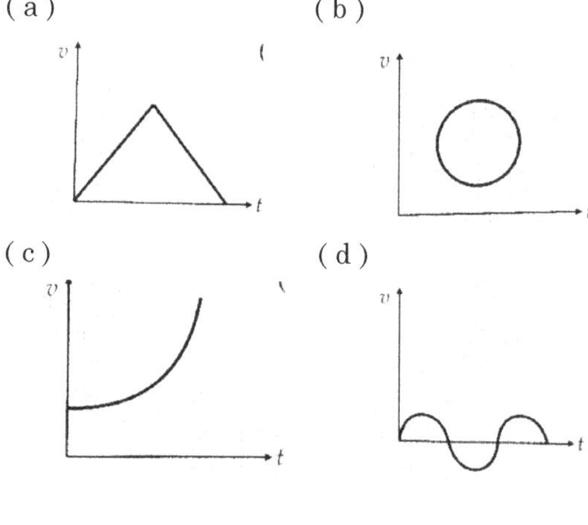

Answer

Kinematics

Topic : Speed-Time Graph and Velocity-Time Graph

(1)	(b)	(6)	(b)	(11)	(a)	(16)	(a)	(21)	(a)
(2)	(d)	(7)	(b)	(12)	(a)	(17)	(d)	(22)	(d)
(3)	(b)	(8)	(d)	(13)	(c)	(18)	(d)	(23)	(d)
(4)	(b)	(9)	(a)	(14)	(d)	(19)	(c)	(24)	(a)
(5)	(c)	(10)	(b)	(15)	(d)	(20)	(d)	(25)	(b)

Physics
MCQ | | Class – XI

Kinematics

Topic : Acceleration-Time Graph

Important Points

Importance of Acceleration-Time Graph :

- **Acceleration** can be read from the graph.
- The area enclosed between the acceleration-time graph and x-axis (i.e. time axis) gives the **change in velocity** of the particle.

Calculation of Change in Velocity & Final Velocity from a-t Graph :

(1) For the acceleration -time graph shown in figure, the change in velocity of particle from t = 0 to t = 6 s is

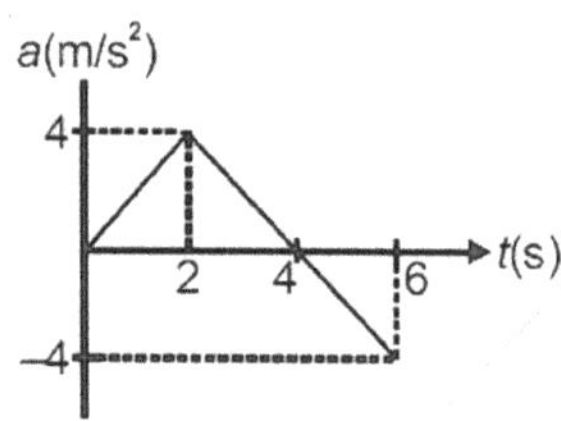

(a) 10 $m\,s^{-1}$
(b) 4 $m\,s^{-1}$
(c) 12 $m\,s^{-1}$
(d) 8 $m\,s^{-1}$

(2) The acceleration-time graph for a particle moving along x-axis is shown in figure. If the initial velocity of particle is – 5 $m\,s^{-1}$, the velocity at t = 8 s is

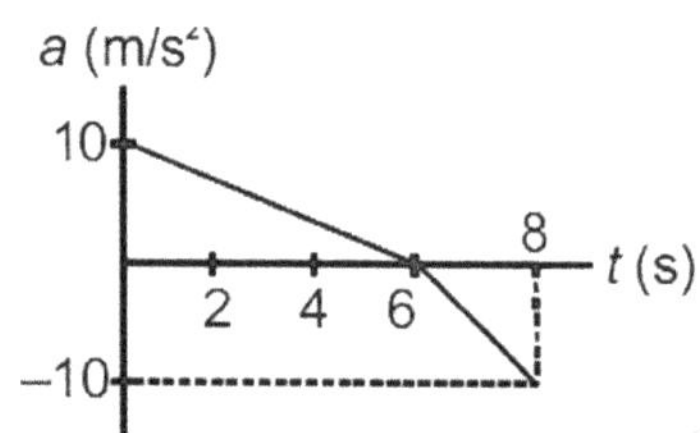

(a) + 15 $m\,s^{-1}$
(b) + 20 $m\,s^{-1}$
(c) – 15 $m\,s^{-1}$
(d) – 20 $m\,s^{-1}$

(3) The acceleration-time graph of a particle moving in a straight line is as shown in figure. At time t=0, the velocity of particle is 10 $m\,s^{-1}$. What is the velocity at t = 8 s ?

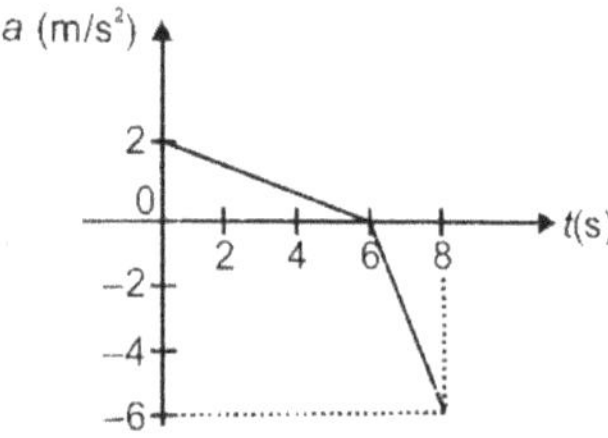

(a) 2 $m\,s^{-1}$
(b) 4 $m\,s^{-1}$
(c) 10 $m\,s^{-1}$
(d) 12 $m\,s^{-1}$

Conversion of a-t Graph to v-t graph :

(4) Acceleration-time graph for a particle is given in figure. If it starts motion at t = 0, distance travelled in 3 s will be

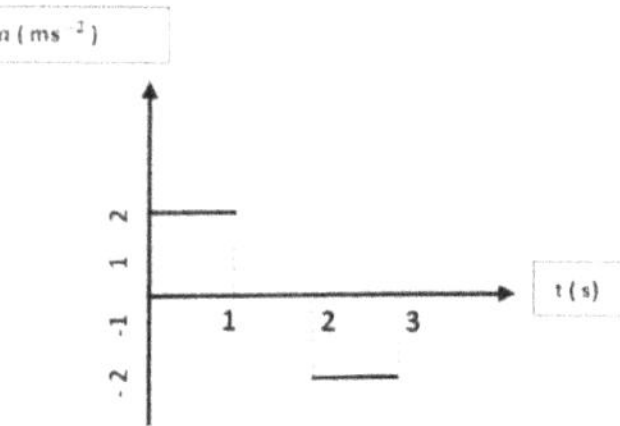

(a) 4 m
(b) 2 m
(c) 0
(d) 6 m

(5) A particle starts from rest at t = 0 and undergoes an acceleration a in $m\,s^{-2}$ with time t in seconds with time t in seconds which is as shown here:

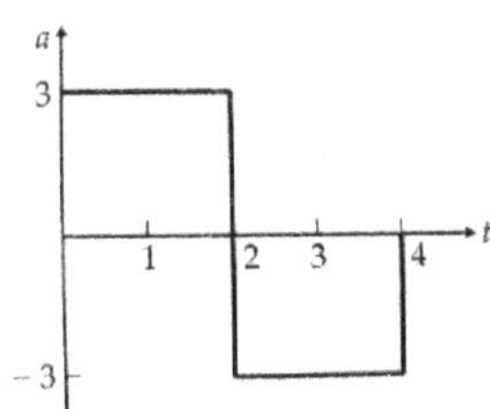

Which one of the following plots represents velocity v in m s^{-1} verses time t in seconds?

(a)

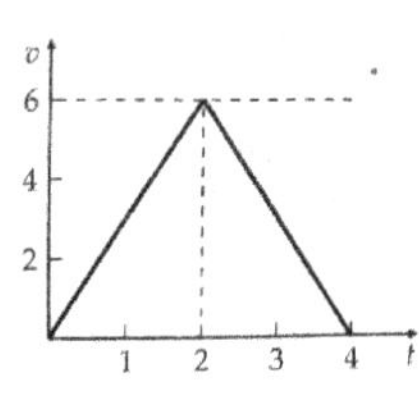

(b)

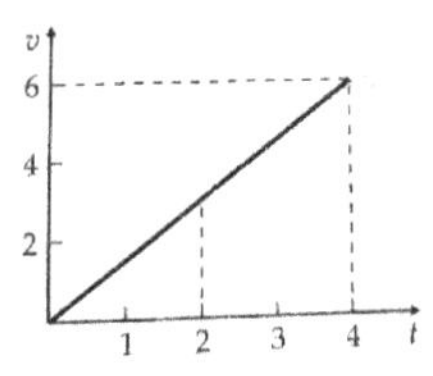

(c)

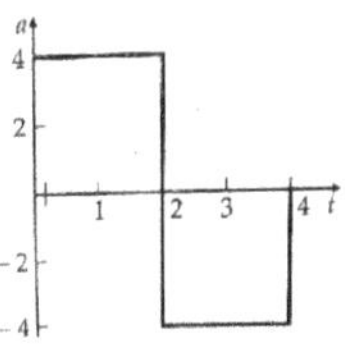

(d)

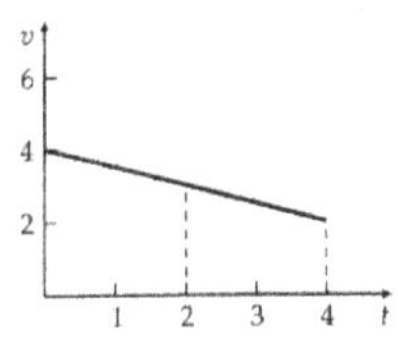

(6) Acceleration-time graph of a body is shown.

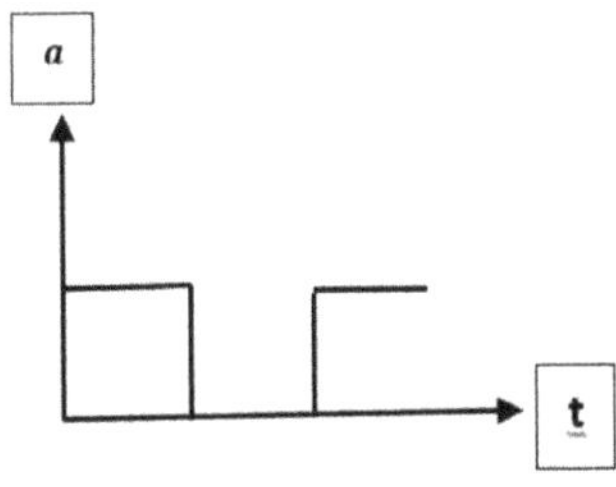

The corresponding velocity-time graph of the same body is

(a)

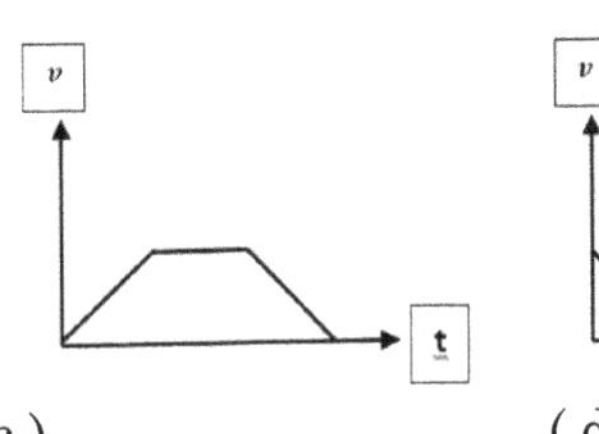

(b)

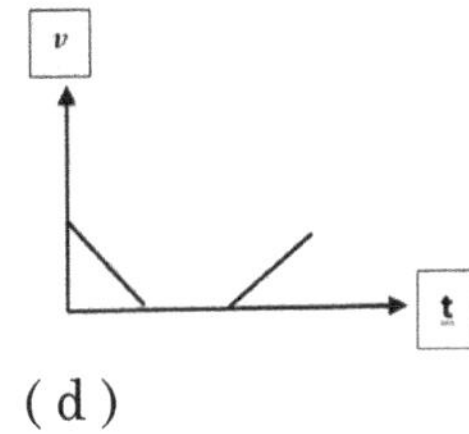

(c)

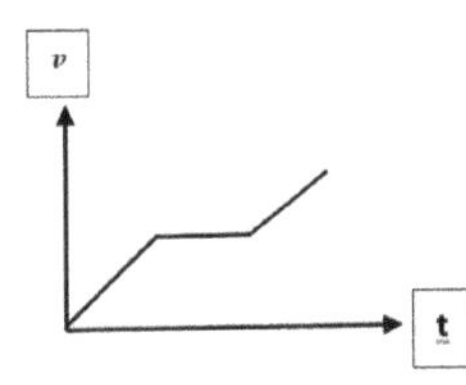

(d)

(7) The velocity v of a particle moving along x-axis varies with its position (x) as $v = \alpha\sqrt{x}$; where α is a constant. Which of the following graph represents the variation of its acceleration (a) with time (t) ?

(a)

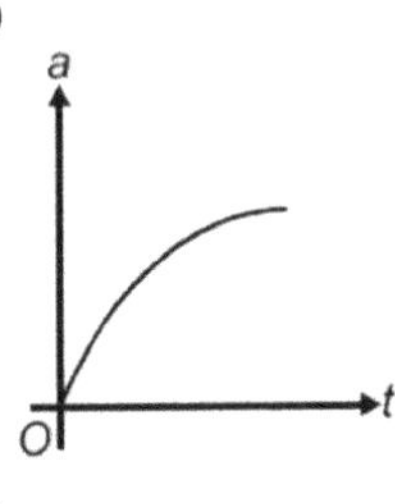

(b)

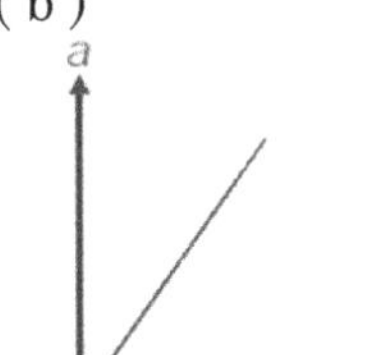

(c)

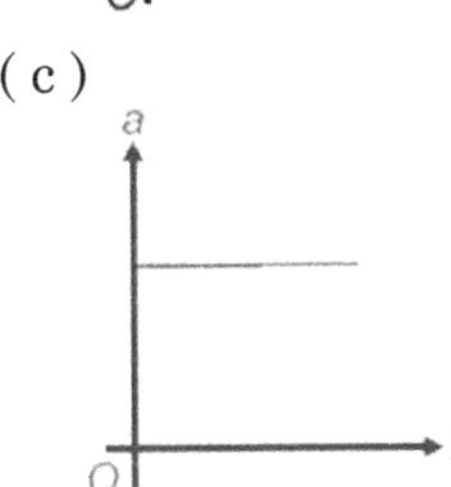

(d)

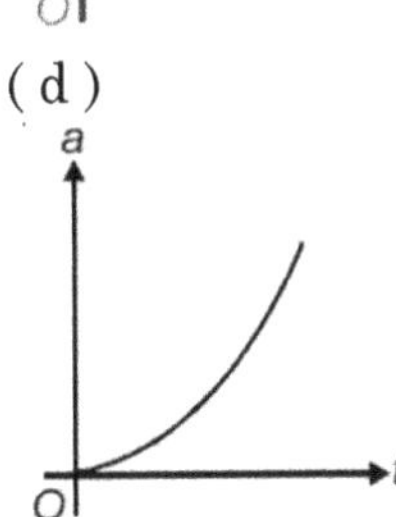

Answer	Kinematics
	Topic : Acceleration-Time Graph

(1)	(b)	(3)	(c)	(5)	(a)	(7)	(c)
(2)	(a)	(4)	(a)	(6)	(c)		

Physics MCQ | | Class – XI	Kinematics
	Topic : Velocity-Position Graph

(1) For a body moving with uniform acceleration along straight line, the variation of its velocity (v) with position (x) is best represented by

(a) (b)

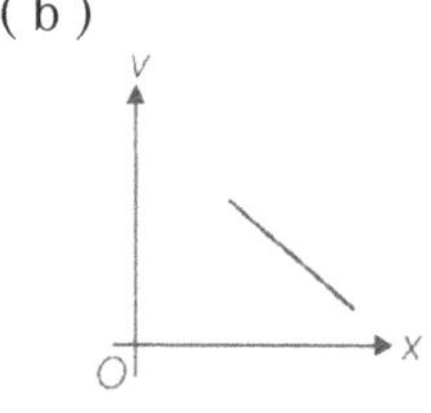

(c) (d)

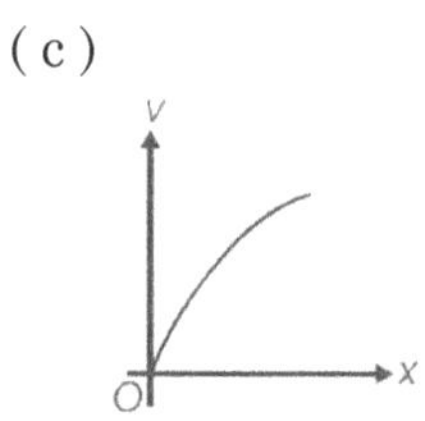

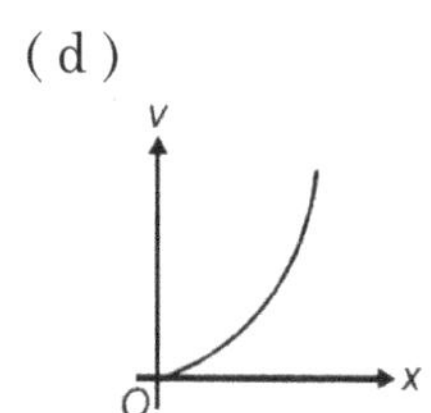

(2) The velocity (v) of a particle moving along x-axis varies with its position x as shown in figure. The acceleration (a) of particle varies with position (x) as

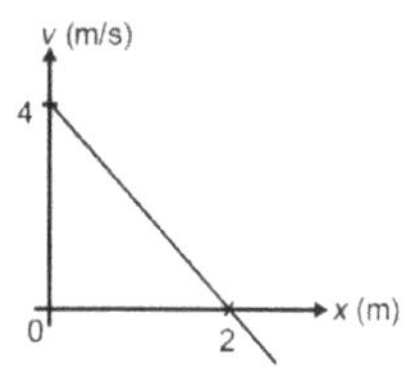

(a) $a^2 = x + 3$
(b) $a = 2x^2 + 4$
(c) $2a = 3x + 5$
(d) $a = 4x - 8$

(3) A body starting from rest moves along a straight line with a constant acceleration. The variation of speed (v) with distance (s) is represented by the graph

(a) (b)

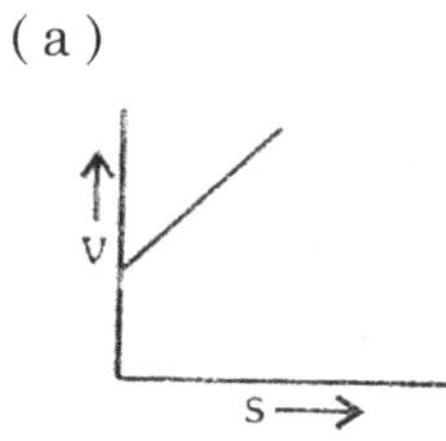

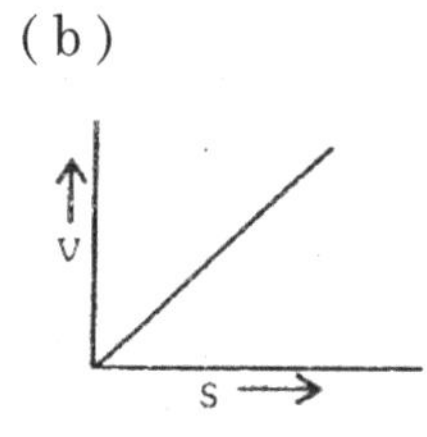

(c) (d)

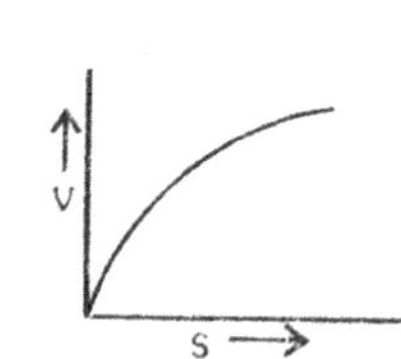

(4) Velocity of a particle depends on displacement travelled by the particle is shown by the graph. Which one of the graph given below represents the variation of acceleration with displacement?

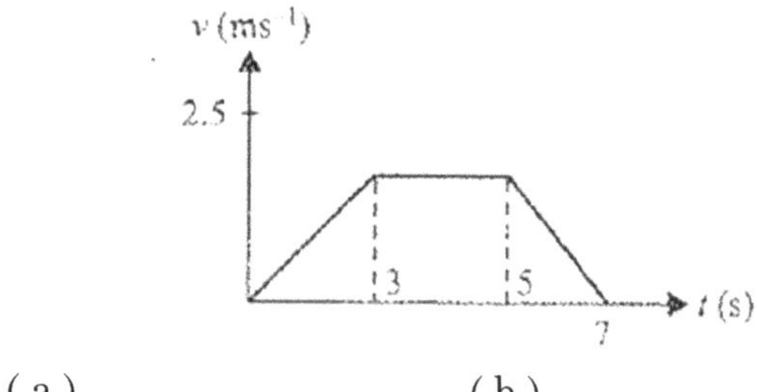

(a) (b)

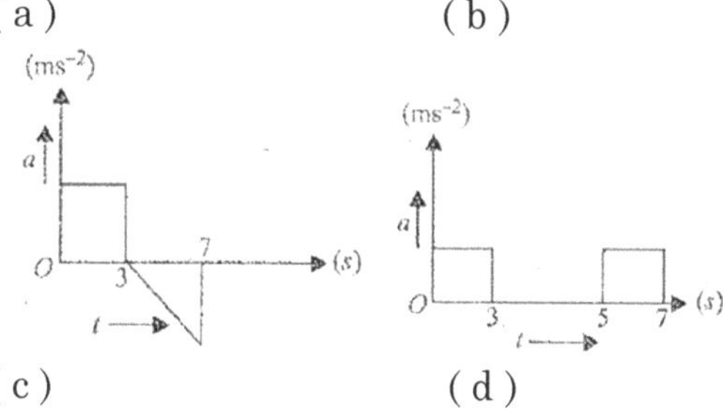

(c) (d)

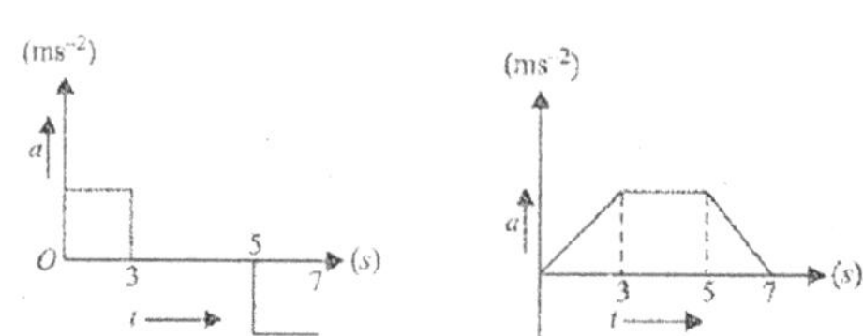

On Graphical Representation of Motion under Gravity

(5) Velocity -time curve for a body projected vertically upwards
(a) Parabola
(b) Ellipse
(c) Hyperbola
(d) Straight line

(6) A body is projected vertically upward from ground. If we neglect the effect of air, then which one of the following is the best representation of variation of speed (v) with time (t) ?

(a) (b) (c) (d)

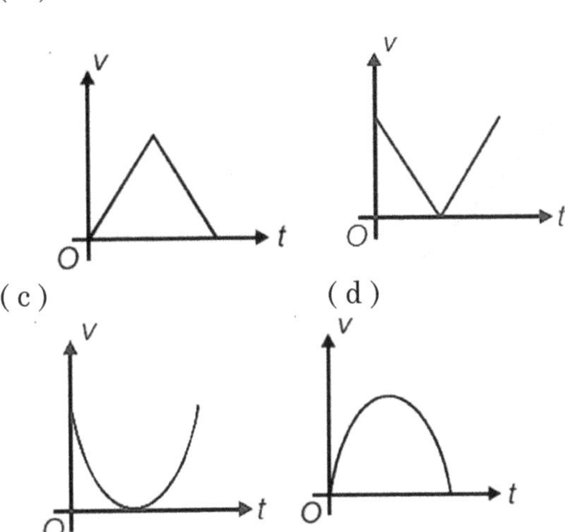

(7) A particle is thrown above, then correct v-t graph will be

(a) (b)

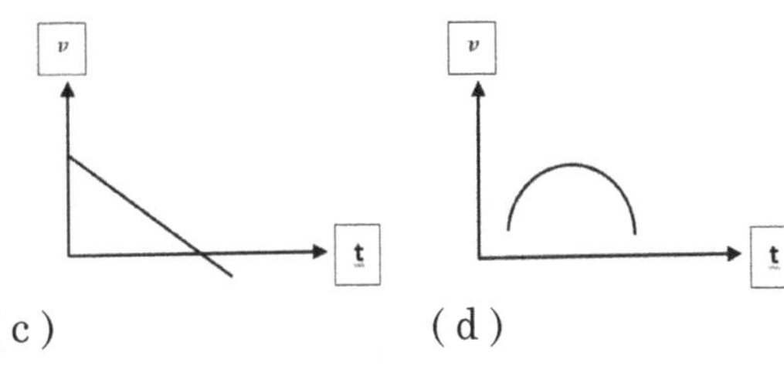

(c) (d)

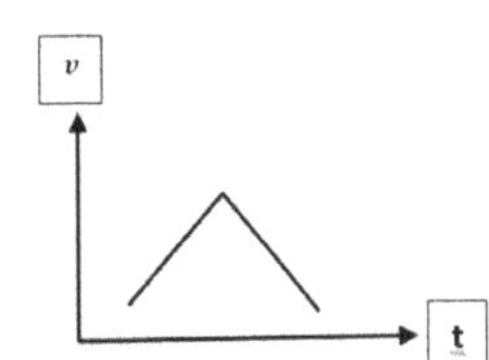

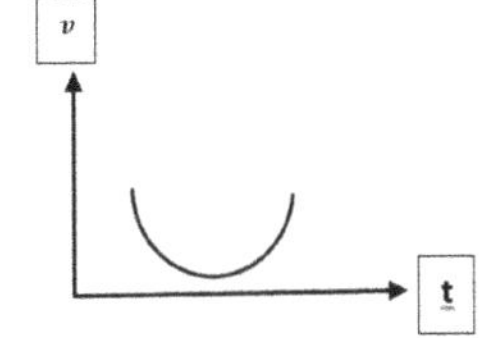

Answer

Kinematics

Topic : Velocity-Position Graph

(1)	(c)	(3)	(d)	(5)	(d)	(7)	(a)
(2)	(d)	(4)	(c)	(6)	(b)		

Dynamics	
1	Discussion on Newton's Laws Motion
2	The Quantities that Determine the Effect of Force
3	Friction

Discussion on Newton's Laws of Motion

(1) Newton's First Law of Motion	**(2) Newton's Second Law of Motion**
(3) Newton's Third Law Motion	**(4) Limitations of Newton's Laws of Motion**
(5) Force	**(6) Types of Force**
(7) Conservation of Linear Momentum	**(8) Apparent Weight in a Lift**

Newton gave three laws of motion that describe the motion of the bodies. These laws are known as Newton's Laws of motion. They describe the relationship between the forces acting on the body and its motion due to those forces. The three laws of motion were first compiled by Sir Isaac Newton in his work Principia Mathematica. First published in 1687. Newton used these laws to explain and investigate the motion of many physical objects and systems.

We shall now learn about Newton's First Law of motion.

(1) Newton's First Law of Motion :

(1) Statement of Newton's First Law of Motion :

An object remains in a state of rest or of uniform motion in a straight line unless it is compelled by an external unbalanced force to change that state.

(2) Importance of Newton's First Law of Motion :

(i) It gives the qualitative definition of force.

(ii) It defines inertia as a fundamental property of every physical object by which the object resists any change in its state of rest or motion.

(iii) It shows an equivalence between the state of rest and state of uniform motion along a straight line as both need a resultant force to change the state.

(3) Inertia :

• *The property of the body by virtue of which the body resists a change in state of rest or of uniform motion along a straight line is known as* ***inertia****.*

• Mass of a body is a measure of its inertia.

• Inertia is of the following three kinds : (a) Inertia of rest
(b) Inertia of motion
(c) Inertia of direction.

(4) Inertia of rest :

Inertia of rest *is that property by virtue of which a body at rest tends to remain at rest.*

Example :

(a) When a train suddenly starts moving forward, the passenger standing in the compartment tends to fall backwards. The reason is that the lower part of the passenger's body is in close contact with the train. As the train starts moving, his lower parts starts the motion at once, but the upper part due to inertia of rest cannot starts the motion simultaneously. Consequently, the lower part of the body moves ahead and the upper part is left behind, so the passenger tends to fall backward.

(b) When a blanket is given a sudden jerk, the dust particle fall off. It is because the blanket is suddenly set in motion but the dust particles tend to remain at rest due to inertia of rest.

(5) Inertia of motion :

Inertia of motion *is that property by virtue of which a body in a state of uniform motion tends to maintain its uniform motion.*

Example :

(a) When a running car stops suddenly, the passenger tends to lean forward. The reason is that in a running car, the whole body of the passenger is in the state of motion. When the car stops suddenly, the lower part of his body, being in contact with the car, comes to rest immediately but his upper part remain in the state of motion, due to inertia. Thus his body leans forward.

(b) An athlete runs for some distance before taking long jump. In this way, the athlete gains momentum and due to inertia of motion, he takes a longer jump.

(6) Inertia of motion :

Inertia of direction *is that property by virtue of which a body tends to maintain its direction.*

Example :
When a stone is rotating in a circle at the end of string, the velocity of the stone at any instant is along the tangent to the circle. When the string is released, the centripetal force whirling the stone vanishes. Due to directional inertia. The stone flies off tangentially.

• Greater the inertia of the body greater will be the force required to bring the change in the state of rest or uniform motion of the body.

(7) Qualitative Definition of Force on the basis of N.F.L. of Motion :

Newton's first law of motion gives us a definition of force. It says that –

Force is an external cause in the form of a push or pull which produces or tries to produce motion in a body at rest, stops or tries to stop a moving body and changes or tries to change the direction of motion of the body.

(2) Newton's Second Law of Motion :

(8) Newton's second law of motion gives the relationship between the force and acceleration.

(9) Concept of Linear Momentum :

Before we discussing about second law of motion we shall first learn about momentum of a moving body. From our daily life experiences like during the game of table tennis if the ball hits a player it does not hurt him. On the other hand, when a fast moving cricket ball hits a spectator, it may hurt. This suggests that impact produced by moving objects depends on both their mass and velocity. So there appears to exist some quantity of importance that combines the object's mass and its velocity called momentum and was introduced by Newton.

- **Definition :** *Linear momentum is the product of mass of an object and its linear velocity.*

- **Mathematical form** : For a body of mass m moving with linear velocity $\vec{v}$, linear momentum $\vec{p}$ is expressed as : $\vec{p} = m\,\vec{v}$

- **Nature of the quantity :** Linear momentum is a vector quantity.

- **Dimensional equation :** $[\,p\,] = [\,M\,L\,T^{-1}\,]$

- **Unit :** CGS unit : g cm s^{-1}
  SI unit : kg m s^{-1}

- Momentum depends on the frame of reference.

- **The momentum of a system :** Total momentum of a system is the **resultant of the momenta** of each of the particle in the system.

- **Change in momentum :** $\Delta\vec{P} = \vec{P_f} - \vec{P_i} = m\,(\vec{v_f} - \vec{v_i})$

(10) Concepts of Resultant Force :

When a number of forces act simultaneously on a body, the combined effect of the multiple forces can be represented by a single force, which is termed as resultant force.
Magnitude and direction of the resultant force depends on – (i) magnitude of the two forces and (ii) the angle between them.
If $\vec{F}$ be the resultant of two forces represented by $\vec{F_1}$ and $\vec{F_2}$, the magnitude of the resultant is given by

$$F = \sqrt{F_1^2 + F_2^2 + 2\,F_1\,F_2\cos\theta}$$

• **Action of** Parallel forces acting in the same direction :

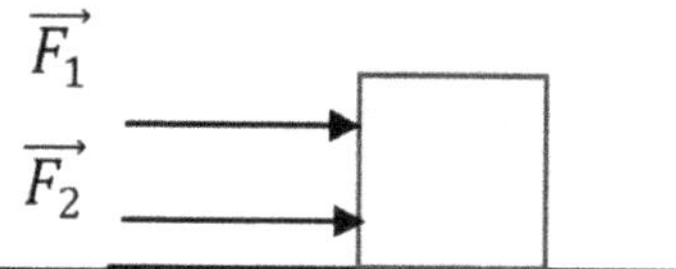

Magnitude of resultant force $|\vec{F}_{net}| = F_1 + F_2$

• **Action of** parallel unequal forces acting in the opposite direction :

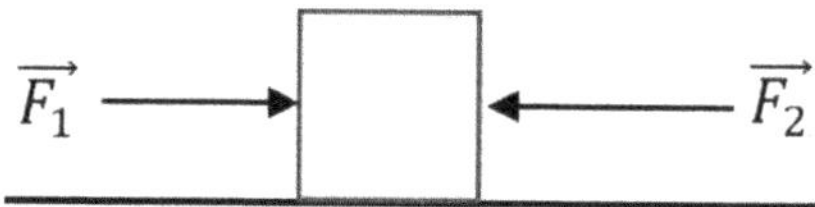

Magnitude of resultant force : $|\vec{F}_{net}| = F_1 - F_2$ (If $F_1 > F_2$)
or, $|\vec{F}_{net}| = F_2 - F_1$ (If $F_2 > F_1$)

$\vec{F}_{net}$ is directed along the greater force.

• Action of parallel forces having equal magnitude acting in opposite direction in the same line of action

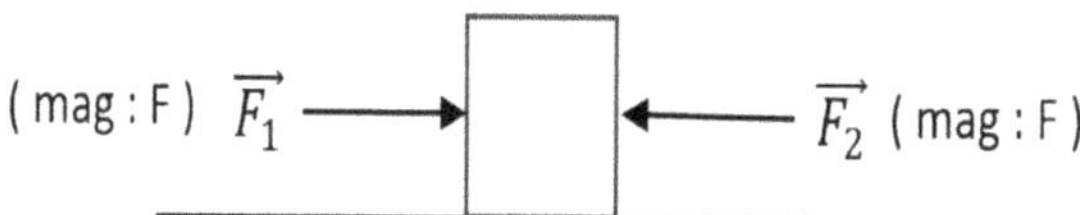

Resultant force : $\vec{F}_{net} = 0$

(11) Concepts of Balanced and Unbalanced Force :

There are two types of forces namely balanced forces and unbalanced forces.
Balanced forces : *If the resultant of all forces acting on a body is zero then the forces are called balanced forces.*

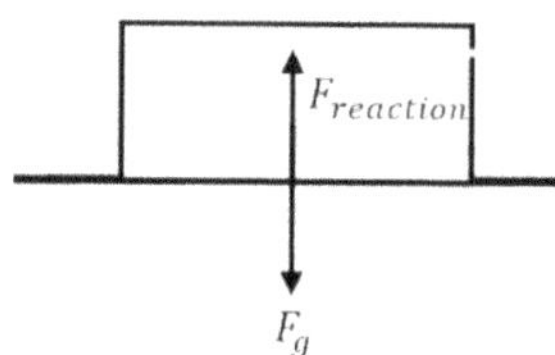

To understand the concept consider an object rests on surface such as a block on the table as shown below in the figure. Weight of the block is balanced by the reaction force from the table. The table pushes up against the block. So the weight of the block lying on a table is balanced by the reaction force from the table top.

If the forces on an object are balanced (or if there is no force acting on it) then the object is not moving, it stays still and the object that is moving continues to move at the same speed in the same direction, i.e. balanced forces cannot produce motion in a stationary body or stop a moving body but they can however change the shape of the body.

Un-balanced forces : *If the resultant of all forces acting on a body is not zero then the forces are called un-balanced forces.*
It produces acceleration in the body.

(12) Newton's Second Law for Variable Mass System

Newton's Second Law of Motion for variable mass system states that – ***The rate of change of linear momentum of an object is directly proportional to the net external force acting on the object and the change in linear momentum takes place in the direction of force.***

Mathematically, $(\vec{F}_{ext})_{net} = \frac{d\vec{P}}{dt}$ [Where, $\vec{P}$ = linear momentum]

(13) Newton's Second Law for Constant Mass System

$$(\vec{F}_{ext})_{net} = \frac{d\vec{p}}{dt}$$
$$= \frac{d}{dt}(m\,\vec{v})$$
$$= \frac{d(m)}{dt}\vec{v} + m\frac{d(\vec{v})}{dt}$$

If mass of the system remains constant, then $\frac{d(m)}{dt} = 0$

$$\therefore (\vec{F}_{ext})_{net} = m\frac{d\vec{v}}{dt} = m\,\vec{a}$$

Therefore, Newton's second law for constant mass states that – ***The acceleration of an object as produced by a net force is directly proportional to the magnitude of the net force, in the same direction, and inversely proportional to the mass of the object.***

(14) Importance of Newton's Second Law of Motion :

(i) It gives mathematical formulation for the measurement of force.
(ii) It defines the unit of force.
(iii) It defines momentum instead of velocity as the fundamental quantity related to motion.

(15) Measurement of force from Newton's second law of motion :

■ Force : $\vec{F} = \frac{\Delta\vec{P}}{\Delta t}$
■ Force : $\vec{F} = m\vec{a}$
From the above equations we come to know that-
(i) Acceleration of the object is in the direction of the force but the force is not always in the direction of the motion or velocity of the object.
(ii) No force is required to move a body uniformly along a straight line with constant speed.
(iii) The force is the cause and acceleration is the effect of it. But the acceleration depends on the force which acts on the body at that instant. Acceleration of the object does not depend on the previous history of the force.

(16) Derivation of Newton's First Law from Second Law of Motion :

Under the conditions (i) velocity of the object is much smaller than the velocity of light and (ii) mass of the object is constant we can write the mathematical form of Newton's second law as –

Resultant force $\vec{F} = m\vec{a}$

$$\text{or, } \vec{F} = m\left(\frac{\vec{v}_f - \vec{v}_i}{t}\right)$$

Where, v_f = final velocity and v_i = initial velocity

If $\vec{F} = 0$ then $m\left(\frac{\vec{v}_f - \vec{v}_i}{t}\right) = 0$

Since m $\neq$ 0 and t $\neq$ 0, therefore, $\vec{v}_f - \vec{v}_i = 0$

$$\text{or, } \vec{v}_f = \vec{v}_i$$

This means that if the resultant force on an object is zero, it will remain moving in the same direction with the same speed.

Again if $\vec{v}_i = 0$, then $\vec{v}_f = 0$, i.e. if the resultant force on an object which is at rest is zero, then it will remain at rest.

Thus, an object not acted upon by any external resultant force, does not change its state of rest or of motion. This statement is Newton's first law of motion.

(3) Newton's Third Law of Motion :

(17) According to Newton's third law, ***To every action, there is always an equal and opposite reaction.***

The terms action and reaction in third law mean nothing else but force. The terms action and reaction in the third law give us a wrong impression as if action is the cause and reaction is the effect, so that action comes always before reaction. In fact, there is no cause effect relationship and the forces act at the same instant or simultaneously. Therefore, a simple and clear way of stating third law is :
Force always occur in pairs. Whenever one body exerts a force on a second body, the second body exerts on force on the first body that is equal in magnitude and opposite in direction to the force exerted by the first body.

Mathematically it can be expressed as : $\vec{F}_{12} = -\vec{F}_{21}$

(18) Newton's third law of motion leads us to a very interesting fact about force. It is that the force never occurs singly in nature. Force always occur in pairs as a result of mutual interaction between two bodies.

(19) Forces of action and reaction act always on different bodies. Hence they can never cancel each other. Each force produces its own effect. [Two forces, equal in magnitude and opposite in direction, acting on the same body balance each other.]

(20) The forces of action and reaction may appear due to actual physical contact of two bodies or even from a distance but they are always equal in magnitude and opposite in direction.

(21) Newton's third law is applicable whether the bodies are at rest or they are in motion. Even it can be applied to all types of forces (e.g. gravitational, electric or magnetic)

(4) Limitations of Newton's Laws of Motion :

(22) Limitations of Newton's Laws of Motion :

(i) Newton's laws are applicable only in the inertial frames of reference. If the object is in a non-inertial frame of reference, we need to use a pseudo force in addition to all the other forces while writing the force equations.
(ii) For objects moving with speeds comparable to that of light. Newton's laws of motion do not give results that much with the experimental results and Einstein special theory of relativity has to be used.
(iii) Behavior and interaction of objects having atomic and molecular sizes cannot be explained using Newton's laws of motion and quantum mechanics has to be used.

(5) Force :

(23) Force

- **Definition of force :** Force is the physical cause which changes or tends to change either the size or shape or the state of rest or motion of the body.

- **Mathematical form of force :** For constant mass : $\vec{F} = m\vec{a}$ **(** Where, $\vec{a}$ = acceleration)

  For variable mass : $\vec{F} = \frac{\Delta\vec{P}}{\Delta t}$ (Where, $\vec{P}$ = linear momentum)

- **Effect of force :**

(a) When a force is applied on a non-rigid body, it changes the inter-spacing between its constituent particles and therefore causes a modification in its dimension and can also generate motion on it.

(b) When a force is applied on a rigid body, it does not change the inter-spacing between its constituent particles and consequently it does not change its dimensions but causes only motion in it.

- **Nature of the quantity of force :** Force is a vector quantity.

- **Dimensional equation of force :** $[F] = [M L T^{-2}]$

- **Unit of force : Absolute unit :** CGS unit : g cm s^{-2} or dyne

SI unit : kg m s^{-2} or N

Gravitational unit : CGS unit : g-f

SI unit : kg -f

• **Definition of dyne :** 1 dyne is the force which acts on a body of mass 1 g, produces an acceleration of 1 cm s^{-2}.

$$\therefore 1 \text{ dyn} = 1 \text{ g} \times 1 \text{ cm s}^{-2}.$$

• **Definition of newton :** 1 N is the force which acts on a body of mass 1 kg, produces an acceleration of 1 m s^{-2}.

$$\therefore 1 \text{ N} = 1 \text{ kg} \times 1 \text{ m s}^{-2}.$$

• **Relationship between newton and dyne :** $1 \text{ N} = 1 \text{ kg} \times 1 \text{ m s}^{-2}$

$$= 10^3 \text{ g} \times 10^2 \text{ cm s}^{-2}$$
$$= 10^5 \text{ g cm s}^{-2}$$
$$= 10^5 \text{ dyne}$$

• **Definition of one gram force :** One gram force is the force due to gravity on a mass of 1 g.

• **Relationship between gf and dyne :** $1 \text{ g f} = \text{Mass } 1 \text{ g} \times g \text{ cm s}^{-2}$

$$= g \text{ dyn}$$
$$= 980 \text{ dyn}$$

• **Definition of one kilogram force :** One kilogram force is the force due to gravity on a mass of 1 kg.

• **Relationship between kgf and N :** $1 \text{ kg f} = \text{Mass } 1 \text{ kg} \times g \text{ m s}^{-2}$

$$= g \text{ N}$$
$$= 9.8 \text{ N}$$

• The absolute units of force remain the same throughout the universe. On the other hand, gravitational units of force are not constant. This is because the gravitational units of force depend upon the value of g which is different at different places.

(6) Types of Force :

(24) Contact and Non-contact forces :

(a) Contact Forces : The forces which act on bodies when they are in physical contact are called contact forces.

Example : Frictional force, Normal force and Force created during collisions.

(b) Field Forces or Range Forces : The forces experienced by bodies even without being physically touched are called non-contact forces or field forces.

Example : Gravitational Force between two masses, Electrostatic force between two charges.

(25) Internal and External forces :

(a) Internal forces : The forces of interaction between portions of a system of bodies being considered are called internal forces.

(b) External forces : The forces exerted on bodies of a given system by bodies not included in the system are called external forces.

Points to Remember :

- To change the state of rest or uniform motion of a body in a straight line, external forces are needed- internal forces cannot do so.
- A system of bodies on which no external forces acts is called a closed system or isolated system.

(26) Fundamental forces in nature :

Though we observe different kinds of force in nature, fundamental forces are of four types. Rest of them is some forms of these fundamental forces. The four fundamental forces which exist in nature are :
(a) Gravitational force : It is the attractive force between two (point) masses separated by a distance. It is the weakest force.
(b) Electromagnetic force : It is the attractive and repulsive force between electrically charged particles.
(c) Weak nuclear force : This is the strongest force that binds the nucleons together inside a nucleus.
(d) Strong nuclear force : It is the interaction between subatomic particles that is responsible for radioactive decay of atoms, in particular β emission.

Name	Relative Strength	Range	Operates among	Exchange particles
Gravitational Force	10^{-39}	Infinite	All objects in universe	Graviton
Weak Nuclear Force	10^{-13}	10^{-16} m	Some elementary particles, particularly electrons and neutrino	W & Z bosons
Electromagnetic Force	10^{-2}	Infinite	Charged particles	Photon
Strong Nuclear Force	1	10^{-15} m	Nucleons	Gluon

(27) Common forces in mechanics :

(a) Weight [$W = mg$] **:** Weight of a body is the force with which earth attracts it.

(b) Normal Force [F_N] **:** When a body is placed on rigid surface, then the body experiences a force which is perpendicular to the surface in contact. This is known as normal force.

(c) Tension [F_T] **:** The force exerted by the end of taut string, rope or chain against pilling or applied force is called tension. The direction of tension is away from the body.

Points to Remember :

- If string is inextensible then the magnitude of acceleration of any number of masses connected through string is always same.
- If string is massless the tension in it is same everywhere.
- If there is no friction between pully and string then tension will be same on both sides of the pulley. But if there is friction between string and pulley then tension will be different on both sides of pulley.

(d) Spring force [$F_s = -kx$] : It is the restoring force exerted by a spring when it is stretched or compressed from its equilibrium position.

(7) Conservation of Linear Momentum :

(28) Principle of conservation of linear momentum for a single particle

Statement : ***If the resultant external force acting on a particle is zero, then its linear momentum remains constant with time.***

Mathematical explanation : According to Newton's second law of motion, resultant external force acting on a particle is given by $\vec{F} = \frac{d\vec{P}}{dt}$

Where, $\vec{P}$ = linear momentum of the particle.

If there is no external force or the resultant external force acting on the particle is zero then,

$\vec{F} = 0$

or, $\frac{d\vec{P}}{dt} = 0$

$\therefore \vec{P}$ = constant.

(8) Apparent Weight in a Lift

(a) When a lift is **accelerating upward**, the apparent weight F_N = m ($a + g$).

i.e. $F_N > mg$

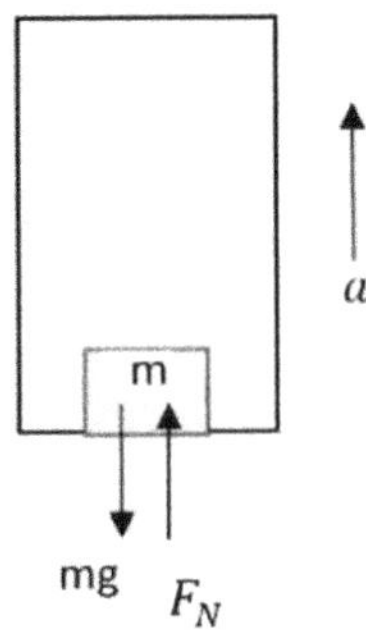

The weighing machine will read the apparent weight, which is more than the actual weight.

(b) When a lift is **accelerating downward**, the apparent weight F_N = m ($g - a$)

i.e. F_N < mg

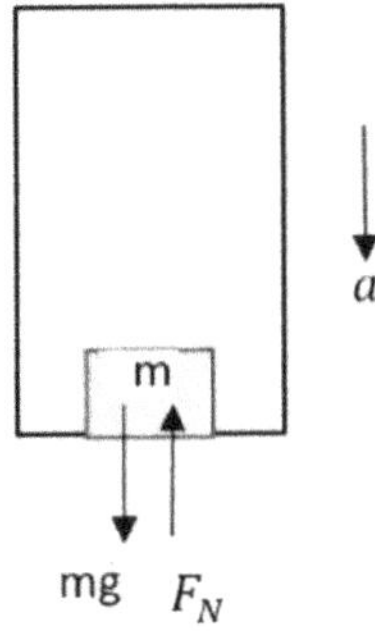

The weighing machine will read the apparent weight , which is less than the actual weight.

(c) When a lift is **falling freely under gravity**, the apparent weight F_N = m ($g - g$) = 0

i.e. The apparent weight of the body becomes zero.

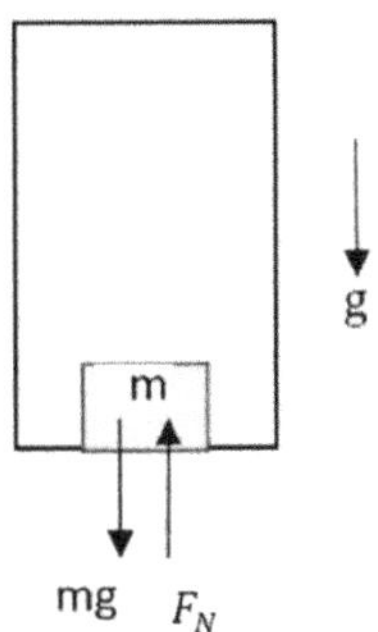

(d) When a lift is **at rest or moving with a constant speed**, the apparent weight F_N =mg

i.e. The weighing machine will read the actual weight of the body.

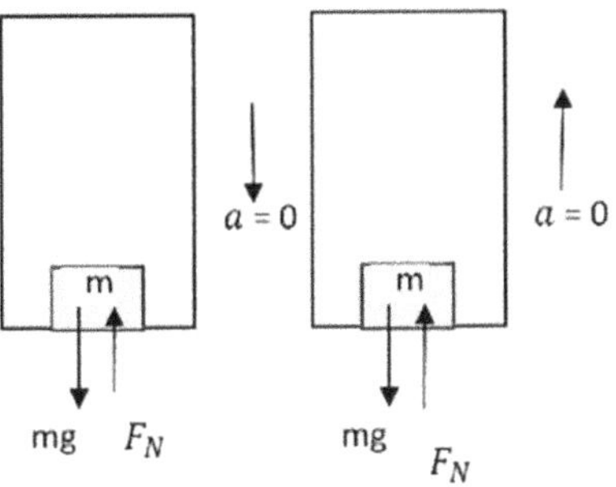

(d) If lift is **accelerating downward with an acceleration greater than acceleration due to gravity**, then the body will be lifted from floor to the ceiling of the lift.

Questions & Answers : Newton's Laws of Motion

Question : Name the physical quantity which cause motion in a body.

Answer : The physical quantity that causes motion in a body is force.

Question : Is force is needed to keep a moving body in motion?

Answer : No force is required to be applied to a moving body unless the direction or the speed is required to be changed.

Question : A ball is moving on a table top eventually stops. Explain the reason.

Answer : A ball moving on a table top is restricted by the force of friction between the ball and the table top as it opposes the motion.

Question : A ball is moving on a perfectly smooth horizontal surface. If no force is applied on it, will its speed decreases, increases or remain unchanged ?

Answer : When no force is applied on a ball moving on a perfectly smooth and horizontal surface, its speed remains unchanged.

Question : What is Galileo's law of inertia?

Answer : Galileo's law of inertia states that – An object, if once set in motion, moves with uniform velocity if no force acts on it.

Question : Name the factor on which inertia of a body depends and state how it depends on the factor stated by you?

Answer : • Inertia of a body depends on its mass.

• Mass and inertia are directly proportional to each other. Greater the mass, greater is the inertia.

Question : Why do bodies of small mass require small initial effort to bring them into motion ?

Answer : The inertia of a body is proportional to its mass. Smaller the mass, lesser is the opposition to change of state of motion.

Question : " More the mass, more difficult it is to move the body from rest". Explain this statement by giving an example.

Answer : Mass is a measure of inertia. More the mass, more is the inertia. If we take the example of a loaded trolley, then we observe that, it is difficult (i.e. larger force is required) to set a loaded trolley (which has more mass) in motion than an unloaded trolley (which has less mass).

Question : Why does a person tend to fall when he jumps out from a moving train and tries to stop immediately ?

Answer : A person falls when he jumps out from a moving train, because inside the train, his whole body was in a state of motion with the train. On jumping out of the moving train, as soon as his feet touch the ground, the lower part of the body comes rest, while the upper part still remains in motion. As a result, he falls in the direction of motion of the train and gets hurt.

To avoid falling, as soon as the passenger's feet touch the ground he should start running on the ground in the direction of motion of the train for some distance.

Question : Why does a coin placed on a card, drop into the tumbler when the card is rapidly flicked with the finger?

Answer : A coin placed on a card, drop into the tumbler when the card is rapidly flicked with the finger, because when the card is flicked the momentary force acts on the card, so it moves away. But the coin kept on it does not share the motion at once and it remain at its place due to inertia of rest. The coin then falls down into the tumbler due to the pull of gravity.

Question : Why does a ball thrown vertically upwards in a moving train, come back to the thrower's hand ?

Answer : A ball thrown vertically upwards in a moving train, comes back to the thrower's hand because when ball was thrown, it was in motion along with the person and the train. It remains in the same state of forward motion even during the time the ball remain in air. The person, inside the train and the ball all move ahead by the same distance due to inertia and so the ball falls back into his palm on its return.

Question : People often shake branches of tree for getting down its fruits. Why ?

Answer : People often shake branches of tree for getting down its fruits because when the branches are shaken, they come in motion, while the fruits due to inertia, remain in the state of rest. Thus, the massive and weakly attached fruits get detached from the branches and they fall down due to the pull of gravity.

Question : Dust particles are removed from a carpet by beating it. Why ?

Answer : Dust particles are removed from a carpet by beating it because the part of the carpet where the stick strikes, comes in motion at once, while the dust particles settled on its fur, remain in position due to inertia of rest. Thus the part of the carpet moves ahead with the stick, leaving behind the dust particles which fall down due to the earth's pull.

Question : Give qualitative definition of force on the basis of Newton's first law of motion.

Answer : Newton's first law of motion gives us a definition of force. It says that –

Force is an external cause in the form of a push or pull which produces or tries to produce motion in a body at rest, stops or tries to stop a moving body and changes or tries to change the direction of motion of the body.

Question : A body of mass m moving with a velocity v is acted upon by a force. Write expression for change in momentum in each cases (i) when $v \ll c$, (ii) when $v \rightarrow c$ and (iii) when $v \ll c$ but m does not remain constant. Here c is the speed of light.

Answer : (i) When $v \ll c$,

change in momentum (Δp) = m Δv

In this case variation of mass with velocity is small enough and mass can be considered to be constant.

(ii) When $v \rightarrow c$,

change in momentum (Δp) = $\Delta(mv)$

In this case mass of the particle does not remain constant, but it increases with velocity, according to the relation

$$m = \frac{m_0}{\sqrt{1-(\frac{v}{c})^2}},$$

where m_0 = mass of the particle when it is at rest.

(iii) When $v \ll c$ but m does not remain constant,

change in momentum (Δp) = $\Delta(mv)$

Question : Two equal and opposite forces act on a stationary body. Will the body move?

Answer : When two equal and opposite forces are acting on a stationary body, the body will not moves as the net force on the body is zero, hence the body will remain stationary. It will be in a state of rest due to inertia.

Question : Two equal and opposite forces act on a moving body. How is its motion affected ?

Answer : When two equal and opposite forces are acting on a moving body, the motion of the body is not affected, it remains unchanged. It is because the net force acting on the body is zero.

Question : Name the two factors on which the force needed to stop a moving body in a given time, depends.

Answer : Velocity and mass are the two factors on which the force needed to stop a moving body depend upon in a given time.

Question : How does Newton's second law of motion differ from first law of motion ?

Answer : Newton's first law of motion defines force only qualitatively. It implies that force is the cause of acceleration. Whereas, Newton's second law of motion gives the quantitative value of force, i.e. it relates force to the measurable quantities like mass and acceleration.

Question : Write the mathematical form of Newton's second law of motion. Under what condition does it take form F = ma ?

Answer : Mathematical form of Newton's second law of motion is –

$$(F_{ext})_{net} = \frac{\Delta P}{\Delta t}$$

Where, P = Linear momentum and

ΔP = change in linear momentum

It takes the form **F = ma** when –

(i) velocity of the object is much smaller that the velocity of light and (ii) mass of the object is constant.

Question : Write two consequences of Newton's second law of motion.

Answer : Two consequences of Newton's second law are –

(i) It gives mathematical formulation for the measurement of force and defines the unit of force.

(ii) It is the real law of motion. Newton's first and third laws of motion can be derived from second law.

Question : How can Newton's first law of motion be obtained from the second law of motion ?

Answer : Under the conditions (i) velocity of the object is much smaller than the velocity of light and (ii) mass of the object is constant we can write the mathematical form of Newton's second law as –

Resultant force F = ma

$$\text{or, } F = m \left(\frac{v_f - v_i}{t}\right)$$

Where, v_f = final velocity and v_i = initial velocity

If F = 0 then $m \left(\frac{v_f - v_i}{t}\right) = 0$

Since m ≠ 0 and t ≠ 0, therefore,

$v_f - v_i = 0$

or, $v_f = v_i$

This means that if the resultant force on an object is zero, it will remain moving in the same direction with the same speed.

Again if v_i = 0, then v_f = 0, i.e. if the resultant force on an object which is at rest is zero, then it will remain at rest.

Thus, an object not acted upon by any external resultant force, does not change its state of rest or of motion. This statement is Newton's first law of motion.

Question : How does the acceleration produced by a given force depend on mass of the body ? Draw a graph to show it.

Answer : When a force is applied on bodies of different masses, the acceleration produced in them is inversely proportional to their masses, i.e. $a \propto \frac{1}{m}$ (for a given mass)

The graph plotted for acceleration against mass is a hyperbola and is shown below :

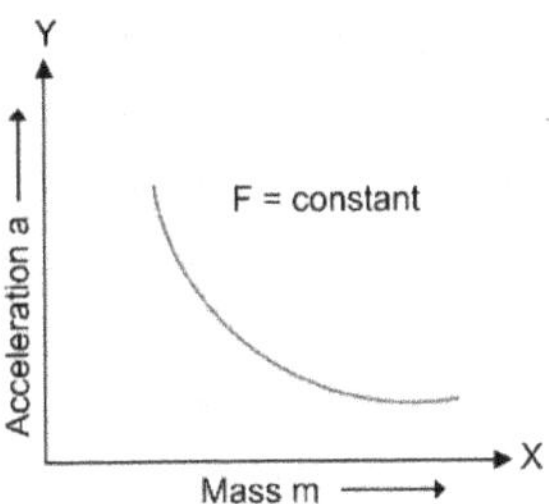

Question : Why does a glass vessel break when it falls on a hard floor, but does no break when it falls on a carpet?

Answer : When glass vessel falls from a height on a hard floor, it comes to rest almost instantaneously (i.e. in a very short time) so the floor exerts a large force on the vessel and it breaks. But if the glass vessel falls on carpet, the time duration in which the vessel comes to rest, increases and so the carpet exerts a less force on the vessel and it does not break.

Question : A cricketer pulls his hand back while catching a fast moving cricket ball.

Answer : If the cricketer does not pull his hands and stop the ball as soon as it touches his hands, he uses very little time (t_1) to stop the ball. Then the force exerted by the ball on the hands of the cricketer is –

$$F_1 = \frac{Chnage\ in\ momentum}{t_1}$$

But if the cricketer pulls back his hands along with the ball, he takes a much longer time (t_2) to stop the ball. The fore now exerted by the ball on his hands is

$$F_2 = \frac{Chnage\ in\ momentum}{t_2}$$

Science, $t_2 > t_1$, therefore, $F_1 > F_2$ or the force exerted on the hands of cricketer by the fast moving ball is less when he withdraws his hands. Thus cricketer avoids the chances of injury to his palms by withdrawing his hands along with the ball while catching it.

Question : Why does an athlete prefer to land on sand instead of hard floor while taking a high jump ?

Answer : When an athlete lands from a height on a hard floor, his feet comes to rest almost instantaneously (i.e. in a very short time) so the floor exerts a large force on the feet and he may hurts. But if he lands on sand, his feet push the sand for some distance, therefore the time duration in which his feet comes rest, increases. As a result, the force exerted on his feet decreases and he is saved from getting hurt.

Question : Classify the following amongst contact and non-contact forces : Frictional force, Normal reaction force, Force of tension in a string, Gravitational force, Electrostatic force, magnetic force.

Answer : Contact forces are : Frictional force, Normal reaction force, Force of tension in a string.

Non-contact forces are : Gravitational force, Electrostatic force, Magnetic force.

Question : State one factor on which the magnitude of a non-contact force depends. How does it depends on the factor stated by you?

Answer : • The magnitude of non-contact force depends on the distance.

• Distance and the magnitude of force are inversely related. The magnitude of force decreases as the distance increases.

Question : State the effect of a force applied on (i) a non-rigid body and (ii) a rigid body.

Answer : • When a force is applied on a non-rigid body, it changes the inter-spacing between its constituent particles and therefore causes a modification in its dimension and can also generate motion on it.

• When a force is applied on a rigid body, it does not change the inter-spacing between its constituent particles and consequently it does not change its dimensions but causes only motion in it.

Question : Give one example in each of the following cases where a force – (1) stops a moving body, (2) moves a stationary body, (3) changes the size of a body and (4) changes the shape of a body.

Answer : The examples are as follows –

(1) Stops a moving body : A fielder on the ground stops a moving ball by applying force with his hands.

(2) Moves a stationary body: A ball lying on the ground moves when it is kicked.

(3) Changes the size of a body : By loading a spring is hanging from a rigid support, the length of the spring increases.

(4) Changes the shape of a body : On pressing a piece of rubber, its shape changes.

Question : Use newton's laws of motion to explain the following : A cricketer pulls his hands back while catching a fast moving cricket ball.

Answer : A cricketer pulls his hands back while catching a fast moving cricket ball because while doing so, time of catching of the ball be increased. In other words, to increase the time to bring about a given change in momentum consequently rate of change of momentum decreases. Hence the ball exerts a small amount of force on our hands.

Question : State the usefulness of Newton's third law of motion?

Answer : Newton's third law of motion explains how the force acts on an object.

Question : A light ball falling on ground, after striking the ground rises upwards. Explain the reason.

Answer : When a falling ball strikes the ground, it exerts a force on the ground. The ground exerts a force back at the ball in the opposite direction. This is the reason the ball rises upwards.

Question : Explain the motion of a rocket with the help of Newton's third law.

Answer : The motion of a rocket can be explained by Newton's third law of motion. In a rocket, fuel burns inside it and they are expelled as burning gases at a higher temperature and pressure through a nozzle of the rocket. Thus the rocket exerts a force on the gases to expel them through the nozzle in the backward direction. The outgoing gases exert an equal and opposite force on the rocket because of which it moves in the forward direction.

Question : When a shot is fired from a gun, the gun gets recoiled. Explain.

Answer : When a bullet is fired from a gun, a force is exerted on the bullet. The gun in return experiences an equal force in opposite direction and hence gets recoiled.

Question : When you step a shore from a stationary boat, it tends to leave the shore. Explain.

Answer : In order to get out of the boat we exert a force (action) on the board of the boat. This creates a force (reaction) which enables us to step out of the boat. At the same instant, the boat tends to leave the shore due to the force exerted by us (i.e. action). For the safety of the passengers the boat man ties the boat to the pole on the shore so that it does not move away.

Question : To move a boat ahead in water, the boatman has push the water backwards by this oar. Explain.

Answer : To move a boat ahead in water, the boatman pushes (action) the water backwards with hi oar and the water exerts an equal and opposite force (reaction) in the forward direction on the boat due to which the boat moves ahead.

Question : A person pushing a wall hard is liable to fall back. Give reason.

Answer : When a person exerts a force (action) on a wall by pushing the palm of his hand against it, he will experience a force (reaction) exerted by the wall on his palm and hence, he may fall back.

Question : A light ball falling on ground, after striking the ground rises upwards. Explain.

Answer : When a light ball strikes the ground it exerts a force on the ground (action) and the ground in turn exerts an equal amount of force (reaction) on the ball, due to which the ball rises up.

Question : When two spring joined at their free ends are pulled apart, both show the same reading. Explain.

Answer : The spring of balance A pulls the spring of balance B due to which we get some reading in balance B. The same reading is seen in balance A because the spring of balance B also pulls the spring of balance A by the same force.

Question : Action and reaction forces do not balance each other. Why ?

Answer : Action and reaction do not balance each other because a force of action and reaction acts always on two different bodies.

Exercise | | Subjective Questions — Newton's Laws of Motion

(1) State Newton's first law of motion ? (1)

(2) Give qualitative definition force on the basis of Newton's first law of motion. (1)

(3) Name the factor on which inertia of a body depends and state how it depends on the factor stated by you. (2)

(4) Why do bodies of small mass require small initial effort to bring them into motion ? (1)

(5) " More the mass, more difficult it is to move the body from rest". Explain this statement by giving an example. (2)

(6) Why does a person tend to fall when he jumps out from a moving train and tries to stop immediately ? (2)

(7) Why does a coin placed on a card, drop into the tumbler when the card is rapidly flicked with the finger?

(8) Why does a ball thrown vertically upwards in a moving train, come back to the thrower's hand ? (2)

(9) Dust particles are removed from a carpet by beating it. Why ? (2)

(10) People often shake branches of tree for getting down its fruits. Why ? (2)

(11) State the effects of force applied on (a) a non-rigid body and (b) a rigid body. (2)

(12) Name the physical quantity which causes motion in a body. (1)

(13) Is force needed to keep a moving body in motion ? (1)

(14) A ball is moving on a table top eventually stops. Explain the reason.

(15) Can there be displacement of an object in the absence of any force acting on it ? (1)

(16) Define linear momentum and state its SI unit. (2)

(17) If 'm' is the mass of the body. 'v' its velocity and 'p' the momentum then write a relationship between change in momentum , mass and velocity of the body when
(a) v is almost equal to c, the velocity of light.
(b) v is very, very less as compared to c, the velocity of light. [2]

(18) Which of the following is scalar quantity ? Mass, force and linear momentum. (1)

(19) Represent the following graphically :
(a) momentum versus velocity when mass is fixed
(b) momentum versus mass when velocity is constant

(20) Name the two factors on which the force needed to stop a moving body in a given time, depends.

(21) A ball is moving on a perfectly smooth horizontal surface. If no force is applied on it, will its speed decreases, increases or remain unchanged ?

(22) What is Galileo's law of inertia?

(23) Two equal and opposite forces act on a stationary body. Will the body move?

(24) Two equal and opposite forces act on a moving body. How is its motion affected ?

(25) State Newton's second law of motion. (2)

(26) Write the mathematical form of Newton's second law of motion. State condition if any. (2)

(27) Draw graphs to show the dependence of (a) acceleration on force for a constant mass and (b) force on mass for a constant acceleration. (2)

(28) What information do you get from Newton's second law of motion ? (1)

(29) Write two consequences of Newton's second law of motion ? (2)

(30) Name the SI unit of force and define it. (2)

(31) Name the CGS unit of force. How is it related to newton. (2)

(32) How can Newton's first law of motion be obtained from the second law of motion. (2)

(33) Give an example of a non-contact force which is always of attractive. (1)

(34) How does the magnitude of the non-contact force on the two bodies depend on the distance of separation between them ? (1)

(35) Soni says that the acceleration in an object could be zero even when several forces are acting on it. Do you agree with her ? Why ? (2)

(36) If force is acting on a moving body perpendicular to the direction of motion, then what will be its effect on the speed and direction of motion of the body ? (1)

(37) Give the magnitude and direction of the net force acting on
(a) A drop of rain falling down with constant speed
(b) A kite skilfully held stationary in the sky.

(38) Action and reaction forces do not balance each other. Why ? (1)

MCQ – 5 : Discussion on Newton's Laws of Motion

Physics
MCQ | | Class – XI

Dynamics

Topic : Newton's First Law of Motion

 # Important Points

• **First Law of Motion (or Law of Inertia) :** Every bodies continues in its state of rest or of uniform motion in a straight line unless compelled by some external force to change that state.

 # Important Definition :

• Inertia is that property of body owing to which the body opposes any change in its state of motion.
• Inertia of rest is the inability of body to change its state of rest by itself.
• Inertia of motion is the inability of the body to change its state of motion by itself.
• Inertia of direction is the inability of the body to change its direction of motion by itself.

(1) The concept of inertia is explained in
(a) Newton's first law
(b) Newton's second law
(c) Newton's third law
(d) All of these

(2) Newton's first law of motion describes the following
(a) Energy
(b) Work
(c) Inertia
(d) Moment of inertia

(3) Inertia of a body has direct dependence on
(a) Impulse
(b) Momentum
(c) Mass
(d) Area

(4) An athletic does not come to rest immediately after crossing the winning line due to the
(a) Inertia of rest
(b) Inertia of Motion
(c) Inertia of direction
(d) None of these

(5) When a bus suddenly takes a turn, the passengers are thrown outwards because of
(a) Inertia of motion
(b) Acceleration of Motion
(c) Speed of Motion
(d) Both (b) and (c)

(6) A person sitting in an open car moving at constant velocity throws a ball vertically up into air. The ball fall
(a) Outside the car
(b) In the car ahead of the person
(c) In the car to the side of the person
(d) Exactly in the hand which threw it up

(7) Newton's first law is applicable
(a) in all reference frames
(b) only in inertial reference frame
(c) only in non-inertial reference frame
(d) none of these

(8) Physical independence of force is a consequence of
(a) third law of motion
(b) second law of motion
(c) first law of motion
(d) all of these laws

(9) A particle is moving with a constant speed along a straight line path. A force is not required to
(a) increase its speed
(b) decrease the momentum
(c) change the direction
(d) keep it moving with uniform velocity

(10) A particle is in a straight line motion with uniform velocity. A force is not required
(a) To increase the speed
(b) To decrease the speed
(c) To maintain the same speed
(d) To change the direction

(11) A ball is dropped from a spacecraft revolving around the earth at a height of 120 km. What will happen to the ball ?
(a) It will continue to move with the same speed along the original orbit of spacecraft
(b) It will move with the same speed, tangentially to the spacecraft
(c) It will fall down to the earth gradually
(d) It will go very far in the space.

(12) When we kick a stone, we get hurt. Due to which of the following properties of stone does it happen ?

(a) Inertia
(b) Momentum
(c) Velocity
(d) Reaction

Physics
MCQ | | Class – XI

Dynamics

Topic : Newton's Second Law of Motion

Important Points

• **Second Law of Motion :** The rate of change of linear momentum of a body is directly proportional to the net applied force on the body and this change takes place always in the direction of the applied force.

Mathematical form : $(\vec{F}_{ext})_{net} = \frac{d\vec{p}}{dt}$

$= \frac{d}{dt}(m\vec{v})$

$= \frac{d(m)}{dt}\vec{v} + m\frac{d(\vec{v})}{dt}$

For constant mass, $(\vec{F}_{ext})_{net} = m\frac{d(\vec{v})}{dt} = m\vec{a}$

• An acceleration motion is the result of application of the force.

(1) Newton's second law of motion connects
(a) Momentum and acceleration
(b) Change of momentum and velocity
(c) Rate of change of momentum and external force
(d) Rate of change of force and momentum

(2) Newton's second law gives the measure of
(a) Acceleration
(b) Force
(c) Momentum
(d) Angular momentum

(3) When a constant force is applied to a body, it moves with uniform
(a) Acceleration
(b) Velocity
(c) Momentum
(d) Speed

(4) From Newton's second law of motion, it can be inferred that
(a) No force is required to move a body uniformly along straight line
(b) Accelerated motion is always due to an external force
(c) Inertial mass of a body is equal to force required per unit acceleration in the body
(d) All of these

(5) A body moving with a constant speed on a horizontal surface does not have
(a) Velocity
(b) Momentum
(c) Acceleration
(d) Kinetic Energy

(6) In non-inertial frame, the second law of motion is written as
[Where, F_p = is a pseudo force while a is the acceleration of the body relative to non-inertial frame]
(a) F = ma
(b) F = m$a + F_p$
(c) F = m$a - F_p$
(d) F = 2ma

(7) According to Newton's 2nd law of motion correct equation is (where symbols have their usual meaning)
(a) $\vec{F} = \frac{d\vec{p}}{dt}$
(b) $\vec{F} = m\,\vec{a}$
(c) $\vec{F} = \vec{v}\,\frac{dm}{dt}$
(d) All of these

(8) Weight is defined as
(a) Force of attraction exerted by the earth
(b) Mass of the body
(c) Nature of the body
(d) None of these

(9) If the force of gravity suddenly disappears
(a) The mass of all bodies will become zero
(b) The weight of all bodies will become zero
(c) Both mass and weight of all bodies will become zero
(d) Neither mass nor weight of all bodies will become zero

(10) A body is acted upon by balanced forces
(a) If it is in rest
(b) If it is moving with constant speed
(c) If even number of force acting on it
(d) It is not accelerating

(11) If a force is constant in magnitude acts in direction perpendicular to the motion of a particle, then its

(a) Speed is uniform
(b) Momentum is uniform
(c) Velocity is uniform
(d) All of these

(12) When a force of constant magnitude acts in direction perpendicular to the motion of a particle, then its path is
(a) circular
(b) parabolic
(c) straight line
(d) either (b) or (c)

(13) When a force of constant magnitude and a fixed direction acts on a moving object, then its path is ?
(a) circular
(b) parabolic
(c) straight line
(d) either (b) or (c)

(14) A particle is acted upon by a force of constant magnitude which is always perpendicular to velocity of the particle, the motion of the particle takes place in a plane, then
(a) its velocity is constant
(b) its acceleration is constant
(c) its kinetic energy is constant
(d) it moves in a straight line

(15) Three forces starts acting simultaneously on a particle moving with velocity $\vec{v}$. These forces are represented in magnitude and direction by the three sides of a triangle ABC (as shown). The particle will now move with velocity

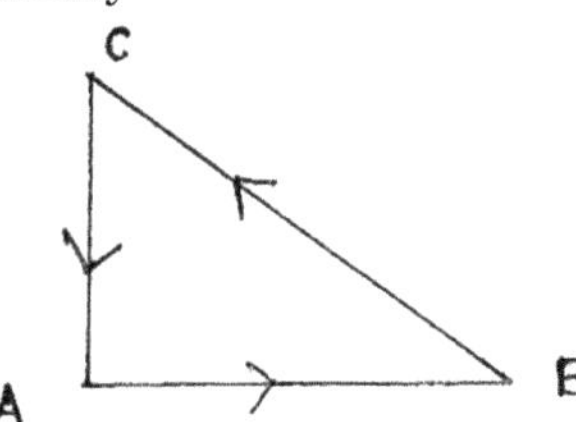

(a) $\vec{v}$ remaining unchanged
(b) Less than $\vec{v}$
(c) Greater than $\vec{v}$
(d) $\vec{v}$ in the direction of the largest force BC

(16) A particle moving with velocity $\vec{v}$ is acted by three forces shown by the vector triangle PQR. The velocity of the particle will

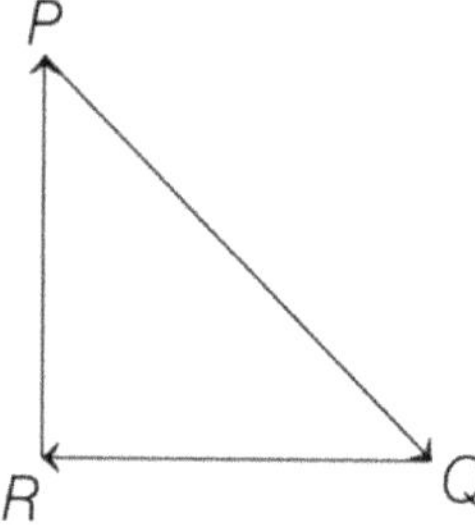

(a) decreases
(b) remains constant
(c) change according to the smallest force QR
(d) increases

(17) The distance x covered in time t by body having initial velocity v_0 and having a constant acceleration a is given by x $=v_0t + \frac{1}{2}at^2$. This result follows from -
(a) Newton's first law
(b) Newton's second law
(c) Newton's third law
(d) Newton's law of gravitation

(18) Three forces acting on a body are shown in the figure. To have the resultant force only along the y-direction, the magnitude of the minimum additional force needed is

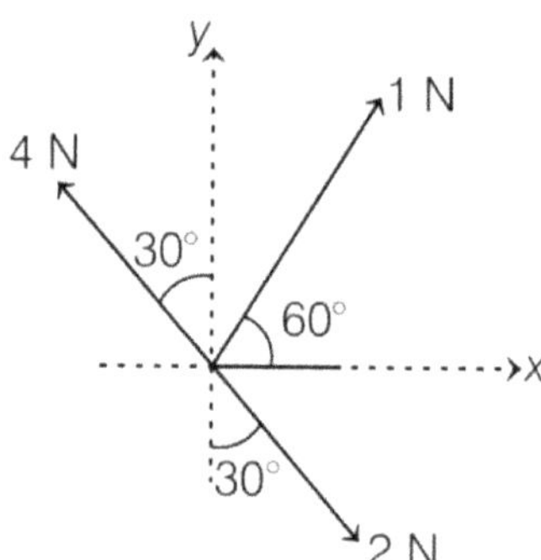

(a) 1.5 N
(b) $\sqrt{3}$ N
(c) 0.5 N
(d) $\frac{\sqrt{3}}{4}$ N

Physics
MCQ | | Class – XI

Dynamics

Topic : Newton's Third Law of Motion

Important Points

• **Third Law of Motion :** To every action, there is always an equal (in magnitude) and opposite (in direction) reaction i.e. when a body exerts a force on any other body, the second body also exerts an equal and opposite force on the first.

Mathematical form, $\vec{F}_{12} = -\vec{F}_{21}$

 # Important Facts :

• Force in nature always occurs in pairs. A single isolated force is not possible.
• Action and reaction never act on the same body.

(1) Action and reaction forces act on
(a) the same body
(b) the different bodies
(c) the horizontal surface
(d) Nothing can be said

(2) In accordance with Newton's third law of motion
(a) action and reaction never balance each other
(b) for appearance of action and reaction, physical contact is not necessary
(c) this law is applicable whether the bodies are at rest or they are in motion
(d) all of these.

(3) For a given system, Action and reaction
(i) act on the two different bodies
(ii) have opposite directions
(iii) have equal magnitude
(i) have zero resultant
(a) (i), (ii), (iii)
(b) (ii), (iii), (iv)
(c) All of the above
(d) None of the above

(4) Swimming is possible on account of
(a) Newton's first law
(b) Newton's second law
(c) Newton's third law
(d) Newton's law of gravitation

(5) Working of rocket or jet is based on
(a) Newton's first law
(b) Newton's second law
(c) Newton's third law
(d) All the three laws

(6) When we jump out of a boat standing in water it moves
(a) Forward
(b) Backward
(c) Sideway
(d) None of the above

(7) On a stationary sail-boat, air is blown at the sails from a fan attached to the boat. The boat will
(a) Remain stationary
(b) Spin around
(c) Move in a direction opposite to that in which air is blown
(d) Move in the direction in which the air is blown

(8) Newton's third law of motion leads to the law of conservation of
(a) Mass
(b) Energy
(c) Angular momentum
(d) Momentum

(9) A man is standing on a balance and his weight is measured. If he takes a step in the left side, then weight
(a) will decrease
(b) will increase
(c) Remains same
(d) First decrease then increase

(10) A man is standing at a spring platform. Reading of spring balance is 55 kg wt. If man jumps outside platform, then reading of spring balance
(a) decreases
(b) increases
(c) Remains same
(d) First increase then decreases to zero

(11) A cold soft drink is kept on the balance. When the cap is open, then the weight
(a) decreases
(b) increases
(c) Remains same

(d) First increases then decreases

(12) A man is at rest in the middle of a pond on perfectly smooth ice. He can get himself to the shore by making use of
(a) Newton's first law
(b) Newton's second law
(c) Newton's third law
(d) Newton's law of gravitation

(13) When a horse pulls a wagon, the force that causes the horse to move forward is the force
(a) He exerts on the wagon
(b) The wagon exerts on him
(c) The ground exerts on him
(d) He exerts on the ground

Physics MCQ || Class – XI

Dynamics

Topic : Change in Linear Momentum

 # Important Points

Change linear momentum : $\Delta\vec{p} = \vec{p}_f - \vec{p}_i$

$= \vec{p}_f + (-\vec{p}_i)$

(1) A particle is moving in a circle with uniform speed v. In moving from appoint to another diametrically opposite point
(a) the momentum changes by mv
(b) the kinetic energy changes by mv
(c) the momentum changes by 2mv
(d) the kinetic energy changes by mv^2

(2) A particle of mass m is projected with velocity v making an angle of 45° with the horizontal. When the particle lands on the level ground, the magnitude of the change in its momentum will be
(a) 2 mv
(b) $\frac{mv}{\sqrt{2}}$
(c) $\sqrt{2}\,mv$
(d) zero

(3) A particle of mass m strikes elastically on a wall with velocity v at the angle of 60° from the wall then magnitude of change in momentum of ball along the wall is
(a) 2 mv
(b) mv
(c) $\sqrt{3}\,mv$
(d) zero

(4) A body of mass m collides against a wall with a velocity v and rebounds with the same speed. Its change of momentum is
(a) 2 mv
(b) mv
(c) $-mv$
(d) zero

Physics MCQ | | Class – XI	Dynamics
	Topic : Force as the time rate of change of linear momentum

Important Points

- Force is an external effect in form of a push or pull which – (a) Produce or tries to produce motion in a body at rest
(b) Stops or tries to stop a moving body
(c) Changes or tries to change the direction of motion of the body.

- Dimensional Formula of force : [M L T^{-2}]

- Unit of force : dyn (CGS unit) , N (SI unit)

- For constant and variable mass system,

Force = Time Rate of change of linear momentum

- Mathematical form of force : $(\vec{F}_{ext})_{net} = \frac{d\vec{p}}{dt}$

(1) A cricket ball of mass 150 g is moving with a velocity of 12 m s^{-1} and is hit by a bat so that the ball is turned back with a velocity of 20 m s^{-1}. The force of blow acts for 0.01 s on the ball. The average force exerted by the bat on the ball is
(a) 480 N
(b) 600 N
(c) 400 N
(d) 500 N

(2) A cricketer catches a ball of mass 150 g in 0.1 s moving with speed 20 m s^{-1}. Then he experiences a force of
(a) 300 N
(b) 30 N
(c) 3 N
(d) 0.3 N

(3) A player catches a ball of 200 g moving with a speed 20 m s^{-1}. If the time taken to complete the catch is 0.5 s, the force exerted on the player's hand is
(a) 8 N
(b) 4 N
(c) 2 N
(d) 0

(4) If n balls hit elastically and normally on a surface per unit time and all balls of mass m are moving with same velocity u, then force on surface is
(a) mnu
(b) 2mnu
(c) $\frac{1}{2}$ mu^2n
(d) mu^2n

(5) A machine gun fires a bullet of mass 65 g with a velocity of 1300 ms^{-1}. The man holding it can exert a maximum force of 169 N on the gun. The number of bullets he can fire per second will be
(a) 1
(b) 2
(c) 3
(d) 4

(6) A body of mass 3 kg hits a wall at an angle of 60° and returns at the same angle. The impact time was 0.2 s. The force exerted on the wall

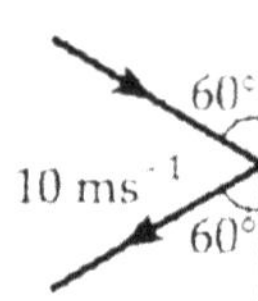

(a) $150\sqrt{3}$ N
(b) $50\sqrt{3}$ N
(c) 100 N
(d) $75\sqrt{3}$ N

(7) A 0.5 kg ball moving with a speed of v = 12 m s^{-1} strikes a hard wall at an angle 30° with the wall. It is reflected with the same speed and at the same angle. If the ball is in contact with the wall for 0.25 s, the average force acting on the wall is

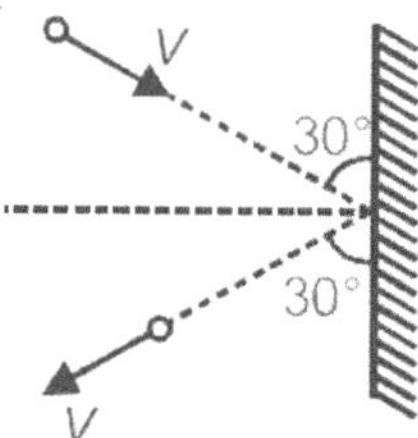

(a) 48 N
(b) 24 N
(c) 12 N
(d) 96 N

(8) The linear momentum p of a body moving in one dimension varies with time according to the equation, p = $a + bt^2$, where a and b are positive constants. The net force acting on the body is
(a) constant
(b) proportional to t^2
(c) inversely proportional to t
(d) proportional to t

(9) The linear momentum p of a body varies with time and is given by the equation, p = $x + yt^2$, where x and y are constants. The net force acting on the body for a one dimensional motion is proportional to
(a) a constant
(b) t^2
(c) t
(d) $\frac{1}{t}$

(10) At time t = 0 a particle starts moving along the x-axis. If its kinetic energy increases uniformly with t, the net force acting on it must be
(a) constant
(b) proportional to t^2
(c) inversely proportional to t
(d) proportional to $\frac{1}{\sqrt{t}}$

(11) A particle moves in the xy plane under the action of a force F such that the components of its linear momentum $\vec{p}$ at any time t are p_x = 2 cos t, p_y = 2 sin t. The angle between $\vec{F}$ and $\vec{p}$ at time t is
(a) 90 °
(b) 0°
(c) 180°
(d) 30°

Physics MCQ | | Class – XI

Dynamics

Topic : Force as a product of mass and acceleration

 # Important Points

For constant mass system, $\vec{F} = m\vec{a} = m\left(\frac{\vec{v_f} - \vec{v_i}}{t}\right)$

Where, m = mass of the system

$\vec{a}$ = acceleration

$\vec{v_i}$ = initial velocity of the system

$\vec{v_f}$ = final velocity of the system

---

(1) A body of mass 2 kg is sliding with a constant velocity of 4 m s^{-1} on a frictionless horizontal table. The force required to keep the body moving with the same velocity is
(a) 8 N
(b) 0 N
(c) 2×10^4 N
(d) $\frac{1}{2}$ N

(2) A body of mass 40 g is moving with constant velocity 2 cm s^{-1} on a horizontal frictionless table. The force on the body (in dyne) is
(a) zero
(b) 3920
(c) 160
(d) 80

(3) A 10 g bullet moving at 200 ms^{-1} stops after penetrating 5 cm of wooden plank. The average force exerted on the bullet will be
(a) 2000 N
(b) – 2000 N
(c) 4000 N
(d) – 4000 N

(4) A 5 kg mass is accelerated from rest to 60 ms^{-1} in 1 s. What force acts on it
(a) 5×60 N
(b) $\frac{5}{60} \times 981$ N
(c) $60^2 \times 52$ N
(d) $\frac{5}{2} \times 60^2 \times 981$ N

(5) A body of mass 2 kg moving on a horizontal surface with an initial velocity of 4 ms^{-1} comes to rest after 2 s. If one wants to keep this body moving on the same surface with a velocity of 4 ms^{-1} , the force required is
(a) 8 N
(b) 4 N
(c) Zero
(d) 2 N

(6) When a 4 kg rifle is fired, the 10 g bullet receives an acceleration of 3×10^6 cm s^{-2}. The magnitude of the force acting on the rifle (in N) is
(a) zero
(b) 120
(c) 300
(d) 3000

(7) A gun of mass 10 kg fires 4 bullets per second. The mass of each bullet is 20 g and the velocity of the bullet when it leaves the gun is 300 m s^{-1}. The force required to hold the gun when firing is
(a) 6 N
(b) 8 N
(c) 24 N
(d) 240 N

(8) A ball of mass 25 g, moving with a velocity of 2 m $s^{-1}$is stopped within 5 cm. The average resistance offered to the ball is
(a) 10 N
(b) 5 N
(c) 2 N
(d) 1 N

(9) A player takes 0.1 s in catching a ball of mass 150 g moving with velocity 20 m s^{-1}. The force imparted by the ball on the hands of the player is
(a) 0.3 N
(b) 3 N
(c) 30 N
(d) 300 N

(10) A man of mass 50 kg carries a bag of weight 40 N on his shoulder. The force with which the floor pushes up his feet will be
(a) 882 N

(b) 530 N

(c) 90 N

(d) 600 N

Physics
MCQ | | Class – XI

Dynamics

Topic : Calculation of Different Parameters from Force

(1) The velocity acquire by a mass m in travelling a certain distance d starting from rest under the action of a constant force is directly proportional to
(a) $\sqrt{m}$
(b) m^0
(c) $\frac{1}{\sqrt{m}}$
(d) m

(2) A material body A of mass m_A exerts a force on another material body B of mass m_B. If the acceleration of B be a_B, the magnitude of the acceleration of A is
(a) zero
(b) $\frac{m_B\ a_B}{m_A}$
(c) $\frac{m_A\ a_B}{m_B}$
(d) a_B

(3) Two bodies of masses 4 kg and 5 kg are acted upon by the same force. If the acceleration of the lighter body is 2 m s^{-2}, then the acceleration of the heavier body is
(a) 4.2 m s^{-2}
(b) 3.6 m s^{-2}
(c) 2.4 m s^{-2}
(d) 1.6 m s^{-2}

(4) An object with mass 10 kg moves at a constant velocity of 10 m s^{-1}. A constant force then acts for 4 s on the object giving it a speed of 2 m s^{-1} in opposite direction. The acceleration produced
(a) 3 m s^{-2}
(b) – 3 m s^{-2}
(c) 0.3 m s^{-2}
(d) – 0.3 m s^{-2}

(5) A force of 6 N acts on a body at rest and of mass 1 kg. during this time, the body attains a velocity of 30 m s^{-1}. The time for which the force acts on the body is
(a) 7 s
(b) 5 s
(c) 10 s
(d) 8 s

(6) A 10 N force is applied on a body to produce in it an acceleration of 1 m s^{-2}. The mass of the body
(a) 15 kg
(b) 20 kg
(c) 10 kg
(d) 5 kg

(7) A ship of mass 3×10^7 kg initially at rest is pulled by a force of 5×10^4 N through a distance of 3 m. Neglecting friction, the speed of the ship at this moment is
(a) 3 m s^{-1}
(b) 1.5 m s^{-1}
(c) 0.1 m s^{-1}
(d) 2 m s^{-1}

(8) A force vector applied on a mass is represented by $\vec{F}$ = (6 $\hat{\imath}$ – 8 $\hat{\jmath}$ + 10 $\hat{k}$) N and acceleration with 1 m s^{-2}. What will be the mass of the body ?
(a) 10 kg
(b) 20 kg
(c) $10\sqrt{2}$ kg
(d) $2\sqrt{10}$ kg

(9) A particle of mass 4 kg is acted upon by steady force of 4 N. Distance travelled by the particle in 4 s is
(a) 16 m
(b) 2 m
(c) 8 m
(d) 4 m

(10) An object of mass 3 kg is at rest. Now a force $\vec{F} = 6t^2\ \hat{\imath} + 4t\ \hat{\jmath}$ is applied on the object then velocity of object at t = 3s is
(a) 18 $\hat{\imath}$ + 3$\hat{\jmath}$
(b) 18 $\hat{\imath}$ + 6 $\hat{\jmath}$
(c) 3 $\hat{\imath}$ + 18 $\hat{\jmath}$
(d) 18 $\hat{\imath}$ + 4 $\hat{\jmath}$

(11) An object of mass 2 kg is at rest at origin starts moving under the action of a force $\vec{F}$ = ($3t^2\ \hat{\imath} + 4t\ \hat{\jmath}$) N . The velocity of the object at t = 2 s will be
(a) (3 $\hat{\imath}$ + 2 $\hat{\jmath}$) m s^{-1}
(b) (2 $\hat{\imath}$ + 4 $\hat{\jmath}$) m s^{-1}
(c) (4 $\hat{\imath}$ + 4 $\hat{\jmath}$) m s^{-1}
(d) (3 $\hat{\imath}$ - 4 $\hat{\jmath}$) m s^{-1}

(12) A body of mass 8 kg is moved by a force F = 3 x N, where x is the distance covered, initial position is x = 2 m and the final position is x = 10 m. The initial speed is 0.0 ms^{-1}. The final speed is
(a) 6 m s^{-1}

(b) 12 m s^{-1}
(c) 18 m s^{-1}
(d) 14 m s^{-1}

(13) A particle of mass 10^{-2} kg is moving along the positive x-axis under the influence of a force, $F(x) = -\frac{k}{2x^2}$, where $k = 10^{-2}$ N m^{-2}. When position of the particle is at x = 1 m, its velocity is v = 0. When x = 0.5 m, its velocity is
(a) 0
(b) 0.5 m s^{-1}
(c) 1 m s^{-1}
(d) 2 m s^{-1}

(14) A block of mass 1 kg starts from rest at x = 0 and moves along the x-axis under the action of a force F = kt, where, t is time and k = 1 N s^{-1}. The distance the block will travel in 6 seconds is
(a) 36 m
(b) 72 m
(c) 108 m
(d) 18 m

(15) The velocity v of a particle (under a force F) depends on its distance (x) from the origin (with x > 0) $v \propto \frac{1}{\sqrt{x}}$. Find how the magnitude of the force (F) on the particle depends on x.
(a) $F \propto \frac{1}{x^{\frac{3}{2}}}$
(b) $F \propto \frac{1}{x}$
(c) $F \propto \frac{1}{x^2}$
(d) $F \propto x$

(16) For a body of 50 kg mass, the velocity-time graph is shown in figure. The force acting on the body is

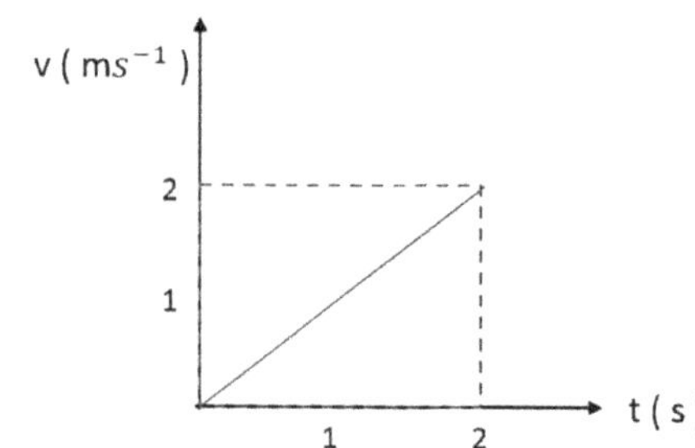

(a) 100 N
(b) 25 N
(c) 50 N
(d) 12.5 N

Physics MCQ | | Class – XI

Dynamics

Topic :Variable Mass System

 # Important Points

Mathematical form : $(\vec{F}_{ext})_{net} = \frac{d\vec{p}}{dt}$

$= \frac{d}{dt}(m\vec{v})$

$= \frac{d(m)}{dt}\vec{v} + m\frac{d(\vec{v})}{dt}$

For constant mass, $(\vec{F}_{ext})_{net} = m\frac{d(\vec{v})}{dt} = m\vec{a}$

(1) A block of metal weighing 2 kg is resting on a frictionless plane. It is struck by a jet releasing water at a rate of 1 kg $s^{-1}$and at a speed of 5 ms^{-1}. The initial acceleration of the block will be
(a) 2 m s^{-2}
(b) 0.5 m s^{-2}
(c)10 m s^{-2}
(d) None of the above

(2) In a rocket of mass 1000 kg fuel is consumed at a rate of 40 kg s^{-1}. The velocity of the gases ejected from the rocket is 5×10^4 ms^{-1}. The thrust on the rocket is
(a) 2×10^3 N
(b) 5×10^4 N
(c) 2×10^6 N
(d) 2×10^9 N

(3) If force on a rocket having exhaust velocity of 300 m s^{-1} is 345 N, then rate of combustion of the fuel is
(a) 1.15 kg s^{-1}
(b) 0.55 kg s^{-1}
(c) 0.75 kg s^{-1}
(d) 2.25 kg s^{-1}

(4) If force on a rocket having exhaust velocity of 300 m s^{-1} is 210 N, then rate of combustion of the fuel is
(a) 0.7 kg s^{-1}
(b) 1.4 kg s^{-1}
(c) 0.07 kg s^{-1}
(d) 10.7 kg s^{-1}

(5) A 5000 kg rocket is set for vertical firing. The exhaust speed is 800 m s^{-1}. To give an initial upward acceleration of 20 m s^{-2}, the amount of gas ejected per second to supply the needed thrust will be(g = 10 m s^{-2})
(a) 127.5 kg s^{-1}
(b) 187.5 kg s^{-1}
(c) 185.5 kg s^{-1}
(d) 137.5 kg s^{-1}

(6) A 600 kg rocket is set for a vertical firing. If the exhaust speed is 1000 m s^{-1}, the mass of the gas ejected per second to supply the thrust needed to overcome the weight of rocket is
(a) 117.6 kg s^{-1}
(b) 58.6 kg s^{-1}
(c) 6 kg s^{-1}
(d) 76.4 kg s^{-1}

(7) For a rocket propulsion velocity of exhaust gases relative to rocket is 2 km s^{-1}. If mass of rocket system is 1000 kg, then the rate of fuel consumption for a rocket to rise up with an acceleration 4.9 m s^{-2} will be
(a) 12.25 kg s^{-1}
(b) 17.5 kg s^{-1}
(c) 7.35 kg s^{-1}
(d) 5.2 kg s^{-1}

(8) A train is moving with velocity 20 ms^{-1}. On this, dust is falling at the rate of 50 kg/min. The extra force required to move this train with constant velocity will be
(a) 16.66 N
(b)1000 N
(c)166.6 N
(d) 1200 N

(9) In a rocket, fuel burns at the rate of 2 kg s^{-1}. This fuel gets ejected from the rocket with a velocity of 80 km s^{-1}. Force exerted on the rocket is
(a)16000 N
(b) 1, 60,000 N
(c)1600 N
(d)12 N

(10) Gravel is dropped onto a conveyer belt at a rate of 0.5 kg s^{-1}. The extra force required in N to keep the belt moving at 2 km s^{-1} is
(a)1 N
(b) 2 N
(c) 4 N
(d) 0.5 N

(11) A rocket is ejecting 50 g of gases per second at a speed of 500 m s^{-1}. The accelerating force on the rocket will be
(a)125 N
(b) 25 N
(c) 5 N
(d) Zero

(12) A rocket of mass 1000 kg exhaust gases at a rate of 4 kg s^{-1} with a velocity 3000 m s^{-1} . The thrust developed on the rocket is
(a)12000 N
(b) 120 N
(c) 800 N
(d) 200 N

(13) A cracker rocket is ejecting gases at a rate of 0.05 kg s^{-1} with a velocity 400 ms^{-1}. The accelerating force on the rocket is
(a) 20 dyne
(b) 20 N
(c) 200 N
(d) zero

(14) A rocket has mass of 100 kg. 90% of this is fuel. It ejects fuel vapours at the rate of 1 kg s^{-1} with a velocity of 50 m s^{-1} relative to the rocket. It is supposed that the rocket is outside the gravitational field. The initial up-thrust on the rocket when it just starts moving upwards is
(a) zero
(b) 5000 N
(c) 1000 N
(d) 2000 N

(15) A balloon has 2 g air. A small hole is pierced into it. The air comes out with a velocity of 4 m s^{-1}. If the balloon shrinks completely in 2.5 s. The average force acting on the balloon is
(a) 0.008 N
(b) 0.0032 N
(c) 8 N
(d) 3.2 N

(16) A rocket of mass 5700 kg ejects mass at a constant rate of 15 kg s^{-1} with constant speed of 12 km s^{-1}. The acceleration of the rocket 1 minute after the blast is (g = 10 m s^{-2})
(a) 34.9 m s^{-2}
(b) 27.5 m s^{-2}
(c) 3.50 m s^{-2}
(d) 13.5 m s^{-2}

(17) A 6000 kg rocket is set for firing. If the exhaust speed is 1000 m s^{-1}, how much gas must be ejected each second to supply the thrust needed to overcome the weight of the rocket?
(a) 30 kg
(b) 40 kg
(c) 50 kg
(d) 60 kg

(18) An open carriage in a goods train is moving with a uniform velocity of 10 m s^{-1}. If the rain adds water with zero velocity at the rate of 5 kg s^{-1} , then the additional force required by the engine to maintain the same velocity of the train is
(a) 0.5 N
(b) 20 N
(c) 50 N
(d) zero

(19) A wagon weighing 1000 kg is moving with a velocity 50 km h^{-1} smooth horizontal rails. A mass of 250 kg is dropped into it. The velocity with which it moves now is
(a) 12.5 km h^{-1}
(b) 20 km h^{-1}
(c) 40 km h^{-1}
(d) 50 km h^{-1}

(20) A block of metal weighing 2 kg is resting on a frictionless plane. It is struck by a jet releasing water at a rate of 1 kg s^{-1} with a speed of 5 m s^{-1}. The initial acceleration of the block will be
(a) 2.5 m s^{-2}
(b) 5 m s^{-2}
(c) 10 m s^{-2}
(d) 15 m s^{-2}

(21) A satellite in force free space sweep stationary interplanetary dust at a rate $\frac{dm}{dt} = +\alpha v$. Here v is the velocity. The acceleration of the satellite of mass M is
(a) $-2\frac{\alpha v^2}{M}$
(b) $-3\frac{\alpha v^2}{M}$
(c) $-\frac{\alpha v^2}{M}$
(d) $-\alpha v^2$

Physics MCQ | | Class – XI

Dynamics

Topic : Conservation of Linear Momentum

 # Important Points

In the absence of any external force, vector sum of the linear momentum of a system of particles remains constant.

(1) The momentum of a system is conserved
(a) Always
(b) Never
(c) In the absence of an external force on the system
(d) None of the above.

(2) A body whose momentum is constant, must have constant
(a) Force
(b) Velocity
(c) Acceleration
(d) All of these

(3) The motion of a rocket is based on the principle of conservation of
(a) Linear momentum
(b) Angular momentum
(c) Kinetic Energy
(d) Mass

(4) Rocket engines lift a rocket from the earth surface because hot gas with high velocity
(a) Push against the earth
(b) Push against the air
(c) React against the rocket and push it up
(d) Heat up the air which lifts the rocket

 # Important Points

Recoil velocity of gun : $|\vec{V}| = \frac{m}{M}\,|\vec{v}|$
Where, M = mass of the gun
m = mass of the bullet
$\vec{v}$ = velocity of the bullet

(5) A bullet of mass 200 g is fired with a velocity 30 m s^{-1} form a gun of mass 100 kg. the recoil velocity of the gun is
(a) 10 m s^{-1}
(b) 5 m s^{-1}
(c) 0.06 m s^{-1}
(d) 0.03 m s^{-1}

(6) A bullet of mass 10 g is fired from a gun of mass 1 kg. If the recoil velocity is 5 m s^{-1} the velocity of the muzzle is
(a) 0.05 m s^{-1}
(b) 5 m s^{-1}
(c) 50 m s^{-1}
(d) 500 m s^{-1}

(7) A man fires a bullet of mass 200 g at a speed of 5 m s^{-1} . The gun is of one kg mass. By what velocity the gun rebounds backward ?
(a) 1 m s^{-1}
(b) 0.01 m s^{-1}
(c) 0.1 m s^{-1}
(d) 10 m s^{-1}

(8) A man of 50 kg mass is standing in a gravity free space at a height of 10 m above the floor. He throws a stone of 0.5 kg mass downward with speed 2 m s^{-1}. When the stone reaches the floor, the distance of the man above the floor will be
(a) 20 m
(b) 9.9 m
(c) 10.1 m
(d) 10 m

(9) A person holding a rifle (mass of person and rifle together is 100 kg) stands on a smooth surface and fires 10 shots horizontally in 5 s. Each bullet has a mass of 10 g with a muzzle velocity of 800 m s^{-1} . The final velocity acquired by the person and the average force exerted on the person are
(a) – 1.6 m s^{-1} , 8 N
(b) – 0.08 m s^{-1}, 16 N
(c) – 0.8 m s^{-1}, 16 N
(d) – 1.6 m s^{-1}, 16 N

(10) A mass of 1 kg is thrown up with a velocity of 100 m s^{-1}. After 5 s, it explodes into two parts. One part of mass 400 g moves down with a velocity 25 m s^{-1} . calculate the velocity of other part just after the explosion (g = 0.05 m s^{-2})
(a) 40 m s^{-1} ↑
(b) 40 m s^{-1} ↓
(c) 100 m s^{-1} ↑
(d) 60 m s^{-1} ↓

(11) A U-238 nucleus originally at rest, decay by emitting an α-particle, say with a velocity v m s^{-1}. The recoil velocity (in m s^{-1}) of the residual nucleus is

(a) $\frac{4v}{238}$

(b) $-\frac{4v}{238}$

(c) $\frac{v}{4}$

(d) $-\frac{4v}{234}$

(12) A shell, in flight, explodes into four unequal parts. Which of the following is conserved ?

(a) Potential Energy

(b) Momentum

(c) Kinetic Energy

(d) Both (a) and (c)

(13) A shell of mass m is at rest initially. It explodes into three fragments having mass in the ratio 2 : 2 : 1. If the fragments having equal mass fly off along mutually perpendicular directions with speed v, the speed of the third (lighter) fragment is

(a) $2\sqrt{2}$ v

(b) 3 $\sqrt{2}$ v

(c) v

(d) $\sqrt{2}$ v

The Quantities that Determine the Effect of Force	
(1) Impulse	**(2) Work**
(3) Power	**(4) Moment of Force**

(1) Impulse

(1.1) The effectiveness of a force in producing motion depends not only upon the magnitude of the force but also on the time.

The **total effect of a force w.r.t. time** is called impulse and is measured by the product of the force and the time for which the force acts on the body.

(1.2) Measurement of impulse :

(i) For constant applied force : $\vec{J} = \vec{F}\,\Delta t$

(ii) For variable applied force : $\vec{J} = \int_{t_1}^{t_2} \vec{F}.dt$

(iii) From graph : The area enclosed by the force-time graph and the time axis gives the impulse of the force.

(iv) From change in linear momentum (**Impulse Momentum Theorem)** : Impulse of a force is equal to the change in linear momentum of the body.

$$\therefore \vec{J} = \overrightarrow{\Delta P} = \vec{P}_f - \vec{P}_i$$

• **Proof of Impulse-momentum theorem for a constant force :**

Impulse of a constant force ($\vec{J}$) = $\vec{F}\,\Delta t$

According to Newton's second law of motion, $\vec{F} = \frac{\Delta \vec{p}}{\Delta t}$ [Where, $\vec{P}$ = linear momentum]

$\therefore \vec{J} = \frac{\Delta \vec{p}}{\Delta t}\Delta t$

or, $\vec{J} = \Delta\vec{p}$

$\therefore \vec{J} = \vec{P_f} - \vec{P_i}$ = change in linear momentum

• **Proof of Impulse-momentum theorem for a variable force :**

Impulse of a variable force ($\vec{J}$) $= \int_{t_1}^{t_2} \vec{F}\, dt$

$$\text{or, } \vec{J} = \int_{t_1}^{t_2} \frac{d\vec{P}}{dt}\, dt \;\left[\because \vec{F} = \frac{\Delta \vec{p}}{\Delta t} \right]$$

$$\text{or, } \vec{J} = \int_{P_i}^{P_f} d\vec{P}$$

$$\therefore \vec{J} = \vec{P_f} - \vec{P_i} \;(= \text{change in linear momentum})$$

[where, $\vec{P_i}$ and $\vec{P_f}$ = linear momenta at time t_1 and t_2]

(1.3) Nature of the quantity : It is a vector quantity. [its (impulse $\vec{J}$) direction is along the direction of the force]

(1.4) Dimensional equation of impulse: [J] = [F] [t]

$= [M L T^{-2}] [T]$

$= [M L T^{-1}]$

(1.5) Unit of impulse : CGS unit : dyne s or g cm s^{-1}

SI unit : N s or kg m s^{-1}

Points to Remember :

• Impulsive Force

(a) Definition : An impulsive force is a **large force** that acts on a body for a **very short interval of time**.

(b) Example : Striking a ball with a bat, hammering a nail etc. are the examples of impulsive force.

(c) Nature of the quantity : vector

(d) Dimensional formula : $[M L T^{-2}]$

(e) Unit : CGS unit : dyne or g cm s^{-2}

SI unit : N or kg m s^{-2}

(2) Effect of force w.r.t. displacement : Work

(2.1) Definition of Work : When a body is displaced from its initial position under the action of a force then work is said to be done.

(2.2) Measurement of Work done : The amount of work done on a body depends on –
(a) magnitude of the force applied
(b) magnitude of the displacement produced by the force and
(c) angle between the force and displacement.

(1) Work done due to constant single force : Work is measured as the scalar product of the applied force ($\vec{F}$) and the displacement ($\vec{r}$) of the body.

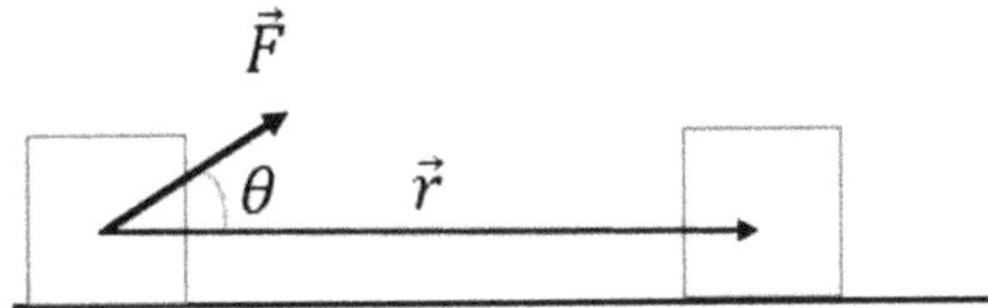

Work done $W = \vec{F} \cdot \vec{r}$ = F r cos θ [Where, θ = angle between the force and displacement]

Measurement of work can be stated in two different ways –

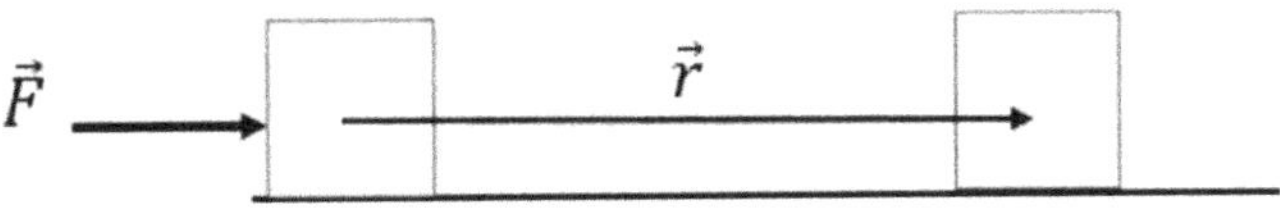

(a) When displacement of the body takes place in the direction of the applied force work is measured by the product of magnitude of the force and magnitude of the displacement of the point of application of the force.

Work done W = F r

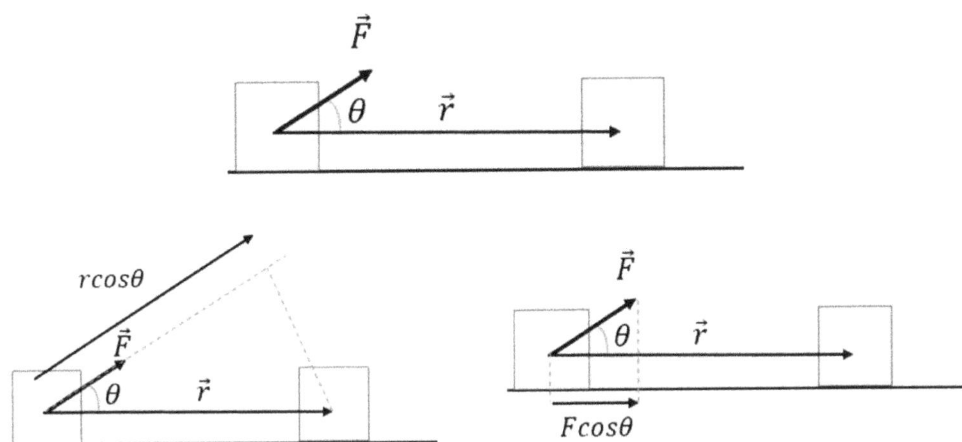

(b) When displacement is not along the force, work done by the force is measured by –

(i) the product of the magnitude of the force and the magnitude of the component of displacement along the direction of force

Work done W = F (r cos θ)

Or, (ii) product of the magnitude of the component of force in the direction of displacement and magnitude of the displacement.

Work done W = (F cos θ) r

Type of Work	Condition	Value of work
Positive work	$\theta = 0°$	+ve
Negative Work	$\theta = 180°$	-ve

Zero Work	$\theta = 90°$	0

(2) Work done due to constant multiple forces : If a number of force $\vec{F}_1, \vec{F}_2, \vec{F}_3 \ldots\ldots \vec{F}_n$ are acting on a body and it shifts from position vector $\vec{r}_1$ to position vector $\vec{r}_2$ then work done

$$W = (\vec{F}_1 + \vec{F}_2 + \vec{F}_3 + \ldots. \vec{F}_n).(\vec{r}_2 - \vec{r}_1)$$

(3) Work force for variable applied force :

$W = \int_A^B \vec{F} . d\vec{r}$

or, $W = \int_A^B (F_x\hat{\imath} + F_y\hat{\jmath} + F_z\hat{k}) . (dx\hat{\imath} + dy\hat{\jmath} + dz\hat{k})$ [In terms of rectangular component]

or, $W = \int_{x_A}^{x_B} F_x dx + \int_{y_A}^{y_B} F_y dy + \int_{z_A}^{z_B} F_z dz$

(4) Work done from Force-Displacement graph : The area enclosed by the force-displacement graph and the displacement axis gives the work.

(a) Force-displacement graph for constant force :

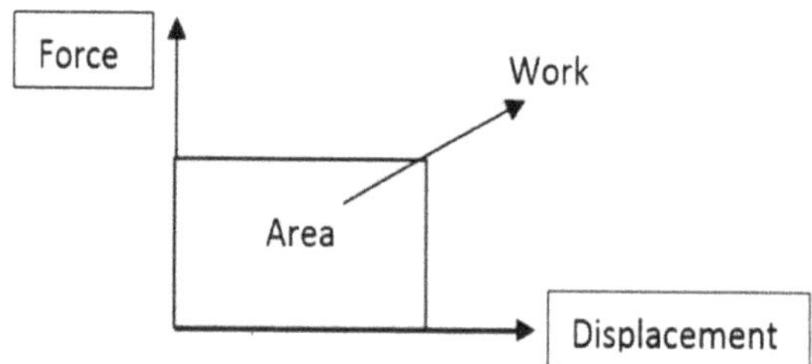

(b) Force-displacement graph for variable force :

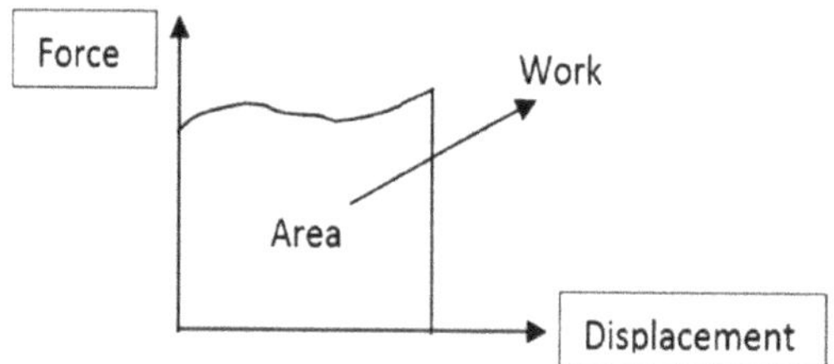

(5) Work done from change in Kinetic Energy (Work-Energy Theorem) :

The work done on a body by a resultant force is equal to change in kinetic energy of the body.

$$W = \Delta E_k = \frac{1}{2} m\, v_f^2 - \frac{1}{2} m\, v_i^2$$

(2.3) Nature of the quantity : It is a Scalar quantity. It has the magnitude only.

(2.4) Dimensional Equation of work : [W] = [Force] × [Displacement]
$= [MLT^{-2}] \times [L]$
$= [M L^2 T^{-2}]$

(2.5) Unit of work : Absolute units : CGS unit : dyne cm or g $cm^2\ s^{-2}$ or erg

SI unit : N m or kg $m^2\ s^{-2}$ or joule (or J)

Gravitational units : CGS unit : g cm

SI unit : kg m

• **Definition of joule :** Work done is said to be one Joule, when 1 Newton force displaces the body through 1 meter in its own direction.

$$1\ J = 1\ N \times 1\ m$$

• **Definition of erg :** Work done is said to be one erg when 1 dyne force displaces the body through 1 cm in its own direction.

$$1\ erg = 1\ dyn \times 1\ cm$$

• **Relation between joule and erg:** 1 joule = 1 N × 1 m

$= 10^5$ dyne $\times 10^2$ cm

$= 10^7$ dyne × cm

$= 10^7$ erg

• **Definition of kg-m [S.I.] :** 1 Kg-m of work is done when a force of 1kg-wt. displaces the body through 1m in its own direction.

• **Relationship between kg-m and J :** 1 kg-m = 1 kg-wt × 1 m

= 9.81 N × 1 m

= 9.81 J

• **Definition of g-cm [C.G.S.] :** 1 g-cm of work is done when a force of 1gm-wt displaces the body through 1cm in its own direction.

• **Relationship between g-cm and erg :** 1 g-cm = 1 g-wt × 1 cm.

= 981 dyne × 1cm

= 981 erg

(2.6) Zero work done situations : Under three conditions, work done becomes zero.

(i) If the force is perpendicular to the displacement $[\vec{F} \perp \vec{r}]$, then work done **(** W) = F r cos 90° = 0

Example : When a coolie travels on a horizontal platform with a load on his head, work done against gravity by the coolie is zero. (Work done against friction is +ve)

(ii) If there is no displacement [r = 0], then work done $W = F\,r\cos\theta = F\,(0)\cos\theta = 0$

Example: When a person tries to displace a wall or heavy stone by applying a force then it does not move, the work done is zero.

(iii) **If there is no force acting on the body [F = 0],** then work done $W = F\,r\cos\theta = (0)\,r\cos\theta$ = 0

Example: Motion of an isolated body in free space.

(2.7) Work Depends on Frame of Reference : With change of frame of reference (inertial) force does not change while displacement may change. So the work done by a force will be different in different frames.

Example : If a person is pushing a box inside a moving train, the work done in the frame of train will $\vec{F}\,.\,\vec{r}$ while in the frame of earth will be $\vec{F}\,.(\vec{r} + \vec{r}_0)$ where $\vec{r}_0$ is the displacement of the train relative to the ground.

(2.8) Path Dependence of Work : If (i) work done by the force (or, line integral of the force i.e. $\int \vec{F}\,.\,d\,\vec{r}$) does not depend on the path joining the points A and B

[Explanation :

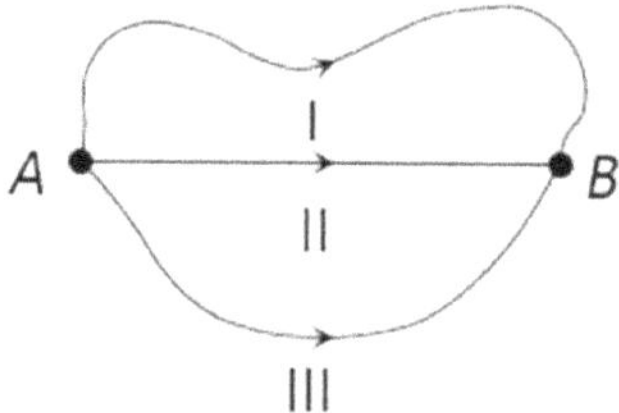

$W_{A\to B} = W_{A\to B} = W_{A\to B}$

Path I Path II Path III

or, $\int \vec{F}\,.d\,\vec{r} = \int \vec{F}\,.d\,\vec{r} = \int \vec{F}\,.d\,\vec{r}$]

Path I Path II Path III

(ii) work done by the force (or, line integral of the force i.e. $\int \vec{F}\,.\,d\,\vec{r}$) over a closed path/loop is zero

[Explanation :

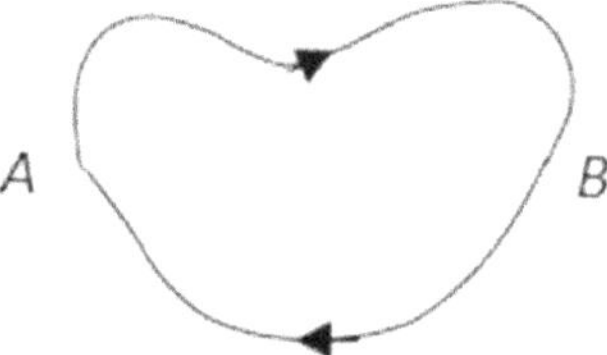

$W_{A\to B} + W_{B\to A} = 0$

or, $\oint \vec{F}\,.\,d\,\vec{r} = 0$]

then the force is said to be conservative and the force field is said to be conservative force field. Again if it (work done) depends on the path joining then the force is said to be non-conservative and its field is termed as non-conservative force field.

(2.9) Conservative Force :

(a) Definition : If the work done by a force in moving a particle from one point to another point is independent of the path joining the points, then the force is said to be conservative and the field of the force is termed as conservative force field.

(b) Alternative definition : If the work done in moving a particle around any closed path in a force field is zero, then the force field is known as conservative force field.

Mathematically, if $\oint \vec{F}.d\vec{r} = 0$, then the force field $\vec{F}$ is conservative.

(c) Example : (i) Gravitational force field and (ii) Electrostatic force field etc.

(d) Properties of conservative force :

(i) Work done by or against a conservative force does not depend upon the nature of the path between initial and final positions of the body but depends only on the initial and final positions of the body.
(ii) Work done by or against a conservative force in a round trip or closed path is zero.
(iii) The work done by a conservative force is completely recoverable.
(iv) When only a conservative force acts within a system, the kinetic energy and potential energy can change. However, their sum, the mechanical energy of the system, does not change.
(v) Conservative forces are central in nature.

(d) Concept of Potential :

A force field $\vec{F}(\vec{r})$ is conservative if the work done in moving a particle round a cyclic path in the field is zero. From the definition we can write, $\oint \vec{F}.d\vec{r} = 0$

Converting this line integral into surface integral by using Stoke's theorem we get,

$$\oint \vec{F}.d\vec{r} = \int (\vec{\nabla} \times \vec{F}).\,d\vec{A} = 0$$

Since the surface element (dA) is arbitrary, we get, $\vec{\nabla} \times \vec{F} = 0$

We know that the curl of the gradient of a scalar point function or scalar field is zero.

Hence, we can write, $\vec{\nabla} \times \vec{F} = \vec{\nabla} \times \vec{\nabla} E_p = 0$

Where E_p is a scalar function, called potential energy

Hence, $\vec{F} = -\vec{\nabla} E_p$

The negative sign of the right hand side indicates that $\vec{F}$ is in the direction of decreasing of potential energy.

Knowledge Plus : • *All central forces are conservative forces.*

• *Central forces are function of position.*

- *The angular momentum of an object moving under a central force is conserved.*

(2.10) Non-Conservative Force :

(a) Definition : If the work done by a force in moving a particle from one point to another point depends upon the path followed by the particle, then the force is said to be non-conservative and the field of the force is termed as non-conservative force field.

(b) Alternative definition : if the work done in moving a particle around any closed path in a force field is not zero, then the force field is known as non-conservative force field.

Mathematically, if $\oint \vec{F}.d\vec{r} \neq 0$, then the force field $\vec{F}$ is non-conservative.

(c) Example : (i) Frictional Force (ii) Viscous Forces

(d) Explanation of Frictional force as a non-conservative force :

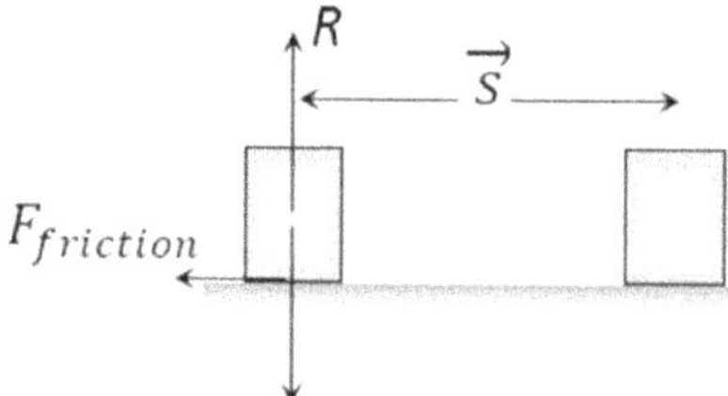

If a body is moved from position A to another position B on a rough table, work done against frictional force shall depends on the length of the path between A and B and not only on the position A and B.

$$W_{AB} = \mu mgs$$

Further if the body is brought back to its initial position A, work has to be done against the frictional force, which always opposes the motion. Hence the net work done against the friction over a round trip is not zero.

$$W_{BA} = \mu mgs$$

∴ Total work done : $W_{total} = W_{AB} + W_{BA}$

$$= \mu mgs + \mu mgs$$

$$= 2\mu mgs \neq 0$$

i.e. the friction is a non-conservative force.

(e) Properties of non-conservative force:

(i) Work done by or against a non-conservative force depends upon the nature of the path between the initial and final positions of the body.
(ii) Work done by or against a non-conservative force in a round trip is not zero.
(iii) The work done by a non-conservative force is not completely recoverable.

(iv) Work done against a non-conservative force may be dissipated as heat energy.
(v) Non-conservative forces are velocity dependent and retarding in nature.

Knowledge Plus : *Work is just the transfer of energy due to the displacement produced by the applied force.*

(2.11) Difference between conservative and non-conservative force :

Conservative Force	Non-conservative Force
(1) Work done by the conservative force does not depend upon the path.	(1) Work done by the non-conservative force depends upon the path.
(2) Work done by the conservative force around a closed path is zero.	(2) Work done by the non-conservative force around a closed path is not zero.
(3) Work done by the conservative force is completely recoverable.	(3) Work done by the conservative force is not completely recoverable.
(4) When only a conservative force acts within a system, the kinetic energy and potential energy can change. However, the sum of potential and kinetic energy i.e. mechanical energy is constant.	(4) When non-conservative force acts within a system, mechanical energy is not constant. Work done against a non-conservative force may be dissipated as heat energy.

(3) Effect of force w.r.t. displacement and time : Power

(3.1) Definition of power : Power is defined as the time rate of work done.

(3.2) Measurement of power :

Average power $P_{av} = \frac{\Delta W}{\Delta t}$

$= \frac{\vec{F} \cdot \Delta\vec{r}}{\Delta t}$ [since work done $\Delta W = \vec{F} \cdot \Delta\vec{r}$]

$= \vec{F} \cdot \vec{v}$ [velocity $\vec{v} = \frac{\Delta\vec{s}}{\Delta t}$]

Instantaneous power $P = \frac{dW}{dt}$

(3.3) Nature of the quantity : It is a scalar quantity.

(3.4) Dimensional equation of power: $[P] = \frac{[W]}{[t]}$

$$= \frac{[M L^2 T^{-2}]}{[T]}$$

$$= [M L^2 T^{-3}]$$

(3.5) Unit of power : Absolute unit : CGS unit : $g\ cm^2\ s^{-3}$ or erg s^{-1}

SI unit : $kg\ m^2\ s^{-3}$ or J s^{-1} or watt (W)

Gravitational unit : CGS unit : g cm s^{-1}

SI unit : kilogram. meter s^{-1} (kg m s^{-1})

(3.6) Definition of watt : If 1 J of work is done in 1 s, the power is said to be 1 watt.

$$1 \text{ watt} = \frac{1\,J}{1\,s}$$

(3.7) Relationship between CGS and SI unit of power : $1 \text{ watt} = \frac{1\,J}{1\,s} = \frac{1\,N\,m}{1\,s}$

$$= \frac{10^5 \text{ dyne} \times 10^2 \text{ cm}}{1\,s}$$

$$= 10^7 \text{ erg } s^{-1}$$

(3.8) Different units of power : (i) kilowatt (kW) [1 kilowatt = 10^3 watt = 10^{10} erg s^{-1}]

(ii) megawatt (MW) [1 megawatt = 10^6 watt = 10^{13} erg s^{-1}]

(iii) gigawatt (GW)

(iv) milliwatt (mW)

(3.9) Relation between kg m s^{-1} and g cm s^{-1}: 1 kg m s^{-1}= 1 kg × 1 m s^{-1}

$$= 10^3 \text{ g} \times 10^2 \text{ cm } s^{-1}$$

$$= 10^5 \text{ g cm } s^{-1}$$

(3.10) Horse power is another unit of power, largely used in mechanical engineering. It is related to the SI unit as below :

1 HP = 746 W

(3.11) Difference between work and power :

Work	Power
(i) Work done by a force is equal to the product of force and displacement in the direction of force.	(i) Power of a source is the rate of work done by the source.

(ii) Work done is independent of time.	(ii) Power spent depends on time in which work is done.
(iii) SI unit of work is joule.	(iii) SI unit of power is watt.

(4) Turning effect

(1) The **turning effect** on the body about an axis is due to the moment of force or torque applied on it. It depends on two factors :
(i) The magnitude of the force
(ii) The perpendicular distance of the line of action of the force from the axis of rotation.(it is called lever arm or moment arm)
The direction of rotation of a pivoted body can be changed by two ways –
(i) by changing the point of application of force
(ii) by changing the direction of force.

(2) Definition of moment of force or torque : Moment of force or torque is the product of the magnitude of the force and perpendicular distance of the line of the action of force from the axis of rotation and its direction is perpendicular to the plane containing the force and perpendicular distance. It is the rotational analogue of a force.

(3) Measurement of moment of force :

(a) Magnitude of moment of force :

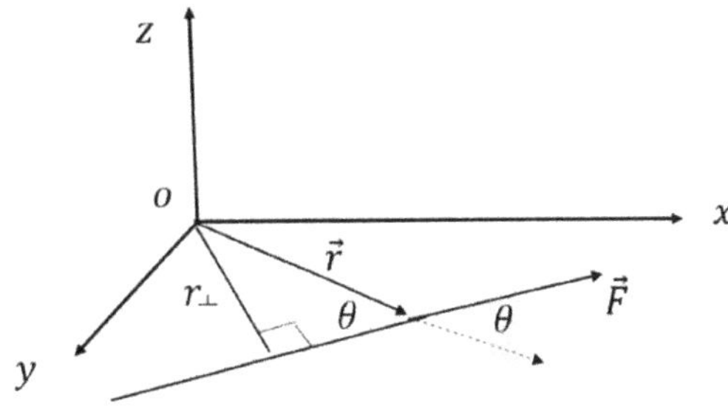

From the figure, moment of force about O is given by $|\vec{\tau}| = F\,r_\perp$

Again, $sin\,\theta = \frac{r_\perp}{r}$

or, $r_\perp$ = r $sin\,\theta$

$\therefore |\vec{\tau}| = F\,r\,sin\,\theta$

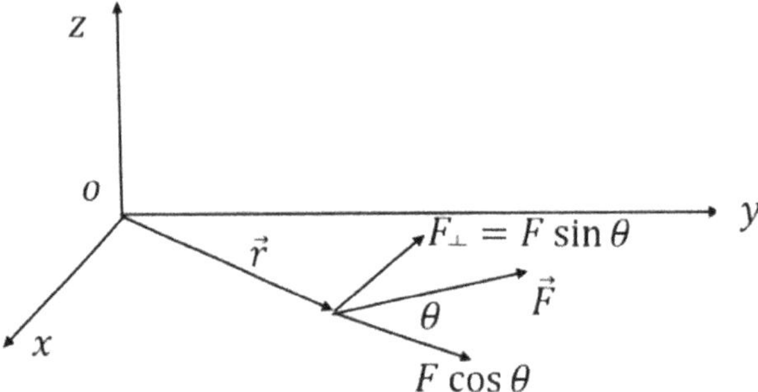

From the figure, moment of force about O is given by $|\vec{\tau}| = r F_\perp = r F \sin\theta$

(b) Vector form of moment of force about origin :

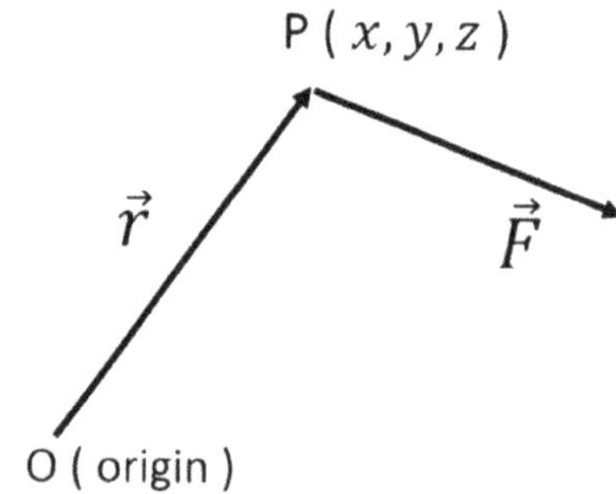

Mathematically, $\vec{\tau} = \vec{r} \times \vec{F}$

Where, $\vec{F}$ = force acting on the particle = $F_x\hat{\imath} + F_y\,\hat{\jmath} + F_z\,\hat{k}$

and $\vec{r}$ = position vector w.r.t. the origin O = $x\hat{\imath} + y\,\hat{\jmath} + z\,\hat{k}$

$$\therefore \vec{\tau} = \vec{r} \times \vec{F} = \begin{vmatrix} \hat{\imath} & \hat{\jmath} & \hat{k} \\ x & y & z \\ F_x & F_y & F_z \end{vmatrix}$$

(c) Vector form of moment of force about any point other than origin :

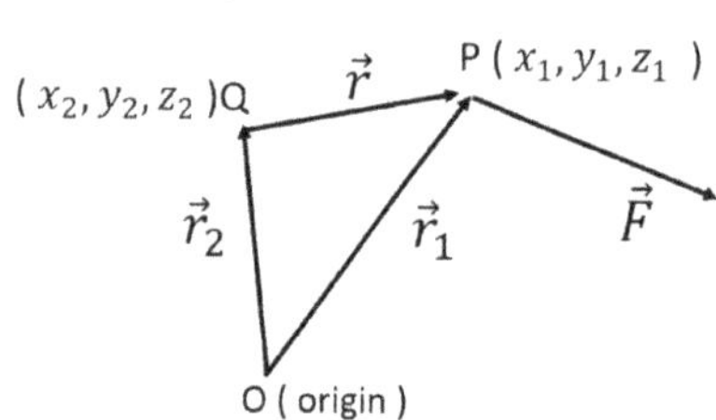

From the figure, the moment of force about O is given by: $\vec{\tau} = \vec{r}_1 \times \vec{F}$

Where, $\vec{r}_1$ = Position vector of the point of application of the force = $x_1\hat{\imath} + y_1\,\hat{\jmath} + z_1\,\hat{k}$
And $\vec{F}$ = force acting on the particle = $F_x\hat{\imath} + F_y\,\hat{\jmath} + F_z\,\hat{k}$

But the moment of force about the point Q is given by : $\vec{\tau} = \vec{r} \times \vec{F}$

Again, $\vec{r}_1 = \vec{r}_2 + \vec{r}$

or, $\vec{r} = \vec{r}_1 - \vec{r}_2$

or, $\vec{r} = (x_1\hat{\imath} + y_1\hat{\jmath} + z_1\hat{k}) - (x_2\hat{\imath} + y_2\hat{\jmath} + z_2\hat{k})$

or, $\vec{r} = (x_1 - x_2)\hat{\imath} + (y_1 - y_2)\hat{\jmath} + (z_1 - z_2)\hat{k}$

Moment of force about the point Q : $\vec{\tau} = \vec{r} \times \vec{F}$

$$= \begin{vmatrix} \hat{\imath} & \hat{\jmath} & \hat{k} \\ (x_1 - x_2) & (y_1 - y_2) & (z_1 - z_2) \\ F_x & F_y & F_z \end{vmatrix}$$

(4) Nature of moment of force : Moment of force is a vector quantity. It is directed along the axis of rotation or perpendicular to the plane containing the force and perpendicular distance.

(5) Types of moment : Conventionally, if the effect of the body is to turn it anticlockwise, the moment of force is taken as positive, while it the effect of the body is to turn it clockwise, the moment of force is taken as negative.

(6) Dimensional formula of moment of force : $[\tau] = [F][r_\perp]$

$= [MLT^{-2}][L]$

$= [ML^2T^{-2}]$

(7) Unit of moment of force : CGS unit : dyne cm or g $cm^2\ s^{-2}$

SI unit : N m or kg $m^2\ s^{-2}$

(8) Couple :

In real life, we apply two equal and opposite forces acting along different lines of action in order to cause rotation. Common examples are – (i) turning of a bicycle handle, (ii) turning the steering wheel, (iii) opening a common water tap, (iv) opening the lid of a bottle (rotational type). Such a pair of forces constitute a couple.

A pair of equal and opposite force acting on a body along two different lines of action constitute a couple.

Properties of couple :

(a) A couple produces or tends to produce only the rotational motion Since there is no resultant force acts on a body, it cannot produce translational motion.

(b) A couple cannot be replaced by a single force.

(c) A couple can be shifted anywhere in its plane.

(9) Moment of Couple :

(a) Definition : The tendency of rotation set up in a body by a couple is called moment of couple or torque.

It is measured by the product of either force and the perpendicular distance between the lines of action between the two forces.

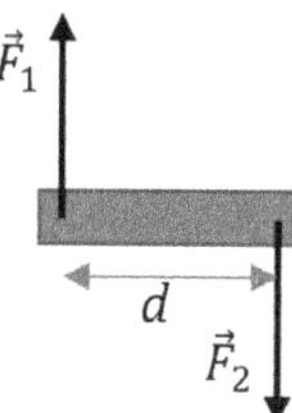

Moment of couple or torque : τ = F d

(b) Nature of the quantity : It is a vector quantity.

(c) Dimensional formula : $[\,M\,L^2\,T^{-2}\,]$

(d) Unit : CGS unit : dyne cm or $g\ cm^2\ s^{-2}$

SI unit : N m or $kg\ m^2\ s^{-2}$

(10) Moment of force and Moment of Couple :

Moment of force	*Moment of couple*
Moment of force depends upon the axis of rotation and the point of application of the force.	Moment of couple depends only upon the two forces, i.e. it is independent of the axis of rotation or points of application of forces.
If the axis of rotation is not fixed or if friction is not enough, it can produce translational acceleration.	It does not produce any translational acceleration, but produces only rotational or angular acceleration.
Its rotational effect can be balanced by a proper single force or by a proper couple.	Its rotational effect can be balanced only by another couple of equal and opposite torque.

Points to Remember :

• Moment of Momentum Or Angular Momentum :

(a) Angular momentum gives a measure of the turning motion of the body.

(b) Magnitude of moment of momentum :

Moment of momentum or angular momentum about an axis is the a vector quantity whose magnitude is equal to the product of the linear momentum and perpendicular distance of the line of action of momentum from the axis of rotation and its direction is perpendicular to the plane containing the linear momentum and the perpendicular distance.

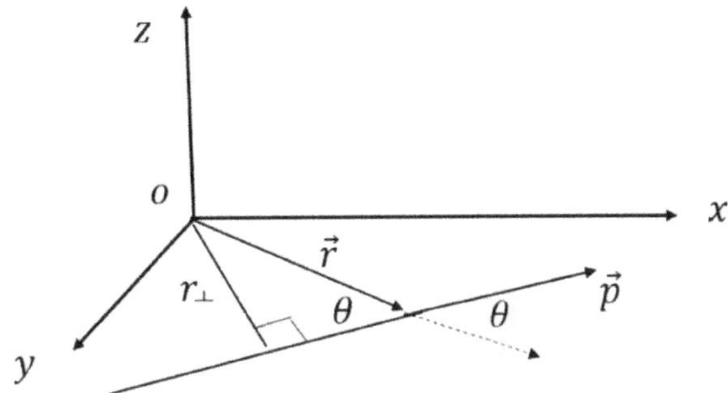

From the figure, moment of momentum about O is given by $|\vec{L}| = P\, r_{\perp}$

Again, $sin\ \theta = \frac{r_{\perp}}{r}$

or, $r_{\perp} = r\ sin\ \theta$

$\therefore |\vec{L}| = P\ r\ sin\ \theta$

(c) Vector form of moment of momentum about origin :

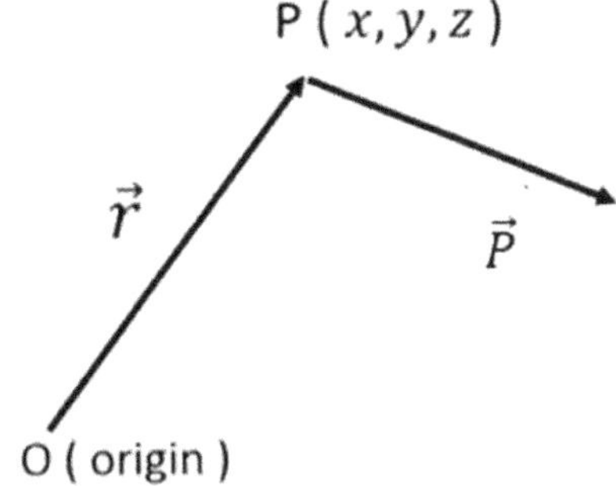

Mathematically, $\vec{L} = \vec{r} \times \vec{P}$

Where, $\vec{r}$ = position vector w.r.t. the origin O = $x_1\hat{\imath} + y_1\,\hat{\jmath} + z_1\,\hat{k}$

and $\vec{P}$ = linear momentum = $P_x\hat{\imath} + P_y\,\hat{\jmath} + P_z\,\hat{k}$

$$\therefore \vec{L} = \vec{r} \times \vec{P} = \begin{vmatrix} \hat{\imath} & \hat{\jmath} & \hat{k} \\ x & y & z \\ P_x & P_y & P_z \end{vmatrix}$$

(d) Vector form of moment of momentum about any point other than origin :

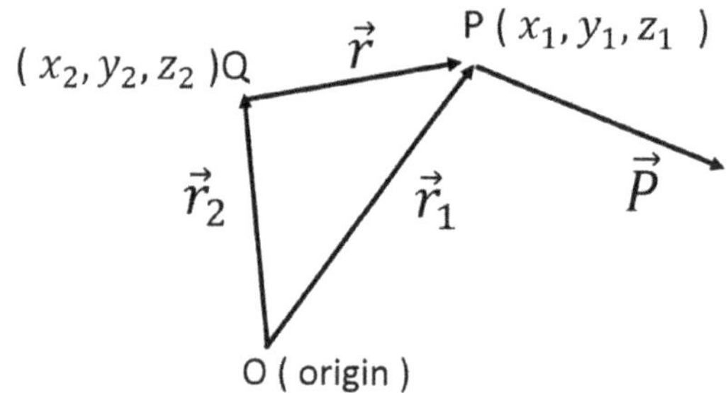

From the figure, the moment of momentum about O is given by: $\vec{L} = \vec{r}_1 \times \vec{P}$

Where, $\vec{r}_1$ = Position vector of the point of application of the force = $x_1\hat{\imath} + y_1\hat{\jmath} + z_1\hat{k}$
and $\vec{P}$ = linear momentum = $P_x\hat{\imath} + P_y\hat{\jmath} + P_z\hat{k}$

But the moment of momentum about the point Q is given by : $\vec{\tau} = \vec{r} \times \vec{P}$

Again, $\vec{r}_1 = \vec{r}_2 + \vec{r}$

or, $\vec{r} = \vec{r}_2 - \vec{r}_1$

or, $\vec{r} = (x_2\hat{\imath} + y_2\hat{\jmath} + z_2\hat{k}) - (x_1\hat{\imath} + y_1\hat{\jmath} + z_1\hat{k})$

or, $\vec{r} = (x_2 - x_1)\hat{\imath} + (y_2 - y_1)\hat{\jmath} + (z_2 - z_1)\hat{k}$

Moment of momentum about the point Q : $\vec{L} = \vec{r} \times \vec{P} = \begin{vmatrix} \hat{\imath} & \hat{\jmath} & \hat{k} \\ (x_2 - x_1) & (y_2 - y_1) & (z_2 - z_1) \\ P_x & P_y & P_z \end{vmatrix}$

(e) Nature of the moment of momentum : It is a vector quantity.

(f) Dimensional formula of moment of momentum : $[L]$ = [P] [$r_\perp$]

$= [\text{M L T}^{-1}][\text{L}]$

$= [\text{M L}^2 \text{T}^{-1}]$

(g) Unit of moment of momentum : CGS unit : $\text{g cm}^2 \text{s}^{-1}$

SI unit : $\text{kg m}^2 \text{s}^{-1}$

(h) Relation Between Angular Momentum And Torque :

If $\vec{P}$ be the linear momentum of the particle and $\vec{r}$ be the position vector w.r.t. the origin, then the angular momentum of the particle about the point O is given by : $\vec{L} = \vec{r} \times \vec{P}$

Now differentiating w.r.t. time, we get, $\frac{d\vec{L}}{dt} = \frac{d}{dt}(\vec{r} \times \vec{P})$

$= \frac{d\vec{r}}{dt} \times \vec{P} + \vec{r} \times \frac{d\vec{P}}{dt}$

$= \vec{v} \times m\vec{v} + \vec{r} \times \vec{F}$

$= \vec{r} \times \vec{F}$ [since $\vec{v} \times m\vec{v} = 0$] = $\vec{\tau}$

i.e. the time rate of change of angular momentum of a particle is equal to the torque acting on it.

Points to Remember :

Principle of conservation of angular momentum for a single particle

Statement : If the total external torque acting on a particle is zero, then its angular momentum remains constant with time.

Mathematical explanation : If the torque $\vec{\tau}$ acting on the particle is zero, we have, $\vec{\tau} = \frac{d\vec{L}}{dt} = 0$

$$\therefore \vec{L} = \text{constant.}$$

Exercise | | Subjective Questions	The Quantities that determine the effect of force

Impulse

(1) What do you mean by impulsive force. Mention its SI unit.

(2) What do you mean by impulse of a force. Write its dimensional formula.

(3) Write down impulse -momentum theorem.

Work

1) When does a force do work ? (1)
Or, define work.

2) How is work done by a force measured when the force (i) is in the direction of displacement (ii) is at an angle to the direction of displacement. (2)
Or, Write an expression for the work done when a force is acting on an object in the direction of its displacement. (1)

3) What should be the angle between the direction of force and the direction of displacement for work to be negative ? (1)

4) What should the angle between forces and displacement be to get the (i) minimum work and (ii) Maximum work ? (2)

5) A toy is acted upon by a force. State two conditions under which the work done could be zero. (2)

6) How can the work done be measured when force is applied at an angle to the direction of displacement ?(1)

7) Write SI unit of work. How is it related to electron volt ? (2)

8) Define 1 J of work. (1)

Conceptual Questions

9) If a force acts perpendicular to the direction of motion of body, what is the amount of work done? (1)

10) A coolie carrying a load on his head and moving on a frictionless horizontal platform does no work. Explain the reason, why ? (2)

11) An object thrown at a certain angle to the ground moves in a curved path and falls back to the ground. The initial and the final points of the path of the object lie on the same horizontal line. What is the work done by the force of gravity on the object ? (1)

12) A coolie moving vertically up the stairs with a suitcase on his head does work. Why ? (2)

13) Does the work done in raising a suitcase on to a platform depend upon how fast it is raised up ? (1)

14) What is the work done by the weight of a body moving at a constant speed on a frictionless surface ? (1)

15) Why does the centripetal force do not work ? (1)

16) State the amount of work done by an object, when it moves in a circular path for one complete rotation. Give your reason to justify your answer. (1)

17) What is the work done by the moon when it revolves around the earth ? (1)

18) In a tug of war, if neither team is able to move the rope, what is the total work done by the teams ?(1)

19) One team in a tug of war pulls the rope and causes the other team to move backward. Which team does positive work and which does negative work ? Explain. (2)

20) A man rowing boat upstream is at rest with respect to the shore. Is he doing work ? (2)

Power

1) Define the term power. State its SI Unit. (2)

2) What is the relationship between work and power ? (1)

3) State and define the SI unit of power. (2)
Or Define 1 W of power.

4) Name the physical quantity measured in horsepower. Define the quantity. [2]

5) How is horsepower related to the SI unit of power ? (1)

6) Define a kilowatt hour. How is it related to the joule? [2]

7) Differentiate between work and Power. (2)

8) State two factors on which power spent by a source depends. (2)

9) What is the relationship between power and velocity ? (2)

Moment of Force

1) What is meant by the term moment of force ? Mention its SI unit. (2)

2) What is the SI unit of moment of force ? (1)

3) Write the relationship between the SI and CGS unit of moment of force. (1)

4) Name the factors affecting the turning effect of a body. (2)

5) If the moment of force is assigned a negative sign, then will the turning tendency of the force be clockwise or anticlockwise ? (1)

6) Why is a jack screw provided with a long arm ? (1)

7) **Define couple. State the SI unit of moment of couple. (2)**

MCQ – 6 : The Quantities that Determine the Effect of Force

Physics MCQ | | Class – XI

Dynamics

Topic : Impulse

 # Important Points

(i) For constant applied force : $\vec{J} = \vec{F}\,\Delta t$

(ii) For variable force : $\vec{J} = \int_{t_1}^{t_2} \vec{F}.dt$

(iii) From graph : The area enclosed by the force-time graph and the time axis gives the impulse of the force.

(iv) From change in linear momentum (**Impulse Momentum Theorem)** :` Impulse of a force is equal to the change in linear momentum of the body.

(1) Impulse of a body is equal to
(a) Change in momentum
(b) Force × time interval
(c) Force × speed
(d) both (a) and (b)

(2) Dimension of impulse are same as that of
(a) Force
(b) Momentum
(c) Energy
(d) Acceleration

(3) Momentum is closely related to
(a) Force
(b) Impulse
(c) Kinetic energy
(d) Velocity

Impulse as a Product of Force and Time

(4) A ball of mass 150 g moving with an acceleration 20 m s^{-2} is hit by a force, which acts on it for 0.1 s. The impulse of the force is
(a) 0.5 N s
(b) 0.1 N s
(c) 0.3 N s
(d) 1.2 N s

(5) A bullet is fired from a gun. The force on the bullet is given by F = 600 – 2 × 10^5t, where, F is in newton and t in second. The force on the bullet becomes zero as soon as it leaves the barrel. What is the impulse imparted to the bullet ?
(a) 9 Ns
(b)1.8 Ns
(c) zero
(d) 0.9 Ns

(6) If force F = 500 – 100 t, then impulse as a function of time will be
(a) 500t – 50 t^2
(b) 50 t - 10
(c) 50 – t^2
(d) $100t^2$

Impulse as the Change in Linear momentum

(7) A particle of mass m is moving with a uniform velocity v_1. It is given an impulse such that its velocity becomes v_2. The impulse is equal to
(a) m [$|v_2| - |v_1|$]
(b) $\frac{1}{2}$ m (v_2^2 - v_1^2)
(c) m ($v_1 + v_2$)
(d) m ($v_2 - v_1$)

(8) A ball strikes a bat with velocity v. The ball has mass m after striking it retraces its path. What is the impulse imparted by the bat ?
(a) 3 mv
(b) mv
(c) zero
(d) 2mv

(9) A body of mass M hits normally a rigid wall with velocity v and bounces back with the same velocity. The impulse experienced by the force
(a) 1.5 Mv
(b) Mv
(c) zero
(d) 2Mv

(10) A ball of mas 0.15 kg is dropped from a height 10 m, strikes the ground and rebounds to the same height. The magnitude of impulse imparted to the ball is nearly :
(a) 0 kg m s^{-1}
(b) 4.2 kg m s^{-1}
(c) 2.1 kg m s^{-1}
(d) 1.4 kg m s^{-1}

(11) A ball of mass M moving with speed v collides perfectly inelastically with another ball

of mass m at rest. The magnitude of impulse imparted to the first ball is
(a) $\frac{Mm}{M+m}$ v
(b) $\frac{M^2}{M+m}$ v
(c) Mv
(d) mv

(12) A rigid ball of mass m strikes a rigid wall at 60° and gets reflected without loss of speed as shown in the figure below. The value of impulse imparted by the wall on the ball will be

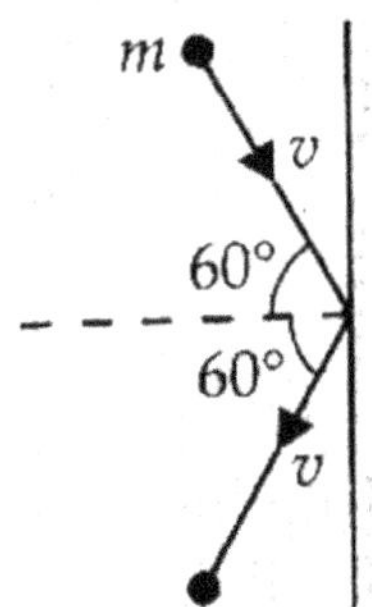

(a) $\frac{mv}{2}$
(b) $\frac{mv}{3}$
(c) mv
(d) 2mv

(13) A particle of mass m strikes a wall with speed v at an angle 30° with elastically as shown in the figure. The magnitude of impulse imparted to the ball by the wall is

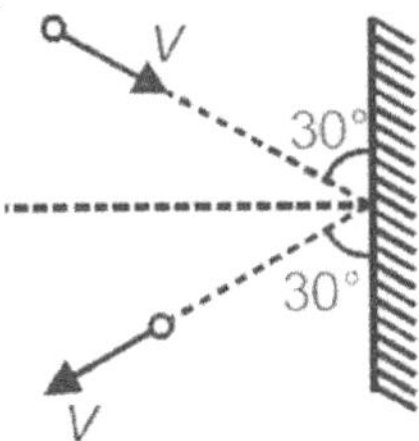

(a) $\frac{mv}{2}$
(b) $\sqrt{3}\,mv$
(c) mv
(d) 2mv

(14) A force of 10 Newton acts on a body of mass 20 kg for 10 seconds. Change in its momentum is
(a) 5 kg m s^{-1}
(b)100 kg m s^{-1}
(c) 200 kg m s^{-1}
(d) 1000 kg m s^{-1}

(15) A force $\vec{F}$ = ($2t\,\hat{i} + 3t^2\hat{j}$) N acts on an object moving in X-Y plane. The change in linear momentum of the object in time interval t = 0 to t = 2 s is
(a) $\sqrt{80}$ N s
(b) $\sqrt{70}$ N s
(c) $\sqrt{100}$ N s
(d) $\sqrt{60}$ N s

(16) A ball of mass 50 g is dropped from a height of 20 m. A boy on the ground hits the ball vertically upwards with a bat with an average force of 200 N, so that it attains a vertical height of 45 m. The time for which the ball remains in contact with the bat is (take g = 10 m s^{-2})
(a) $\frac{1}{20}$ th of a second
(b) $\frac{1}{40}$ th of a second
(c) $\frac{1}{80}$ th of a second
(d) $\frac{1}{120}$ th of a second

Impulse (or change in momentum) from Force-time graph

(17) A graph is drawn with force along Y axis and time along X-axis. The area under the graph represents
(a) Linear momentum
(b) Couple
(c) Impulse of the force
(d) moment of the force

(18) A body is initially at rest on a smooth surface. A force F, whose time variation is shown in the figure acts on it for a duration of 4 s. The momentum of the ball at the end of the 4 s (in Ns is)

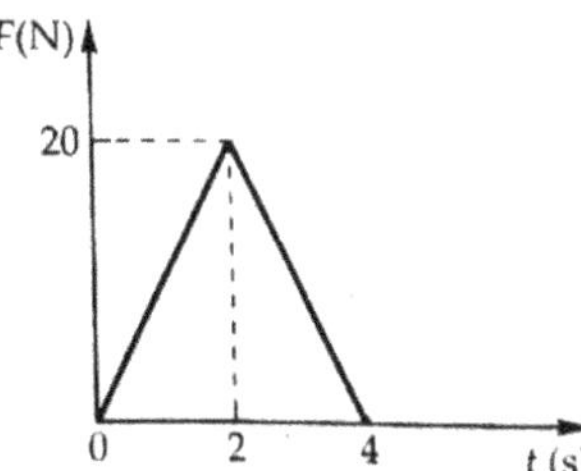

(a) 10
(b) 20
(c) 30
(d) 40

(19) The force F acting on a particle of mass m is inclined by the force-time graph shown below. The change in momentum of the particle over the time interval from zero to 8 s is

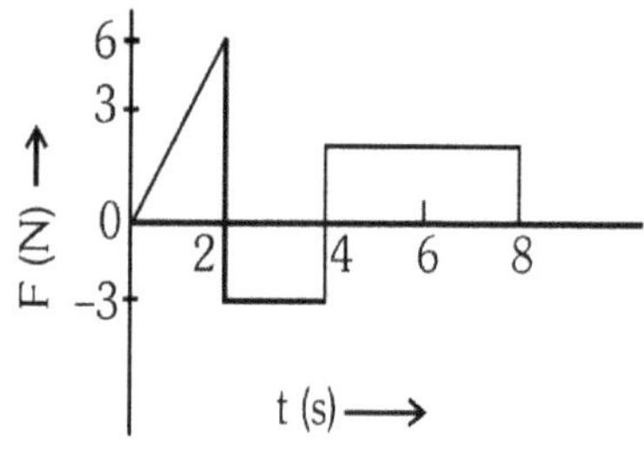

(a) 24 N s
(b) 20 N s
(c)12 N s
(d) 6 Ns

(20) The force-time (F–t) curve of a particle executing linear motion is as shown in the figure. The momentum acquired by the particle in time interval from zero to 8 second will be

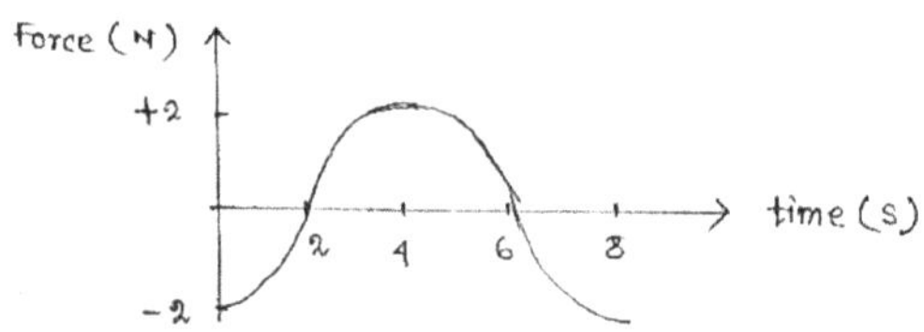

(a) – 2 N s
(b) + 4 N s
(c) 6 N s
(d) 0

(21) In which of the following graphs, the total change in momentum is zero?

(a)

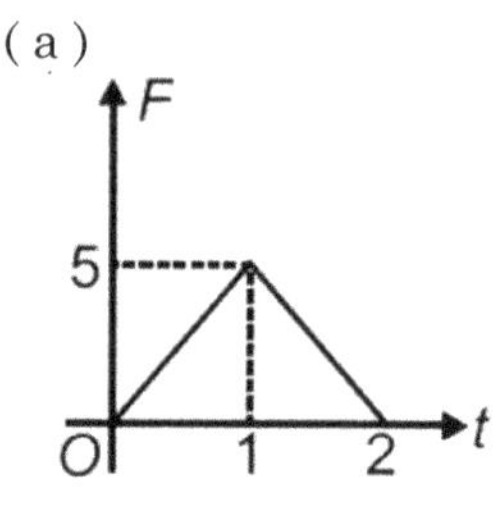

(b)

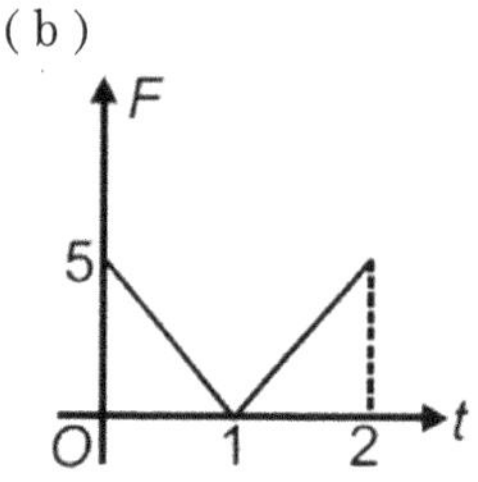

(c)

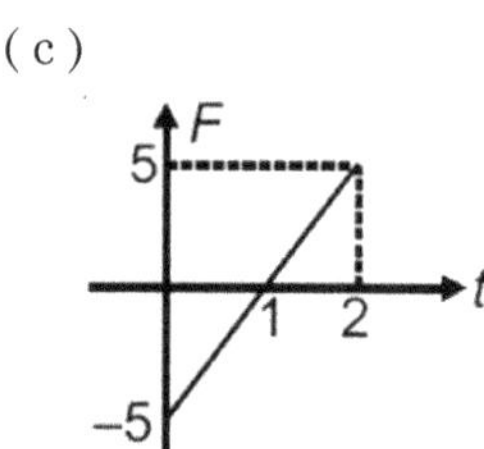

(d)

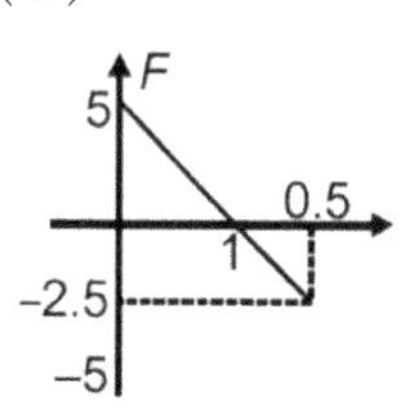

(22) Force acting on a body varies with time as shown below. If initial momentum of the body is $\vec{p}$ then the time taken by the body to retain its linear momentum $\vec{P}$ again is

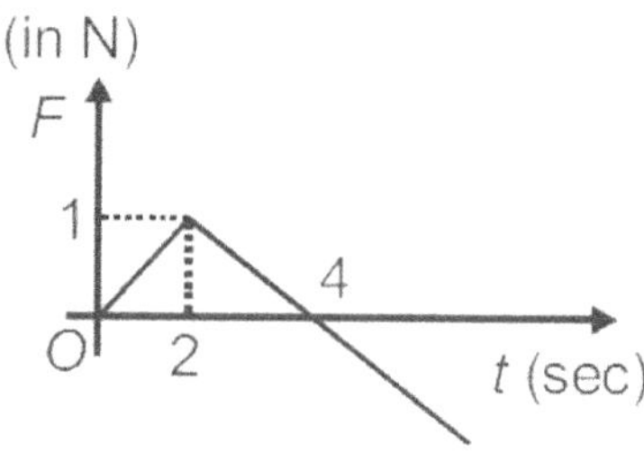

(a) 8 s
(b) ($4 + 2\sqrt{2}$) s
(c) 6 s
(d) can never obtain

(23) The magnitude of force acting on a particle moving along x-axis varies with time (t) as shown in figure. If at t = 0 the velocity of particle is v_0, then its velocity at t = T_0 will be

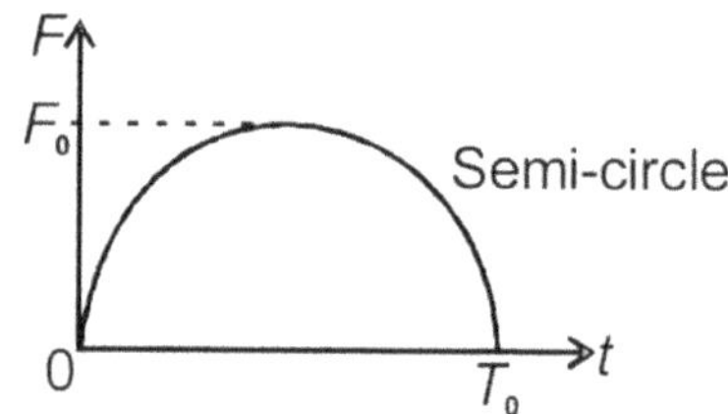

(a) $v_0 + \frac{\pi F_0 T_0}{4m}$
(b) $v_0 + \frac{\pi F_0}{2m}$
(c) $v_0 + \frac{\pi T_0^2}{4m}$
(d) $v_0 + \frac{\pi F_0 T_0}{m}$

On Displacement-Time graph

(24) The displacement-time graph of a particle of mass 0.1 kg is shown in the figure. The impulse at t = 2 s is

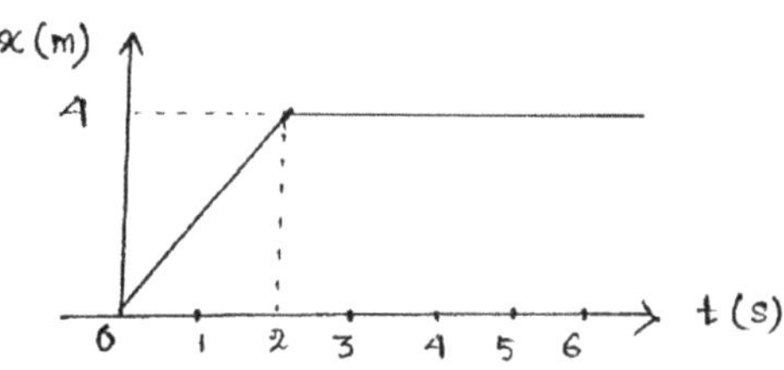

(a) 0.02 kg m s^{-1}
(b) 0.2 kg m s^{-1}
(c) 0.1 kg m s^{-1}
(d) 0.4 kg m s^{-1}

Physics MCQ || Class – XI	Dynamics
	Topic : Work & work done by constant force

Important Points

For constant applied force : $W = \vec{F} \cdot \vec{s} = F\,s\cos\theta$

(1) Which of the following is a scalar quantity
(a) Displacement
(b) Electric field
(c) Acceleration
(d) Work

(2) A man pushes a wall and fails to displace it. He does
(a) Negative work
(b) Positive but not maximum work
(c) Now work at all
(d) Maximum work

(3) If the unit of force and length each be increased by four times, then the unit of energy is increased by
(a) 16 times
(b) 8 times
(c) 2 times
(d) 4 times

(4) A body of mass m kg is lifted by a man to a height of one meter in 30 s. Another man lifts the same mass to the same height in 60 s. The work done by them are in the ratio
(a) 1 : 2
(b) 1 : 1
(c) 2 : 1
(d) 4 : 1

On Work done by Constant Force

(5) A ball is released from the top of a tower. The ratio of work done by the force of gravity in first, second and third second of the motion of the ball is
(a) 1 : 2 : 3
(b) 1 : 4 : 9
(c) 1 : 3 : 5
(d) 1 : 5 : 3

(6) A body of mass 5 kg is placed at the origin, and can move only on the x-axis. A force of 10 N is acting on it in a direction making an angle of 60° with the x-axis and displaces it along the x-axis by 4 metres. The work done by the force is
(a) 2.5 J
(b) 7.25 J
(c) 40 J
(d) 20 J

(7) The work done against gravity in taking 10 kg mass at 1 m height in 1 s will be
(a) 49 J
(b) 98 J
(c) 196 J
(d) None of these

(8) A body moves a distance of 10 m along a straight line under the action of a force 5 N. If the work done is 25 joule, the angle which the force makes with the direction of motion of the body is
(a) 0°
(b) 30°
(c) 60°
(d) 90°

(9) A particle of mass m starts moving from origin along x-axis and its velocity varies with position (x) as $v = k\sqrt{x}$. The work done by force acting on it during first t second is
(a) $\frac{m k^4 t^2}{4}$
(b) $\frac{m k^2 t}{2}$
(c) $\frac{m k^4 t^2}{8}$
(d) $\frac{m k^2 t^2}{4}$

(10) A force $\vec{F} = (5\,\hat{\imath} + 3\,\hat{\jmath})$ N is applied over a particle which displaces it from its origin to the point $\vec{r} = (2\,\hat{\imath} - 1\,\hat{\jmath})$ metres. The work done on the particle is
(a) –7 J
(b) +13 J
(c) +7 J
(d) +11 J

(11) A body constrained to move in z-direction is subjected to a force given by $\vec{F} = (3\,\hat{\imath} - 10\,\hat{\jmath} + 5\,\hat{k})$ N. What is the work done by this

force in moving the body through a distance of 5 m along z-axis ?
(a) 15 J
(b) – 15 J
(c) – 50 J
(d) 25 J

(12) A body moves from a position $\vec{r}_1 = (2\hat{i} - 3\hat{j} - 4\hat{k})$ m to a position $\vec{r}_2 = (3\hat{i} - 4\hat{j} + 5\hat{k})$ m under the influence of a constant force $\vec{F} = (4\hat{i} + \hat{j} + 6\hat{k})$ N. The work done by the force is
(a) 57 J
(b) 58 J
(c) 59 J
(d) 60 J

(13) A particle is displaced from a position $(2\hat{i} - \hat{j} + \hat{k})$ m to another position $(3\hat{i} + 2\hat{j} - 2\hat{k})$ m action of force $(2\hat{i} + \hat{j} - \hat{k})$ N. The work done by the force is
(a) 8 J
(b) 10 J
(c) 12 J
(d) 36 J

(14) A horizontal force of 5 N is required to maintain a velocity of 2 m s^{-1} for a block of 10 kg mass sliding over a rough surface. The work done by this force in one minute is
(a) 600 J
(b) 60 J
(c) 6 J
(d) 6000 J

(15) A force $\vec{F} = (3\hat{i} + 4\hat{j})$ N acts on a particle moving in x-y plane. Starting from origin, the particle first goes along x-axis to the point (4, 0) m and then parallel to the y-axis to the point (4,3) m. The total work done by the force on the particle is

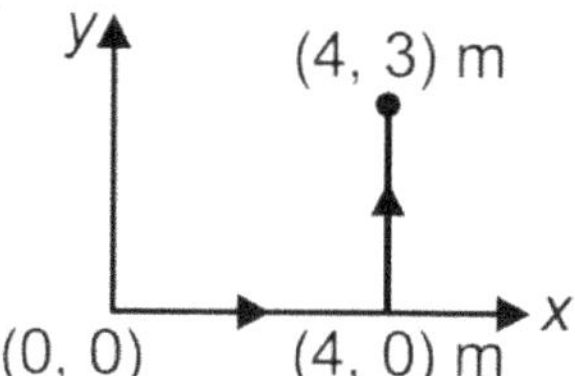

(a) + 12 J
(b) – 6 J
(c) + 24 J
(d) – 12 J

(16) A box of mass 1 kg is pulled on a horizontal plane of length 1 m by a force of 8 N then it is raised vertically to a height of 2m, the net work done
(a) 28 J
(b) 8 J
(c) 18 J
(d) None of above

Physics MCQ | | Class – XI	Dynamics
	Topic : Work done by variable force

 # Important Points

For variable force : $W = \int_A^B \vec{F} . \vec{ds}$

(1) A position dependent force $F = (7 - 2x + 3x^2)$ N acts on a small abject of mass 2 kg to displace it from $x = 0$ to $x = 5$ m. The work done in joule is

(a) 70 J
(b) 270 J
(c) 35 J
(d) 135 J

(2) A particle moves along x-axis from $x = 0$ to $x = 1$ m under the influence of a force given by $F = (3x^2 + 2x - 10)$ N. Work done in the process

(a) + 4 J
(b) – 4 J
(c) + 8 J
(d) – 8 J

(3) A particle moves under the effect of a force F = Cx from x = 0 to x = x_1. The work done in the process is

(a) C x_1^2
(b) $\frac{1}{2}$ C x_1^2
(c) C x_1
(d) zero

(4) The vessels A and B of equal volume and weight are immersed in water to a depth h. The vessel A has an opening at the bottom through which water can enter. If the work done in immersing A and B are W_A and W_B respectively, then

(a) $W_A = W_B$
(b) $W_A < W_B$
(c) $W_A > W_B$
(d) $W_A \leq W_B$

(5) A force of (5 + 3x) N acting on a body of mass 20 kg along the x-axis displaces it from x = 2 m to x = 6 m. The work done by the force is

(a) 20 J
(b) 48 J
(c) 68 J
(d) 86 J

(6) When a spring is stretched by a distance x, it exerts a force, given by $F = (-5x - 16x^3)$N. The work done, when the spring is stretched from 0.1 m to 0.2 m is

(a) 8.7×10^{-2} J
(b) 12.2×10^{-2} J
(c) 8.7×10^{-1} J
(d) 12.2×10^{-1} J

Physics	Dynamics
MCQ | | Class – XI	Topic : Work done from force-displacement graph

 # Important Points

Work done From graph : The area enclosed by the force-displacement graph and the displacement axis gives the work.

(1) The area under the displacement-force curve gives
(a) Distance travelled
(b) Total force
(c) Momentum
(d) Work done

(2) A force F acting on an object varies with distance as shown here. The force is in N and x is in m. The work done by the force in moving the object from x = 0 to x = 6 m is

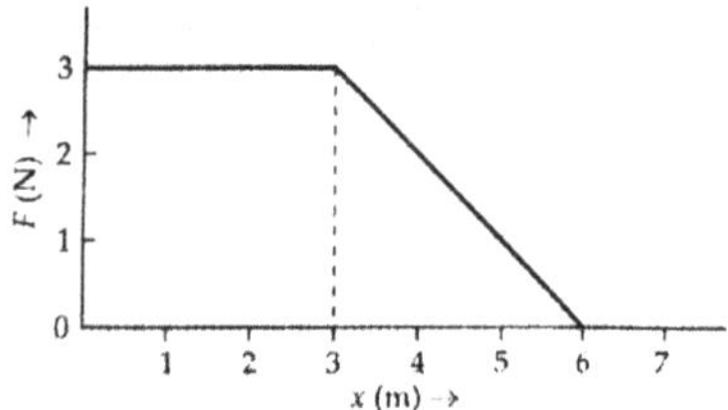

(a) 18.0 J
(b) 13.5 J
(c) 9.0 J
(d) 4.5 J

(3) A 10 kg mass moves along x-axis. Its acceleration as a function of its position is shown in the figure. What is the total work done on the mass by the force as the mass moves from $x = 0$ to $x =$ 8cm

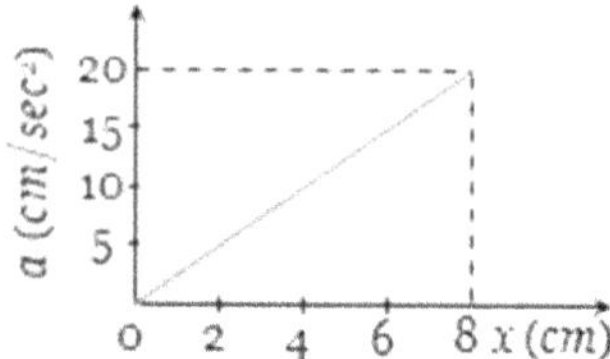

(a) 8×10^{-2} J

(b) 16×10^{-2} J

(c) 4×10^{-4} J

(d) 1.6×10^{-3} J

(4) The relationship between force and position is shown in the figure given (in one dimensional case). The work done by the force in displacing a body from $x = 1$ cm to $x =$ 5cm is

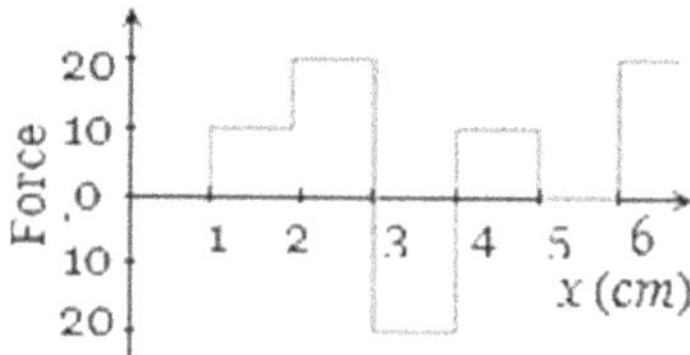

(a) 20 erg
(b) 60 erg
(c) 70 erg
(d) 700 erg

(5) The graph between the resistive force F acting on a body and the distance covered by the body is shown in the figure. The mass of the body is 25 kg and initial velocity is 2 m/s. When the distance covered by the body is $5m$, its kinetic energy would be

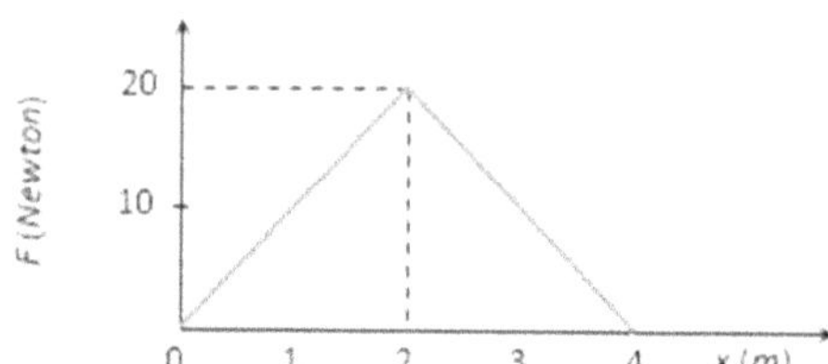

(a) 50 J
(b) 40 J
(c) 20 J
(d) 10 J

(6) Force F on a particle moving in a straight line varies with distance d as shown in the figure. The work done on the particle during its displacement of 12 m is

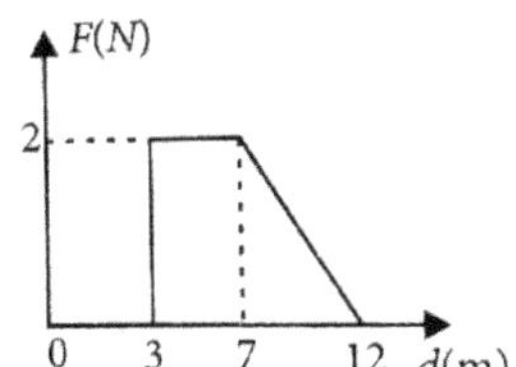

(a) 18 J

(b) 21 J

(c) 26 J

(d) 13 J

Physics MCQ | | Class – XI	Dynamics
	Topic : Work done in Conservative and Non-conservative Field

(1) Which of the following is non-conservative force ?
(a) Interatomic Force
(b) Gravitational Force
(c) Electrostatic Force
(d) Viscous Force

(2) If W_1, W_2 and W_3 represent the work done in moving a particle from A to B along three different paths 1, 2 and 3 respectively (as shown) in the gravitational field of a point mass m, find the correct relation

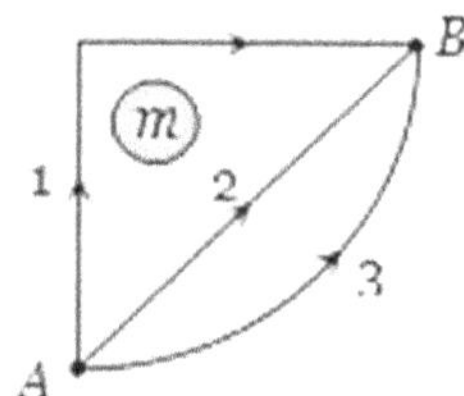

(a) $W_1 > W_2 > W_3$
(b) $W_1 = W_2 = W_3$
(c) $W_1 < W_2 < W_3$
(d) $W_2 > W_1 > W_3$

(3) A man is slipping on a frictionless inclined plane and a bag falls down from the same height. Then the velocity of both is related as (v_B = velocity of bag and v_m = velocity of man)
(a) $v_B > v_m$
(b) $v_B = v_m$
(c) $v_B < v_m$
(d) v_B and v_m can't be related

(4) If 250 J of work is done in sliding a 5 kg block up an inclined plane of height 4 m. Work done against friction is
(a) 50 J
(b) 100 J
(c) 200 J
(d) zero

(5) A man carries a load on his head through a distance of 5 m. The maximum amount of work is done when he
(a) Moves it over an inclined plane
(b) Moves it over a horizontal surface
(c) Lifts it vertically upwards
(d) None of these

Physics MCQ | | Class – XI	Dynamics
	Topic : Power

Important Points

Important Definition :

- **Power** is defined as the time rate of work done.

Important Formulae :

Average power $P_{av} = \frac{\Delta W}{\Delta t}$

$= \frac{\vec{F} \cdot \Delta\vec{s}}{\Delta t}$ [since $\Delta W = \vec{F} \cdot \vec{s}$]

$= \vec{F} \cdot \vec{v}$ [velocity $\vec{v} = \frac{\Delta\vec{s}}{\Delta t}$]

Instantaneous power $P = \frac{dW}{dt}$

Power Developed against Resistive & Driving Force

(1) A car of mass 'm' is driven with acceleration 'a' along a straight level road against a constant external resistive force 'R'. When the velocity of the car is 'v', the rate at which the engine of the car is doing work will be
(a) Rv
(b) m a v
(c) (R + ma) v
(d) (m a – R) v

(2) A car of mass 1250 kg experience a resistance of 750 N when it moves at 30 m s^{-1}. If the engine can develop 30 kW at this speed, the maximum acceleration that the engine can produce is
(a) 0.8 m s^{-2}
(b) 0.2 m s^{-2}
(c) 0.5 m s^{-2}
(d) 0.4 m s^{-2}

Power as a Time Rate of Work

(3) A bus weighing 100 quintals moves on a rough road with a constant speed of 72 km s^{-1}. The friction of the road is 9% of its weight and that of air is 1% of its weight. What is the power of the engine. Take g = 10 m s^{-2}
(a) 50 kW
(b) 100 kW
(c) 150 kW
(d) 200 kW

(4) A pump motor is used to deliver water at a certain rate from a given pipe. To obtain twice as much water from the same pipe in the same time, power of the motor has to be increased to
(a) 16 times
(b) 4 times
(c) 8 times
(d) 2 times

(5) The power of a pump, which can pump 500 kg of water to height 100 m in 10 s is
(a) 75 kW
(b) 25 kW
(c) 50 kW
(d) 500 kW

(6) From a water fall, water is falling at the rate of 100 kg s^{-1} on the blades of turbine. If the height of the fall is 100 m then the power delivered to the turbine is approximately equal to
(a) 100 kW
(b) 10 kW
(c) 1 kW
(d) 1000 kW

(7) Two men with weights in the ratio 5 : 3 run up a staircase in times in the ratio 11 : 9. The ratio of power of first to that of second is
(a) $\frac{15}{11}$
(b) $\frac{11}{15}$
(c) $\frac{11}{9}$
(d) $\frac{9}{11}$

(8) A dam is situated at a height of 550 metre above sea level and supplies water to a power house which is at a height of 50 metre above sea level. 2000 kg of water passes through the turbines per second. The maximum electrical power output of the power house if the whole system were 80% efficient is
(a) 8 MW
(b) 10 MW
(c) 16 MW
(d) 12.5 MW

(9) The power of water pump is 4 kW. If g =10 m s^{-2}, the amount of water it can raise in 1 minute to a height of 20 m is
(a) 100 L
(b) 1000 L
(c) 1200 L
(d) 2000 L

(10) How much water a pump of 2 kW can rise in one minute to a height of 10 m ? (Take g =10 m s^{-2})
(a) 1000 L
(b) 1200 L
(c) 100 L
(d) 2000 L

(11) A pump is used to pump a liquid of density ρ continuously through a pipe of cross section area A. If liquid is flowing with speed V, then power of pump is
(a) $\frac{\rho A V^3}{3}$
(b) $\frac{\rho A V^2}{2}$
(c) $\rho A V^2$
(d) $\frac{1}{2}\rho A V^3$

Power as a Dot Product of Force and Velocity

(12) A particle moves with a velocity $\vec{v} = 5\hat{\imath} - 3\hat{\jmath} + 6\hat{k}$ m s^{-1} under the influence of a constant force $\vec{F} = 10\hat{\imath} + 10\hat{\jmath} + 20\hat{k}$ N. The instantaneous power applied to the particle is
(a) 200 J s^{-1}
(b) 40 J s^{-1}
(c) 140 J s^{-1}
(d) 170 J s^{-1}

(13) A particle moves with the velocity $\vec{v} = 5\hat{\imath} + 2\hat{\jmath} - \hat{k}$ m s^{-1} under the influence of a constant force $\vec{F} = 2\hat{\imath} + 5\hat{\jmath} - 10\hat{k}$ N. The instantaneous power applied to the particle is
(a) 5 W
(b) 10 W
(c) 20 W
(d) 30 W

(14) A body of mass 1 kg begins to move under the action of time dependent force $\vec{F} = 2t\hat{\imath} + 3t^2\hat{\jmath}$ N where $\hat{\imath}$ and $\hat{\jmath}$ are unit vectors along x and y axis. What is the power will developed by the force at the time t ?
(a) ($2t^2 + 4t^4$) W
(b) ($2t^3 + 3t^4$) W
(c) ($2t^3 + 3t^5$) W
(d) ($2t^2 + 3t^3$) W

(15) A body is projected from ground obliquely. During downward motion, power delivered by gravity to it
(a) Increase
(b) Decrease
(c) Remain constant
(d) First decreases and then becomes constant

Instantaneous Power

(16) A body of mass m accelerates uniformly from rest to v_1 in time t_1 . The instantaneous power delivered to the body as a function of time t is
(a) $\frac{m v_1 t}{t_1}$
(b) $\frac{m {v_1}^2 t}{{t_1}^2}$
(c) $\frac{m v_1 t^2}{t_1}$
(d) $\frac{m {v_1}^2 t}{t_1}$

(17) A body of mass m accelerates uniformly from rest to v_1 in time T_1 . The instantaneous power delivered to the body as a function of time t is
(a) $\frac{m {v_1}^2 t}{{T_1}^2}$
(b) $\frac{m v_1 t}{{T_1}^2}$
(c) $(\frac{m v_1}{T_1})^2 t$
(d) $\frac{m {v_1}^2 t}{T_1}$

(18) A constant force F is applied on a body. The power (P) generated is related to the time elapsed (t) as
(a) $P \propto t^2$
(b) $P \propto t$
(c) $P \propto \sqrt{t}$
(d) $P \propto t^{\frac{3}{2}}$

(19) A car of mass m starts from rest and accelerates so that the instantaneous power delivered to the car has a constant magnitude P_0 . the instantaneous velocity of this car is proportional to
(a) $P_0 t^2$
(b) $t^{\frac{1}{2}}$
(c) $t^{-\frac{1}{2}}$
(d) $\frac{t}{\sqrt{m}}$

(20) A car of mass m has an engine which can deliver power P. The minimum time in which car can be accelerated from rest to a speed v is
(a) $\frac{m V^2}{2P}$

(b) $\frac{m v^2}{2} P$
(c) $P m v^2$
(d) $2 P m v^2$

Mechanical Power Received by Wind Mill

(21) A wind-powered generator converts wind energy into electrical energy. Assume that the generator converts a fixed fraction of the wind energy intercepted by its blades into electrical energy. For wind speed v, the electrical power output will be proportional to
(a) v
(b) v^2
(c) v^3
(d) v^4

(22) The blades of a wind mill sweep out a circle of area A. If wind flows with velocity v perpendicular to blades of wind mill and its density is ρ , then the mechanical power received by wind mill is
(a) $\frac{\rho A V^3}{2}$
(b) $\frac{\rho A V^2}{2}$
(c) $\rho A V^2$
(d) $2\rho A V^2$

Physics MCQ | | Class – XI	Dynamics
	Topic : Turning effect of force

Important Points

Important Formulae :

Torque Applied on a Particle

- Torque (in vector) : $\vec{\tau} = \vec{r} \times \vec{F}$

Where, $\vec{F}$ = Force

$\vec{r}$ = position vector of the point of application of force about which we are calculating the torque or moment of force

- Magnitude of torque : $\tau = r\,F\,sin\theta$

$= r_{\perp}\,F$

Where, $r_{\perp}$ = perpendicular distance of line of application of force from the point or axis about which we are calculating the torque.

Important Facts :

- Torque or moment of force is an axial vector, i.e. its direction is always perpendicular to the plane containing vectors $\vec{r}$ and $\vec{F}$ in accordance with right-hand screw rule.

---

(1) A couple produces
(a) Linear and rotational motion
(b) No motion
(c) Purely linear motion
(d) Purely rotational motion

Calculation of Torque about Origin

(2) The torque of a force $\vec{F} = 2\,\hat{\imath} - 3\,\hat{\jmath} + 4\,\hat{k}$ N acting at a point $\vec{r} = 3\,\hat{\imath} + 2\,\hat{\jmath} + 3\,\hat{k}$ meter about origin is
(a) $(- 6\,\hat{\imath} - 6\,\hat{\jmath} + 12\,\hat{k}\ )$ Nm
(b) $(- 6\,\hat{\imath} + 6\,\hat{\jmath} - 12\,\hat{k}\ )$ N m
(c) $(17\,\hat{\imath} - 6\,\hat{\jmath} - 13\,\hat{k}\ )$ N m
(d) $(- 17\,\hat{\imath} + 6\,\hat{\jmath} + 13\,\hat{k}\ )$ N m

(3) A force $\vec{F} = - 3\,\hat{\imath} + \hat{\jmath} + \hat{k}$ is acting on a body at a point located at $\vec{r} = 7\,\hat{\imath} + 3\,\hat{\jmath} + \hat{k}$. The torque about the origin is
(a) $2\,\hat{\imath} - 10\,\hat{\jmath} + 16\,\hat{k}$
(b) $14\,\hat{\imath} - 38\,\hat{\jmath} + 16\,\hat{k}$
(c) $- 14\,\hat{\imath} + 38\,\hat{\jmath} - 16\,\hat{k}$
(d) $- 21\,\hat{\imath} + 3\,\hat{\jmath} - 5\,\hat{k}$

(4) Find the torque about the origin when a force of $3\,\hat{\jmath}$ acts on the particle whose position vector is $2\,\hat{k}$ m
(a) $6\,\hat{\jmath}$ N-m
(b) $- 6\,\hat{\imath}$ N-m
(c) $6\,\hat{k}$ N-m
(d) $6\hat{\imath}$ N-m

Calculation of Torque about a Point other than Origin

(5) A particle is acted upon by a force $\vec{F} = (\hat{\imath} - 3\,\hat{\jmath} + \hat{k}\ )$ N. If the particle is at P (−1 m, 2 m, 3 m), the torque of the force about Q (1 m, 2 m, 3 m) is
(a) $-2\,\hat{\imath} + 6\,\hat{k}$
(b) $2\,\hat{\jmath} + 6\,\hat{k}$
(c) $-\hat{\jmath} + 6\,\hat{k}$
(d) $\hat{\imath} + 6\,\hat{k}$

(6) A force $\vec{F} = 2\,\hat{\imath} - 3\,\hat{k}$ acts on a particle at $\vec{r} = 0.5\,\hat{\jmath} - 2\,\hat{k}$. the torque $\vec{\tau}$ acting on the particle relative to a point with co-ordinates (2.0 m, - 3.0 m) is
(a) $(- 3.0\,\hat{\imath} - 4.5\,\hat{\jmath} - \hat{k}\ )$ Nm
(b) $(3\,\hat{\imath} + 6\,\hat{\jmath} - \hat{k}\ )$ N m
(c) $(- 20\,\hat{\imath} + 4.0\,\hat{\jmath} + \hat{k}\ )$ N m
(d) $(- 1.5\,\hat{\imath} - 4.0\,\hat{\jmath} - \hat{k}\ )$ N m

(7) A force $\vec{F} = (2\hat{\imath} + 3\,\hat{\jmath} - 5\,\hat{k}\ )$ N acts at a particle $\vec{r_1} = (2\hat{\imath} + 4\,\hat{\jmath} + 7\,\hat{k}\ )$ m. The torque of the force about the point $\vec{r_2} = (\hat{\imath} + 2\,\hat{\jmath} + 3\,\hat{k}\ )$ m is
(a) $(17\,\hat{\jmath} + 5\,\hat{k} - 3\,\hat{\imath}\ )$ Nm
(b) $(2\,\hat{\imath} + 4\,\hat{\jmath} - 6\hat{k}\ )$ N m
(c) $(12\,\hat{\imath} - 5\,\hat{\jmath} + 7\,\hat{k}\ )$ N m
(d) $(13\,\hat{\jmath} - 22\,\hat{\imath} - \hat{k}\ )$ N m

(8) Two like parallel forces 20 N and 30 N act at the ends A and B of a rod 1.5 m long. The resultant of the forces will act at the point
(a) 90 cm from A
(b) 75 cm from B
(c) 20 cm from B
(d) 85 cm from A

Physics MCQ || Class – XI	Dynamics
	Topic : Angular momentum & its conservation

Important Points

Important Formulae :

- Angular momentum (in vector) : $\vec{L} = \vec{r} \times \vec{p} = \vec{r} \times m\vec{v}$

Where, $\vec{p}$ = Linear momentum

$\vec{r}$ = position vector of the particle about the point about which we are calculating the angular momentum

- Magnitude of angular momentum : L = $r\ p\ sin\theta$

$= r_{\perp}\ p$

$= r_{\perp}\ (mv)$

Where, $r_{\perp}$ = perpendicular distance of line of direction of velocity from the point or axis about which we are calculating the angular momentum.

Important Facts :

- Angular momentum is an axial vector, i.e. its direction is always perpendicular to the plane containing vectors $\vec{r}$ and $\vec{p}$ in accordance with right-hand screw rule.

(1) Angular momentum is
(a) Axial vector
(b) Polar vector
(c) Scalar
(d) None of the above

(2) A particle of mass m is moving along the positive x-direction with velocity v. the angular momentum about A and B is

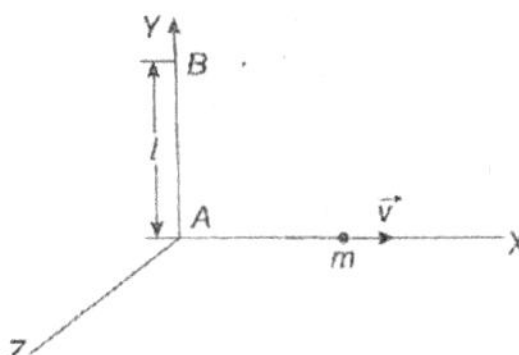

(a) 0, $mlv\,\hat{j}$
(b) $mv\,\hat{\imath}$, $mlv\,\hat{j}$
(c) 0, $mlv\,\hat{k}$
(d) $mv\,\hat{\imath}$, 0

(3) A particle of mass m is moving with constant velocity v parallel to the x-axis as shown in the figure. Its angular momentum about origin O is

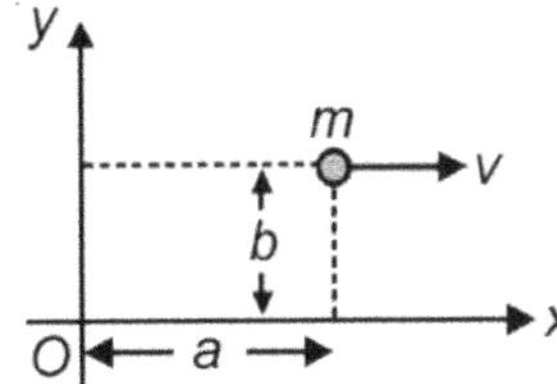

(a) mvb
(b) mva
(c) mv $\sqrt{a^2 + b^2}$
(d) mv (a + b)

(4) A particle of mass 5 kg is moving with a uniform speed 3 $\sqrt{2}$ in XOY plane along the line Y = X + 4. The magnitude of its angular momentum about the origin is

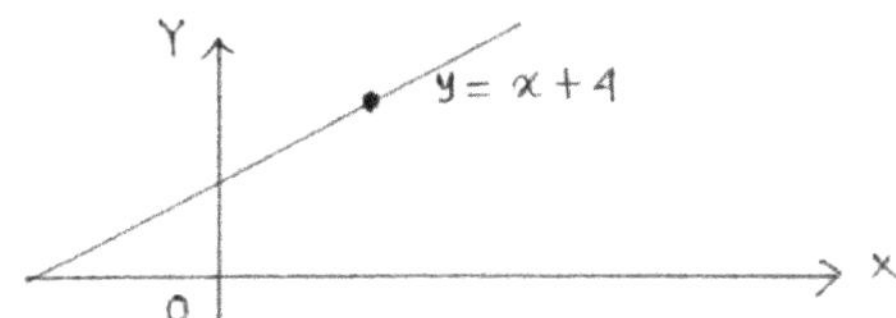

(a) 40 units
(b) 60 units
(c) Zero
(d) 40$\sqrt{2}$ units

(5) A particle P is moving along a straight line as shown in the figure. During the motion of the particle from A to B the angular momentum of the particle about O

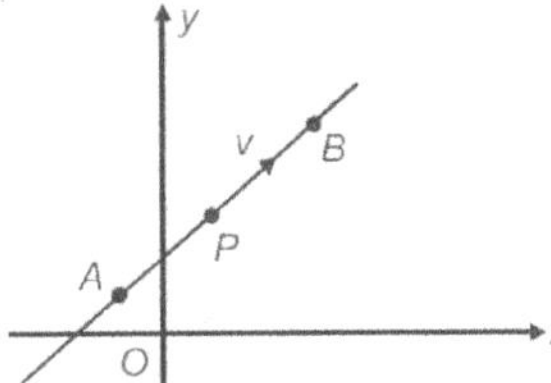

(a) Increases
(b) Decreases
(c) Remains constant
(d) First increases and then decreases

(6) In an orbital motion, the angular momentum vector is
(a) along the radius vector
(b) parallel to the linear momentum

(c) in the orbital plane
(d) perpendicular to the orbital plane

(7) A body of mass m is moving with constant velocity parallel to x-axis. The angular momentum with respect to origin
(a) Increases with time
(b) Decreases with time
(c) Does not change
(d) None of the above

(8) A particle undergoes uniform circular motion. About which point in the plane of the circle, will the angular momentum of the particle remain conserved ?
(a) Centre of the Circle
(b) On the circumference of the circle
(c) Inside the circle other than centre
(d) Outside the circle

(9) When a mass is rotating in a plane about a fixed point, its angular momentum is directed along
(a) a line perpendicular to the plane of rotation
(b) the line making an angle of 45° to the plane of rotation
(c) the radius
(d) the tangent to the orbit

(10) A force $\vec{F} = \alpha\hat{i} + 3\hat{j} + 6\hat{k}$ is acting at a point $\vec{r} = 2\hat{i} - 6\hat{j} - 12\hat{k}$. The value of α for which angular momentum about origin is conserved
(a) 2
(b) – 1
(c) zero
(d) 1

Friction

(1) Friction

When two surfaces are in contact with each other and there exists a relative motion between them, or an attempt is made to impart a relative motion, then a force comes into play that resists the movement. This force is called the force of friction, or simply friction.

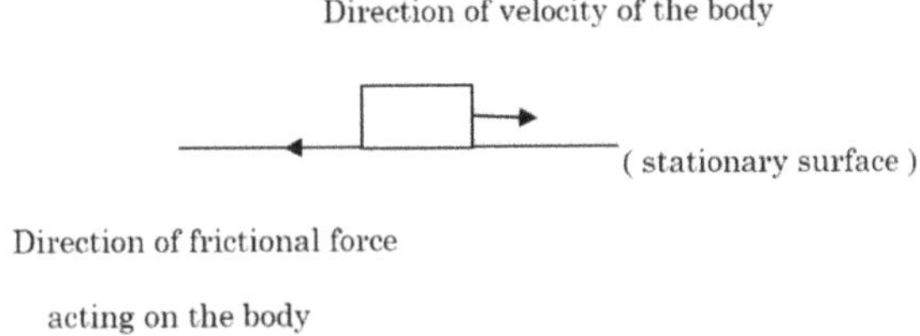

A frictional force opposes even the attempted sliding/rolling of a body over surface. When there is no attempt at sliding / rolling, there is no friction.

(2) Cause of Friction:

Old View: The surfaces of bodies are never perfectly smooth but have irregularities. Even if the surface of a body appears smooth, it is not actually so. When such a surface is minutely observed under a powerful microscope, it shows irregularities.

When a body is placed on another body, there is an interlocking of the irregular projections of the two surfaces. When some force is applied to make one of the body moves over the surface of another body, the motion is resists due to the interlocking of the large number of irregularities. The opposing force is called friction. The direction of the force of friction is always opposite to the direction of motion.

Modern Theory Of Friction Or Surface Adhesion Theory Of Friction: Friction arises on account of strong atomic or molecular force of attraction between the two surfaces at that points of actual contact.

Frictional force will be independent of the area of contact. This is because with increase in area of contact, force of adhesion also increases (in the same ratio). And the adhesive pressure responsible for friction, remains the same.

When the surface in contact are extra smooth, distance between the molecules of the surfaces in contact decreases, increasing the adhesive force between them. Therefore, the adhesive pressure increases, and so does the force of friction.

(3) Classification of Friction :

Friction may be classified as : (i) Static friction, (ii) Sliding friction or Kinetic friction and (iii) Rolling friction.

(4) Static friction :

• The opposing force that comes into play when one body tends to move over the surface of the another but the actual motion yet not started called static friction.

• Static friction is a self adjusting force because it changes itself in accordance with the applied force and is always equal to the net external force.

• **Limiting Friction :** The maximum force of static friction which comes into play when a body just starts sliding over the surface of another body is called limiting friction.

(5) Laws of static friction :

(i) The direction of the force of friction is always in a direction opposite to which the body moves or tends to move.

(ii) The force of friction is a self-adjusting force and increases with the applied force, so as to be equal and opposite to it, until the motion is just about to start.

(iii) When one body just tends to move, the force of friction between the surfaces in contact is maximum. The force of friction is called limiting friction.

(iv) The limiting friction depends on the nature of surfaces in contact but is independent of the area of surface in contact.

(v) The limiting friction is independent of the extent of the area of the surfaces in contact so long as the normal reaction remains the same.

(vi) Limiting friction is directly proportional to the normal between the two surfaces in contact.

i.e. $F_S \propto F_N$

$\therefore F_S = \mu_S F_N$

Where, μ_S = co-efficient of static friction

(6) Co-efficient of static friction :

• The co-efficient of static friction for any two surfaces in contact is defined as the ratio of the limiting frictional force and the normal reaction between them.

i.e. $\mu_S = \frac{F_S}{F_N}$

- It is the ratio of two forces, hence it is a pure number and has no unit and dimension.
- It depends on the materials and roughness of the surface in contact.
- Its value is generally found to be less than 1 but under special circumstances, it may be more than 1. Such as the value of μ_s may be more than 1 between two specially cleaned metallic surface in vacuum.

(7) Variation of frictional force with applied force :

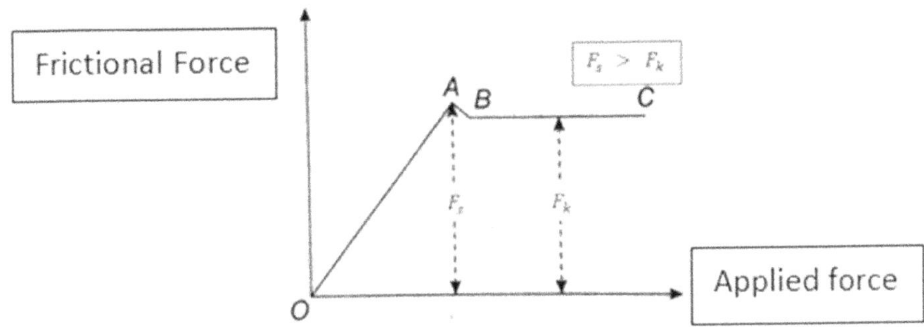

Explanation :

- When there is no relative motion between the bodies in contact, the frictional force increases proportionately with the applied force.
- The maximum value of static friction is known as limiting friction.
- When the applied force exceeds the value of limiting friction, the body commences to move. At this stage, frictional force suddenly decreases by a small amount and then becomes constant. The constant value represents the kinetic or sliding frictional force.

(8) Angle of friction :

It is the angle which the resultant of force of limiting friction and the normal reaction makes with the normal reaction.

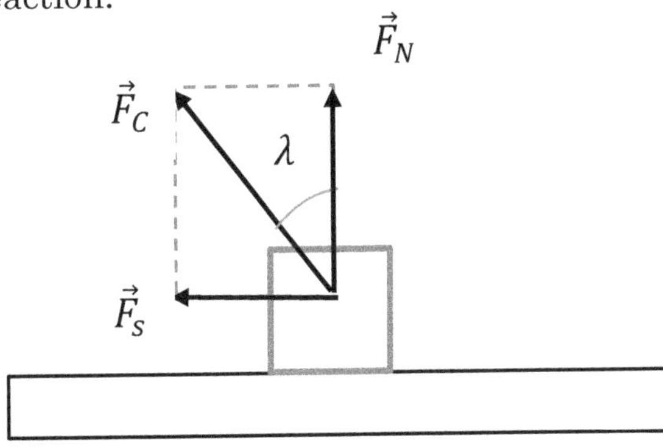

In this figure, λ = angle of friction

If F_C be the resultant force of limiting friction and the normal reaction, then

$F_c \sin\lambda = F_s$ and $F_c \cos\lambda = F_N$

$\therefore$ Co-efficient of static friction : $\mu_s = \frac{F_S}{F_N} = \frac{F_C \sin\lambda}{F_C \cos\lambda} = \tan\lambda$

i.e. the tangent of the angle of friction is equal to the co-efficient of friction. [$\lambda = \tan^{-1} \mu_s$]

(9) Resultant force exerted by the surface on the block :

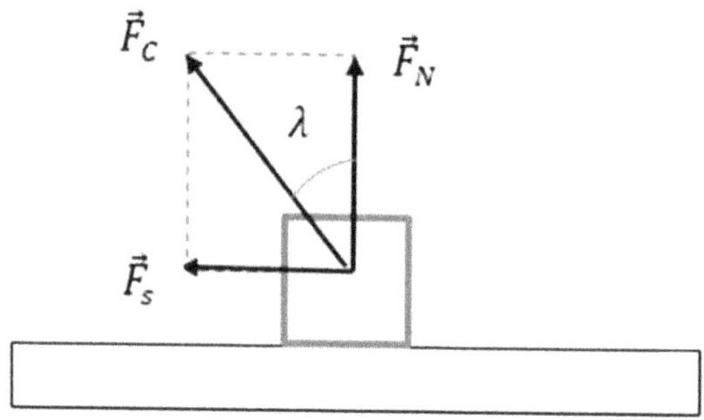

From the figure, the resultant force exerted by the surface on the block is given by $\vec{F}_c = \vec{F}_N + \vec{F}_s$

Magnitude of the resultant force $F_c = \sqrt{F_N^{\,2} + F_s^{\,2}}$

$$= \sqrt{(mg)^2 + (\mu_s mg)^2}$$

$$= mg\sqrt{1 + \mu_s^{\,2}}$$

When there is no friction, the resultant force is minimum and $(F_c)_{min} = mg$

(10) Acceleration of a block against friction on a horizontal surface :

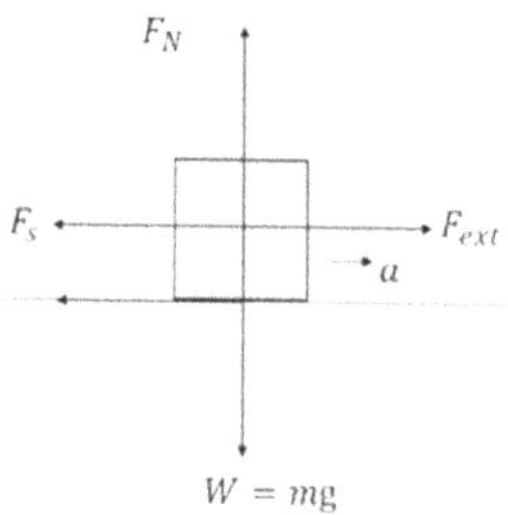

When a block is moving under the application of an external force F_{ext}, then kinetic friction opposes its motion.

Now, the resultant force on the block is given by $F_{net} = F_{ext} - F_k = F_{ext} - \mu_k F_N$

If a be the net acceleration of the block , then we can write, m $a = F_{ext} - \mu_k F_N$

$$\therefore a = \frac{F_{ext} - \mu_k F_N}{m}$$

(11) Angle of sliding or angle of repose :

It is the angle that an inclined plane makes with the horizontal when a body placed on it just starts sliding down.

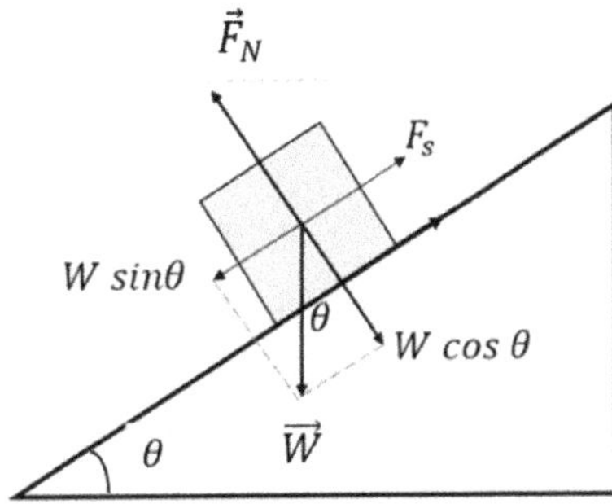

In this figure, θ = angle of repose

Considering the equilibrium of the block, we can write F_N = W cos θ and F_s = W sin θ

∴ Co-efficient of static friction : $\mu_s = \frac{F_s}{F_{reaction}} = \frac{W \sin\theta}{W \cos\theta}$ = tan θ

i.e. the tangent of the angle of repose is equal to the co-efficient of friction. [θ = $\tan^{-1} \mu_s$]

(12) Relation between angle of friction and angle of repose :

We know that, Co-efficient of static friction : μ_s = tan λ [Where, λ = angel of friction]

Again, μ_s = tan θ [Where, θ = angel of friction]

So, λ = θ i.e. the angle of friction is equal to the angle of repose.

(13) Kinetic friction :

Kinetic friction or dynamic friction is the opposing force that comes into play when one body is actually moving over the surface of another body.

Kinetic friction is always slightly less than the limiting value.

(14) Laws of sliding friction :

(i) The direction of the force of sliding friction is always in a direction opposite to which the body moves.

(iv) The sliding friction depends on the nature, condition and material of the surfaces in contact but is independent of the area of surface in contact.

(v) The sliding or kinetic friction does not depend on the relative velocity of the surfaces, provided the velocity is not too large.

[When the relative velocity of the surfaces becomes too large, considerable amount of heat is produced due to friction. This heat alters the condition of the surfaces in contact in which case the law does not hold good.]

(vi) The force of sliding friction is directly proportional to the normal force between the two surfaces in contact and it is less than the force of static friction.

i.e. $F_k \propto F_N$

$\therefore F_k = \mu_k F_N$

Where, μ_k = co-efficient of sliding (or kinetic) friction

(15) Acceleration of a block sliding down over a rough inclined plane :

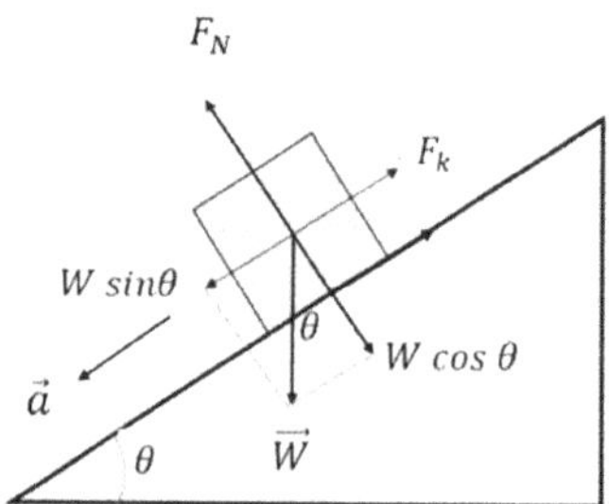

When angle of inclined plane is more than angle of repose, the block placed on the inclined plane slides down over an acceleration a.

Resolving the weight of the block into two perpendicular components, we get $W \cos\theta = F_N$ (since there is no motion perpendicular to the plane.)

If F_k be the frictional force acting up the plane, the resultant force responsible for the downward sliding of the block $F_{net} = W \sin\theta - F_k$

$$= W \sin\theta - \mu_k F_N$$

$$= W \sin\theta - \mu_k W \cos\theta$$

$$= W (\sin\theta - \mu_k \cos\theta)$$

$$= mg (\sin\theta - \mu_k \cos\theta)$$

$\therefore$ Acceleration of the block down the plane $a = \frac{F_{net}}{m}$

$$= \frac{mg (\sin\theta - \mu_k \cos\theta)}{m}$$

$$= g (\sin\theta - \mu_k \cos\theta)$$

For frictionless inclined plane, $a = g \sin\theta$ ($\because \mu_k = 0$)

i.e. Friction reduces the acceleration of the block by an amount equal to $\mu_k g \cos\theta$.

(16) Rolling friction :

- Motion of a body over another surface is said to be rolling if its point of contact with the other keeps on changing continuously and its centre of gravity advances forward.

• When one body rolls over another, the frictional force developed is called force of rolling friction.

• Force of rolling friction is directly proportional to the normal force (F_N) and inversely proportional to the radius (R) of the rolling body.

Mathematically, force of rolling friction $F_r = \mu_r \frac{F_N}{R}$
Where, μ_r = co-efficient of rolling friction.

• Co-efficient of rolling friction has the dimension of length and its SI unit is m.

• Rolling friction is small as compared to the sliding friction. That's why heavy bodies are transported by placing on carts with wheels.

• The expression for rolling friction is applicable only if the motion is purely rolling. If there is slipping, the expression is not valid.

(17) Advantages of friction :

• Friction helps in the generation of heat.
• Friction helps in stopping bicycle or any vehicle by applying brakes.
• Friction helps to write and to walk.
• Friction helps in ignition of matchsticks.
• Friction provide support to the ladder against the wall.

(18) Disadvantages of friction :

• Friction produces heat which may damage machine and cause the wastage of energy.
• Friction resists motion.
• The cause of forest fires is the friction between tree branches.
• Production of noise in machines due to friction.
• Consumption of more fuel in vehicles

(19) Ways to increase friction :

• Friction may be increased my making the surfaces rougher. The roughness of the surfaces in contact can be enhanced to increase friction.
• Friction may be increased by increasing the mass of the object that is moving.
• The treads (a series of patterns) present on the tyres of car, buses and trucks help to increase friction.
• The grooves on the sole of shoes help to increase friction and provide better grip to the ground.
• The brake shoes in automobiles are used to increase friction.

(20) Ways to reduce friction :

- Use of lubricants (substance like oil or grease polish on the surface of a machines to reduce friction and the process of applying lubricants to machines is known as lubrication.)
- The use of wheels also helps to reduce friction.
- The use of ball bearings between machine part generally helps to reduce friction as rolling friction is less than sliding friction.
- Sprinkling power on dholak can reduce friction.
- Polishing surfaces that come into contact with one another to way to reduce friction. Polishing the surfaces eliminates imperfections and thereby smooths the surface.

MCQ – 7 : Friction

Physics

MCQ || Class – XI

Dynamics

Topic : Concept of friction and coefficient of friction

Important Points

- If we slide or try to slide a body over a surface, the motion is resisted by a bonding between the body and the surface. The resistance is represented by a single force, called frictional force.
- It acts parallel to the surface and opposite to the direction of intended motion.
- The opposing force that comes into play when one body tends to move over the surface of another, but the actual motion yet to be started is called static friction.
- Static friction is a self-adjusting force because it changes itself in accordance with the applied force and is always equal to net external force.
- The maximum value of static friction upto which body does not move is called limiting friction.
- The magnitude of limiting friction between any two bodies in contact is directly proportional to the normal reaction between them.

---

(1) Which of the following is self-adjusting force?
(a) Static friction
(b) Limiting friction
(c) Kinetic friction
(d) Rolling friction

(2) Maximum force of friction is called
(a) Static friction
(b) Limiting friction
(c) Sliding friction
(d) Rolling friction

(3) The limiting friction between two bodies in contact is independent of
(a) Nature of the surface in contact
(b) The area of the surface in contact
(c) Normal reaction between the surface
(d) The material of the bodies

(4) Which is a suitable method to decrease friction?
(a) Polishing
(b) Lubrication
(c) Ball bearing
(d) All of these

(5) Which of the following is the dimension of coefficient of friction ?
(a) $[M L T^{-2}]$
(b) $[M^0 L^0 T^{-2}]$
(c) $[M^2 L T^{-2}]$
(d) $[M^2 L T]$

(6) If the normal force is doubled, then co-efficient of friction is
(a) halved
(b) tripled
(c) doubled
(d) not changed

(7) Co-efficient of kinetic friction and coefficient of static friction between two block is μ_s and μ_k respectively. In general
(a) $\mu_s < \mu_k$
(b) $\mu_s > \mu_k$
(c) $\mu_s = \mu_k$
(d) None of these

(8) If μ_s is coefficient of static friction and and μ_k is coefficient of kinetic friction, then
(a) generally, $\mu_s < \mu_k$
(b) generally, $\mu_s > \mu_k$
(c) generally, $\mu_s = \mu_k$
(d) There is no relation between μ_s and μ_k

(9) Static friction between two surfaces
(a) Prevents the relative motion between them
(b) Opposite to the direction of motion of them
(c) Acts in opposite direction of applied force
(d) Both (a) & (b)

(10) The limiting value of static friction between two contact surfaces is
(a) Proportional to normal force between the surface in contact
(b) Independent of apparent area of contact
(c) Depends on the microscopic area of contact
(d) All of these

(11) It is easier to roll a barrel than to pull it along the road. This statement is
(a) not possible
(b) uncertain
(c) false
(d) true

(12) Which of the following statements is incorrect ?

(a) Frictional force opposes the relative motion
(b) Limiting value of static friction is directly proportional to normal reaction
(c) Rolling friction is smaller than sliding friction
(d) co-efficient of sliding friction has dimensions of length

Answer

Dynamics

Topic : Concepts of Friction and Co-efficient of Friction

(1)	(a)	**(4)**	(d)	**(7)**	(b)	**(10)**	(d)
(2)	(b)	**(5)**	(b)	**(8)**	(b)	**(11)**	(c)
(3)	(b)	**(6)**	(d)	**(9)**	(d)	**(12)**	(d)

Physics MCQ | | Class – XI	Dynamics
	Topic : Motion on a Rough Horizontal surface

(1) An object is moving on a plane surface with uniform velocity 10 m s^{-1} in the presence of a force 10 N. The frictional force between the object and the surface is
(a) 1 N
(b) – 10 N
(c) 10 N
(d) 100 N

(2) An object of mass 1 kg moving on a horizontal surface with initial velocity 8 m s^{-1} comes to rest after 10 s. If one wants to keep the object moving on the same surface with velocity 8 m s^{-1} the force required is
(a) 0.4 N
(b) 0.8 N
(c) 1.2 N
(d) zero

(3) On the horizontal surface of a truck, a block of mass 1 kg is placed ($\mu = 0.6$) and truck is moving with acceleration 5 m s^{-2} then the frictional force on the block will be
(a) 5 N
(b) 6 N
(c) 5.88 N
(d) 8 N

(4) A block of mass 10 kg is moving on a rough horizontal surface having coefficient of friction $\mu = 0.5$. If a horizontal force of 100 N is acting on it, then acceleration of the block will be
(a) 10 m s^{-2}
(b) 5 m s^{-2}
(c) 15 m s^{-2}
(d) 0.5 m s^{-2}

(5) A body of mass m is kept on a rough horizontal surface (coefficient of friction = μ). Horizontal force is applied on the body, but it does not move. The resultant of normal reaction and the frictional force acting on the object is given by F, where F is
(a) $|\vec{F}| = mg + \mu\, mg$
(b) $|\vec{F}| = \mu\, mg$
(c) $|\vec{F}| = mg$
(d) $|\vec{F}| \le mg\,\sqrt{1+\mu^2}$

(6) What is the maximum value of the force such that the block shown in the arrangement, does not move ?

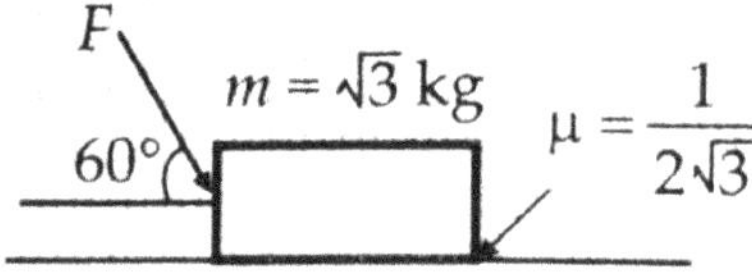

(a) 20 N
(b) 10 N
(c) 12 N
(d) 15 N

(7) The frictional force acting on 1 kg block is

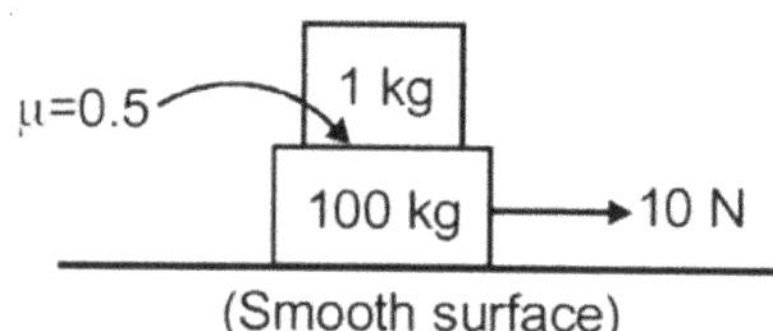

(a) 0.1 N
(b) 2 N
(c) 0.5 N
(d) 5 N

(8) If reaction is R and coefficient of friction is μ, What is work done against the friction in moving a body by distance d ?

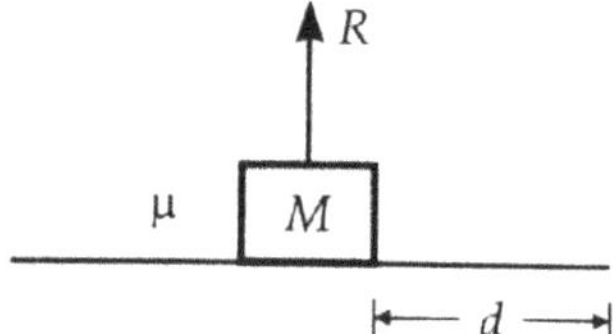

(a) $\frac{\mu Rd}{4}$
(b) $2\mu Rd$
(c) μRd
(d) $\frac{\mu Rd}{2}$

(9) A block B is pushed momentarily along a horizontal surface with an initial velocity v. If μ is the coefficient of sliding friction between B and the surface, block B will come to rest after a time

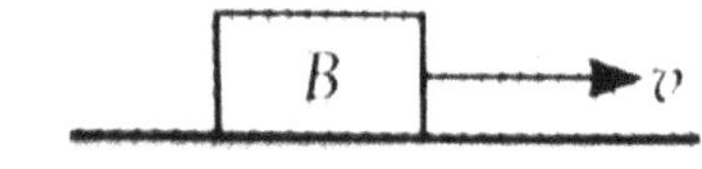

(a) $\frac{\mu g}{v}$
(b) $\frac{g}{v}$

(c) $\frac{v}{g}$
(d) $\frac{v}{\mu g}$

(10) A cylinder of mass 10 kg is rolling on a place with initial velocity of 10 m s^{-1}. If co-efficient of friction between surface and cylinder is 0.5, then before stopping, the cylinder will cover a distance of
(a) 10 m
(b) 5 m
(c) 7.5 m
(d) 2.5 m

(11) A car of mass 400 kg is pulling a coach of mass 300 kg with a force of 4500 N. If the coefficient of friction is 0.001, what is tension ?
(a) 2100 N
(b) 2126 N
(c) 1929 N
(d) 2750 N

(12) A body of mass 2 kg is kept stationary by pressing to a vertical wall by a force of 100 N. The coefficient of friction between wall and body is 0.3. Then the frictional force is equal to (a) 6 N
(b) 20 N
(c) 600 N
(d) 700 N

(13) A horizontal force 10 N is necessary to just hold a block stationary against a wall. The co-efficient of friction between the block and the wall is 0.2, the weight of the block is

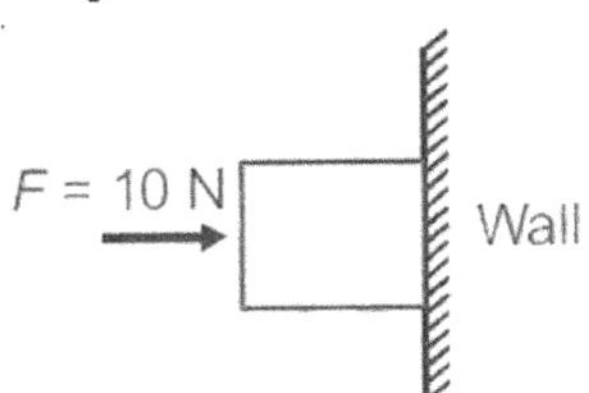

(a) 20 N
(b) 50 N
(c) 100 N
(d) 2 N

(14) Calculate the acceleration of the block and trolly system shown in the figure. The co-efficient of kinetic friction between the trolly and the surface is 0.05 (g = 10 m s^{-2}, mass of the string is negligible and no other friction exists)

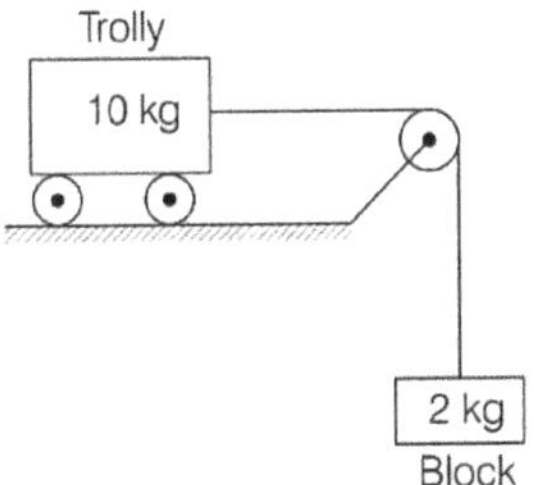

(a) 1.25 m s^{-2}
(b) 1.50 m s^{-2}
(c) 1.66 m s^{-2}
(d) 1.00 m s^{-2}

(15) A block A of mass m_1 rests on a horizontal table. A light string connected to it passes over a frictionless pulley at the edge of table and from its other end another block B of mass m_2 is suspended. The co-efficient of kinetic friction between the block and the table is μ_k . When the block A is sliding on the table, the tension in the string is
(a) $\frac{(m_2+\mu_k m_2)g}{(m_2+m_2)}$
(b) $\frac{(m_2-\mu_k m_2)g}{(m_2+m_2)}$
(c) $\frac{m_1 m_2(1+\mu_k)g}{(m_2+m_2)}$
(d) $\frac{m_1 m_2(1-\mu_k)g}{(m_2+m_2)}$

(16) Work done by frictional force
(a) is always negative
(b) is always positive
(c) is zero
(d) May be positive, negative or zero

Answer

Dynamics

Topic : Motion on a Rough Horizontal surface

(1)	(b)	**(5)**	(d)	**(9)**	(d)	**(13)**	(d)
(2)	(b)	**(6)**	(a)	**(10)**	(a)	**(14)**	(a)
(3)	(a)	**(7)**	(a)	**(11)**	(c)	**(15)**	(c)
(4)	(a)	**(8)**	(c)	**(12)**	(a)	**(16)**	(a)

Physics	Dynamics
MCQ	| Class – XI	Topic : Motion along rough inclined plane

(1) $\sqrt{3}$. The angle through which the plane be inclined to the horizontal so that the block just slides down will be
(a) 30°
(b) 45°
(c) 60°
(d) 75°

(2) A plank with a box on it at one end is gradually raised about the other end. As the angle of inclination with the horizontal reaches 30° , the box starts to slip and slides 4.0 m down the plank in 4.0 s. The co-efficient of static and kinetic friction between the box and the plank will be, respectively

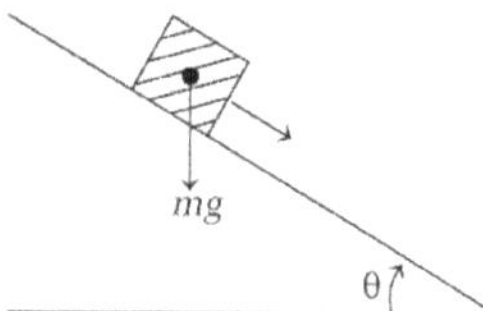

(a) 0.6 and 0.6
(b) 0.6 and 0.5
(c) 0.5 and 0.6
(d) 0.4 and 0.3

(3) A body of mass M starts sliding down on the inclined plane where the critical angle is $\angle ABC = 30°$ as shown in figure. The co-efficient of kinetic friction will be

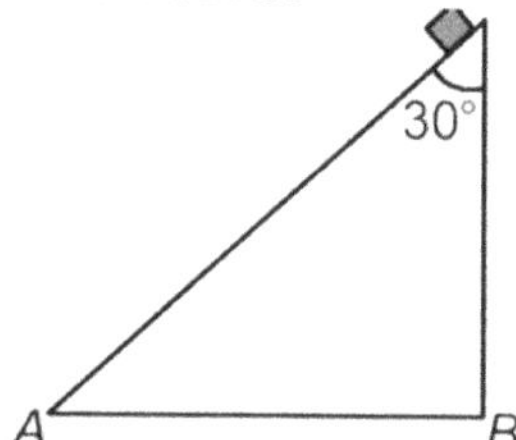

(a) $\frac{Mg}{\sqrt{3}}$
(b) $\sqrt{3}$ Mg
(c) $\sqrt{3}$
(d) None of these

(4) Starting from rest, a body slides down a 45° inclined plane in twice the time it takes to slide down the same distance in the absence of friction. The co-efficient of friction between the body and the inclined plane is
(a) 0.80
(b) 0.75
(c) 0.25
(d) 0.33

(5) A block of mass 10 kg is moving on inclined plane with constant velocity 10 m/s. The coefficient of kinetic friction between inclined plane and block is
(a) 0.57
(b) 0.75
(c) 0.5
(d) None of these
A cubic block rests on a plane of μ =
(6) A block of mass 1 kg is projected from the lowest point up along the inclined plane. If $g = 10$ m s^{-2}, the retardation experienced by the block is

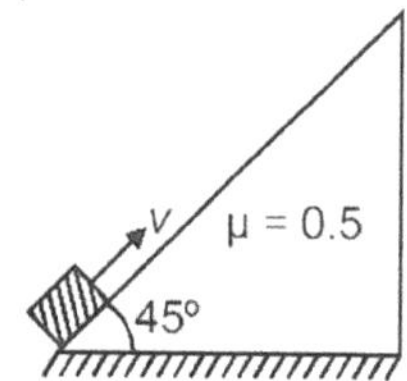

(a) $\frac{15}{\sqrt{2}}$ m s^{-2}
(b) $\frac{5}{\sqrt{2}}$ m s^{-2}
(c) $\frac{10}{\sqrt{2}}$ m s^{-2}
(d) zero

(7) A cubic block rests on a plane of $\mu = \sqrt{3}$. The angle through which the plane be inclined to the horizontal so that the block just slides down will be
(a) 30°
(b) 45°
(c) 60°
(d) 75°

(8) 300 J of work is done in sliding a 2 kg block up an inclined plane of height 10 m. Taking g = 10 m s^{-2}, work done against friction is
(a) 200 J
(b) 100 J
(c) zero
(d) 1000 J

Answer

Dynamics

Topic : Motion along Rough Inclined Plane

(1)	(c)	**(3)**	(c)	**(5)**	(b)	**(7)**	(c)
(2)	(b)	**(4)**	(b)	**(6)**	(a)	**(8)**	(b)

Energy

(1) Energy

• **Definition of energy :** The energy of a body is defined as its capacity for doing work. So, the body which is able to work has energy in it and the body that does not have energy in it cannot work. It gives the idea of the total amount of work that the body can do. It has nothing to do with the time taken to do the work.

• **Nature of the quantity :** It is a scalar quantity.

• **Dimensional equation of energy:** [E] = $[\mathrm{M\,L^2T^{-2}}]$
Note : It is same as that of work or torque.

• **Unit of energy :** SI unit : joule (or, J) or, N m
CGS unit : erg or dyn cm

• **Relationship between J and erg :** 1 joule = 1 N × 1 m
= 10^5 dyne × 10^2 cm
= 10^7 dyne × cm
= 10^7 erg

• **The bigger units of energy are :** (a) watt hour (Wh)
(b) kilowatt hour (kWh).

• **Definition of watt hour :** One watt hour (i.e.1 Wh) is the energy spent (or work done) by a source of power 1 W in 1 hour.

• **Relationship between Wh and J :** 1 Wh = 1 watt × 1 hour
= 1 J $\mathrm{s^{-1}}$ × 3600 s
= 3.6×10^3 J

• **Definition of kilowatt hour :** One kilowatt hour (i.e.1 kWh) is the energy spent (or work done) by a source of power 1 kW in 1 hour.

• **Relationship between kW-h and J :** 1 kW h = 1 kilowatt × 1 hour
= 1000 J $\mathrm{s^{-1}}$ × 3600 s
= 3.6×10^6 J
= 3.6 MJ

• Heat energy is usually measured in **calorie (cal).**

Definition of calorie : 1 cal is the energy required in raising the temperature of 1 g of water from 14.5°C to 15.5°C (or through 1°C).

• The energy transfer in case of atomic particles is very small, so it is measured in **electron volt (eV).**

Definition of electron volt : 1 eV is the energy gained by an electron when it is accelerated through a potential difference of 1 V.

• **Relationship between different units of energy :** 1 joule = 10^7 erg

1 eV = 1.6×10^{-19} joule

1 kWh = 3.6×10^6 joule

1 calorie = 4.18 joule $\approx$ 4.2 J

1 kcal = 4180 joule

• **Various forms of energy :** (i) Mechanical energy (Kinetic energy and Potential energy)

(ii) Chemical energy

(iii) Electrical energy

(iv) Magnetic energy

(v) Nuclear energy

(vi) Sound energy

(vii) Light energy

(viii) Heat energy

• **Transformation of energy :** Conversion of energy from one form to another is possible through various devices and processes. Mass can also be transformed into energy and vice-versa.

• **Mass energy equivalence :** Einstein's special theory of relativity shows that material particle itself is a form of energy. The relation between the mass of a particle m and its equivalent energy E is given as $E = mc^2$

Where, c = speed of light in vacuum.

= 3×10^8 m s^{-1}

(2) Kinetic Energy

• **Definition of kinetic energy :** The energy possessed by a body by virtue of its motion is called kinetic energy.

• **Examples of kinetic energy :**

(i) Flowing water possesses kinetic energy which is used to run the water mills.

(ii) Moving vehicle possesses kinetic energy.

(iii) Moving air (i.e. wind) possesses kinetic energy which is used to run wind mills.

(iv) The hammer possesses kinetic energy which is used to drive the nails in wood.

(v) A bullet fired from the gun has kinetic energy and due to this energy the bullet penetrates into a target.

- **Measurement of kinetic energy:**

(i) The kinetic energy of a moving body is equal to the amount of work that must be done to bring the body form rest into the state of motion; or,

(ii) The kinetic energy of a moving body is the amount of work that we must do in order to bring a moving body to rest.

- **Expression for kinetic energy :** If a particle of mass m is moving with velocity v then, its kinetic energy is given by :

$$E_k = \frac{1}{2}mv^2 = \frac{1}{2}m(\vec{v}\,.\,\vec{v})$$

Deduction : Non-calculus Method

Let us consider, a body of mass m is moving with a velocity v. A force F is applied against the motion of the body. This would produce a retardation on the body which will finally come to rest.

Let us consider, the retardation produced be a and r the distance travelled by the body before it comes to rest.

From $v_f{}^2 = v_i{}^2 + 2\,a\,s$ we get, $0 = v^2 + 2\,(-\,a\,)\,r$

$$\therefore r = \frac{v^2}{2a}$$

So, work done by the body is given by $W = F\,r$

$$\text{or, } W = ma \times \frac{v^2}{2a}$$

$$\text{or, } W = \frac{1}{2}mv^2$$

This work done is the kinetic energy of the body.

Therefore, kinetic energy : $E_k = \frac{1}{2}mv^2$

Alternative approach :

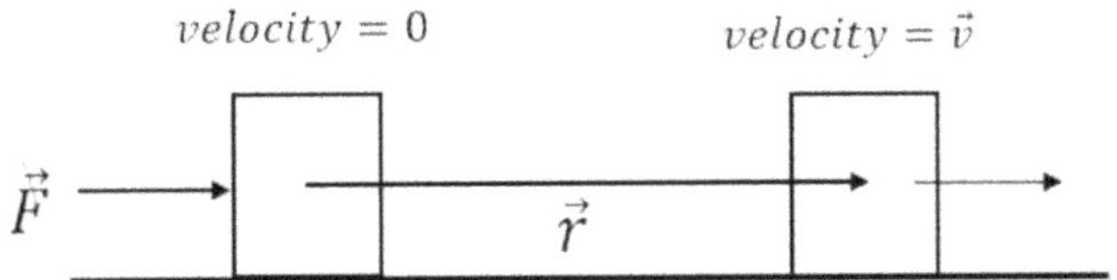

Let us consider, a body of mass m lying on a smooth horizontal surface and a constant force F displace this body in its own direction through r. After travelling distance r, velocity of the body becomes v.

From $v_f^2 = v_i^2 + 2\,a\,s$ we get, $v^2 = 0 + 2\,a\,r$

$$\therefore r = \frac{v^2}{2a}$$

Since the displacement of the body is in the direction of the applied force, then work done by the force is given by

$W = F\,r\cos 0°$

or, $W = ma \times \frac{v^2}{2a}$

or, $W = \frac{1}{2}mv^2$

This work done appears as the kinetic energy of the body.

Therefore, kinetic energy : $E_k = \frac{1}{2}mv^2$

Calculus method :

Let us consider, a body of mass m is initially at rest on a smooth horizontal surface. A force $\vec{F}$ is applied on the body to displace it through $d\bar{r}$ along its own direction then small work done is given by

$dW = \vec{F}.d\vec{r} = Fdr\cos 0°$

or, $dW = (ma)\,dr$ [$\because$ F = ma]

or, $dW = m\frac{dv}{dt}dr\left[\because a = \frac{dv}{dt}\right]$

or, $dW = m\,dv.\frac{dr}{dt}$

or, $dW = mvdv\left[\because \frac{dr}{dt} = v\right]$

Therefore total work done on the body in order to increase its velocity from zero to v is given by

$W = \int_0^v mvdv$

or, $W = m\int_0^v vdv$

or, $W = m\left[\frac{v^2}{2}\right]_0^v$

or, $W = \frac{1}{2}mv^2$

This work done appears as the kinetic energy of the body.

Therefore, kinetic energy : $E_k = \frac{1}{2}mv^2$

• Kinetic energy of a body depends on frame of reference. For example, the kinetic energy of a person sitting in a moving train is zero in the frame of train but it has kinetic energy in the frame of the earth.

• **Kinetic energy according to relativity :** As we know $E_k = \frac{1}{2}mv^2$.

But this formula is valid only for v << c. If v is comparable to speed of light in free space (= 3×10^8 m s^{-1}) then according to Einstein theory of relativity

$$E_k = \frac{mc^2}{\sqrt{1-\left(\frac{v}{c}\right)^2}} - mc^2$$

• **Work-Energy Theorem:**

Statement : The work done on a body by a resultant force is equal to increase in kinetic energy of the body.

Mathematical Form : W = $\Delta E_k = \frac{1}{2} m\, v_f^2 - \frac{1}{2} m\, v_i^2$

Deduction :

Non-calculus method :

Let us consider, a body of mass m moves in a straight line with velocity v_i. A constant force F is applied on the body in the direction of the motion.
Hence, an acceleration a is produced and after a further displacement s the body gets velocity v_f.

Form $v_f^2 = v_i^2 + 2\,as$ we get, s = $\frac{1}{2\,a}\left(v_f^2 - v_i^2\right)$

Now, work done by the force is given by, W = F s

$$\begin{aligned} &= \text{m}\, a\, \text{s} \\ &= \frac{1}{2a}\, m\, a\left(v_f^2 - v_i^2\right) \\ &= \frac{1}{2}\, m\, v_f^2 - \frac{1}{2}\, m\, v_i^2 \\ &= (E_k)_f - (E_k)_i \\ &= \text{Change in kinetic energy} \end{aligned}$$

Calculus Method :

If dW be the small amount work done in giving an infinitesimally small displacement dr to the body in the direction of the force F, then dW = F dr
Let us consider, m be the mass of the body and a is the acceleration of the body then, F = ma

$$\begin{aligned} \therefore \text{dW} &= \text{m}\, a\, \text{dr} \\ &= \text{m}\frac{\text{dv}}{\text{dt}}\text{dr} \\ &= \text{m}\frac{\text{dr}}{\text{dt}}\text{dv} \\ &= \text{m v dv} \end{aligned}$$

If W be the work done in increasing the velocity from v_i to v_f, then W = $\int_{v_i}^{v_f} m\,v\,dv$

or, W = m $\int_{v_i}^{v_f} v\,dv$

or, W = m $\left[\frac{v^2}{2}\right]_{v_i}^{v_f}$

or, W = $(E_k)_f - (E_k)_i$

∴ W = Change in kinetic energy

Therefore, The work done on a body by a resultant force is equal to increase in kinetic energy of the body.

Discussion :

(i) This theorem is valid for a system in presence of all types of forces (external or internal, conservative or non-conservative).

(ii) If kinetic energy of the body increases, work is positive i.e. body moves in the direction of the force (or field).

Example : In case of vertical motion of body under gravity when the body is projected up, force of gravity is opposite to motion and so kinetic energy of the body decreases and when it falls down, force of gravity is in the direction of motion so kinetic energy increases.

If kinetic energy decreases work will be negative and object will move opposite to the force (or field).

Example : When a body moves on a rough horizontal surface, as force of friction acts opposite to motion, kinetic energy will decrease and the decrease in kinetic energy is equal to the work done against friction.

If kinetic energy remains unchanged, then work done is zero.

Example : Circular motion.

(iii) The work-energy theorem is not independent of Newton's second law. It may be viewed as scalar form of second law.

(iv) The work-energy theorem holds in all inertial frames. It can be extended to non-inertial frames provided we include the pseudo force in the calculation of the net force acting on the body under consideration.

(v) In deriving the work-energy theorem, it has been assumed that the work done by the force is effective only in changing the kinetic energy of the body. However, the work done on a body may also be stored as the potential energy of the body.

- **Relation of Kinetic Energy with Linear Momentum:**

If a particle of mass m is moving with velocity v then, its kinetic energy is $E_k = \frac{1}{2}mv^2$

and its linear momentum is $P = mv$

Now, $E_k = \frac{1}{2}mv^2$

or $E_k = \frac{1}{2m}(mv)^2$

$\therefore E_k = \frac{P^2}{2m}$

or, $P^2 = 2mE_k$

$\therefore P = \sqrt{2m E_k}$

Knowledge Plus : A body cannot have kinetic energy without having momentum and vice-versa..

- **Various Graphs of Kinetic Energy :**

Variation of K.E. w.r.t velocity	Variation of K.E. w.r.t mass	Variation of K.E. w.r.t. momentum	Variation of square root of K.E. w.r.t. momentum
When mass is constant, $E_k \propto v^2$	When momentum is constant, $E_k \propto \frac{1}{m}$	When mass is constant, $E_k \propto P^2$	When mass is constant, $\sqrt{E_k} \propto P$
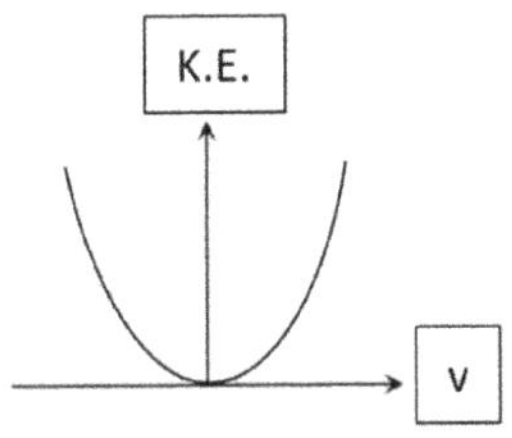 K.E. v	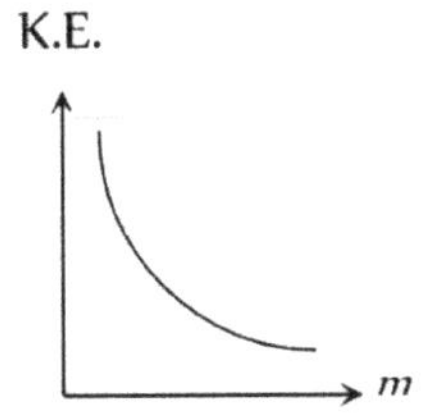 K.E. m	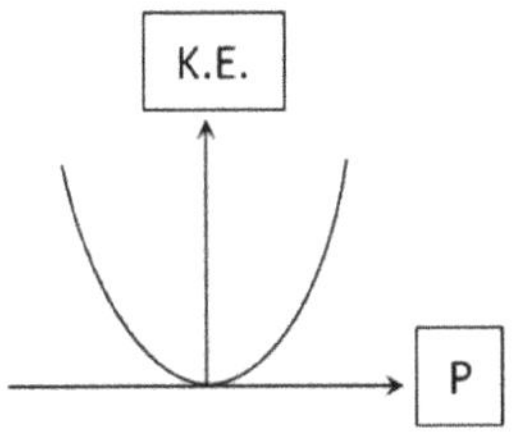 K.E. P	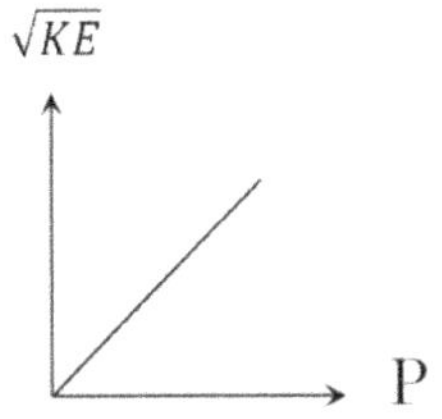 $\sqrt{KE}$ P

- **Forms of kinetic energy :**

There are three types of kinetic energy : (a) Translational kinetic energy
(b) Rotational kinetic energy
(c) Vibrational kinetic energy

Depending upon its state of motion, a moving body may possess either one or more than one form of kinetic energy simultaneously. For example, a rolling ball and a wheel of a moving car have kinetic energies both in translational and rotational forms simultaneously.

(3) Potential Energy

- **Definition of Potential Energy :**

The energy stored in a body or system by virtue of its configuration or its position in a field of conservative force is called potential energy.

• Measurement of Change in Potential Energy :

Change in potential energy between any two points is defined as the negative work done by the associated conservative force in displacing a particle between those two points without any change in kinetic energy.

$$\Delta E_p = -W_{conservative} = -\int_{r_1}^{r_2} \vec{F}.d\vec{r} \text{ .....(1)}$$

• Measurement of Potential Energy:

To define a unique value of potential energy we assign some arbitrary value to a fixed point called the reference point. Whenever and wherever possible, we take the reference point at infinite and assume potential energy to be zero there, i.e. if take $r_1 = \infty$ and $r_2 = r$ then equation (1) becomes

$$E_p = -W_{\infty\, r} = -\int_{\infty}^{r} \vec{F}.d\vec{r}$$

Therefore, potential energy is defined as the negative work done by the associated conservative force in displacing a particle from reference position or reference point to given position or reference point.

Knowledge Plus : *Potential energy should be considered to be a property of the entire system, rather than assigning it to any specific particle.*

• Conservative Force and Potential Energy:

Potential energy is defined only for conservative forces. In the space occupied by conservative forces every point is associated with certain energy which is called the energy of position or potential energy. It does not exist for non-conservative force.

Mathematically, Conservative force $\vec{F} = -\vec{\nabla} E_p$

$$\text{or, } \vec{F} = -\left[\frac{\partial E_p}{\partial x}\hat{\imath} + \frac{\partial E_p}{\partial y}\hat{\jmath} + \frac{\partial E_p}{\partial z}\hat{k}\right]$$

$$\text{or, } F_x\,\hat{\imath} + F_y\,\hat{\jmath} + F_z\hat{k} = -\left[\frac{\partial E_p}{\partial x}\hat{\imath} + \frac{\partial E_p}{\partial y}\hat{\jmath} + \frac{\partial E_p}{\partial z}\hat{k}\right]$$

Therefore, the components of force are given by : $F_x = -\frac{\partial E_p}{\partial x}$

$$F_y = -\frac{\partial E_p}{\partial y}$$

$$F_z = -\frac{\partial E_p}{\partial z}$$

• Potential Energy Depends on Position of Reference Level :

(i) For gravitational force and electrostatic force, we select reference level at infinity (At infinity F = 0 and E_p = 0)

(ii) For springs, we take natural length of spring as reference level because at x = 0, F = 0.

(iii) For intermolecular forces reference level is at infinity.

• Important Points Related to P.E.:

(i) Potential energy can be positive, negative or zero.

Explanation : In a conservative field (say gravitational or electric), if the particle moves opposite to the field, work done by the field will be negative and so change in potential energy will be positive i.e. potential energy will increase.

When the particle moves in the direction of field, work will be positive and change in potential energy will be negative i.e. potential energy will decrease.

(ii) Potential energy depends on frame of reference.

(iii) A moving body may or may not have potential energy.

• Potential Energy Curve :

A graph plotted between the potential energy of a particle and its displacement from the centre of force is called potential energy curve.

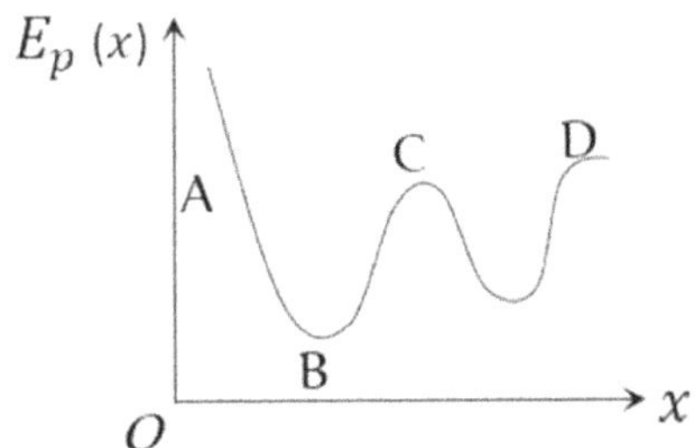

Figure shows a graph of potential energy function E_p(x) for one dimensional motion.

Importance of Potential-Energy Curve : As we know that negative gradient of the potential energy gives force.

$$\therefore\ -\frac{dE_p}{dx} = F$$

(i) On increasing x, if E_p increases $\frac{dE_p}{dx}$ = positive then F is negative in direction i.e. **force is attractive** in nature. In graph this is represented in region BC.

(ii) On increasing x, if E_p decreases $\frac{dE_p}{dx}$ = negative then F is positive in direction i.e. **force is repulsive** in nature. In graph this is represented in region AB.

(iii) On increasing x, if E_p does not changes $\frac{dE_p}{dx} = 0$ then F is zero i.e. no force works on the particle. Point B, C and D represents the point of zero force or these points can be termed as position of equilibrium.

• Types of Potential Energy :

Potential energy generally are of three types: (a) Elastic potential energy,

(b) Electric potential energy

and (c) Gravitational potential energy etc.

• Elastic Potential Energy :

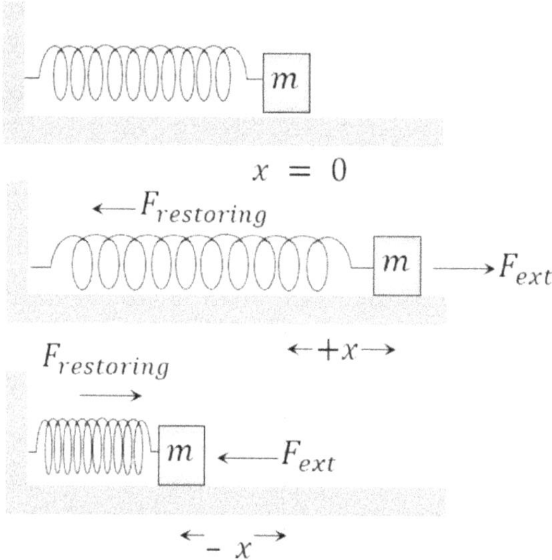

When a spring is stretched or compressed from its normal position (x = 0) by a small distance x, then a restoring force is produced in the spring to bring it to the normal position. According to Hooke's law this restoring force is proportional to the displacement x and its direction is always opposite to the displacement.

i.e. $\vec{F}_{restoring} \propto -\vec{x}$

or, $\vec{F}_{restoring} = -k\,\vec{x}$ [Where k is called spring constant]

Points to Remember :

• Spring Constant :

(a) Definition : If x = 1, k = F (Numerically)

Hence spring constant is numerically equal to force required to produce unit displacement (compression or extension) in the spring.

(b) If required force is more, then spring is said to be more stiff and vice-versa. Actually k is a measure of the stiffness/softness of the spring.

(c) Dimensional formula : $[k] = \frac{[F]}{[x]} = \frac{[\text{MLT}^{-2}]}{\text{L}} = [\text{MT}^{-2}]$

[Dimension of force constant is similar to that of surface tension.]

(d) Unit : CGS unit : dyn cm^{-1}

SI unit : N m^{-1}

Expression for Elastic Potential Energy of a Spring :

When a spring is stretched or compressed from its normal position (x = 0), work has to be done by external force against restoring force.

When extension is zero, $F_{restoring}$ = 0 and after completion of extension restoring force is F.

Therefore, average restoring force : $(F_{restoring})_{av} = \frac{0+F}{2} = \frac{F}{2}$

Now total work done to stretch the spring through a distance Δx from its mean position is given by :

$$W = \frac{F}{2}\,\Delta x$$

$$= \frac{1}{2}k\,(\Delta x)^2$$

This work done is stored as the potential energy of the stretched spring.

∴ Elastic potential energy : $(E_p)_{spring} = \frac{1}{2}k\,(\Delta x)^2$

• Gravitational Potential Energy :

(a) It is the usual form of potential energy. Gravitational potential energy is the energy associated with the state of separation between two bodies that interact via gravitational force.

(b) Expression for gravitational potential energy for any mass system :

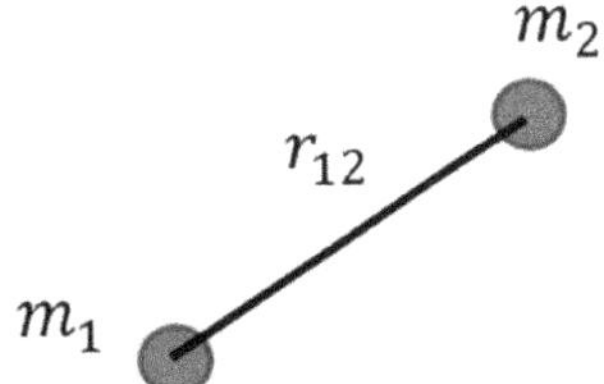

For two particles of masses m_1 and m_2 separated by a distance r_{12}, Gravitational potential energy of the system is given by : $\boldsymbol{E_p} = -\frac{Gm_1m_2}{r_{12}}$

(c) Expression for gravitational potential energy near the earth surface :

(i) Taking the surface of the Earth as reference level :

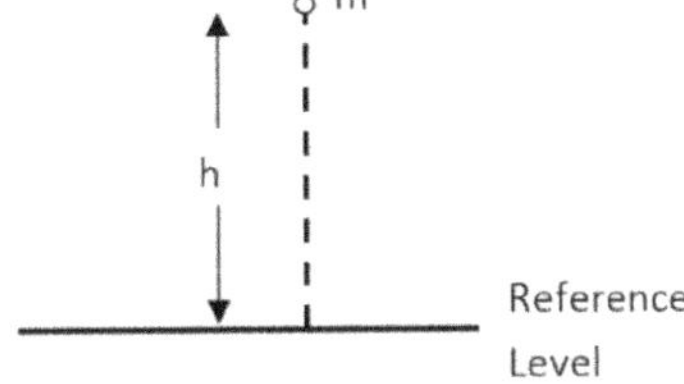

Let us consider, a body of mass m lying on the surface of the earth. Now, the work done in order to lift the body to a height h against the gravitational force will be

$W_{conservative} = \vec{F_g}\,.\vec{h}$

$= (mg)h\cos 180°$

$= -mg\,h$

∴ Gravitational potential energy of the body will be : $\boldsymbol{E_p} = -W_{conservative} = \boldsymbol{m\,g\,h}$

If we do not take the surface of the earth as reference level or zero potential energy level, then the work done should be considered as the change in potential energy of the body.

Therefore, $\boldsymbol{m\,g\,h} = \Delta \boldsymbol{E_p}$

Note : The variation of acceleration due to gravity (g) with height is ignored.

(ii) Taking the reference level or zero potential energy level at infinity :

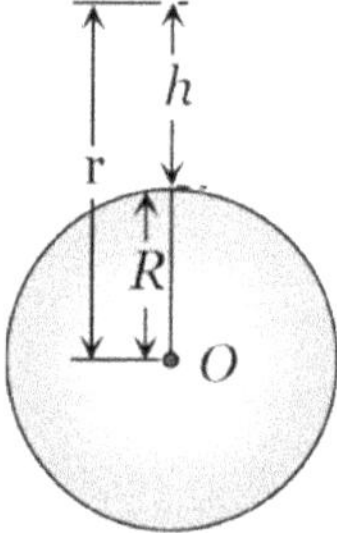

Let us consider, a body of mass m lying on the surface of the earth. Now, if we lift the body to a height h from the surface against the gravitational force then change in gravitational potential energy is given by :

$\Delta E_p = E_p(\mathrm{R+h}) - E_p(\mathrm{R})$ [Where R = radius of the earth]

$= \mathrm{G\,M\,m}\left[\frac{1}{\mathrm{R}} - \frac{1}{\mathrm{R+h}}\right]$ [Where M = mass of the earth]

$= \frac{\mathrm{GMm}}{\mathrm{R}}\left[1 - \frac{\mathrm{R}}{\mathrm{R+h}}\right]$

$= \frac{\mathrm{GMm}}{\mathrm{R}}\left[1 - \frac{1}{1+\frac{\mathrm{h}}{\mathrm{R}}}\right]$

$= \frac{\mathrm{GMm}}{\mathrm{R}}\left[1 - \left(1+\frac{\mathrm{h}}{\mathrm{R}}\right)^{-1}\right]$

$= \frac{\mathrm{GMm}}{\mathrm{R}}\left[1 - \left(1-\frac{\mathrm{h}}{\mathrm{R}}+\cdots\right)\right]$ [If h << R]

$= \frac{\mathrm{GMm}}{\mathrm{R^2}}\,\mathrm{h}$

$= \mathrm{m}\,g\,\mathrm{h}$ [∵ Acceleration due to gravity at the surface of the earth $g = \frac{\mathrm{GM}}{\mathrm{R^2}}$]

(d) Relation between Gravitational Potential & Gravitational Potential Energy : If V is the gravitational potential at a point, the potential energy of a particle of mass m at that point will be

$$E_p = \mathrm{mV}$$

(e) Energy height graph :

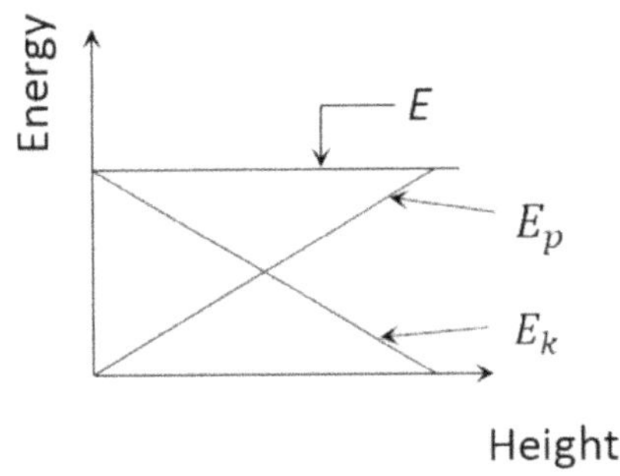

When a body projected vertically upward from the ground level with some initial velocity then it possess kinetic energy but its potential energy is zero.

As the body moves upward its potential energy increases due to increase in height but kinetic energy decreases (due to decrease in velocity). At maximum height its kinetic energy becomes zero and potential energy maximum but through out the complete motion total energy remains constant as shown in the figure.

• Electrostatic Potential Energy :

(a) Electrostatic potential energy is the energy associated with state of separation between charged particles that interact via electric force.

(b) **Expression for electrostatics potential energy for charge system :** Electrostatic potential energy for two point charges q_1 and q_2, separated by distance r is given by : $E_p = \frac{1}{4\pi\varepsilon_0} \cdot \frac{q_1 q_2}{r}$

(c) **Electrostatic potential energy in terms of potential :** While for a point charge q at a point in an electric field where the potential is V, the electrostatic potential is given by : E_p = qV

(d) As charge can be positive or negative, electric potential energy can be positive or negative.

(4) Equilibrium & Different Types of Equilibrium

If net force acting on a particle is zero, it is said to be in equilibrium.

For equilibrium $\frac{dE_p}{dx} = 0$, but the equilibrium of particle can be of three types :

(a) Stable Equilibrium :

(i) Definition : When a particle is displaced slightly from a position, then a force acting on it brings it back to the initial position, it is said to be in stable equilibrium position.

(ii) Example : A marble placed at the bottom of a hemispherical bowl.

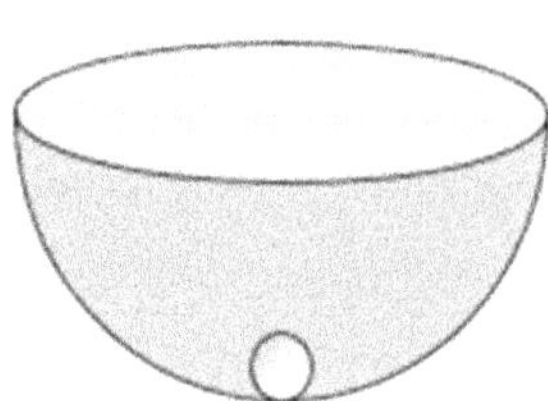

(iii) Potential energy is minimum.

(iv) Mathematical Condition :

Force : $F = -\frac{dE_p}{dx} = 0$ and rate of change of $\frac{dE_p}{dx}$ is positive i.e. $\frac{d^2E_p}{dx^2}$ = Positive

(b) Unstable Equilibrium :

(i) Definition : When a particle is displaced slightly from a position, then a force acting on it tries to displace the particle further away from the equilibrium position, it is said to be in unstable equilibrium.

(ii) Example : A marble balanced on top of a hemispherical bowl.

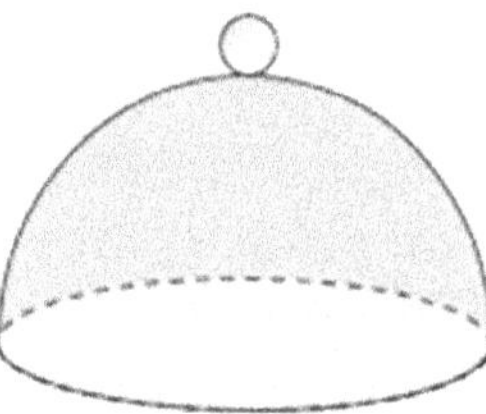

(iii) Potential energy is maximum.

(iv) Mathematical Condition :

Force : $F = -\frac{dE_p}{dx} = 0$ and rate of change of $\frac{dE_p}{dx}$ is negative i.e. $\frac{d^2E_p}{dx^2}$ = negative

(c) Natural Equilibrium :

(i) Definition : When a particle is slightly displaced from a position then it does not experience any force acting on it and continues to be in equilibrium in the displaced position, it is said to be in neutral equilibrium.

(ii) Example : A marble placed on horizontal table.

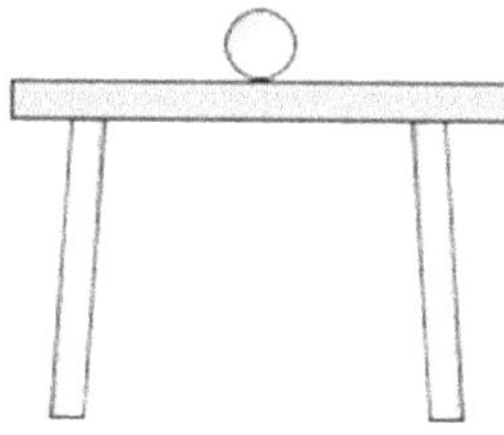

(iii) Potential energy is constant.

(iv) Mathematical Condition :

Force : $F = -\frac{dE_p}{dx} = 0$ and rate of change of $\frac{dE_p}{dx}$ is zero i.e. $\frac{d^2E_p}{dx^2}$ = zero.

(5) Law of Conservation of Energy

(a) **Law of conservation of mechanical energy**

Statement :

For an isolated system or body in presence of conservative forces the sum of kinetic and potential energies at any point remains constant throughout the motion. It does not depends upon time.

Alternative statement :

If there is only an interchange between potential energy and kinetic energy, the total mechanical energy remains constant in the absence of all kinds of frictional forces.

Alternative statement :

The total mechanical energy of a system is conserved if the force, doing work on it, are conservative.

Explanation :

For a body or an isolated system by work-energy theorem we have

$$(E_k)_f - (E_k)_i = \int \vec{F}.d\vec{r} \text{ .... } (1)$$

But according to definition of potential energy in a conservative field

$$(E_p)_f - (E_p)_i = -\int \vec{F}.d\vec{r} \text{ ...... } (2)$$

So from equation (1) and (2) we have $(E_k)_f - (E_k)_i = -\{(E_p)_f - (E_p)_i\}$

or, $(E_k)_f + (E_p)_f = (E_k)_i + (E_p)_i$

i.e. $E_k + E_p = \text{constant.}$

Now, $\Delta(E_k + E_p) = \Delta E = 0$ [As E is constant in a conservative field]

$\therefore \Delta E_k + \Delta E_p = 0$

i.e. if the kinetic energy of the body increases its potential energy will decrease by an equal amount and vice-versa.

If some non-conservative force like friction is also acting on the particle, the mechanical energy is no more constant. It changes by the amount of work done by the frictional force.

$\Delta(E_k + E_p) = \Delta E = W_f$ [where W_f is the work done against friction]

The lost energy is transformed into heat and the heat energy developed is exactly equal to loss in mechanical energy.

We can, therefore, write $\Delta E + Q = 0$ [where Q is the heat produced]

This shows that if the forces are conservative and non-conservative both, it is not the mechanical energy alone which is conserved, but it is the total energy, may be heat, light, sound or mechanical etc., which is conserved.

The law of conservation of energy may be stated as follows :

"Energy may be transformed from one kind to another but it cannot be created or destroyed. The total energy in an isolated system is constant".

Deduction

Mathematical explanation of principle of conservation of energy for a single particle :

The work done by the force in moving a particle from position 1 to position 2 is given by

$W_{12} = \int_1^2 \vec{F}.\vec{dr}$

$= \int_1^2 m \frac{d\vec{v}}{dt}.\vec{dr}$

$= m \int_1^2 \frac{d\vec{v}}{dt} . \vec{dr}$ [since m = constant]

$= m \int_1^2 \frac{d\vec{v}}{dt} . \frac{d\vec{r}}{dt} dt$

$= m \int_1^2 \frac{d\vec{v}}{dt} . \vec{v}\, dt$

$= \frac{m}{2} \int_1^2 \frac{d v^2}{dt} . dt$

$= \frac{m}{2} \int_{v_1}^{v_2} d(v^2)$

$= \frac{1}{2} m v_2^2 - \frac{1}{2} m v_1^2$

$= (E_k)_2 - (E_k)_1$ ....(1)

Where, $(E_k)_1$ and $(E_k)_2$ are the kinetic energies of the particle in position 1 and 2 respectively.

For conservative force field, $\oint \vec{F}.\vec{dr} = 0$

Converting this line integral into surface integral by using Stoke's theorem we get,

$\oint \vec{F}.\vec{dr} = \iint (\vec{\nabla} \times \vec{F}) . d\vec{A} = 0$

Since dA, the surface element is arbitrary, we get $\vec{\nabla} \times \vec{F} = 0$.

We know that the curl of the gradient of a scalar point function or scalar field is zero.

Hence we can write, $\vec{F} = - \vec{\nabla} E_p$ [where E_p is a scalar function or potential energy of the particle at the point and the negative sign of the right hand side indicates that $\vec{F}$ is in the direction of decreasing E_p]

We can write the expression for W_{12} as

$W_{12} = \int_1^2 \vec{F}. d\vec{r}$

$= - \int_1^2 \vec{\nabla} E_p . d\vec{r}$

$= - \int_1^2 (\frac{\partial E_p}{\partial x} \hat{i} + \frac{\partial E_p}{\partial y} \hat{j} + \frac{\partial E_p}{\partial z} \hat{k}).(dx\, \hat{i} + dy\, \hat{j} + dz\, \hat{k})$

$= - \int_1^2 (\frac{\partial E_p}{\partial x} dx + \frac{\partial E_p}{\partial y} dy + \frac{\partial E_p}{\partial z} dz)$

$= - \int_1^2 dE_p$

$= (E_p)_1 - (E_p)_2$ ....(2)

Thus the work done by the force in displacing the particle from position 1 to position 2 is equal to the difference between the P.E. of the particle in those positions.

From (1) and (2) we get,

$(E_k)_2 - (E_k)_1 = (E_p)_1 - (E_p)_2$

or, $(E_p)_1 + (E_k)_1 = (E_k)_2 + (E_p)_2$

i.e. total energy (kinetic energy and potential energy) of a particle moving in a conservative force field is constant.

Exercise | | Subjective Questions — Energy

1) Define energy and state its SI unit. (1)

2) What is the SI unit of energy? How is the electron volt (eV) related to it? [2]

3) 1 kWh = ….. J ? (1)

4) Name two forms of mechanical energy. (1)

5) What is the kinetic energy of an object ? (1)

6) Can the kinetic energy of a body be negative ? Explain. (2)

7) Name the form of energy which a body may possess even when it us not in motion. (1)

8) Write an expression for the kinetic energy of an object. (1)

9) Derive the expression of kinetic energy of a body of mass m and moving with a velocity v.

10) The kinetic energy of a body of mass m is E_k, show that its linear momentum p = $\sqrt{2\,mE_k}$ (2)

11) If the kinetic energy of a body moving with velocity v is E, show that its linear momentum p = $2Ev$. (2)

12) State work energy theorem. (1)

13) The kinetic energies of two bodies (one heavy and one light) are equal. Which one has the higher linear momentum ? (2)

14) The linear momentum of two bodies (one heavy and one light) are equal. Which one has the higher kinetic energy ? (2)

15) A body of mass m is moving with constant acceleration from rest. Its velocity is v after t seconds. What is its kinetic energy at time T ?

16) Define potential energy ? (1)

17) Write an expression for gravitational potential energy of a body of mass m kept at a height h above the ground. (1)

18) Can potential energy of a body be negative ? (1)

19) Can any object have mechanical energy even if its momentum is zero ? (1)

20) Is it possible that a body may possess energy even when it is not in motion ? Explain with an example. (1)

21) Name the physical quantity obtained using the formula $\frac{U}{h}$, where U is the potential energy and h is the height. (1)

22) State the principle of conservation of energy. (1)

23) Give two examples in which mechanical energy is conserved. (2)

24) Verify that the total mechanical energy is always conserved in the case of a freely falling body under gravity. (3)

MCQ – 8 : Energy

Physics MCQ | | Class – XI	Energy
	Topic : Kinetic Energy of a Body

Important Points

Energy :

The energy of an object is defined as its capacity of doing work.

- Nature of the quantity : Scalar
- Dimensional Formula : [M L^2 T^{-2}]
- Unit : CGS Unit : erg
  SI unit : J

Important Formulae :

- If a point object of mass m has velocity v, then its kinetic energy is given by $E_k = \frac{1}{2}\, m\, v^2$
- Relation between K.E. and linear momentum :

$$p = \sqrt{2\, m\, E_k}$$

Important Facts :

- K.E. is always positive and does not depend on the direction of motion of the point object.
- K.E. depends on the frame of reference.

(1) Consider the following two statements (1) Linear momentum of a system of particles is zero (2) Kinetic energy of a system of particles is zero. Then
(a) 1 implies 2 and 2 implies 1
(b) 1 does not imply 2 and 2 does not imply 1 (c) 1 implies 2 but 2 does not imply 1
(d) 1 does not imply 2 but 2 implies 1

(2) A running man has half the kinetic energy of that of a boy of half of his mass. The man speeds up by 1 m s^{-1} so as to have same K.E. as that of boy. The original speed of the man will be

(a) $\sqrt{2}\,ms^{-1}$
(b) $(\sqrt{2}-1)ms^{-1}$
(c) $\frac{1}{(\sqrt{2}-1)}ms^{-1}$
(d) $\frac{1}{\sqrt{2}}ms^{-1}$

(3) A body of mass 10 kg at rest is acted upon simultaneously by two forces 4 N and 3 N at right angles to each other. The kinetic energy of the body at the end of 10 s is
(a) 100 J
(b) 300 J
(c) 50 J
(d) 125 J

(4) A ball of mass 2 kg and another of mass 4 kg are dropped together from a 60 ft tall building. After a fall of 30 ft each towards earth, their respective kinetic energies will be in the ratio of

(a) $\sqrt{2}$: 1
(b) 1 : 4
(c) 1 : 2
(d) 1 : $\sqrt{2}$

(5) If the momentum of a body increases by 0.01%, its kinetic energy will increase by
(a) 0.01 %
(b) 0.02 %
(c) 0.04 %
(d) 0.08 %

(6) If the momentum of a body is increased by 100 %, then the percentage increase in the kinetic energy is
(a) 150 %
(b) 200 %
(c) 225 %
(d) 300 %

(7) When momentum of a body increases by 200%, its K.E. increases by
(a) 200 %
(b) 300 %
(c) 400 %
(d) 800 %

(8) If kinetic energy of a body is increased by 300 % then percentage change in momentum will be
(a) 100 %
(b) 150 %
(c) 265 %
(d) 73.2 %

(9) K.E. of a body is increased by 44%. What is the percent increase in the momentum ?
(a) 10 %
(b) 20 %
(c) 30 %
(d) 44 %

(10) If the kinetic energy of a body is increased 2 times, its momentum will
(a) half
(b) remain unchanged
(c) be doubled
(d) increased $\sqrt{2}$ times

(11) A body of mass 5 kg is moving with a momentum of 10 kg-m s^{-1}. A force of 0.2 N acts on it in the direction of motion of the body for 10 seconds. The increase in its kinetic energy is
(a) 2.8 J
(b) 3.2 J
(c) 3.8 J
(d) 4.4 J

(12) The kinetic energy of two masses m_1 and m_2 are equal . The ratio of their linear momentum will be
(a) $\frac{m_1}{m_2}$
(b) $\frac{m_2}{m_1}$
(c) $\sqrt{\frac{m_2}{m_1}}$
(d) $\sqrt{\frac{m_1}{m_2}}$

(13) Two bodies of masses m_1 and m_2 are moving with same kinetic energy. If P_1 and P_2 are their respective momentum, the ratio $\frac{P_1}{P_2}$ is equal to
(a) $\frac{m_1^2}{m_2^2}$
(b) $\frac{m_1}{m_2}$
(c) $\sqrt{\frac{m_2}{m_1}}$
(d) $\sqrt{\frac{m_1}{m_2}}$

(14) The bodies of masses m_1 and m_2 have same momentum. The ratio of their kinetic energy is
(a) $\frac{m_1}{m_2}$
(b) $\frac{m_2}{m_1}$
(c) $\sqrt{\frac{m_2}{m_1}}$
(d) $\sqrt{\frac{m_1}{m_2}}$

(15) Two masses of 1 g and 9 g are moving with equal kinetic energies. The ratio of the magnitudes of their respective linear momenta is
(a) 1 : 9
(b) 9 : 1
(c) 1 : 3
(d) 3 : 1

(16) Two bodies with kinetic energies in the ratio of 4 : 1 are moving with equal linear momentum. The ratio of their masses is
(a) 4 : 1
(b) 1 : 1
(c) 1 : 2
(d) 1 : 4

(17) A body of mass 2 kg is thrown upward with an energy 490 J. The height at which its kinetic energy would become half of its initial kinetic energy will be [$g = 9.8\ ms^{-2}$]

(a) 35 m
(b) 25 m
(c) 12.5 m
(d) 10 m

(18) A 300 g mass has a velocity of $(3\hat{\imath} + 4\hat{\jmath})\ m\,s^{-1}$at a certain instant. What is its kinetic energy

(a) 1.35 J
(b) 2.4 J
(c) 3.75 J
(d) 7.35 J

(19) A body initially at rest, breaks up into two pieces of masses 2M and 3M respectively, together having a total kinetic energy E. The piece of mass 2M, after breaking up, has a kinetic energy

(a) $\frac{2E}{5}$
(b) $\frac{E}{2}$
(c) $\frac{E}{5}$
(d) $\frac{3E}{5}$

Answer	Energy
	Topic : Kinetic Energy of a Body

(1)	(d)	(5)	(b)	(9)	(b)	(13)	(d)	(17)	(c)
(2)	(c)	(6)	(d)	(10)	(d)	(14)	(b)	(18)	(c)
(3)	(d)	(7)	(d)	(11)	(d)	(15)	(c)	(19)	(d)
(4)	(c)	(8)	(b)	(12)	(d)	(16)	(d)		

Physics MCQ | | Class – XI

Energy

Topic : Work-Energy Theorem

Important Points

Statement :` Work done by a force (it may be external or internal and conservative or non-conservative) acting on a body is equal to the change in the kinetic energy of the body.

$\therefore W = \Delta E_k$

(1) K.E. acquire by a mass m is travelling a certain distance d, starting from rest, under the action of a constant force F is

(a) directly proportional to $\sqrt{m}$
(b) directly proportional to m
(c) directly proportional to $\frac{1}{m}$
(d) None of these

(2) The K.E. acquired by a mass m in travelling a certain distance d, starting from rest, under the action of a constant force is directly proportional to

(a) $\sqrt{m}$
(b) m
(c) $\frac{1}{m}$
(d) Independent of m

(3) The total work done on a particle is equal to the change in kinetic energy. This is applicable

(a) Always
(b) Only if the conservative forces are acting on it
(c) Only in inertial frame
(d) Only when pseudo force are absent

(4) Work done in time t on a body of mass m which is accelerated from rest to a speed v in time t_1 as a function of time t is given by

(a) $\frac{1}{2}m\frac{v}{t_1}t^2$
(b) $m\frac{v}{t_1}t^2$
(c) $\frac{1}{2}\left(\frac{mv}{t_1}\right)^2 t^2$
(d) $\frac{1}{2}m\frac{v^2}{t_1^2}t^2$

(5) Under the action of a force, a 2 kg body moves such that its position x as a function of time t is given by $x = \frac{t^2}{3}$, where x is in metre and t in second. The work done by the force in first two seconds is

(a) 1600 J
(b) 160 J
(c) 16 J
(d) $\frac{16}{9}$ J

(6) A rifle bullet loses $\left(\frac{1}{20}\right)$th of its velocity in passing through a plank. Assuming that the plank exerts a constant retarding force, the least number of such planks required just to stop the bullet is

(a) 11
(b) 20
(c) 21
(d) Infinite

(7) A bullet of mass 20 g leaves a riffle at an initial speed 100 m s^{-1} and strikes a target at the same level with speed 50 m s^{-1}. The amount of work done by the resistance of air will be

(a) 100 J
(b) 25 J
(c) 75 J
(d) 50 J

(8) A bullet of mass 10 g leaves a riffle at an initial velocity 1000 m s^{-1} and strikes

the earth at the same level with a velocity 500 m s^{-1}. The work done in joule to overcome the resistance of air will be
(a) 375
(b) 3750
(c) 5000
(d) 500

(9) A particle of mass 2 kg travels along a straight line with velocity v = $a\sqrt{x}$, where a is a constant. The work done by net force during the displacement of the particle from x = 0 to x = 4 m is
(a) a^2
(b) $2a^2$
(c) $4 a^2$
(d) $\sqrt{2}a^2$

(10) The position x of a particle moving along x-axis at time (t) is given by the equation t = $\sqrt{x}$ + 2, where x is in meters and t in seconds. Find the work done by the force in first four seconds
(a) zero
(b) 2 J
(c) 4 J
(d) 8 J

(11) A 2 kg mass is displaced from rest by a force $\vec{F} = 2\,x\,\hat{\imath} + 4y\,\hat{\jmath}$ N from origin to the point P(1 m, 2 m). The final velocity is
(a) 1 m s^{-1}
(b) 3 m s^{-1}
(c) 2 m s^{-1}
(d) 4 m s^{-1}

(12) A particle of mass 0.01 kg travels along a curve with velocity given by $4\hat{\imath} + 16\hat{k}$ m s^{-1}. After some time, its velocity becomes $8\hat{\imath} + 20\hat{\jmath}$ m s^{-1} due to the action of a conservative force. The work done on particle during this interval of time is
(a) 0.32 J
(b) 6.9 J
(c) 9.6 J
(d) 0.96 J

(13) A stone with weight W is thrown vertically upward into the air from ground level with initial speed v_0. If a constant force f due to air drag acts on the stone throughout its flight. The maximum height attained by the stone is
(a) $h = \frac{v_0^2}{2g(1+\frac{f}{W})}$
(b) $h = \frac{v_0^2}{2g(1-\frac{f}{W})}$
(c) $h = \frac{v_0^2}{2g(1+\frac{W}{f})}$
(d) $h = \frac{v_0^2}{2g(1-\frac{W}{f})}$

(14) A time dependent force F = 6t acts on a particle of mass 1 kg. If the particle starts from rest, the work done by the force during the first 1 s will be
(a) 4.5 J
(b) 22 J
(c) 9 J
(d) 18 J

(15) A block of mass 10 kg, moving in x-direction with a constant speed of 10 m s^{-1}, is subjected to a retarding force F = 0.1 x J m^{-1} during its interval from x = 20 m to 30 m. Its final kinetic energy
(a) 475 J
(b) 450 J
(c) 275 J
(d) 250 J

(16) Power supplied to a particle of mass 1 kg is P = 4t. If it is at rest t = 0, its velocity at t = 2 s is
(a) 2 m s^{-1}
(b) 4 m s^{-1}
(c) 6 m s^{-1}
(d) 8 m s^{-1}

(17) A particle of mass m is driven by a machine that delivers a constant power k

watt. If the particle starts from rest the force on the particle at time t is

(a) $\sqrt{\frac{mk}{2}}\, t^{-\frac{1}{2}}$
(b) $\sqrt{mk}\, t^{-\frac{1}{2}}$
(c) $\sqrt{2\, mk}\, t^{-\frac{1}{2}}$
(d) $\frac{1}{2}\sqrt{km}\, t^{-\frac{1}{2}}$

(18) A body is moved in a straight line by machine with constant power. The distance travelled by it in time duration t is proportional to

(a) $t^{\frac{3}{2}}$
(b) $t^{\frac{1}{2}}$
(c) t^2
(d) t

(19) A particle of mass m is moving in a circular path of radius r so that the centripetal acceleration varies with time as, $a_c = k^2\, rt^2$. Work done by the resultant force acting on it in time t is given by

(a) $\frac{1}{2} m\, r^2\, t^2$
(b) $\frac{1}{2} m\, k^2\, t^2$
(c) $\frac{1}{2} m\, k\, t^2$
(d) $\frac{1}{2} m\, k^2\, r^2\, t^2$

(20) A force applied by an engine of a train of mass 2.05×10^6kg changes its velocity from 5 m s^{-1} to 25 m s^{-1} in 5 minutes. The power of the engine is

(a) 1.025 MW
(b) 2.05 MW
(c) 5 MW
(d) 6 MW

(21) The kinetic energy K of a particle moving along x-axis varies with its position (x) as shown in figure. The magnitude of force acting on particle at x = 9 m is

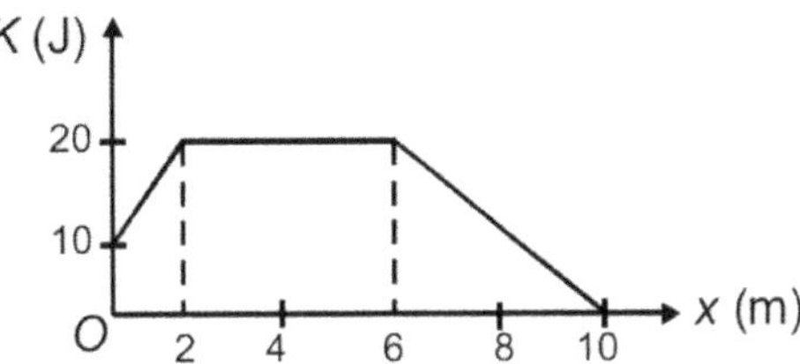

(a) zero
(b) 5 N
(c) 20 N
(d) 7.5 N

(22) A block of mass 4.5 kg is free to move along the x-axis. It is at rest at t = 0. If the force on the particle varies with time, then its kinetic energy at t = 4.5 s is

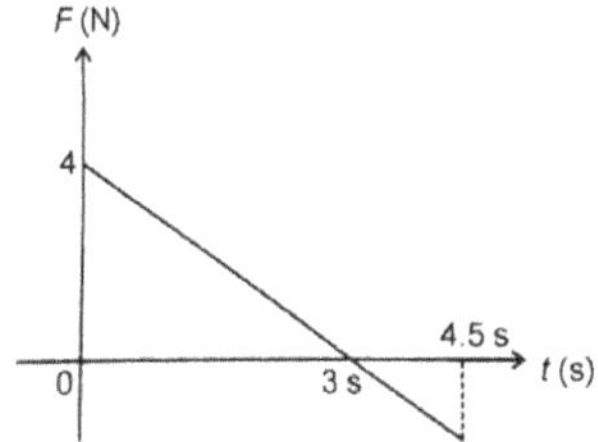

(a) 2.25 J
(b) 1.25 J
(c) 5 J
(d) zero

(23) The graph of force versus displacement is shown in figure. A body of mass 2 kg has a velocity of 20 m s^{-1} at x = 0. Find the kinetic energy of the body at x = 10 m

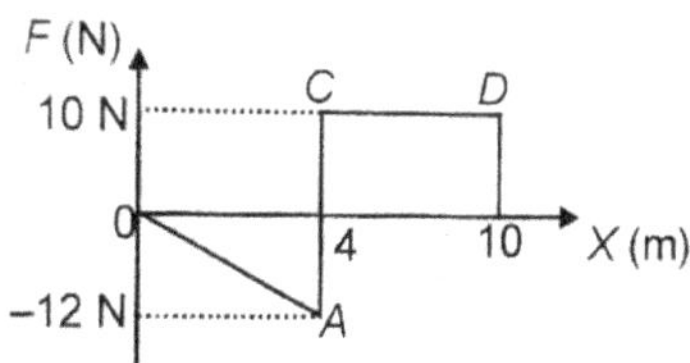

(a) 436 J
(b) 460 J
(c) 484 J
(d) 282 J

(24) A particle of mass 0.5 kg is subjected to a force which varies distance as shown in graph. If the speed of the particle

at x = 0 is 4 m s^{-1}, then its speed at x = 8 m is

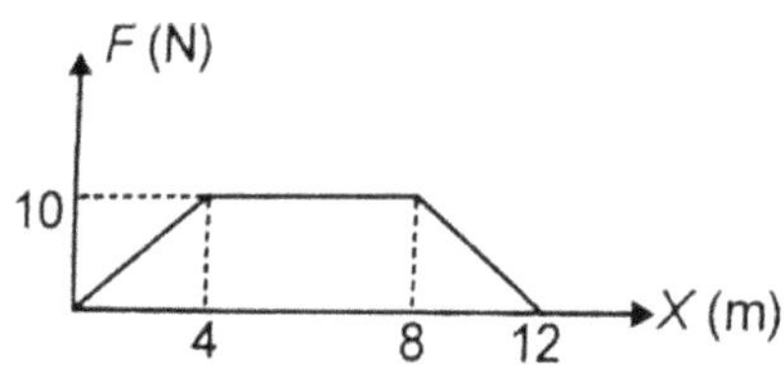

(a) 8 m s^{-1}
(b) 16 m s^{-1}
(c) 32 m s^{-1}
(d) 4 m s^{-1}

(25) A particle of mass 0.1 kg is subjected to a force which varies with distance as shown. If it starts its journey from rest at x = 0, then its velocity at x = 12 m is

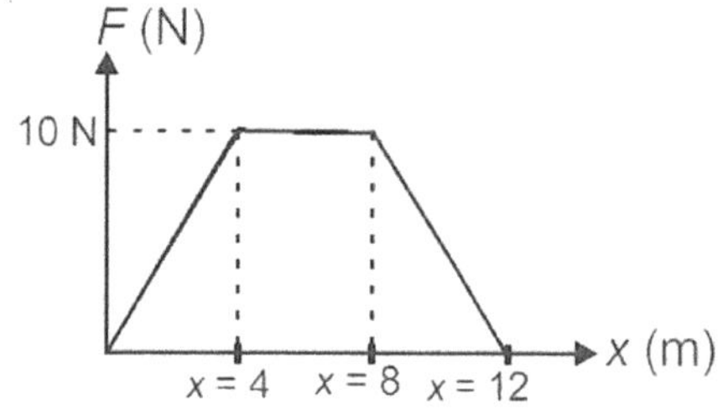

(a) 0 m s^{-1}
(b) $20\sqrt{2}$ m s^{-1}
(c) $20\sqrt{3}$ m s^{-1}
(d) 40 m s^{-1}

(26) A body starts moving unidirectionally under the influence of a source of constant power. Which one of the graph correctly shows the variation of displacement (s) with time (t) ?

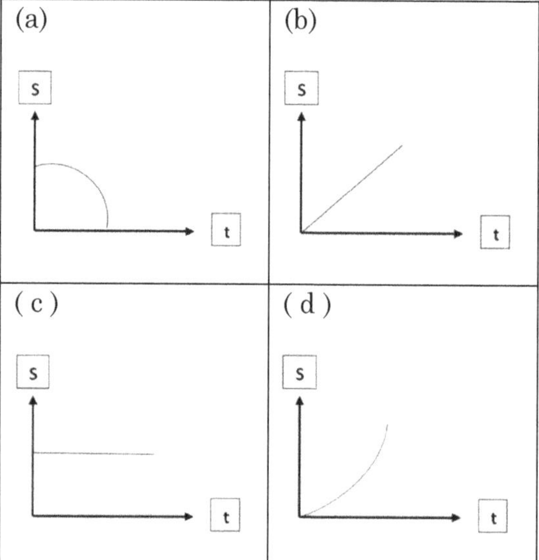

Answer	Energy
	Topic : Work-Energy Theorem

(1)	(d)	(7)	(c)	(13)	(a)	(19)	(d)	(25)	(d)
(2)	(d)	(8)	(b)	(14)	(a)	(20)	(b)	(26)	(d)
(3)	(a)	(9)	(a)	(15)	(a)	(21)	(b)		
(4)	(d)	(10)	(a)	(16)	(b)	(22)	(a)		
(5)	(d)	(11)	(b)	(17)	(a)	(23)	(b)		
(6)	(a)	(12)	(d)	(18)	(a)	(24)	(b)		

Physics MCQ || Class – XI	Energy
	Topic : Potential Energy & Equilibrium

Important Points

• Potential Energy is defined only for conservative forces.

• Potential energy generally are of three types :
(i) Elastic Potential Energy
(ii) Electric Potential Energy
(iii) Gravitational Potential Energy

(1) Potential energy is defined
(a) Only in conservative fields
(b) As the negative of work done by conservative forces
(c) As the negative work done by external forces when $\Delta K = 0$
(d) All of these

(2) The potential energy of a system increases if work is done
(a) upon the system by a non-conservative force
(b) by the system against a conservative force (c) by the system against a nonconservative force
(d) upon the system by a conservative force

(3) Once a choice is made regarding zero potential energy reference state, the changes in potential energy
(a) Are same
(b) Are different
(c) Depend strictly on the choice of the zero of potential energy
(d) Become indeterminate

Important Points

If net force acting on a particle is zero, it said to be in equilibrium.
For equilibrium, F = $-\frac{dU}{dx} = 0$

Types of equilibrium :

(1) Stable equilibrium : P.E. is minimum and $\frac{d^2U}{dx^2}$ = Positive
(2) Unstable equilibrium : P.E. is maximum and $\frac{d^2U}{dx^2}$ = Negative
(3) Neutral equilibrium : P.E. is constant and $\frac{d^2U}{dx^2} = 0$

(4) If U represents the potential energy of a system in one dimensional motion along x axis, then $-\frac{dU}{dx}$ represents

(a) power
(b) Force
(c) momentum
(d) work

(5) If F = $2x^2 - 3x - 2$, then select the correct statement

(a) $x = -\frac{1}{2}$ is the position of stable equilibrium
(b) $x = 2$ is the position of stable equilibrium
(c) $x = -\frac{1}{2}$ is the position of unstable equilibrium
(d) $x = 2$ is the position of neutral equilibrium

(6) The variation of potential energy U of a body moving along x axis varies with its position (x) as shown in figure. The body is in equilibrium state at

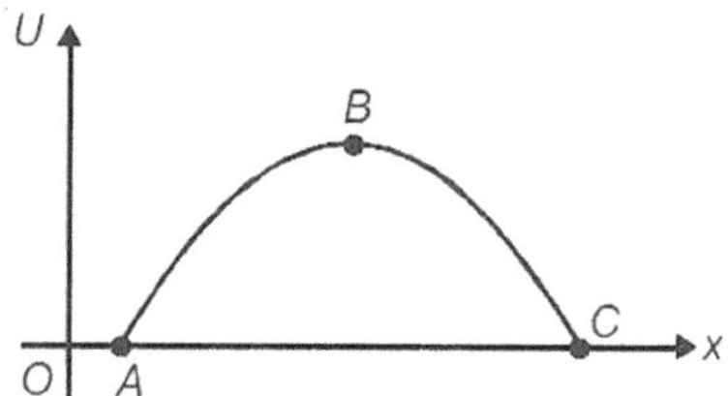

(a) A
(b) B
(c) C
(d) Both A and C

(7) A particle which is constrained to move along the x-axis, is subjected to a force in the same direction which varies with the distance x of the particle from the origin as $F(x) = -kx + ax^3$. Here k and a are positive constants. For $x \geq 0$, the functional from of the potential energy $U_{(x)}$ of the particle is

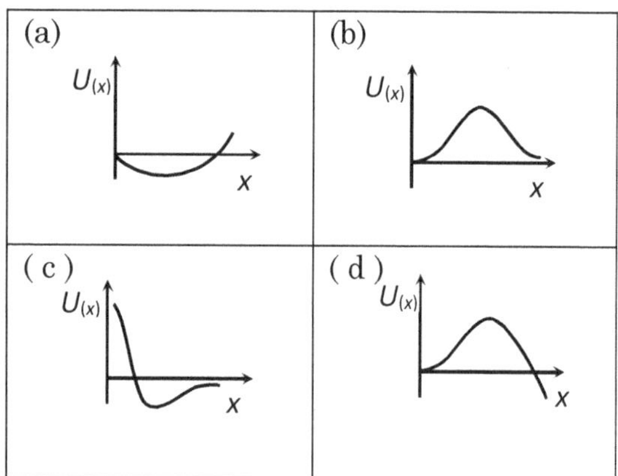

(8) The potential energy of a body is given by $A - Bx^2$ (where x is the displacement). The magnitude of force acting on the particle is
(a) Constant
(b) Proportional to x
(c) Proportional to x^2
(d) Inversely proportional to x

(9) The potential energy of a conservative system is given by U = ay^2 – by, where y represents the position of the particle, both a and b are constants. What is the force acting on the system ?
(a) $-ay$
(b) $-by$
(c) $2ay - b$
(d) $b - 2ay$

(10) On a particle at origin a various force F = – ax (where a is positive constant) is applied. If U (0) = 0, the graph between potential energy of the particle U (x) and x is best represented by

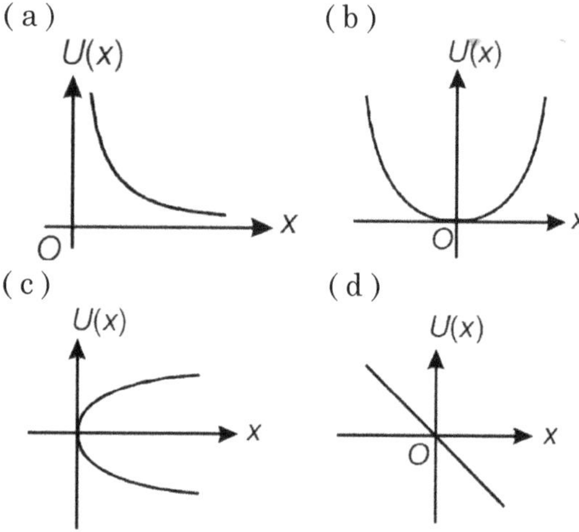

(11) The potential energy of a system is represented in the first figure. The force acting on the system will be represented by

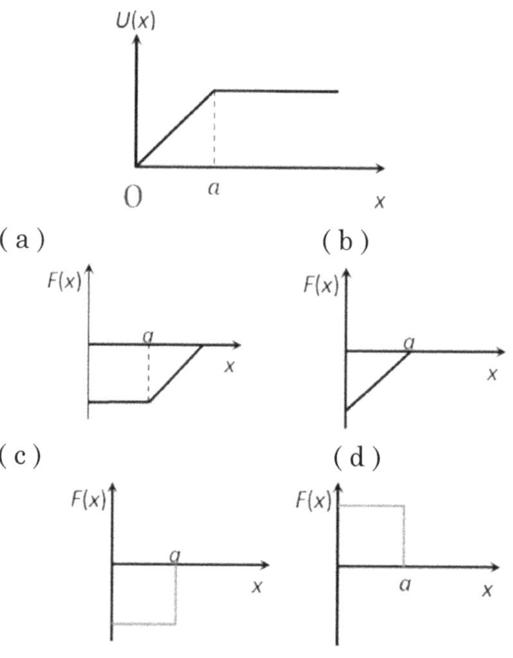

(12) The variation of potential energy U of a system is shown in the first figure. The

force acting on the system is best represented by

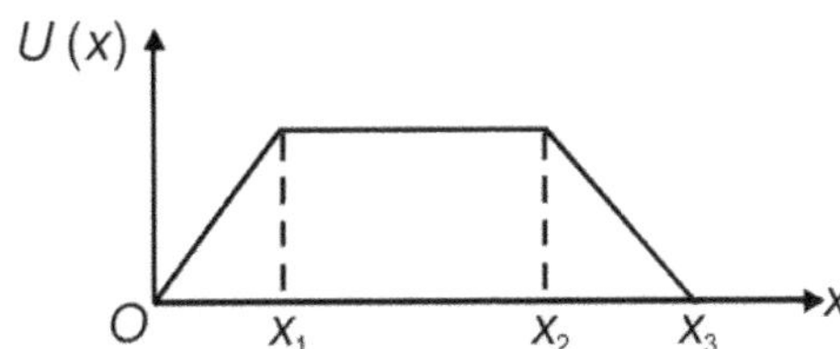

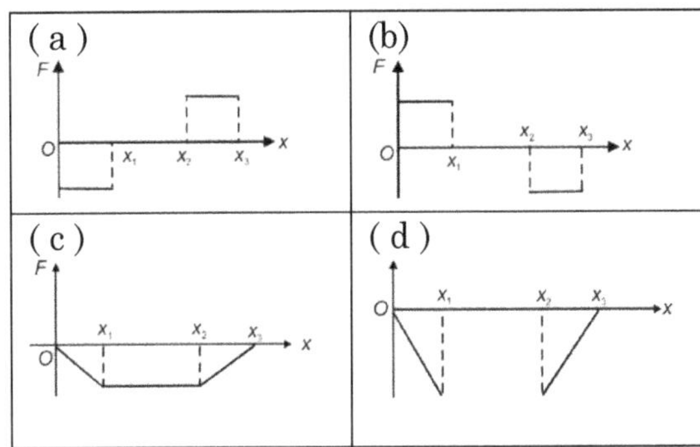

(13) A particle moves in a potential region given by $U = 8x^2 - 4x + 400$ J. Its state of equilibrium will be

(a) $x = 25$m

(b) $x = 0.25$m

(c) $x = 0.025$m

(d) $x = 2.5$m

(14) The potential energy of a particle in a force field U $= \frac{A}{r^2} - \frac{B}{r}$ where, A and B are constants and r is the distance of particle from the centre of the field. For stable equilibrium, the distance of the particle is

(a) $\frac{A}{B}$

(b) $\frac{B}{A}$

(c) $\frac{B}{2A}$

(d) $\frac{2A}{B}$

(15) A particle located in one dimensional U(x) $= \frac{a}{x^2} - \frac{b}{x^3}$ where, a and b are positive constants. The position of equilibrium corresponding to x =

(a) $\frac{3a}{2b}$

(b) $\frac{2b}{3a}$

(c) $\frac{2a}{3b}$

(d) $\frac{3b}{2a}$

(16) In a certain field, the potential energy is U = $a\,x^2 - b\,x^3$, where a and b are constants. The particle is in stable equilibrium at x equal to

(a) zero

(b) $\frac{a}{3b}$

(c) $\frac{2a}{3b}$

(d) $\frac{2a}{b}$

(17) The potential energy function for the force between two atoms in a diatomic molecule is approximately given by U (x) = $\frac{a}{x^{12}} - \frac{b}{x^6}$ where, a and b are constants and x is the distance between the atoms. If the dissociation energy of the molecule is D = [U (x = ∞) – U $_{\text{at equilibrium}}$], D is

(a) $\frac{b^2}{2a}$

(b) $\frac{b^2}{12a}$

(c) $\frac{b^2}{4a}$

(d) $\frac{b^2}{6a}$

(18) The potential energy of a 2 kg particle, free to move along x-axis is given by V(x) = ($\frac{x^3}{3} - \frac{x^2}{2}$) J. The total mechanical energy of the particle is 4 J. Maximum speed (in m s^{-1}) is

(a) $\frac{1}{\sqrt{2}}$

(b) $\sqrt{2}$

(c) $\frac{3}{\sqrt{2}}$

(d) $\frac{5}{\sqrt{6}}$

(19) The force acting on a particle moving along x-axis varies with position on x-axis as shown in figure. The particle is in stable equilibrium at

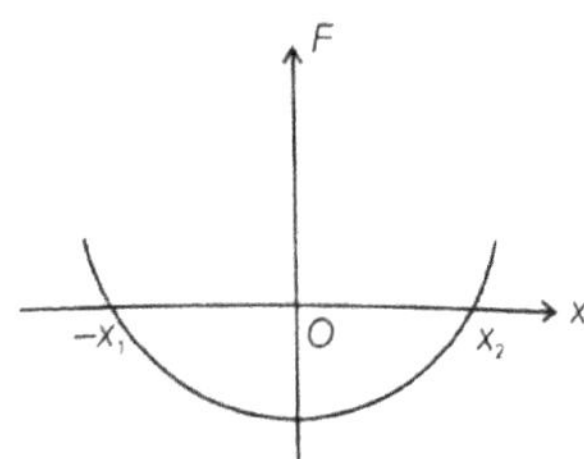

(a) $x = -x_1$
(b) $x = x_2$
(c) $x = 0$
(d) Both (a) and (b)

(20) A particle is moving in a circular path of radius a under the action of an attractive potential $U = -\frac{k}{2r^2}$. Its total kinetic energy is

(a) zero

(b) $-\frac{3}{2}\frac{k}{a^2}$

(c) $-\frac{k}{4a^2}$

(d) $\frac{k}{2a^2}$

Answer	Energy
	Topic : Potential Energy & Equilibrium

(1)	(a)	(5)	(a)	(9)	(d)	(13)	(d)	(17)	(d)
(2)	(d)	(6)	(b)	(10)	(b)	(14)	(a)	(18)	(b)
(3)	(a)	(7)	(d)	(11)	(c)	(15)	(b)	(19)	(c)
(4)	(b)	(8)	(b)	(12)	(d)	(16)	(a)	(20)	(b)

Physics MCQ | | Class – XI

Energy

Topic : Electric & Gravitational Potential Energy

On Electric Potential Energy

(1) A particle of mass 'm' and charge 'q' is accelerated through a potential difference of 'V' volt. Its energy is
(a) qV
(b) mqV
(c) $\left(\frac{q}{m}\right)V$
(d) $\frac{q}{mV}$

(2) The energy required to break one bond in DNA is 10^{-20} J. This value (in eV) is nearly
(a) 0.6
(b) 0.06
(c) 0.006
(d) 6

(3) A proton has a positive charge. If two protons are brought near to one another, the potential energy of the system will
(a) Increase
(b) Decrease
(c) Remain the same
(d) Equal to the kinetic energy

(4) Two protons are situated at a distance of 100 fermi from each other. The potential energy of this system will be in eV
(a) 1.44
(b) 1.44×10^3
(c) 1.44×10^2
(d) 1.44×10^4

(5) $^{208}_{80}$Hg nucleus is bombarded by α - particles with velocity 10^7 m/s. If the α - particle is approaching the Hg nucleus head-on then the distance of closest approach will be
(a) 1.115×10^{-13}m
(b) 11.15×10^{-13}m
(c) 111.5×10^{-13}m
(d) Zero

On Gravitational Potential Energy

(6) The work done in pulling up a block of wood weighing 2 kN for a length of 10 m on a smooth plane inclined at an angle of $15^o$with the horizontal is (sin 15° = 0.259)
(a) 4.36 k J
(b) 5.17 k J
(c) 8.91 k J
(d) 9.82 k J

(7) If g is the acceleration due to gravity on the earth's surface, the gain in the potential energy of an abject of mass m raised from the surface of earth to a height equal to the radius of the earth R, is

(a) $\frac{1}{2}mgR$
(b) $2mgR$
(c) mgR
(d) $\frac{1}{4}mgR$

(8) The work done in raising a mass of 15 g from the ground to a table of 1 m height is

(a) 15 J
(b) 152 J
(c) 1500 J
(d) 0.15 J

(9) A body is falling under gravity. When it loses a gravitational potential energy by U, its speed is v. The mass of the body shall be

(a) $\frac{2U}{v}$
(b) $\frac{U}{2v}$
(c) $\frac{2U}{v^2}$
(d) $\frac{U}{2v^2}$

Answer	Energy
	Topic : Electric & Gravitational Potential Energy

(1)	(a)	(3)	(a)	(5)	(a)	(7)	(a)	(9)	(c)
(2)	(b)	(4)	(d)	(6)	(b)	(8)	(d)		

Physics MCQ | | Class – XI	Energy
	Topic : Conservation of Energy

(1) Two stones each of mass 5 kg fall on a wheel from a height of 10 m. The wheel stirs 2 kg water. The rise in temperature of water would be
(a) 2.6° C
(b) 1.2° C
(c) 0.32° C
(d) 0.12° C

(2) A boy is sitting on a swing at a maximum height of 5 m above the ground. When the swing passes through the mean position which is 2 m above the ground its velocity is approximately
(a) 7.6 m s^{-1}
(b) 9.8 m s^{-1}
(c) 6.26 m s^{-1}
(d) None of these

(3) A body of mass 1 kg is thrown upwards with a velocity 20 m s^{-1}. It monetarily comes to rest after attaining a height of 18 m. How much energy is lost due to air friction ? Take $g = 10$ m s^{-2}
(a) 20 J
(b) 30 J
(c) 40 J
(d) 10 J

(4) A block of mass M slides along the sides of a bowl as shown in the figure. The walls of the bowl are frictionless and the base has coefficient of friction 0.2. If the block is released from the top of the side, which is 1.5 m high, where will the block come to rest ? Given that the length of the base is 15 m

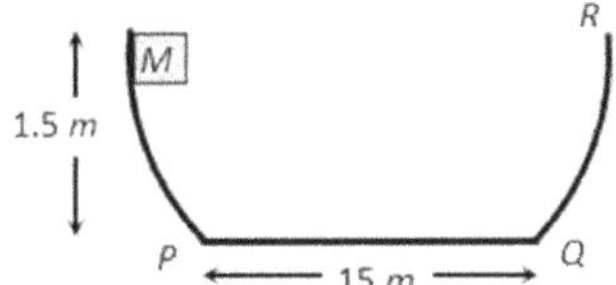

(a) 1 m from P
(b) Mid point
(c) 2 m from P
(d) At Q

(5) If we throw a body upwards with velocity of 4 m s^{-1} at what height its kinetic energy reduces to half of the initial value ? Take $g = 10$ m s^{-2}
(a) 4 m
(b) 2 m
(c) 1 m
(d) None of these

(6) A body of mass 2 kg is thrown up vertically with kinetic energy of 490 J. the height at which the kinetic energy of the body becomes half of its original value is
(a) 50 m
(b) 12.5 m
(c) 25 m
(d) 10 m

(7) A block of mass 2 kg is released from A on the track that is one quadrant of a circle of radius 1m. It slides down the track and reaches B with a speed of 4 ms^{-1} and finally stops at C at a distance of 3m from B. The work done against the force of friction is

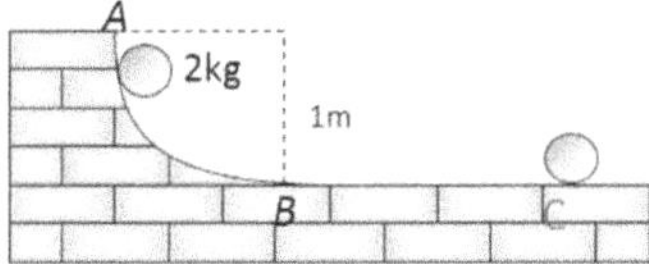

(a) 10 J
(b) 20 J
(c) 2 J
(d) 6 J

(8) A stone projected vertically upwards from the ground reaches a maximum height h. When it is at a height

$\frac{3h}{4}$, the ratio of its kinetic and potential energies is
(a) 3 : 4
(b) 1 : 3
(c) 4 : 3
(d) 3 : 1

(9) Bernoulli's principle is based on the law of conservation of
(a) Angular momentum
(b) Energy
(c) Linear momentum
(d) Mass

(10) A particle is released from height S from the surface of the Earth. At a certain height its kinetic energy is three times its potential energy. The height from the surface of earth and the speed of the particle at that instant are respectively
(a) $\frac{S}{4}, \frac{3gS}{2}$
(b) $\frac{S}{4}, \frac{\sqrt{3gS}}{2}$
(c) $\frac{S}{2}, \frac{\sqrt{3gS}}{2}$
(d) $\frac{S}{4}, \sqrt{\frac{3gS}{2}}$

Answer	Energy
	Topic : Conservation of Energy

(1)	(d)	(3)	(a)	(5)	(d)	(7)	(b)	(9)	(b)
(2)	(a)	(4)	(b)	(6)	(b)	(8)	(b)	(10)	(d)

www.ingramcontent.com/pod-product-compliance
Ingram Content Group UK Ltd.
Pitfield, Milton Keynes, MK11 3LW, UK
UKHW061959290726
14090UKWH00021B/1295